8⁰⁰

ENEMIES OF THE PEOPLE

ENEMIES
OF THE
PEOPLE

The Ordeal
of the Intellectuals
in China's Great
Cultural Revolution

ANNE F. THURSTON

Harvard University Press
Cambridge, Massachusetts,
and London, England
1988

PUBLISHED BY ARRANGEMENT WITH ALFRED A. KNOPF, INC.

EXCERPTS FROM *In Exile from the Land of Snows,* by John F.
Avedon. Copyright © 1979, 1984 by John F. Avedon.
Reprinted by permission of Alfred A. Knopf, Inc.
Harcourt Brace Jovanovich, Inc. and *Faber and Faber Publishers:*
Excerpt from "Journey of the Magi," from *Collected Poems,*
1909–1962 by T. S. Eliot. Copyright 1936 by Harcourt Brace
Jovanovich, Inc. Copyright © 1963, 1964 by T. S. Eliot.
Reprinted by permission of the publishers.

Portions of this work were originally published in different form
in *Pacific Affairs,* as "Victims of China's Cultural Revolution:
The Invisible Wounds," by Anne Thurston. Part I, Vol. 57, No.
4. Winter 1984–85, pp. 599–620, and Part II, Vol. 58, No. 1,
Spring 1985, pp. 5–27.

Library of Congress Cataloging-in-Publication Data

Thurston, Anne F.
Enemies of the people / Anne F. Thurston.
p. cm.
Reprint. Originally published: New York : Knopf, 1987.
Bibliography: p.
Includes index.
1. China–History–Cultural Revolution, 1966–1969.
I. Title.
[DS778.7.T46   1988]   951.05'6–dc19   88-7210   CIP
ISBN 0-674-25375-2 (pbk.)

To those whose voices are recorded
here; to the millions more for whom
they speak; to those who did not live
to tell their tales—

Our spiritual sources are poisoned,
and . . . the whole of our vaunted
social system is founded upon a cesspit
of lies.

Dr. Stockman,
in Ibsen's *An Enemy of the People*

CONTENTS

ACKNOWLEDGMENTS

My deepest debt of gratitude is to those courageous, articulate, and honest people who shared with me their experiences during the Cultural Revolution. This book is not only about them but is also in fundamental ways by them and for them. It is to them that the book is dedicated.

I would also like to thank the Institute of Sociology, the Foreign Affairs Office, and the Institute of Literature at the Chinese Academy of Social Sciences in Peking for arranging the affiliations that made my research in China possible. Special appreciation should be given to Jiang Shouqian of the Institute of Literature for guiding my reading of the "literature of the wounded" about the Cultural Revolution and to the tireless, good-humored, gracious, and unfailing help of my colleague, friend, and research assistant Liu Yuehua. Burton Pasternak has also been a source of continuing encouragement and help at every step of this project, including the lengthy period spent in China.

For assistance with translations and for

many useful insights, I am indebted to Chiang Yung-chen. Arthur Kleinman made extremely valuable comments on early drafts of that part of the manuscript dealing with the psychological consequences of the Cultural Revolution, and I profited greatly from the comments of colleagues at seminars presented at Harvard and Columbia universities and at the University of California, Berkeley. John King Fairbank, Donald Klein, Patrick Maddox, Andrew Walder, and Lynn White made thorough, insightful, and helpful comments on the entire draft. I would also like to thank Charles Elliott for his support and Sharon Zimmerman for her attention in seeing the manuscript through to production.

Funding for research conducted in China in 1981–82 was provided by a fellowship from the National Endowment for the Humanities. The American Philosophical Society granted me funds to travel to various parts of the United States and conduct interviews with Chinese residing here. Support to complete the book was provided by the Wang Institute of Graduate Studies Fellowship Program in Chinese Studies.

I alone am responsible for the contents of this book and for whatever mistakes and misinterpretations remain.

A.F.T.

PREFACE

You Xiaoli was standing, precariously balanced, on a stool. Her body was bent over from the waist into a right angle, and her arms, elbows stiff and straight, were behind her back, one hand grasping the other at the wrist. It was the position known as "doing the airplane." Around her neck was a heavy chain, and attached to the chain was a blackboard, a real blackboard, one that had been removed from a classroom at the university where You Xiaoli, for more than ten years, had served as a full professor. On both sides of the blackboard were chalked her name and the myriad crimes she was alleged to have committed. She was accused of being a bourgeois academic authority and a follower of Liu Shaoqi—the former chief of state of the People's Republic of China, now labeled a traitor and a scab and a lackey of the imperialists, the Soviet revisionists, and the Chinese Nationalist reactionaries. She was accused of being a spy and a counterrevolutionary, and opposed to Party Chairman Mao Zedong.

The stool on which You Xiaoli stood

was balanced in turn on an ordinary wooden chair, and underneath the chair was a heavy wooden desk, the kind professors in China stand behind while lecturing. Both chair and desk had also come from a university classroom.

The scene was taking place at the university, too, in a sports field at one of China's most prestigious institutions of higher learning. In the audience were You Xiaoli's students and colleagues and former friends. Workers from local factories and peasants from nearby communes had been bused in for the spectacle. From the audience came repeated, rhythmic chants. *"Dadao You Xiaoli! Dadao You Xiaoli!"* "Down with You Xiaoli! Down with You Xiaoli!"

"I had many feelings at that struggle session," recalls You Xiaoli. "I thought there were some bad people in the audience. But I also thought there were many ignorant people, people who did not understand what was happening, so I pitied that kind of person. They brought workers and peasants into the meetings, and they could not understand what was happening. But I was also angry."

After doing the jet airplane for several hours, listening to the endless taunts and jeers and the repeated chants calling for her downfall, the chair on which You Xiaoli had been balancing was suddenly kicked from under her and she tumbled from the stool, hitting the table, and onto the ground. Blood flowed from her nose and from her mouth and from her neck where the chain had dug into the flesh. As the fascinated, gawking audience looked on, You Xiaoli lost consciousness and was still.

"They left her there to die," says one of her colleagues.

"They thought she was dead," says another.

Zhao Shuli, one of China's leading twentieth-century novelists, had died as a result of a similar incident. A rib had broken and punctured his lung when the chair had been knocked from beneath the stool on which he had been standing. Accused of being a counterrevolutionary, he was not eligible for medical treatment. Instead, he was dragged to another city to face yet another struggle session against him. He died several days later.

It was dark when You Xiaoli awoke, and she was all alone on the field. The pain in her back was excruciating. Her legs were numb. She could not stand or walk. Her apartment, located on the campus grounds, was a mere three-minute walk away, but it took You Xiaoli hours, crawling, her jacket and trousers tearing to shreds, the skin ripping off her flesh, to arrive at the entrance to her three-story garden-style apartment building.

No member of her family was there to help. Her husband had also been accused of a multitude of counterrevolutionary crimes and been dispatched to forced labor in the countryside. Their eight-year-old son had been delivered into the care of a relative in a distant city—You Xiaoli and her husband were unable to care for him. You Xiaoli had access to only one small room in her apartment. The other rooms were occupied by two "revolutionary rebel" families who, in the rare moments when You Xiaoli was allowed to return home, took it upon themselves to taunt her, reminding her always of the crimes of which she stood accused.

The time it took for You Xiaoli to crawl up the three flights of stairs seemed interminable, the pain unbearable. The tiny room into which she finally crawled was empty of anything but a torn, tattered quilt, its cotton padding protruding from numerous holes. Months earlier, the young Red Guards had searched her apartment and removed its entire contents. The possessions of "counterrevolutionaries" were considered "bourgeois."

You Xiaoli lay down on a barren wood floor to recuperate.

The next day, a kindly neighbor, suspecting You Xiaoli's plight, took a brick and heated it, wrapped it in a towel, and applied it to her swollen back, blackened with bruises. Twelve years later, when You Xiaoli was finally able to see a doctor, X-rays would show that a disk in her back had been ruptured by the fall, but at the time a heated brick wrapped in a towel was the only treatment she received. As a counterrevolutionary, she was ineligible for medical care.

Even had she been able to find a doctor willing to risk his own political standing by treating an enemy of the people, she would have been unable to pay. Her salary had been reduced from some $60 a month to a mere $7.50. With that, You Xiaoli could barely buy food. She subsisted on one salty pickle each day and bread made of coarse sweet-potato flour. She was thin and emaciated and weak.

You XIAOLI's tribulations, with numerous variations, were being experienced by countless others throughout the length and breadth of China. The year was 1967, and it was in the name of Communist Party Chairman Mao Zedong and his Great Proletarian Cultural Revolution that thousands upon tens of thousands of China's citizens were being dragged to repeated, innumerable "struggle sessions" as public, defenseless, helpless spectacles to be taunted and jeered at and hurt.

As an episode in the history of man's inhumanity to man, China's Great Proletarian Cultural Revolution is surpassed only by the Nazi Holocaust, the Stalinist purges, and the recent genocide in Cambodia. As a tumultuous revolutionary upheaval, it is rivaled only by the French and the Russian revolutions and by China's own revolution of 1949 which brought the Communist Party to power. As an incident in the cruelty of Chinese leaders to their own people, it can be compared, as victims of the period are wont to do, to the behavior of Qin Shi Huangdi, the despotic first emperor of the Qin dynasty, in the third century B.C., the man credited with having buried alive the intellectuals of his day.

In its scale and in its scope, the tragedy of the Cultural Revolution is so vast as to be almost incomprehensible. Hu Yaobang, general secretary of the Chinese Communist Party and himself purged during the Cultural Revolution, has been quoted as saying that between the antirightist campaign of 1957 that presaged the Cultural Revolution and the conclusion of the Cultural Revolution itself, a hundred million people, a tenth of the Chinese population, were rendered victims, directly and adversely affected. How many died during that period we will probably never know. Perhaps as many as a million. Maybe more. Possibly fewer. China is not a country where such statistics are easy to collect. Whatever the figures, the Cultural Revolution was a human tragedy of untold proportions, a catastrophe that brought China to the brink of collapse.

It had begun quietly, almost benignly, as what appeared to many at first as mere academic, if vitriolic, debate. In the fall of 1965, the Shanghai-based Communist Party theorist and ideologue Yao Wenyuan published an attack on a morality play by the leading historian Wu Han, who was then vice-mayor of Peking. For months the pages of China's newspapers were filled with defenses of and attacks on Wu Han. Then, in late May 1966, the Communist Party committee that governed Peking, including Vice-Mayor Wu Han and the mayor himself, Peng Zhen, was purged.

The purge of Mayor Peng signaled a political crisis of a higher order of magnitude. For Peng Zhen was not only mayor of his country's capital city but a member of the Communist Party Politburo as well, one of a handful of the country's highest leaders. The Communist Party of China had not been in the habit of purging its highest leaders.

In early June, the leading nationally circulated Communist Party newspaper, the *People's Daily*, began calling for mass participation in purges of all those in Chinese society who had opposed Party Chairman Mao Zedong's policy and thought. Universities and middle schools first in Peking and then throughout China were closed as students attacked administrators and teachers and "counterrevolutionary" students as well. In many parts of China during the summer months of 1966, the Communist Party sent teams into universities to direct the Cultural Revolution on college campuses. It was a period of upheaval, violence, and terror—but the upheaval was nonetheless tightly controlled.

Early in August, the Eighth Central Committee of the Chinese Communist Party held a plenary session, and the decisions emanating from that meeting pushed the Cultural Revolution in a decidedly leftist, and ultimately more violent, direction. Whereas heretofore the primary targets of attack had been allegedly "bourgeois" academics and intellectuals, who had often served as targets in the past, now the enemies were said to include members of the

Communist Party of China as well—members deemed to be "following the capitalist road." This, too, was new. Since "liberating" the country in 1949, the party had led the populace in campaign after campaign against a variety of "enemies," but had itself remained relatively immune to attack. Mao Zedong was now turning against the very party he himself had built. To spearhead the attacks, the chairman called upon the young of China, the students of the country's universities and middle schools. The Red Guard revolutionaries, soon to number some twenty million strong, were born.

Within months, the young Red Guards had spread their attacks from academic and party leaders within their own educational institutions to society at large. At the height of the upheaval, in the spring and summer of 1967, and again in the spring of 1968, large parts of the country hovered around anarchy as government in China's major cities and provincial capitals was paralyzed. In the winter and spring of 1966–67, all but one of China's ambassadors abroad were called home, and foreign relations ground nearly to a halt. A number of embassies in Peking were stormed by the young Red Guards, and the British Chancellery was burned to the ground. Having severed ties with the Soviet "revisionists" and those allied with them, and scorning and being scorned by American "imperialism" and its many "lackeys," China's closest ties were with Albania. With a population of only slightly more than two million, Albania is somewhat larger than the state of Maryland. The crowds in Peking which turned out to greet visiting dignitaries from Albania were often nearly as large as the country itself. For years, Albania was the country about which the Chinese population was told most.

The scope of the purge of the Chinese Communist Party during the Cultural Revolution rivaled the Stalinist purges of the mid-1930s. Liu Shaoqi, former president of the People's Republic of China and Mao's longtime heir apparent, was purged, as was the party's former general secretary, Deng Xiaoping. Over 70 percent of the members and alternate members of the Central Committee were either purged or forced to undergo criticism from the "revolutionary masses." But victims of the Cultural Revolution were not confined to members of the Communist Party. They were to be found in many walks of life, and they numbered in the millions, even the tens of millions of people.

Beginning in the summer of 1967, the Chinese military, headed by Lin Biao, was brought in to reestablish order. The price of order was a new wave of persecutions, as the young whom Mao had earlier called upon to rebel became themselves the objects of attack. Between 1967 and 1971, persecution followed upon persecution as China's young were betrayed—repeatedly brought to heel for the rebellion in which they had so exultantly participated in the name of and upon the encouragement of their great leader, Chairman Mao. Between 1968 and 1970, some five or six million urban young people— nearly a third of the Red Guards—were sent, ostensibly permanently, to live and work in sometimes remote and often backward areas of the Chinese countryside. By 1975, some twelve million urban young had been dispatched to rural areas.

Educated urban adults, too, in numbers massive but still unknown, were sent to the countryside to live and work in what were euphemistically referred to as "May Seventh Cadre Schools,"* but were in fact labor camps where study classes for "political reeducation"—taught by soldiers or peasants markedly inferior to their students in education certainly and intellect often—occupied a substantial portion of each day.

By the late summer of 1971, the country was settling into a sustained period of routinized oppression. Then, in an incident exemplifying anew the old adage that truth is stranger than fiction, Minister of Defense Lin Biao, Chairman Mao's celebrated closest comrade-in-arms and the heir apparent replacing Liu Shaoqi, died when his plane crashed in Outer Mongolia in flight to the Soviet Union. Lin Biao's planned coup d'état against Mao had been discovered just before its scheduled execution.

By 1973, the country had disintegrated to the point where the practical-minded and pragmatic Deng Xiaoping was called back as vice-premier. It was under his aegis, and with the support and cooperation of the moderate, balanced Premier Zhou Enlai, that numerous party members previously purged began tentatively to be rehabilitated and new attention came to be paid to the economic modernization of one of the world's most impoverished nations.

But Deng Xiaoping and Zhou Enlai were stymied by the growing power and audacity of high-ranking revolutionaries more interested in waging attacks on such improbable, intangible targets as Confucius, Beethoven, and Jonathan Livingston Seagull than in the fact of poverty and backwardness in their own country, more preoccupied with "cutting the tail of capitalism"—ridding the country of all vestiges of free and private enterprise—than with questions of the basic sustenance, health, and well-being of their country's people.

In the spring of 1974, Zhou Enlai entered the hospital with cancer. For nearly a year and a half, growing weaker by the month, he conducted the affairs of state from his hospital bed, as the power of the radicals grew.

On January 8, 1976, Zhou Enlai was dead. Now, increasingly, the radicals turned their attacks openly and directly against the hardnosed moderate Deng Xiaoping. In early April, millions in Peking took to the streets in grief over the death of Zhou Enlai, in support of Deng Xiaoping, and in protest against both the radicals, Party Chairman Mao Zedong included, and the radical policies that had led their country to the brink of disaster. But the radicals, temporarily at least, retained the upper hand. The spontaneous demonstration was declared a counterrevolutionary incident, and Deng Xiaoping was purged again.

Six months later, in October 1976, extremist rule in China—the "ten years of great disaster"—finally came to an end. Mao Zedong died in early

---

*Mao had decreed their establishment in a directive to Lin Biao on May 7, 1966.

September. Within a month, some thirty high-ranking party leftists—including the so-called Gang of Four, which counted Mao's wife as its leading and most ostentatious member—were arrested, imprisoned, and stripped of all political power.

As a tumultuous, revolutionary, violent upheaval, the Great Proletarian Cultural Revolution lasted approximately three years, from the summer of 1966 to the spring of 1969. As a period of ideological extremism, routinized oppression, gross mismanagement, and egregious misrule, it dragged on for ten, ending only in the fall of 1976 with the death of Mao Zedong and the arrest of the Gang of Four. It left in its wake a wounded, crippled society. The world's most populous nation lay in shambles.

THE Great Proletarian Cultural Revolution has already been examined by Westerners from a wide variety of perspectives. It has been seen as a struggle for power between Party Chairman Mao Zedong and the country's chief of state, Liu Shaoqi; as an ideological struggle between the revolutionary, egalitarian line of Mao Zedong and the stultifying bureaucratic line of Liu Shaoqi; as Mao's quest for revolutionary immortality; as a factional struggle between rival young Red Guards; as the rise to power of Minister of Defense Lin Biao and the People's Liberation Army; as a radical experiment in social, political, and economic egalitarianism. It has been seen as a case of a leader and a society gone mad. Some have seen its roots in events as distant as the Chinese defeat by Great Britain in the Opium War of 1839, others in events as recent as the Socialist Education Campaign of the early 1960s, just preceding the outbreak of the Cultural Revolution.

As the truth about the Great Proletarian Cultural Revolution has gradually filtered through to the West, most observers have come to agree that it was also a "human tragedy on the grand scale."

But no one has attempted systematically to examine that grand-scale tragedy —to learn precisely how the political upheaval of the Cultural Revolution affected the lives of those who were its victims, how political events became tragedy writ large. This book provides a view of the Cultural Revolution less as politics than as tragedy. It examines what happened to individual Chinese during that tumultuous, violent, and oppressive decade and what the long-term human consequences of that period—both for China as a society and for individual Chinese—have been. It presents the Cultural Revolution as a failure of morality.

Harold Lasswell has argued that "revolutions are ruptures of conscience," that the violence against existing symbols of authority which revolutions necessitate means that those who have a hand in revolution must almost inevitably face a crisis of conscience. Mao Zedong would agree. One purpose of the Cultural Revolution was precisely to compel a rupture of conscience with the

Chinese past. The movement was often referred to as a "revolution that touches people to their very souls."

The Cultural Revolution was indeed a revolution that touched people to their very souls, and for some it was a rupture of conscience. But what the Cultural Revolution failed utterly to do was to establish a new system of morality against which the Chinese conscience could measure its behavior. Many of those who, during the Cultural Revolution, would have had others regard their behavior as "revolutionary" appear here in retrospect as crass, rank opportunists. Youth raised during that period of revolutionary upheaval remain even now illiterate with respect to basic tenets of morality. And many of those whose consciences never fully ruptured during the Cultural Revolution remain burdened today by a profound sense of guilt. China remains a country morally adrift.

This book is based largely on interviews conducted in China during the years 1981 and 1982, and the story is told in substantial measure by victims of the Cultural Revolution themselves. I offer it above all, with profound and heartfelt gratitude, to those courageous Chinese who share their experiences here, in the fervent hope that despite the fears that continue to haunt, the revelations recorded in this book will help in some small measure to reduce the possibility of the Cultural Revolution ever happening again. And I offer the book to friends in this country not just for what it teaches about China and the Chinese but for what it tells us about ourselves.

CHRONOLOGY

1839–42
The Opium War

1850–64
The Taiping Rebellion

1911
Collapse of the Last Chinese dynasty,
the Qing

1919
Student demonstrations launch the
nationalistic May Fourth Movement

October 1, 1949
Establishment of the People's
Republic of China

1950
Thought reform of China's
leading intellectuals begins

1951
The Three-anti Campaign—against
corruption, waste, and bureaucratism

1952
The Five-anti Campaign—against bribery, tax evasion, fraud,
theft of state secrets, and leakage of economic secrets

1955
Movement for the Suppression of Counterrevolutionaries

May 1957
Following Mao's declaration "Let a hundred flowers bloom,"
liberals begin speaking out

June 1957
Anti-rightist campaign begins, striking first at those
who had taken Mao's "Hundred Flowers" remark literally;
movement to Root Out the "White Flags" follows

1959
Anti-right Deviationist Campaign

1959–61
The "three bad years" of economic crisis and starvation
in the wake of the abortive Great Leap Forward

1962
Beginning of the Socialist Education Campaign
in the countryside

June 2, 1966
Publication of Nie Yuanzi's "big character poster"
signaling the start of the Great Cultural Revolution

1967
People's Liberation Army intervenes for the first time
in the Cultural Revolution, ostensibly on the side of
the leftists; First Movement to Ferret Out May
Sixteenth Elements gets under way

July 28, 1968
Mao meets with Red Guard leaders at Qinghua University;
two days later, first Mao Zedong Propaganda Team moves
into Qinghua

August 1968
Start of Movement to Purify Class Ranks;
students ordered to return to universities

December 1968
Call for urban youth to go to the countryside

October 1969
Evacuation of deposed high-ranking Communist Party
members from Peking; adults start being shipped to May
Seventh Cadre Schools for political reform

November 1969
Deaths of Liu Shaoqi and Tao Zhu

Late 1969–1971
Second Movement to Ferret Out May Sixteenth Elements

Autumn 1971
Death of Lin Biao following a failed coup attempt

January 8, 1976
Death of Zhou Enlai

April 4, 1976
Qing Ming festival,
demonstration in memory of Zhou Enlai

April 5, 1976
Demonstrations at Tiananmen Square
turn violent

July 6, 1976
Death of Zhu De

July 28, 1976
Tangshan earthquake

September 9, 1976
Death of Mao Zedong

October 1976
Arrest of the Gang of Four, including Mao's widow,
Jiang Qing; ostensible end of the Cultural Revolution

ENEMIES OF THE PEOPLE

O N E

THE PEOPLE OF PEKING REBEL AT LAST: TIANANMEN SQUARE, QING MING FESTIVAL, APRIL 1976

On March 23, 1976, a single wreath of white paper flowers, China's traditional symbol of mourning, was placed at the foot of the Monument to the Revolutionary Heroes in the center of Peking's Tiananmen Square. The two broad ribbons streaming from the wreath bore an inscription in commemoration of Zhou Enlai, China's late premier. During the day, another wreath, similarly inscribed and also dedicated to the memory of the late Zhou Enlai, appeared before the same monument. At night, under cover of darkness, the wreaths disappeared.

In the week that followed, more wreaths bearing similar inscriptions and also dedicated to Zhou Enlai were placed before the monument. They, too, disappeared.

On March 30, at shortly after six o'clock in the morning, a group of soldiers marched in cadence across Tiananmen Square and through the crowd already assembled before the Monument to the Revolutionary Heroes. The wreath they presented was signed by twenty-four men and bore the insignia of a prestigious unit of the Chinese military, the People's Liberation Army.

Later on the same day, another wreath appeared, its memorial message to Premier Zhou signed by twenty-nine mourners from the Peking Municipal Labor Union. Above the wreath, pasted to the monument itself and surrounded by paper flowers, was a eulogy to China's deceased premier.

That evening, the wreaths were protected by an informal contingent of self-selected watchmen, members of yet another unit of the People's Liberation Army, who had come to guard the monument around the clock. The following morning, the wreaths were still there.

The wreaths were a signal, a call to mourning.

THE traditional festival of Qing Ming—its precise date determined by the ancient lunar calendar which continues to govern the pulse of ordinary Chinese life—was approaching. The Qing Ming festival is that time of year the Chinese set aside to honor their dead, the day when families pay homage to their deceased by sweeping and cleaning the graves of their ancestors and placing upon them various offerings of food. The link between death and life was a continuous flow in traditional China, the dead relying on the living to provide them with the necessities of afterlife, the living at the mercy of the dead, who could, and frequently did, return to torment in the form of ghosts.

With the dramatic increase in population and the shortage of land for both buildings and crops, the state in revolutionary China had prohibited burial of the dead. The urban dead were supposed to be cremated. With the introduction of cremation, the traditional mode of homage to the dead had changed, with only minor alterations in spirit. At the Babaoshan Cemetery in the western outskirts of Peking, along peaceful courtyards shaded with evergreens, are housed the ashes of the city's dead. Social stratification persisting even in death, the ashes of Peking's ordinary citizens are stored in one section of the cemetery, the tightly crowded boxes and narrow shelves duplicating in death the housing shortage with which they had to contend in life. Before being reclaimed by the family, the boxes of ashes are allowed to remain for three years, the period of time that children in traditional China ordinarily withdrew from active life to mourn their parents. The ashes of revolutionary cadres and heroes, a category determined less by actual contribution than by position on the government pay scale, are housed along more spacious shelves within grander, more impressive edifices. Their ashes remain indefinitely.

With the coming of Communist rule, the Qing Ming festival had been designated the time for schoolchildren to honor the revolutionary heroes. At Babaoshan, the festival had come to be observed not by sweeping the graves but by dusting the boxes of ashes and cleaning the black-bordered photographs of the deceased that identified the remains within. Flowers were substituted for the offerings of food. China was still a country that believed in paying respect to its dead. In 1976 the Qing Ming festival fell on Sunday, April 4.

THE year 1976 had begun, on January 8, with the death of Zhou Enlai. His demise had long been expected. Zhou had been confined to hospital, able to make only rare public appearances, since the spring of 1974, cancer slowly eating away at his body. But his death was no less a shock because it was expected.

The news was delayed for the good part of a day. Most heard it first early in the morning of January 9, shortly after they had wakened and before they left for work. The announcement had come first on the radio—broadcast by the ubiquitous outdoor loudspeakers that hang on trees and poles in residential units throughout Peking, loudspeakers that serve to wake one up in the morning, to call one to exercise and meals, to ensure that no one misses any of the important announcements that might be made during the day. The announcement had begun with the playing of a few bars of "The East Is Red," the martial ode to Mao. Then a voice, slow, solemn, and steeped in grief, began reciting the myriad official positions of the deceased, followed by his name, reading the joint communiqué from the Party Central Committee, the State Council, and the People's Congress. Throughout the day, at half-hour intervals, the loudspeakers continued to play the slow, solemn music of funeral dirges.

Urban Chinese still remember today exactly where they were, what they were doing, and how they felt when they heard the news. It is a memory analogous in incandescence and pain to the American memory of the assassination of President John Fitzgerald Kennedy. People wept at the death of Zhou Enlai, wept bitterly and openly. And the memory of grief and pain is often accompanied by an equally strong memory that the grief was shared, that the tears, the black armbands so publicly and defiantly displayed, had served, however transiently, to bridge the gulf that had long divided the Chinese people.

"At that time, people often felt frustrated, harassed, agonized," remembers one about the period just prior to Zhou's death. "In buses, people always used to quarrel. If someone stepped on someone else's toes, the people would shout at each other. In our work units, we were annoyed and humiliated, but we could say nothing. The only outlet for frustration was the bus. So buses were very depressing.

"But when Premier Zhou died, many people were weeping—in the streets, on the buses. A mournful silence reigned on the buses. It was uplifting, really uplifting. There was a sense of relief. In the past, for so long in China, there had been no occasion when you could feel your feelings uplifted. But when Zhou died, people were kind, considerate of each other. If people saw you had a black band on your arm or saw you weeping, you found out that other people felt the same way. Before, you didn't know what other people thought. But with Zhou's death, you came to realize when other people were weeping that your grief was their grief, too. We were isolated before, but then people became close."

URBANE, sophisticated, handsome, cosmopolitan, and educated, Zhou Enlai had served as premier of China since the inception of the People's Republic. He had come to stand, in symbol and in practice, for all that was civilian, civil, and orderly in China, for what was literate, cultured, and refined, for what was good and kind—for what the Chinese describe as *wen*. He had come to stand for much of what had collapsed in China in the decade preceding his death.

Still burdened by superstitions that had attached to the imperial court of dynastic China, peasants in remote areas of the countryside had continued to regard Zhou, as they had once regarded the emperor himself and those closest to him, as part man, part god, a being descended from a star, still quite visible in the sky, to which he had returned after fulfilling his mortal mission on earth.

Lest doubt be raised about the place of Premier Zhou in China's history and mythology, the heavens had obliged those who still believed in omens, as so many in the countryside still so tenaciously did, with a sign that was unmistakable. On March 8, exactly two months after Zhou's death, a huge meteorite blazed its trail across the sky and fell to earth in Jilin province in China's northeast. Weighing 3,894 pounds, it was the largest meteorite to have crashed to earth in recorded history. When Zhuge Liang, master strategist, dazzling intellect, immortal hero of the epic classic *Romance of the Three Kingdoms*, and China's ancient symbol of *wen*, had died some seventeen hundred years before, another meteorite had flashed its way across the sky and fallen to earth. So deeply ingrained a part of China's historical myth that his story seems almost to be transmitted through the genes, Zhuge Liang had set a precedent for other great men to follow. The death of those whose legend will endure is signaled by a meteorite. Zhou Enlai in life, master strategist and dazzling intellect, had often been compared to Zhuge Liang. They had both descended from the same star.

Urban Chinese—better educated, more sophisticated, less burdened by folk superstition—were more prone to judge Zhou Enlai on the basis of his perceived contributions to his country than his relationship to the celestial galaxy. China's urban intellectuals, in particular, credit Zhou with a special grace. They point to the fact that it was Zhou, in a speech in January 1975 to China's National People's Congress, ostensibly the highest organ of state power, who first put forth the slogan of the "four modernizations"—of industry, agriculture, science and technology, and the military. It was Zhou who set the goal of modernization for the year 2000. They distinguish Zhou from Mao by pointing to the fact that the friends of Mao—his wife, Jiang Qing, Zhang Chunqiao, Yao Wenyuan—were the enemies of Zhou, arguing that it was Mao and his friends who blocked the implementation of the four modernizations, insisting on political struggle over the economic development of their country. They say that when Zhou was dying, confined to hospital, Mao never once visited the man who had stood by him so faithfully, so loyally, so long.

They argue that Zhou Enlai had not supported the Cultural Revolution, launched by Mao in 1966, but that he cooperated with it, refusing directly to challenge Mao, in order to retain his control over the state apparatus, to use that power to protect his associates under attack and to minimize political interference in economic production. They argue that the Cultural Revolution would have been worse without Zhou Enlai. Far worse. They believe that he was a friend and patron of China's intellectuals and that without him their fate, too, would have been worse.

China's urban intellectuals saw much of themselves in Zhou Enlai, for they were people who had wished and worked for the modernization of their country, who had stood faithfully and loyally by the party chairman, who had often sacrificed the integrity of their own beliefs in order to remain loyal to the chairman's cause. Just as many believed that Zhou had been betrayed by Mao, so many more ordinary Chinese had come by 1976 to believe that they too had been betrayed by the party chairman. Mao had let them down. Many felt that with Zhou Enlai still alive and in power, there was hope for them and their country. With his death, many lost hope.

And many were angry when Zhou Enlai died. They were angry because they believed that Zhou had not been properly mourned, that the people of China had been prohibited from mourning. They were furious with Mao's wife, Jiang Qing, for daring to appear in the guise of a mourner at the official memorial ceremonies, for at the time of Zhou's death, Jiang Qing, it is said, was directing a campaign, rife with innuendo, against him. It was not just that she had dared publicly to pretend to mourn the death of Zhou Enlai. On national television with the entire country watching, she had, on approaching the late premier's bier, refused to remove her cap.

"When Premier Zhou died," recounts one of the capital's residents, "they wouldn't let us mourn him. We couldn't even wear black armbands. On the television, on the radio, after the very first day, the programs continued as usual, as though nothing had happened, as though there had been no change. A directive came that we weren't even to hold our own memorial meetings in our own work units. There was to be no recognition of this historic passing."

"In my work unit," relates another, "there was a telephone notice saying not to do much for Zhou's death, telling us not to cry. So the man who took the call said, 'Okay, I will take this order. From now on, there will be no tears of grief when anyone dies.' He meant that when Mao died no one would cry either."

True, there was an outpouring of public grief when Zhou left the scene, but it was largely spontaneous and without official sanction. Official homages were minimal and tightly controlled. People did place wreaths before the Monument to the Revolutionary Heroes, and they gathered in Tiananmen Square to share their grief and their tears. Huge crowds lined the route from the Peking Hospital, where Zhou had lain briefly in state, to the crematorium at Babaoshan. Thousands waited in teary silence from the early hours of the morning until late at night, braving the chill and windy weather of January in Peking for a glimpse of the funeral bus that would transport Zhou's remains to the crematorium and return his ashes to the Great Hall of the People in Tiananmen Square, whence they would be scattered across the land and the rivers of the country he had served so long. But that was not enough. Zhou Enlai remained insufficiently mourned.

Within the grief-stricken crowd that lined the streets of Peking in homage to the late premier, the silence was broken only by the whispering of three words that spread like electricity along a telegraph wire from one end of the crowd to the other: "Qing Ming festival." "Since Qing Ming is the traditional time for paying homage to the dead and for paying respect to revolutionary heroes, it seemed appropriate that we use that time to pay our respects to Premier Zhou," remembers one participant.

But how?

PEKING is a city where life is lived and work performed behind walls, walls that even in the best of times serve to compartmentalize and divide, walls that render communication difficult. Telephones in 1976 were the preserve of officialdom. Communication between ordinary people was best conducted in person. But entrance to the residential and office buildings behind the city's walls is through gates, and those gates are guarded by personnel whose task it is to register any outsider and to inquire as to whom he is visiting and the purpose of the call. Such visits may be reported to one's "leader," who may not look with favor upon unauthorized, unwarranted calls. Peking is a city suspicious of strangers.

For most residents of Peking, March of 1976 was not the best of times. Communication even among family and friends was often strained, guarded, distant. People were isolated, one from the other. "You felt lonely even in a crowd," recalls one.

And the walls that even in the best of times served to divide had been officially imbued with purpose. "Interunit ties," communication across and over the city's walls, had been forbidden.

Tiananmen Square, located in the very heart of the city, is an anomaly in Peking. There are no walls. It is a huge open space, a square so vast that it is reputed to hold upwards of half a million people.

An uncertain fusion of China's imperial past and its socialist present, Tiananmen is bordered on the east by the Museum of Revolutionary History and on the west by the equally massive and Stalinesque Great Hall of the People, meetingplace for the highest echelons of the Chinese Communist Party and court for the country's highest leaders. China's highest leaders, in March 1976, were deeply divided. They included:

- At the pinnacle, Mao Zedong, then eighty-two years old, chairman of the Chinese Communist Party since 1935, aging, autocratic, and delphic, feeble of body and mind and probably suffering from Parkinson's disease. Mao Zedong had had the misfortune to become both the Lenin and the Stalin of China, responsible both for leading the Chinese Communist Party to victory over the Guomindang of Chiang Kai-shek and establishing thereby a new China and for building the new order in the wake of military victory. It was his radical insistence that the revolution at all costs must continue that brought him into confrontation first with his own lieutenants and ultimately with the people he ruled.
- Mao's neurotic fourth wife, Jiang Qing, a former Shanghai actress and once a woman of considerable beauty. Catapulted into power by the Great Proletarian Cultural Revolution, Jiang Qing had exercised power through control over China's literature and arts and her vindictive and vitriolic personal attacks against prominent Chinese intellectuals and officials. She was widely reviled.
- Zhang Chunqiao, a radical bureaucrat and close associate of Jiang Qing, similarly thrust to power by the Great Proletarian Cultural Revolution. Zhang Chunqiao had become a member of the ruling Politburo in April 1969 and was the party boss in Shanghai, the largest of China's cities.
- Yao Wenyuan, close friend of both Jiang Qing and Zhang Chunqiao and the Communist Party's leading leftist ideologue. The Propaganda Department of the Chinese Communist Party had disintegrated during the course of the Cultural Revolution, but to the extent that anyone in 1976 was in charge of party propaganda, it was Yao Wenyuan. It was the Shanghai publication in 1965 of Yao's bitter attack on a play by Wu Han—leading historian, writer, and then vice-mayor of Peking—which had presaged the opening of the Great Proletarian Cultural Revolution.
- Hua Guofeng, enigmatic acting premier since the death of Zhou Enlai and member of the Politburo since 1973. Hua Guofeng's political career was rooted in Mao's home province of Hunan, where Hua had been sent at the time of Liberation in 1949 and where he had stayed, weathering even the worst storms of the Cultural Revolution, until 1971, and where he had never

taken a lead in initiating policies but had always faithfully, loyally, and honestly responded to the shifting dictates of Peking.

· Deng Xiaoping, tough, resilient, and outspoken, purged by Mao at the start of the Cultural Revolution in 1966 but officially reinstated as deputy premier in 1973 upon the urging of Zhou Enlai. In the late 1950s and early 1960s, when much of China was locked in famine and the country was on the brink of economic collapse, Deng Xiaoping had justified the introduction of policies that Mao and his supporters would later describe as capitalist by arguing that "any cat, whether black or white, is a good cat so long as it catches mice." It was for this philosophy that he was purged in 1966. In March 1976, another campaign of vilification against Deng Xiaoping was in full swing. Upon being reinstated in 1973, Deng had worked to exonerate numerous party officials who had been purged with him early in the Cultural Revolution and had sought to reverse the extremism of that period. Far from being chastened by his period as a political pariah, Deng continued to place the necessity of economic production and the modernization of his country ahead of ideological purity. The campaign against Deng was being led by Mao's wife and her friends, with the tacit support of the chairman.

On the south, Tiananmen Square is edged by the ancient, graceful, and stately Zhengyang Gate, popularly known as Qianmen, the Front Gate, one of the few of the city's gates which has not been demolished to make way for modernity. Opposite the Front Gate, to the north across the wide expanse, is another ancient gate from whence the square takes its name, Tiananmen, the Gate of Heavenly Peace, entrance to the Forbidden City, the magnificent imperial palace where China's former emperors once lived and held court.

In March 1976, the red façade of the Gate of Heavenly Peace was bedecked with larger-than-life portraits of Communist Party Chairman Mao Zedong and slogans invoking the longevity of both the People's Republic of China and the international solidarity of the working class. Beneath these testimonials stood the reviewing stands from which, on October 1, 1949, the party chairman had proclaimed to the world the establishment of a new government in China, and where, on a number of occasions throughout the late summer and fall of 1966, he had sanctified China's Great Proletarian Cultural Revolution by reviewing several million young Red Guards from middle schools and universities throughout the country to whom he had assigned the exulting task of rebelling against the very authority he had taken credit for establishing.

The most notable object of the Red Guards' rebellion had been one of the men who had stood next to Mao in October 1949 when the People's Republic was proclaimed—Liu Shaoqi, once the president of the People's Republic and until 1966 Mao's anointed successor. Maimed and crippled from the beatings he had suffered at the hands of Cultural Revolution rebels, Liu Shaoqi had died in prison in November 1969, isolated and alone and without intervention on his behalf by any of the men with whom he had once shared the podium. In 1976, his death was still officially a secret.

The man who had risen to replace Liu Shaoqi as Mao's successor and closest comrade-in-arms was also dead by 1976. Lin Biao, appointed China's minister of defense in 1959, had died in a plane crash in Outer Mongolia, in flight to the Soviet Union, after his plot to overthrow Mao had been discovered in the late summer of 1971.

In front of the reviewing stands, separating the Gate of Heavenly Peace from the square itself, is Changan Avenue, the Avenue of Eternal Peace, a wide, eight-lane boulevard linking Peking east to west.

The Monument to the Revolutionary Heroes stands roughly in the center of the vast open space that is Tiananmen Square. It is an obelisk, so unprepossessing in scale that it is nearly dwarfed by both the space and the edifices surrounding it. The bas-relief at the base of the monument depicts a series of several revolutionary struggles, extending over more than a century, that culminated in the victory of the Communist Party in 1949: the Opium War that began in 1839, during which Britain successfully insisted by force of arms on its right to sell opium to China and to use the country's ports; the May Fourth Movement of 1919, during which the people of Peking rose against their own leaders for acceding to the terms of the Versailles Treaty, which ceded parts of Shandong province to Japan; the Northern Expedition that began in 1926, during which Chiang Kai-shek led a combined force of Nationalist and Communist troops to reunify the country, which had splintered into contentious warlord satrapies following the collapse of the last of China's dynasties, the Qing, in 1911, and during the course of which Chiang had turned against the very Communists with whom he had earlier cooperated; and the civil war between the Nationalists and the Communists. This last scene depicts the Communist troops crossing the vast eastward-flowing Yangtze River, which divides China north from south, sealing thereby their victory over Chiang Kai-shek. The calligraphy on one side of the monument, reading "The people's heroes are immortal," is that of Mao. The characters of the eulogy for the revolutionary martyrs to whom the monument is dedicated had been written by Zhou.

It was fitting that memorial wreaths to Zhou Enlai should have been placed before this, the most modest, most honest of China's monuments—not just because a monument to the dead was a proper place to mourn, or because the monument itself was dedicated to revolutionary heroes, of whom Zhou was one, or because it was inscribed with his own calligraphy, but also because part of Zhou Enlai's own monument, in the eyes of many of his countrymen, lay in the fact that he had seemed to behave as a man among men, no bigger than life, unprepossessing, even modest.

There was another reason that the Monument to the Revolutionary Heroes was a particularly appropriate spot to place memorial wreaths for Zhou Enlai.

If the signal carried and the call to mourning was heeded, the citizens of Peking might need a vast open space to express their grief.

They did. The wreaths transcended walls. The signal carried. The call was heeded.

"When we learned about the wreaths at Tiananmen Square," one resident of Peking explained, "we all began planning. We made our wreaths days in advance, getting ready to take them to the square. And many people began composing poetry." To construct the wreaths of mourning, they used the thin, multicolored onionskin paper that for so many years had been used for the big character posters of the political campaigns and that even then was being used in the attacks against Deng Xiaoping.

After the first wreaths appeared in Tiananmen in late March 1976, people began coming from disparate parts of the city, singly at first or with small groups of family or friends, to visit the square. Some wore handmade white paper flowers in their lapels, and these simple flowers soon covered the pine bushes surrounding the monument, bathing the evergreens in a mantle of white. In the first two days of April, the crowds in the square began swelling, from the hundreds, to the thousands, to the tens of thousands. The hours of crowding grew longer and longer. The number of wreaths grew larger and larger.

On April 2, a telephone directive was sent to all of Peking's work units, forbidding participation in the Qing Ming activities at Tiananmen Square. Telephone directives are quicker, more urgent, than written ones. The directive declared that the Qing Ming festival was superstitious, a festival of "ghosts," that the practice of cleaning the tombs was to be classified among the "four olds"—old ideas, old customs, old culture, and old habits—that the Cultural Revolution was supposed to have eliminated. "Don't go to Tiananmen to present your wreaths," the directive urged. "Don't fall into the trap of the class enemy." And it threatened, "Whoever sends wreaths will be severely punished."

Saturday, April 3, the day before Qing Ming festival, was a working day for most residents of Peking, and it was rainy and unseasonably cold. Leaders of some work units, in an attempt to enforce the ban against going to the square, called mandatory all-day meetings of the staff. The captive audiences clandestinely arranged shifts to allow a series of small groups to leave and return together. "I was wondering what to do, how to get to the square," remembers one member of such an audience, "when I realized that two or three of my good friends had disappeared and another was motioning to me. We met in the bathroom and went to Tiananmen together."

At Peking University, China's most prestigious institution of higher education and the one that had figured most prominently in all other outpourings of popular sentiment in twentieth-century China, students, faculty, and staff were ordered to spend the weekend in their dormitories or homes, a directive that many feared would be enforced through house checks by the surveillance personnel with which the campus was said to abound. It is said that the huge iron gates of the walled campus were closed and locked, passage to and from the grounds being confined to openings large enough for only one person to traverse at a time, and those wishing to pass were subject to questioning by a loyal gatekeeper. Peking University, at the time, was a stronghold of elements unsympathetic to the late premier. Rumor has it that one of those arrested during the Qing Ming festival was a compatriot of the university's captives, a man who caught a wreath tossed over the campus wall which he had agreed to take to the square.

In other work units, leaders warned their subordinates to go to the square by eight in the morning of Saturday, April 3, before the workday had officially begun. The directive of April 2 prohibiting people from going to the square would not be read until the start of official business on Saturday. By seven-thirty on the morning of Saturday, April 3, Tiananmen Square was already full.

In still other units, the political leadership responsible for conveying the directive was frankly complicitous with the mourners, and many marched together with their units to the square. "At my institute," recalls a member of the prestigious Chinese Academy of Sciences, an organization controlled by colleagues of Deng Xiaoping, "at first we had just gone by ourselves, individu-ally or with a few friends. But then we decided we wanted to go together, as a group. So we planned and made wreaths. Then the leadership called a meeting for eight-thirty in the morning of April 3, just before we were sched-uled to start out. We all had to attend. At first, one cadre read a document forbidding us to go, saying there was danger of counterrevolutionary activity. Then, right after that, another cadre, standing right next to him, said that we would assemble at nine o'clock to begin our march to the square. We all walked together as a group, down Changan Avenue, carrying our wreath."

It was to Mao's wife, Jiang Qing, that most mourners attributed responsi-bility for the ban they were so boldly defying. "Who is it," demanded one poem, quoting from the directive, "who says that presenting wreaths is an old habit? When *she* dies, she won't get any flowers."

Defy her they did. From early in the morning until late at night on Saturday, April 3, Tiananmen Square remained crowded with a sea of people and of wreaths. When the rain began, some of the wreaths were covered in clear plastic wrapping, umbrellas went up, and scarves covered heads, but the crowds did not appreciably thin.

On Sunday, April 4, the day of the Qing Ming festival itself, some went by bus, the banners along the vehicles' sides proclaiming the mourning of the passengers within. Tens of thousands went by bicycle, and the street in front of the Workers' Cultural Palace on Changan Avenue, to the east of Tianan-men, was covered with a sea of bikes, an unexpected and not insubstantial bonus to the enterprising attendants, who charged a penny per bike to guard them against theft. Tens of thousands went by foot, collectively, starting in formation from work units scattered throughout the city, converging finally from the east and the west on Changan Avenue, in front of Tiananmen, their wreaths and banners held high, reciting their poems in unison, rendering Peking's main boulevard a huge parade. Workers from a heavy electrical machine factory in the suburbs of the city began their march in the early morning, carrying a huge wreath weighing over a thousand pounds, finally arriving triumphantly, to cheers from the waiting crowd, at five o'clock in the afternoon. They knew, as everyone in the square must have known, that the wreaths would ultimately be removed. The workers from this factory wanted to make that task as difficult as possible.

Whole classes of schoolchildren, from kindergarten through senior middle school, arrived together, standing in disciplined formation, their heads bowed or their right hands raised in clenched fists, to chant their poems in harmony. Toddlers were accompanied by their parents, and little children, too, presented wreaths. "Who says the premier left no descendants?" read a wreath presented by a five-year-old child and referring to the fact that Zhou had died childless. "This wreath will present to him the heart of a loyal son."

The sole representative of Peking University, a female assistant professor in the Department of History, arrived at ten o'clock in the morning, escorted by a friend. She carried not a wreath but a basket of fresh flowers, bought near the Dongdan section of Peking, to the east of the square—a few daffodils, some boughs of evergreen, and some horseshoe lotus, Premier Zhou's favorite flower. She did not enter the square itself, but placed her tribute at the foot of the flagpole directly opposite the Gate of Heavenly Peace, at the northern entrance to the square. She came and departed quickly, but those who saw her were awed to silence by her special courage. People swarmed around the humble, brave, and heartfelt offering, everyone wanting to photograph it, people literally climbing on top of each other's shoulders to see and get a good shot. "We were so disappointed that Peking University could not take more of a part," explains a graduate from that university. "The students and faculty of Peking University had played such an important role in all of China's twentieth-century protests. We had hoped they would be able to play more of a role in this. We looked for them, waited for them, during those two days."

A young worker bit through his own finger. Sitting on the shoulders of one of his comrades, he displayed and read the poem, his "letter of determination," he had written on cloth with his own blood, pledging to defend the premier with blood and life. The crowd roared its approval, shouting his name. "You are my representative. I feel the same," they yelled, rewarding him with a bouquet of flowers. They sang the "Internationale."

Before the Monument to the Revolutionary Heroes were hundreds and thousands of wreaths, constantly shifting wreaths, as those that had already been duly noted, registered, and appreciated by the crowd were moved to make way for the new arrivals. The monument, as described by one Westerner who was there, seemed strangled, the wreaths climbing higher and higher as if reaching for the peak. Daring young men scaled the pile, attempting to place their unit's wreath at the top. From the height of the monument, the view was remarkable, a sheet of humanity reaching all the way to Changan Avenue.

Poems composed in honor of the occasion were posted and read aloud, to be copied and shared by the appreciative crowd. Relay teams were formed to shout the poems to the audience, line by line, each line echoing slowly from the hub along the spokes of a wheel, as people wrote on one another's back, recording the messages.

Many were poems of grief, simple, even childlike, in their innocence:

> The people loved their premier.
> The people's premier loved the people.
> The premier and people shared weal and woe;
> Their hearts were always linked.

Some, such as the poem to be chosen by the Public Security Bureau as exhibit number one in the case of the Tiananmen counterrevolutionary incident, were superb:

> In our grief we hear the devils shrieking;
> We weep while wolves and jackals laugh.
> Shedding tears, we come to mourn our hero;
> Heads raised we unsheathe our swords.

The Tiananmen demonstrations of Qing Ming festival 1976 were an expression of collective grief for China's late premier, but they were also an expression of anger, an act of protest, of outrage, against the country's highest leaders, against those leaders who had destroyed the *wen* for which Zhou had stood and who had led the country to civil disaster.

It was against Jiang Qing that the strongest popular revulsion was directed.

> This woman is really crazy.
> She even wants to be an empress!
> Look at yourself in the mirror
> And see what you are.
> You've got a small gang of henchmen
> Who make trouble all the time,
> Trying to kid the people, capering about.
> But your days are numbered.

Not that Jiang Qing was ever named in the poems directed against her. She never had to be. Neither in traditional nor in modern China have top-ranking officials still in power ever been attacked by name. Allegory and metaphor have been sufficient both to launch a political attack and to bring retribution when criticisms failed to result in the dismissal of the person attacked.

And, yes, if the demonstrations of Tiananmen in 1976 were attacks against Jiang Qing, Zhang Chunqiao, and their associates, then underneath the allegorical attacks, unspoken but nonetheless there, they were also protests against the emperor himself, against the previously unimpeachable and infallible Party Chairman Mao Zedong. For who among them could forget that it was Chairman Mao's "little red book" that the young Red Guards had held high, that it was before his image that all working adults had had to bow in the morning to ask for their day's instructions and in the evening to confess their day's mistakes, that it was in his name and with his blessing that the movement that brought the country to the brink of disaster had been launched?

The Qing Ming festival of 1976 was also an expression of support for Deng Xiaoping—purged by Mao as the "number-two capitalist roader" early in the Cultural Revolution, brought back by Zhou himself in 1973—against whom yet another campaign of vilification was now in full swing. Deng's given name, Xiaoping, is a homophone for the Chinese characters that mean "little bottle"; and adorning the trees around the Monument to the Revolutionary Heroes were not only the paper flowers that people had removed from their lapels but hundreds of little bottles, surreptitiously removed from scientific laboratories and pharmacies throughout the city. Eight young workers locked arms and, without camouflage of innuendo or allegory, chanted their support for Deng, declaring that the situation had improved measurably since his restoration. Word of their action spread quickly to those who had missed the performance.

IN those two days when the crowds were at their height, between the recitations of poetry, the cheers that greeted the waves of new contingents arriving in the square, and the applause with which each new wreath was welcomed, there was time for talk—talk about forbidden matters, dangerous subjects, topics that were ordinarily discussed only in private among family and closest friends, and often, even then, only in code. Jiang Qing was only referred to in such surreptitious conversations in code. In the gossip of Tiananmen, she was at last named openly.

There was much to be learned in the talk that spread through the square. Many of the participants in the demonstrations, those in fact who had worked behind the scenes to organize it, were the sons and daughters of high-ranking party officials, officials who had been disgraced during the Cultural Revolution, but who, in the rehabilitations that had left them cleared but still without official position, remained privy to the scandal, the intrigue, the lapses of integrity within the highest circles of power.

It was against Mao's wife that the most delectable of Tiananmen scandals were directed. That some of the revelations fell short of the truth, that some of the accusations could not have been true, hardly diminished the fascination with which the stories were greeted. Scatology had long been employed in China as the finishing touch in accusations designed to discredit foes. It was the contrast between her public presentation of self and the alleged reality of her life in private that was the source of greatest wonder.

At a time when asceticism was the official norm, when people vied with each other to adorn themselves in ever more humble accouterments of poverty, Jiang Qing had assumed a life of luxury, taking up residence behind the walls of the privileged haven of Diaoyu Tai, the estate reserved for visiting heads of state, where President Nixon and entourage had stayed in 1972. It contained elegant, cavernous guest houses scattered through vast gardens, and ponds lined with graceful weeping willows. Jiang Qing is said to have spent her days in Diao Yutai riding horseback, galloping through its open fields. It was a sport she had learned in Yenan, the guerrilla base area from which the Communist Party launched its final bid for power and where Jiang Qing had captured the heart of Mao.

At a time when the viewing pleasure of China's hundreds of millions had been limited to eight revolutionary operas in which the heroes were ever both glorious and victorious and the villains unabashedly and unremittingly evil, operas reworked into stilted caricatures of reality by Jiang Qing herself, Mao's wife enjoyed American—and sometimes, it was rumored, obscene—movies by night.

At a time when Jiang Qing was presenting herself in public as her husband's representative and most faithful spokesman, Jiang Qing's affair with Zhang Chunqiao was said to be already of long standing. The assertion that she had borne a child by her paramour at the start of the Cultural Revolution failed to take into account that she was fifty-two years old at the time.

The chairman of the Communist Party and the most powerful man in China was said to be powerless to control his wife, for reasons that did not reflect favorably upon him. Mao, it was alleged, had a private secretary with whom he had often gone to bed, and the result of one such episode had been a child. However carefully guarded the secret, Jiang Qing had discovered the truth. Had Mao attempted to rein in his wife, to control her politically and personally errant ways, the price would have been the image he had cultivated so assiduously, so long. For Jiang Qing would have revealed the secret of his illegitimate child, threatening thereby both the cult and the legitimacy of Mao. The party chairman was helpless before his wife.

Or so the story went.

"We all heard these things," a young female participant in the demonstrations said. "Everyone I know heard the same thing. How much is true, probably we never will know." Women had often been blamed in traditional China for the failures of men in power.

True or not, the stories had an effect. With the revelations in Tiananmen Square, something changed—something fundamental to how China's leaders were perceived by those over whom they ruled.

True, the undertone of anger had long been present. "By the time of Tiananmen," one participant said, "anyone who still supported the 'gang' was either evil or a fool." But with the opportunity to talk openly about the moral and political turpitude of their leaders, the few remaining shreds of legitimacy were finally and decisively snapped.

Residents of Peking say that something about the city changed in those few days surrounding Qing Ming festival 1976, that the people became united as rarely before. Salespeople, known ordinarily for their surly rudeness, became polite, cooperative, even helpful. Lines for ever-crowded buses became orderly, the people waiting, patient. Arguments and altercations were fewer, and when they did occur, a whispered "Remember Premier Zhou" was enough to settle the dispute. Lost articles were returned to their rightful owners, and when the rightful owner was not apparent, advertisements were placed to find him.

True, some went to Tiananmen for the profits to be reaped from such a huge and various crowd: the city's pickpockets were out in force. Hundreds of others were there because it was their job: the secret police were liberally dispersed. And some were there for the spectacle. Entertainment in the city of Peking was sparse in 1976, and the city had not witnessed such splendid diversion since . . . few could remember when.

But pickpockets, secret police, and spectators aside, a singular fact remained. If it is true that Tiananmen Square holds half a million people, then in the square, from morning until night, at any given time, on April 3 and April 4, were close to half a million people, the composition of the crowd changing as people came and went by the tens and hundreds of thousands. It was the largest spontaneous demonstration in the history of China.

THE crowd that arrived in the square shortly after dawn on Monday, April 5, was different in character from the crowds of the earlier days—younger and predominantly, indeed overwhelmingly, male. Its numbers were smaller—in the tens of thousands rather than the hundreds of thousands. It is said that many who went to the square that day had been young Red Guards or "revolutionary rebels" during the early stages of the Cultural Revolution, young militants whose dissensions had sometimes led to violence. Others were students from Peking's middle schools, teenagers whose formative years had been spent under the shadow of the Cultural Revolution, too young to have participated, too old to have remained unaffected—the generation whose parents had spent so much time in political meetings or on rural work stints that they had been deprived of many of the benefits of parental supervision. Members of the older generation who came to the square that day went largely to bear witness to history in the making.

No work units marched collectively to the square that day. People came alone or with small groups of friends. A few wreaths did appear before the Monument to the Revolutionary Heroes, but Monday, April 5, was not a day for bringing wreaths. The most famous poem of Tiananmen 1976 would be pasted to the monument shortly before dusk, but the poetry of Qing Ming had evaporated.

This crowd had come to the square not out of grief but out of anger, not to commemorate or to demonstrate but to protest. They had come to exercise once more both the right of rebellion that had its origins deep in Chinese history and the right that had so captured the hearts of the young some ten years earlier when none other than Chairman Mao himself had declared that "to rebel is justified." That many in the crowd were the same young men who had earlier practiced what Mao had preached, had exercised that right some-times to the point of violence, and that others were their younger brothers who had looked on in envy as their teenage seniors had reveled in their newfound power and importance, no doubt had an effect on the day's events.

Under cover of darkness during the early-morning hours of Monday, April 5, it had taken more than a hundred of the city's largest trucks and fire engines to cart the tens of thousands of wreaths away—a task so burdensome that cranes had finally to be called into service.

The removal of the wreaths was a signal of a different sort. It was a provocation to rebel. Historical coincidence, moreover, was on the side of the rebels.

Nearly sixty years earlier, on May 4, 1919, the most significant mass demon-stration in twentieth-century China, a demonstration that ultimately turned to violence, had begun at Tiananmen, the Gate of Heavenly Peace, just opposite and in full view of the Monument to the Revolutionary Heroes around which the wreaths had been massed. It was that very incident that was sculptured in one of the scenes at the base of the monument. During the First World War, China had entered the conflict on the side of the Allies, inspired by Wilson's promises of self-determination for all nations, the end of extrater-ritoriality in China, and the assurance that control of Chinese land usurped by foreign powers would be returned to its rightful governors. The Chinese, however, were betrayed at Versailles by both the Allies and their own diplo-mats, who had acceded to the further parceling out of the country's territory. Angered, patriots of China's capital city, led by university students and most notably those from Peking University, had taken to the streets in protest.

The Chinese assign numbers rather than names to the months of the year, and they delight in numerical juxtaposition. That the protest of 1919 had reached its height on the fourth day of the fifth month and the wreaths of 1976 had been removed on the fifth day of the fourth month was not entirely insignificant. Historical coincidence lent the anger of those in the square on April 5, 1976, a certain legitimating élan. Many in the crowd that day were the sons and grandsons of those who had participated in the May Fourth protest. May Fourth was part of their familial lore. It was not at the Monument to the Revolutionary Heroes that people began gathering on the morning of April 5, but in front of the Gate of Heavenly Peace.

By eight in the morning, the area in front of Tiananmen was already full, tens of thousands of people having come to join the protest. When two public security vans sped into the area announcing that Qing Ming was over and ordering the crowds to leave the square, the vans were surrounded by hostile youths. One vehicle was overturned, its passengers fleeing to the Sun Yat-sen Park that borders the Imperial Palace.

Shortly thereafter, alternately shouting slogans calling for the return of the wreaths and the release of their arrested comrades and singing the "Internationale," the crowd began moving toward the Great Hall of the People in the mistaken hope that someone within that seat of Chinese government and diplomacy would be willing to negotiate with a crowd that threatened to become unruly, a crowd whose demands were unlikely to be negotiable. When a young man unsympathetic to their cause yelled slogans challenging the crowd, he was surrounded, seized, and paraded through the square. When the head of the local police appeared on the steps of the Great Hall of the People, in an effort to subdue and disperse the crowd, he, too, was surrounded and besieged. At eleven in the morning, the first ineffectual contingent of the workers' militia, many of whom had themselves brought wreaths to the square the day before, arrived to subdue the crowd. "Have you no shame?" the crowd jeered. "Are you still Chinese?" Ill at ease with their officially assigned mission, the militia were not entirely united.

By noon, the protesters had managed to select five representatives to the "Committee of the People of the Capital for Commemorating the Premier" and had drawn up three demands: the return of all the wreaths, the release of those who had been arrested, the severe punishment of those who had been responsible for destroying the wreaths and arresting the demonstrators, and a guarantee of the democratic right of the masses to commemorate their dead premier. That the demands were contradictory—wreaths that have been destroyed cannot be returned—and that there were actually four demands rather than three, did not really matter. Demands composed by crowds in anger are rarely either entirely coherent, completely rational, or very likely to be met.

Negotiations with representatives at the Public Security Bureau's "command post" proved fruitless. The crowd grew angrier. When reinforcements from the police, the militia, and the capital police force arrived, the crowd surrounded an automobile, turned it over, and set it on fire. The police and militia fanned out, encircling the square. Demonstrators were allowed to leave the square, but no one was permitted to enter. The crowd toppled and burned three more cars. Hundreds of mounds of steamed bread rolled across the pavement. One of the cars had been delivering food to the police and militia.

The violence escalated. A small group of militants, young people of middle school age, broke through the police lines and into the Public Security Bureau's barracks, a three-story brick building along the eastern edge of the square, to the south of the Museum of Revolutionary History. Doing battle with the guards, the teenagers smashed and looted the interior. Then they set the barracks on fire. Being of brick, it could not burn to the ground, but smoke filled the square.

It was nearly dusk, and the air was still filled with smoke, when the last of the Tiananmen poems was pasted on the Monument to the Revolutionary Heroes. Written on eight separate pages, it was not markedly different in tone or in content from many of the poems that had been read in the square over the Qing Ming festival. But of its forty-four lines, three attracted particular attention from the crowd. A shock wave rippled through the square as the three lines were read and repeated in relays, the young who wanted to preserve the moment for posterity hastily copying the poem into notebooks. Aside from the reading, no one spoke. The crowd was silent. For the unspoken had finally been said, the thought that had lain barely below the surface had become manifest, the undertow had merged with the current.

> China is no longer the China of yore
> Its people are no longer wrapped in ignorance
> Gone for good is the feudal society of Qin Shi Huang.

In 221 B.C., Qin Shi Huang had unified a host of small warring states and proclaimed himself first emperor of the Qin dynasty (Chin in more traditional forms of spelling), the dynasty from which the Middle Kingdom that Westerners know as China takes its name. Qin Shi Huang had unified into one the series of small walls that numerous heads of numerous warring states had constructed to keep out the barbarians from the north—the wall, rebuilt over the centuries, that still stands, the symbol of China, the Great Wall. Qin Shi Huang had unified the diverse weights and measures of the empire he had conquered, and the currency and the written language. It was Qin Shi Huang who had begun a dynastic tradition that was to continue, almost uninterrupted, for more than two thousand years. He was the founding father of imperial, unified China.

His legacy, however, is not altogether benign. Qin Shi Huang had also, in 213 B.C., ordered the notorious burning of the books, "an act for which," as

Derk Bodde points out, "he has gained the undying odium of Chinese schol-ars." Many intellectuals were sentenced to death by Qin Shi Huang. By the educated classes he has been remembered above all as the man who burned the books, the man who murdered the intellectuals, despotic, brutal, and cruel.

In 1957, during that brief period when the Communist Party of China had pursued a policy of letting "one hundred flowers bloom, one hundred schools of thought contend," when intellectuals were urged to make criticisms of the party and government, some had guardedly compared Party Chairman Mao to Emperor Qin Shi Huang. Mao, too, had unified China. Mao, too, had killed intellectuals.

Mao, it is said, had responded favorably to the comparison. "Yes, we are Qin Shi Huang," he is reported to have said. "We are Qin Shi Huang, Qin Shi Huang. But Qin Shi Huang only killed several hundred intellectuals. We have killed four hundred thousand."

The last of the Tiananmen poems had turned the tide of protest. It was directed now against the party chairman himself.

FROM inside the Great Hall of the People overlooking the square, Zhang Chunqiao, Yao Wenyuan, and other top Chinese leaders had been surveying the situation all day. At six-thirty in the evening, in the gathering darkness, the voice of the mayor of Peking, Wu De, came over the hundreds of loud-speakers attached to the darkened lightposts along the perimeter of the square, loudspeakers ordinarily reserved for announcing to officially approved crowds yet another amazing victory in China's glorious march through socialism. Over and over the message was repeated, broadcast as well on Peking radio and television.

> In the past few days while we were studying our great leader Chairman Mao's important instructions . . . a handful of bad elements, out of ulterior motives, made use of the Qing Ming festival to deliberately create a political incident, directing their spearhead at Chairman Mao and the Party Central Committee in a vain attempt to change the general orientation of the struggle to criticize the unrepentant capitalist roader Deng Xiaoping's revi-sionist line and beat back the right deviationist attempt. . . .
>
> Today, there are bad elements carrying out disruptions and engaging in counterrevolutionary sabotage at Tiananmen Square. Revolutionary masses must leave the square at once and not be duped by them.

The crowd in the square thinned substantially, but thousands of the boldest remained.

Sometime after nine o'clock, the elaborate bulbous lights around Tianan-men Square flashed on, lighting the massive area like a playing field at night. From staging areas on the grounds of the Workers' Cultural Palace and Sun Yat-sen Park, north of Changan Avenue and to the east and west of the Gate of Heavenly Peace, some ten thousand worker-militiamen, people's policemen, and soldiers of the People's Liberation Army rushed south across Changan Avenue, clubs ready, and encircled the square. In a divide-and-conquer tactic as old as the ancient military strategist Sun Tzu and reminiscent of nothing so much as Chinese chess, the guardians of social order quickly formed one grid of police lines running north and south, across the length of the square, and another running east and west across its width, their bodies tracing the lines of a gigantic checkerboard, tens of small, discrete squares within the massive square of Tiananmen. Within the squares, surrounded and isolated, were small groups of demonstrators, overwhelmed in numbers by the guardians of social order, the prisoners being led back to the staging areas whence the protectors of law and order had come.

How many were arrested, how many were injured, how many may have died, has never been publicly stated. But it is said that there were parents in Peking who went for several years before hearing again from the children to whom they had bid goodbye on the morning of April 5. It is even said that there are some who never heard from their children again.

THE buses that ordinarily stop at the four corners of Tiananmen Square sped past those stops on April 6, the passengers gaping in silence at the empty expanse, the stone pavement still wet. The fire engines had returned the night before to hose the spots that others had scrubbed.

But by the evening of Wednesday, April 7, the square was full once more with throngs of people, with hundreds of thousands of people, with soldiers from the People's Liberation Army and members of the people's militia, with students and teachers from Peking and Qinghua universities—units under control of the radical leftist leaders. Workers and peasants were there, too, and many of the same people who had brought their wreaths and presented their poems during the weekend of the Qing Ming festival. They were brought there again on April 8 and April 9, their numbers totaling two million, in an endless flow of buses and trucks, their red flags unfurled, their banners held high, marching to the rhythmic beat of drums and gongs interspersed with the celebratory popping of firecrackers.

"We'll defy death to defend Chairman Mao," read the banners. "We'll defy death to defend Chairman Mao's proletarian revolutionary line."

"Resolutely carry the struggle against the right deviationist attempt to reverse correct verdicts through to the end!" shouted the crowd. "Long live the dictatorship of the proletariat! Long live the great leader Chairman Mao!" they yelled.

The radical leftists against whom the Qing Ming demonstrators had protested were in control again. The loudspeakers had resumed their usual function, proclaiming yet another set of victories for the Chinese revolution that
refused to stop, the class struggle that would not die—the successful overthrow,
his second in a decade, of the unrepentant capitalist roader Deng Xiaoping,
the promotion of Hua Guofeng to the permanent position of premier, replacing Zhou Enlai, and the welcome suppression of the Qing Ming counterrevolutionary incident in the same Tiananmen Square.

Many in the square on April 9, while marveling at the efficiency with which
the square had been cleaned, believed they could still see faint traces of
brownish-pink blood on the pavement. Few actually saw it, of course, but
everyone knew that on the Monument to the Revolutionary Heroes, gleaming
like a red neon light, was one stain of blood that had somehow been missed.

"The situation is excellent," proclaimed Peking Mayor Wu De over the
loudspeakers at the rally of 100,000 people.

"The terror had returned," said one who was there.

But the reassertion of leftist control, the reinstitution of the routinized
terror that had come over the years to characterize life in China, was temporary. For the next six months, the period that in retrospect would come to be
known as the "ten years of great disaster," the period of the Great Proletarian
Cultural Revolution, careened inevitably, helplessly, toward its final dénoue-
ment. They were months rich with omen and portent.

On July 6, three months after the Tiananmen incident and six months after
the death of Zhou Enlai, Marshal Zhu De, the cofounder of the People's
Liberation Army, the general who had led the Communist revolution to
victory, died at the age of ninety. Symbolizing the military and force, what the
Chinese describe as *wu*, Zhu De was the precise counterpoint to Zhou Enlai.
With the death of the symbols of both *wen* and *wu*, so some peasants reasoned,
the death of the emperor himself could not be far behind.

Indeed, they were right.

But the death of Marshal Zhu De was followed immediately not by the
death of Mao but by yet another portent, a portent that suggested that the
transition of power would not be entirely smooth, that a certain amount of
disorder was at hand.

As millions slept in the early-morning hours of July 28, a massive earthquake,
registering 7.5 on the Richter scale, leveled the entire city of Tangshan in a
matter of seconds, its tremors waking the residents of Peking and Tianjin as
well. Estimates as to how many were killed range from a quarter to three
quarters of a million people. Even if the improbable lowest estimates are
accepted, more people died in less time in the city of Tangshan on July 28,
1976, than from any other disaster, natural or man-made, in the history of
humankind.

The military units flown in for the rescue first began feverishly burying the dead in shallow, improvised mass graves. When the health implications of such massive burials in the heat of July became all too apparent, when the stench of flesh from tens of thousands of corpses rotting so close to the surface had begun to take its toll on the rescue workers, when the city's surviving and hungry dogs gathered in packs to dig corpses out of their graves, the military concentrated on rebuilding the crematoria first. The process of digging up and burning the dead went on for months. The populations of Peking, Tianjin, and other major and minor cities located in the earthquake's wake—tens of millions of people—spent the next several weeks living outside, in the sidewalks and streets, in improvised shelters, through rains that seemed never to end, lest an afterquake bring similar catastrophe to the cities of Peking and Tianjin. In late 1981, the tiny brick earthquake shelters could still be seen along the sidewalks of Tianjin. In the press of overcrowding, the shelters, for many, had become home.

In imperial China, the weather reports received by the emperor were among the state's most carefully guarded secrets, for the emperor ruled by mandate from the same heaven that also dictated the weather. Natural disasters stood as the signal that the emperor's mandate was slipping. If the citizens of China had the obligation to be loyal and obedient subjects when the emperor's mandate was intact, they had the right to rebel when the mandate came into question. Leaders of traditional Chinese rebellions, and emperors, too, had often read their future from signs that nature gave. The earthquake in Tangshan, officially downplayed, the magnitude of its devastation not reported for years, stood as further mute but mocking testimony that the contemporary emperor's mandate was on the wane, that heaven was siding with the rebels of Tiananmen.

Then on September 9, 1976, just after the people of Peking had moved inside, the danger of another earthquake apparently passed, Chairman of the Chinese Communist Party Mao Zedong, architect of both the party's greatest victories and its worst defeats, the man who had led a revolution designed to eradicate forever the hold of China's feudalist past only to install himself in the role of emperor, met the inevitable fate of emperors and men.

For many in China, Mao's death was a deliverance. "There was a sense of apprehension about what would come, yes," recalls one, "but also a sense of relief."

It took less than a month for China's Great Proletarian Cultural Revolution, its "ten years of great disaster," the Maoist era itself, to be finally brought to an end. In the dark of night between October 6 and October 7, some thirty high-ranking party and government officials, close adherents of Mao's tenets, including the four ranking members of the Chinese Politburo who came to be known as the Gang of Four—Mao's widow, Jiang Qing; Shanghai party boss

Zhang Chunqiao; ideologue Yao Wenyuan; and a young worker risen to the most exalted reaches of power, Wang Hongwen—were arrested and imprisoned. China took its first step in the slow and painful ascent from an abyss of darkness, ignorance, terror, and fear.

1976 is a year rich in memory for most Chinese. But what they remember most is the death of Zhou Enlai and those days during the Qing Ming festival when millions converged, spontaneously and defiantly, to honor him in Tiananmen Square. There are those in China who believe that the legacy of what happened in Tiananmen Square during the Qing Ming festival of 1976 will come in time to rival the legacy of the May Fourth Movement of 1919. There are those who believe that the overthrow of the Gang of Four would not have been possible had not the people of Peking taken to the streets in protest, that Deng Xiaoping could not so quickly have been reinstated to power had not so many so clearly supported him at Tiananmen, that the new reforms and liberalizations that have brought new hope to so many Chinese were propelled by the actions of the demonstrators of April 1976. There are those who see in Tiananmen an unquenchable cry for the democratization of their country.

"Tiananmen is a very great event in Chinese history," asserts one participant. "In all of twentieth-century China, this was the most significant act of protest."

"I am proud of this demonstration," said another. "It cleansed the people of the shame of their earlier compliance."

"You must understand how unimaginable an event like Tiananmen was for a nation as centralized, as totalitarian as China," says another. "The capacity of the Chinese people to endure is so great that it is fearful. During the Cultural Revolution, the situation became so intolerable that people couldn't stand up. But still they kept silent. You must remember how great was Mao's prestige, how much faith the Chinese had in him. And in the party. The Communist Party had very high prestige. For the whole three decades following Liberation, any sign of discontent had been ruthlessly suppressed. And remember that there was a major campaign against Deng Xiaoping going on at the very time of Tiananmen. So how could such a thing happen? Even for us Chinese, even for those of us who participated, it was a great surprise. We couldn't believe it had happened. There were so many people who weren't afraid of death."

IT was grief above all that had brought so many to Tiananmen Square during the Qing Ming festival of 1976. But it was not grief for Zhou Enlai alone. Behind the expressions of grief for China's late premier stood a deeper sense of mourning. Zhou Enlai was not alone in China in having died without being properly mourned. In the ten years that preceded his death, many had died without being properly mourned. They had died of beatings, of torture, of suicide. They had died of the refusal to grant medical care to those labeled "counterrevolutionary." They had died when the factional fighting among the young Red Guards had turned to violence. They had died in official disgrace. And because the state had come to intercede even in death, their ashes had never reached Babaoshan. Sometimes their ashes had never even reached their families. No memorial services had been held. It was not only for Zhou Enlai that the state had forbidden them to weep. It was for their relatives, their colleagues, their friends. Qing Ming festival of 1976 was an outpouring of grief, an act of mourning, not only for Zhou Enlai but for all who had died in China and who had yet to be properly mourned.

And it was an outpouring of grief for the loss of that for which Zhou Enlai had stood—for Zhou Enlai as the symbol of *wen* and for the values so many Chinese believed he embodied, values that they shared, too. For much in addition to life had been lost in the ten years that preceded Zhou's death— much that gives meaning to life. The people of Peking had come to mourn not just Zhou Enlai but everyone who had died and all that had been lost.

Underlying it all, the demonstrations in Tiananmen Square were an outcry, an act of protest, against the oppression and injustice of the leaders who had led them into "ten years of great disaster," and against the disaster itself, the "Great Proletarian Cultural Revolution." For, to borrow a metaphor from Arthur Miller, the Cultural Revolution that had once "pranced on the scene like a pure white horse . . . flashing its beauty and its promise" had reared instead a vicious head, turning into "an ugly monster trampling on every-thing." During the Qing Ming festival of 1976, the people of Peking rebelled at last against that ugly monster.

T W O

"THIS IS A MEMORY BOOK": LOOKING BACK ON THE GOLDEN YEARS

MY first visit to China was in the summer of 1978. The evening before I left, in the darkened ballroom of a decaying downtown New York hotel, I and the group with whom I would be traveling were shown a film. The filmmaker, hewing narrowly to what he thought was the party line, had gone to considerable lengths to ensure that the China he presented conformed closely to the China its leaders wanted the world to believe.

There is only one scene I remember. It was an interview with an aging senior scholar, a professor at one of China's major universities. The professor was discussing his experiences during China's Great Proletarian Cultural Revolution. As a result of the Cultural Revolution, the professor explained, he had come to realize that for years he had unwittingly, but nonetheless consistently, been following the "bourgeois," "capitalist" educational "line" so stridently advocated by Liu Shaoqi, the man who had once been Party Chairman Mao Zedong's heir apparent and had been labeled during the

Cultural Revolution as "China's Khrushchev," the "number-one party person in authority taking the capitalist road." Unbeknownst to the elderly professor, the elitist, revisionist educational line of Liu had been in conflict with the more egalitarian, democratic line of Mao for years, and he, like so many of his colleagues, had sided with Liu Shaoqi. Upon receiving the education of the masses during the course of the Cultural Revolution, however, the professor had come to recognize his mistakes. He had, enthusiastically and voluntarily, chosen to transform himself by taking leave from his academic duties and undergoing labor reform at a "May Seventh Cadre School" deep in the countryside of China, engaging in agricultural production and receiving political reeducation from the perhaps less cosmopolitan and sophisticated but nonetheless allegedly politically wiser poor-and-lower-middle peasants, soldiers of the People's Liberation Army, and ordinary workers.

As a result of his "reeducation," the professor claimed to be a new man. He had returned to teaching at his university, but now, far from following the line of Liu Shaoqi, the professor was now using the thought of Mao Zedong to guide his work and his thinking, to guide, indeed, his every act. The professor spoke enthusiastically not only of the efficacy of Mao's thought in stimulating academic endeavor but of his new students. Gone from his campus were the sons and daughters of China's capitalists, intellectuals, and high party officials. Even university entrance exams were gone. The new students were workers from China's factories, peasants from the countryside, soldiers from the People's Liberation Army. They had not been chosen on the basis of standard academic criteria. They could not have made the grade. Some had graduated only from primary school. They had been chosen on the basis of their political commitment, their devotion to Chairman Mao.

The room in which the professor was being filmed was in shadows, his jacket barely distinguishable from the darkness that surrounded him. Only his hands and face were visible, dimly lit from within. He was sitting stiffly, speaking quietly. I studied his performance, searching his face, listening to his voice, watching his hands, attempting to interpret his body language, for signs that the position he was so doggedly presenting and his own personal convictions might somehow be at odds. The man's speech was formulaic, to be sure. As a regular reader of the *People's Daily,* the nationally circulated, official newspaper of the Chinese Communist Party, I could, with little effort, have written his presentation myself. He seemed tense, tight, perhaps even a trifle nervous. But whether his tension was natural stage fright or fear of straying from the elaborate political formula it was his task to present was impossible to fathom.

YEARS later, I would tell my friend Huang Chaoqun about the professor in the film, about how I studied his face, listened to his voice, watched his body in an effort to determine whether he was telling the truth.

"Could you tell?" he wanted to know.

"No."

"He was lying." Huang Chaoqun had no doubt. "He had to lie. We all had to lie."

And because they had to lie, the truth of what happened during the Cultural Revolution, in particular the truth about the suffering so many endured, has been difficult for outsiders to learn. We have had to wait until the official line on the Cultural Revolution changed, until men like the professor on film no longer had to lie.

The line changed slowly, in stages. By the summer of 1978, the political formula so fervently adhered to by the professor on film was already out of date. The Great Proletarian Cultural Revolution that the professor had spoken of only in the most glowing terms had taken on a new aura—dark, inchoate, evil. Foreigners who had once thought that the Cultural Revolution had lasted only three years, from 1966 to 1969, were told that it had lasted a full ten years, the whole decade from 1966 to 1976. It was a decade in which Party Chairman Mao Zedong had seemed to outsiders to be clearly in the ascendancy, the period when his "little red book" had held a position more exalted than the Bible, when every action had to be justified on the basis of Mao's sayings, when jewelry was confined exclusively to buttons bearing the image of Mao, when working adults began their mornings by bowing before a portrait of Mao, reciting his sayings, and asking his instructions for their daily tasks. But in the summer of 1978, the decade of the Cultural Revolution was no longer presented as Mao's but was being labeled instead the "rule of the Gang of Four." In October 1976, less than a month after the death of Mao, the Gang of Four, including its ringleader, Mao's widow, Jiang Qing, had been arrested, imprisoned, and stripped of all political power. In the summer of 1978, all of China's ills were being ascribed to the evil rule of the Gang of Four, and judging from the "brief introductions and tea" to which we were treated wherever we went, and in contrast to the script of the Cultural Revolution which clearly specified that everything happening in China was "good," China's ills were myriad and manifold. The policies of the Cultural Revolution had yet to come fully unraveled, but the threads were already pulling loose. The truth was beginning to change, but what exactly had happened during the "rule of the Gang of Four," what really had happened to professors like the one on film, remained shrouded still in mystery.

EIGHT months later, the veil began to lift. In April 1979, in the wake of good feeling left by the normalization of relations between China and the United States in January, it was my official duty to be one of those to greet the first delegation of Chinese social scientists and humanists, thirteen distinguished members of the Chinese Academy of Social Sciences, to visit the United States in more than thirty years.

What is most memorable about their visit is not the information officially conveyed but the knowledge that was transferred almost wordlessly, through some peculiar form of psychic osmosis, chilling the bones. Their stories were different from that of the professor on film—terrifyingly different.

There were the limbs that had never fully healed, the legs that did not quite work, the missing parts of stomachs and intestines, the vague bodily complaints of men who had been tortured but survived. There were the years in jail, sometimes in solitary confinement. There were the wasted years, the men struck down in the prime of their lives, men, some of towering intellect, who had had so many contributions to make. There were the disbanded academic disciplines, like anthropology and sociology, political science and law, some of which had been defunct since 1952, now in the painful process of revival. There was Fei Xiaotong, China's best and internationally renowned anthropologist, who had been declared a "rightist" in 1957 and disappeared from Western view. Wilma Fairbank, who had arranged his last visit to the United States in the early 1940s, had been so convinced of Fei's death that she had released her private correspondence with the man now so miraculously and ebulliently revived. There was Oxford-educated Qian Zhongshu, seventy years old, dazzlingly brilliant, witty, sardonic, handsome, China's most learned classicist. During the Cultural Revolution, Qian's intellect had earned for him the role of postman in a remote and impoverished area of rural Henan, hundreds of miles from his home in Peking. Rural Henan was not an area noted for the volume of its mail. There was a different picture of the May Seventh Cadre Schools—of the hardships endured by intellectuals who did not know how to farm assigned to cultivate land that nature had never intended to be sown, of the petty, unintelligent narrow-mindedness of those assigned to reeducate the scholars. There were the family members and friends who had not survived.

There was a certain bravado, too, for their successful imitation of the bamboo they so admired, bending always but never breaking. There was humor at the expense of the strutting, swaggering, vain, and ignorant men to whose tutelage they had until so recently been assigned. There was contempt toward colleagues who had stooped to play the game, attacking and betraying friends in the interest of their own aggrandizement. They carried the wounds of the survivor, but the elation and the anger, too.

In the winter of 1979–80, I was in China again, this time as a member of an academic fact-finding delegation. It was our task to investigate the state of the social sciences and humanities, to determine what effect the Cultural Revolution had had. We spent three weeks in meetings and banquets with academics and professors—professors like the one on film. Several scenes remain indelibly etched on my mind.

One member of my delegation had brought a tape of Beethoven's Ninth Symphony as a gift to a friend in China. Sometime after delivering the tape, my colleague had had a chance to meet with his Chinese friend again. He learned that on the day the tape had been delivered, his Chinese friend had not slept. He had stayed up all night listening to Beethoven's Ninth Symphony over and over again. He had not heard it in nearly twenty years.

There was the meeting between two of my American colleagues and an elderly, Western-educated, and once famous and highly respected Chinese scholar. The scholar had suffered grievously during the Cultural Revolution. His suffering, in fact, had begun long before the Cultural Revolution, and even in 1980 he was not fully restored to public grace. He was disoriented at the meeting, having to be steered into the room by two younger colleagues and physically turned and pointed in the direction of the Americans; who they were and the purpose of the visit had to be explained and then explained again. Upon understanding at least that the men before him were the first Americans he had seen in decades, the gentleman had only one question to raise. He wondered whether a book he had submitted to a major university press in the United States, shortly before Chinese-American relations were finally severed more than thirty years before, had ever been published.

There was the visit to Peking University, the walk around the lake, on a bitterly cold and dreary winter day.

"You see the lake?" the Chinese professor had asked. Even in the desolate barrenness of the Peking winter, it was a beautiful lake, lined by graceful weeping willows. "During the Cultural Revolution, people committed suicide in that lake."

Toward the end of that visit some of our hosts asked me what my impressions of China had been. I tried, ineptly, inelegantly, to explain that I had not previously appreciated the human costs of the Cultural Revolution, that so many we met in the universities and research institutes seemed to have suffered so much. I was still having difficulty reconciling the professor on film, China on stage, with the impact of those more recent scenes. I still could not grasp the enormity of what lay behind those scenes. I told the story of the tape. I said how easy it was for me as an American to take music for granted, how difficult life would be without it. "Yes," replied one of my hosts, a young woman, "I know what you mean. When the Cultural Revolution began, I was studying music. But then my family came under attack, and the Red Guards came to search our home. They destroyed most of my phonograph records—not all of them, though. Some they took for themselves. And they ripped up all my musical scores. They tried to destroy my piano, too. With an ax."

I asked another of our hosts what he had done during the Cultural

Revolution. Like the professor on film, he had spent much of it—some six years —in a May Seventh Cadre School in a remote and backward area of the Chinese countryside, doing agricultural labor and receiving "political reeducation." I wondered what he had done wrong. "I asked myself that question for ten years," my host replied. "I never found the answer. Now they tell me I did nothing wrong." What he regretted most was not so much the suffering that he and his family had had to endure but that so many of his friends and colleagues had died before being rehabilitated, before their names had been cleared.

THE definitive history of China's Great Proletarian Cultural Revolution has yet to be written. When it is, when the full story is told, the final facts and figures compiled, the scale of the tragedy is likely to obscure its human meaning. The brain is capable of absorbing only so much tragedy before it shuts down in self-protection, turning numb. It is through the small scenes, the individual evidence, the private testimony, that human tragedy on this scale can be reduced to manageable, meaningful proportions. That is why novelists—and playwrights—make such fine historians.

But the *War and Peace* of the Cultural Revolution has also yet to be written. Perhaps it never will be. Chinese, historically, have not made memorable novelists.

A single, passing thought implanted itself in my mind during that second visit to China. It took root, and against all odds, it flourished and grew. It is Camus who insists that human evidence must be preserved. *They must be allowed to bear witness,* I thought.

"I THINK you will have difficulty doing your research in China," Fan Yinghua began. We were sitting in my New York apartment, but she was speaking quietly, tensely, as though looking over her shoulder, afraid of being overheard. "I don't think people will be willing to talk to you. People will be afraid. During the hundred flowers campaign in 1956, people talked, but then look what happened. There was the antirightist campaign. Let me give you an example about why people won't talk. I have a friend who was an English teacher. One day she saw a small crowd gathered around a foreigner. The foreigner seemed very confused, and it was clear he didn't speak any Chinese and no one in the crowd spoke his language. So my friend went to see if she could help. He turned out to speak English, so she asked him what he wanted. He wanted directions to the section in Peking where all the antique stores are. So she gave him the directions. He thanked her and went on his way.

"As she was walking away after giving him directions, she felt a tap on her shoulder. A man said, 'Comrade, come with me.' He showed her identification that said he was with the police. He said they were going to the police station. She had no choice but to go. She couldn't say no.

"At the police station, they asked her what she had said to the foreigner. She told them that he had wanted directions, and since he didn't know Chinese, she had given him directions in English. They asked her to repeat the conversation word for word, so she did. Then they asked her again. They kept saying, 'Comrade, you must be forgetting something. Think again. Think some more. There must have been something else. Repeat the conversation again.' So she did. They kept her there all night. Her husband and son didn't know where she was, so they were very worried. They didn't let her go home until the next morning.

"A week later, someone knocked on her door and identified himself as being with the police. He asked her to come to the police station. They kept her there all day. They kept making her repeat the conversation and kept saying, 'Comrade, try to remember. There must be something you are forgetting.' But there was nothing she was forgetting. They wanted her to say she had given away state secrets, that she was a spy. But all she had done was give directions.

"For the next six weeks, every week someone would knock at her door, and then she would have to go to the police station and spend the whole day repeating the conversation while they kept saying, 'Comrade, you must have forgotten something.' She couldn't understand why they wouldn't believe her.

"That happened in 1971 or 1972. Yes, it's true that was under the rule of the Gang of Four. It's true they are gone now. But things like that could happen again."

I HAD dinner with Liu Fusheng at the Fairmont Hotel in downtown San Francisco shortly before departing. He was uncomfortable that evening, not only because of the unaccustomed opulence of the place but because we had simply walked in past the uniformed bellman without being questioned or required to register our presence. He worried that we did not have proper permission to enter and that there was thus a tinge of illegality to our meal. Liu Fusheng had been in the United States only a few months. He echoed Fan Yinghua's concerns. "I think you will have a very difficult time doing your research in China," he said. "I don't think you should try to do your research now. When you go to China, you should just study your Chinese and be a good student. You shouldn't let them know you are doing a study of the Cultural Revolution. If you tell them, they will make trouble for you. They will follow you and watch you very closely. You should never leave any of your notes lying around in your room, because someone may come to read them. And you should be very careful about what you write in letters. You shouldn't mention your research on the Cultural Revolution, because your letters will be opened and read. In the Soviet Union, every letter that goes out is microfilmed. They don't read them then, but all the letters are on file, on microfilm, so if the need ever arises, they can go back and read all your letters.

"Often, when trying to understand China, I use the Soviet Union as the model. I know China is backward technologically, that it would be difficult for China to microfilm all the letters. But this is the type of thing China would spend its money on.

"In Peking, you could say that you are doing research on the Cultural Revolution, that you want to speak to someone about the Cultural Revolution. They might even arrange an interview. They would tell the person what to say and what not to say, and then, after the interview was over, they would question the person about what he had said. If you then asked for another interview, they would be very suspicious. They would wonder why you want to know so much about the Cultural Revolution. China doesn't want foreigners to know too much about the Cultural Revolution.

"My advice to you would be to make lots of friends, to tell people you are there to learn more Chinese, to learn more about Chinese culture. Maybe the question of the Cultural Revolution will come up naturally. If it does, you can just say, 'Oh, really?' and ask a polite question. But don't say you are studying the Cultural Revolution. If you do, they will think you are the CIA or the FBI —a spy. You could jeopardize the people who talk to you. They could be arrested, punished, sent to the countryside, to another May Seventh Cadre School.

"When I first came to San Francisco, I would go all the time to Golden Gate Park. The pigeons in Golden Gate Park are not afraid of people. They just walk right up to you, and you can feed them. They want you to feed them. The squirrels are the same way. They want me to feed them. That was incredible to me, almost inconceivable. In China, pigeons and squirrels are afraid of people. They run away from people. Because in China, people kill pigeons and squirrels. With stones. People in China are like squirrels. People run away from people. Because people hurt people. In China, people are always smiling, and you don't know why they are smiling. They smile when it is not appropriate to smile. Inside, they are thinking one thing, and outside they are smiling. For no reason. Outwardly, people are smiling, nodding. But inwardly, everyone is throwing stones.

"That is the way it will be for you, too, so you must be prepared. Outwardly, everyone will be smiling at you, but inwardly they will be throwing stones."

I RETURNED to China in June of 1981 as a student at Peking Normal University, part of a small program organized by my alma mater, the University of

California at Berkeley. My request to conduct "field research" in China—to be allowed to interview victims of the Cultural Revolution under the auspices of the Institute of Sociology at the Chinese Academy of Social Sciences—had been refused. However well the new academic exchanges between China and the United States were progressing, the issue of field research, of deep and sustained immersion by outsiders in Chinese life, remained singularly delicate. One of the first Americans to have been granted the opportunity to conduct field research had not acquitted himself well, his alleged misconduct reverberating to the detriment of others who had hoped to follow him into the field. And despite the official labeling of the Cultural Revolution in the summer of 1981 as "ten years of great disaster," the episode remained wrapped in an aura of extreme political sensitivity. No outsider was going to be given the public opportunity to risk shattering the delicate official explanation that had already taken several years to construct. Going to China as a student was my only hope of gaining the informal access to people who might be willing to talk privately but candidly. I hoped that during the two-month program I might be able to meet and to interview a few people about their experiences. But I also intended during that time to try once more to obtain formal permission to conduct my research. Shortly after arriving in Peking, I made contact with my colleagues at the Academy of Social Sciences.

We were able to reach a compromise. I would affiliate with the Institute of Literature, and the official purpose of my stay would be to study a new genre of Chinese literature—*shanghen wenxue*, the "literature of the wounded." Dating back to the Tiananmen poems of April 1976, the literature of the wounded contains accounts, sometimes fictionalized, often real, of people's experiences during the Cultural Revolution. That literature, together with published reminiscences about the Cultural Revolution and memorial speeches to those who died, is a vital part of the human evidence. Moreover, the Institute of Literature would arrange for me to interview some of the authors.

Neither the institute nor the academy, however, could arrange for the wider range of interviews they knew I wanted to conduct.

But I was in China, after all, and I was to stay for nine months. I was surrounded by survivors of the Cultural Revolution. If, on my own, I was able to conduct such interviews, then there was nothing the academy could do or wanted to do to prevent me. My sponsors asked only that I remember how profoundly those with whom I might speak had already suffered and urged that care be taken in whatever I might later write to protect them from further harm.

In China, I was in a particularly advantageous position to strike out and conduct interviews on my own, without, as Fan Yinghua and Liu Fusheng had feared, jeopardizing those with whom I spoke. My informal contacts and friendships with Chinese were already good, and I had brought with me a number of letters of introduction. The life-style I had chosen was simple, even spartan, more conducive to private exchanges than that of many foreigners living in China. In 1981–82, in the Western-style hotels where most foreigners in China resided, Chinese visitors were ordinarily either excluded altogether or required to register at a service desk, giving their names, the name and address of their work unit, and the name of the foreigner they were visiting. Such visits, in turn, might be reported to the leader of the Chinese visitor's work unit. Lurking in the shadow of every recorded but unauthorized visit was the possibility that the leader would frown upon such contact and the visitor would "get into trouble," punishment ranging, or so rumor had it, from mere reprimand to forced exile in the Chinese countryside. In the best of cases, the contact might merely be recorded in the permanent but secret dossier that is part of the invisible baggage carried by every Chinese—a blot on his record to be used against him at some appropriate future date.

WHETHER the opportunities presented me in China were the result of fortuitous accident or hidden design would be foolish to speculate. I believe that there were senior officials at the Chinese Academy of Social Sciences who agreed both that the human evidence of the Cultural Revolution ought to be preserved and that the task of preservation was still too politically risky for most Chinese. I believe that they trusted that I would be a fair and sympathetic reporter and would do everything in my power to protect the people who would share their stories with me. I do not believe my Chinese sponsors knew how eager their countrymen would be to talk or what their countrymen might say.

I interviewed nearly anyone who was willing to share his story with me— some thirty-four people in China and, both before leaving and upon my return, an additional fifteen people in the United States, twelve of whom were here on a long-term but temporary basis and three of whom, including Fan Yinghua and Liu Fusheng, have left China permanently. The vast majority of the interviews were conducted privately, in depth, and over extended periods of time.

Those in China who shared their stories with me did so at potentially serious personal risk. On a few occasions, contact had to be terminated. But the summer of 1981 was a particularly open and liberal period in recent Chinese history, and in the student dormitory at Peking Normal University where I lived, the potentially embarrassing sign-in procedures that ordinarily discourage Chinese from visiting foreign friends had been relaxed. Guests could enter my dormitory freely. In the small, old-fashioned hostel into which I moved upon affiliation with the Chinese Academy of Social Sciences, I was the only American and one of only two foreign guests; sign-in procedures were similarly lax. The interviews were private. I have returned to China many times and currently reside there half my time, and no one who had contact with me has suffered from that contact. The most dire predictions of Fan Yinghua and Liu Fusheng have yet to come to pass.

THOSE who shared their stories were special—exceptionally articulate, intelligent, educated, and self-aware, and hardly representative of Chinese society at large. From the variety of their stories, it is possible to grasp some of the diversity with which educated and relatively privileged Chinese initially greeted and later succumbed to the Cultural Revolution. With a sample so special and numbers so small, the orderliness of theory necessarily bows before the kaleidoscope of contradiction and mystification that human evidence entails. But themes inevitably do force themselves to the surface—testimonies to the pervasiveness of human frailty and to the tenacity of the human spirit. It is possible to discern patterns in how these individuals, in the long term, have been affected, indeed wounded, by their experiences. To a large degree, their experiences are representative of the way any group of human beings, anywhere in the world, similarly educated and with similar demographic characteristics, would have responded in similar situations of adversity. They teach us something about ourselves, about how we would behave for better or for worse— and mostly for worse—in situations of extremity.

Who were they? They were very much like the Chinese whom many Americans now have the opportunity to meet—like the many visitors and scholars from China who come to the United States or the Chinese with whom American tourists, businessmen, students, and scholars come into contact while visiting there. In the United States, their backgrounds might not be considered particularly remarkable. In China, they are. In a society where less than 5 percent of the college-age population can go on to receive a university education and where the vast majority of people labor with their hands, all the people I interviewed were intellectuals—at least in the Chinese sense of the word, meaning simply people who have received a middle school education or more and who work not with their hands but with their minds. Not all had graduated from college, and one, because her schooling had been interrupted by the Cultural Revolution, had not even graduated from middle school, but the majority were college-educated. Today, they are middle school teachers and college professors, researchers and doctors, scientists, editors, writers, lawyers, artists, and students.

In a country where 80 percent of the population lives in the countryside, many had spent considerable periods of time in rural parts of their country, but at the time I talked with them, all were living and working, rooted, in urban areas. In a nation governed by the Communist Party but where only 4 percent of the population are members of the party, some 25 percent of those with whom I spoke were.

The nearly fifty people were roughly equally divided between male and female. There was a spread of ages, too. The youngest had been only eight years old when the Cultural Revolution began and remembered the period without continuity, as a series of confused and broken images—disparate, disconnected, colorful, and often fearful flashes. The eldest were in their early seventies when they spoke with me and had been in their mid-fifties at the onset of the Cultural Revolution, which for them often represented only one more catastrophe, and not necessarily the worst, in lives that had been rich in catastrophe.

Politically, the group was diverse, running nearly the entire gamut of the Chinese political spectrum—from people who had barely "escaped through the net" during the antirightist campaign of 1957 and who therefore were the "natural" and among the first victims of the Cultural Revolution, to young people who had been radical "revolutionary rebels" *(zaofan pai)* in the early stages of the movement and who continue today to look back on some phases of the Cultural Revolution with a degree of nostalgia. Some who had been fully grown and nearly all who had been young in 1966 had supported the movement at its inception, with varying degrees of enthusiasm. Particularly among the young, some had begun as persecutors in the early stages, engaging in violence against others, only to become victims when their parents came under attack. Other young people had remained active throughout the most turbulent phases of the Cultural Revolution, to become victimized by the often brutal assertion of military control. Political commitment was hardly a reliable indicator of who would be cut down by the Cultural Revolution's scythe. Each new phase of the movement, each change in the prevailing line, brought a new wave of persecutions, as the "revolutionaries" of one phase became the "counterrevolutionaries" of the next. People became victims for a wide variety of reasons, at very different times.

They were all Chinese patriots. They all loved their country—tenaciously and often bitterly. Of those old enough to remember the Communist takeover of 1949, only Song Erli, merely seven years old at the time, remembers it with relative indifference. "I remember a corpse lying on the street. The stink. There was such a stink. In my hometown, there wasn't much fighting. But still there was some. I just remember the stink of the corpse. It was a corpse from the Guomindang side. The victorious side would bury their dead very quickly. It was important for morale. I didn't know which side I supported. I was too young."

OTHERS remember 1949 literally as the Communists have labeled it—as Liberation. Some had worked for that Liberation, risking their lives. "I suffered in the old society," You Xiaoli recalls. You Xiaoli had grown up desperately poor. In 1947, during the civil war between Nationalists and Communists, her mother had died of starvation on the streets of Shanghai, and You Xiaoli had fled to one of the areas already liberated by the Communists. Somewhere in

You Xiaoli's young mind, Chairman Mao, her father, and the Messiah had gotten all jumbled up, merging finally into the single image of Mao. For You Xiaoli was the illegitimate offspring of a rape by a landlord of his maidservant, and You Xiaoli had never known her father. When You Xiaoli's father died, while Xiaoli was still a child, she and her mother were expelled from the landlord's opulent house, living thereafter in bitter, dire, and grating poverty. You Xiaoli grew up believing that if only she had a father, life would be better. She prayed for a father, to any God, in any place of worship, Christian or Buddhist, she could find.

One of You Xiaoli's tiny playmates, Xiao Pingping, had also been fatherless and bitterly poor. But when Xiao Pingping's mother married a rickshaw driver, "they lived okay. They had a much better life that way," recalls You Xiaoli. "Before, they were just as poor as us. They wore torn rags for clothes. And then her mother got married, and things were better, so I asked my mother why she didn't get married, too." You Xiaoli's mother was furious and slapped her daughter across the face.

But You Xiaoli's mother was also deeply religious, pious to a fault. She believed in the second coming of Christ and wanted You Xiaoli to believe in it, too. And You Xiaoli did. "You know, the first time I was told about Chairman Mao in 1942," she remembers, "I thought maybe he was the Messiah, Jesus Christ coming the second time. My mother always talked about the second time Jesus would come and said that when he came we would be saved. The oldest song of the revolution is 'The East Is Red.' Do you know that song?

> The East is red.
> The sun rises.
> China has brought forth a Mao Zedong.

That song says that Mao Zedong is the *dajiuxing*, the great star in the sky who will save us, the great liberator, the Messiah. So when I heard about Chairman Mao, I thought maybe he was the second coming of the Messiah."

You Xiaoli remembers the period she spent in the liberated areas, before the Communist Party had come to power, as one of the most impoverished but also the happiest of her life. She was at the front with the Communist troops during the civil war, serving together with peasant women as a stretcher bearer bringing the Communist wounded to makeshift mobile hospitals set up under tents. She carried hand grenades and used them when the Nationalist troops got too close. "At that time," she says, "we had only four ounces of rice a day to eat. I never thought we would be liberated. But I was so happy. I think that was the happiest time in my life. Life was hard, but you had a dream, you had a future. You could work for the future. You were poor, but the

Communist Party was the party of the poor people. I always thought that Chairman Mao was the Messiah, the Savior. So in the future, we would no longer be poor. It would be the end of exploitation.

"I joined the revolution because I wanted a better society established, a society based on equality, where there weren't that many gaps—in wealth, between men and women. I wanted our country to be strong and powerful and free. It was easy for someone with my background to believe. I was so poor and I suffered so much, and I was looked down on by those rich people. So of course I had always been longing for a society with more equality.

"Then suddenly in 1949, I was liberated. It was Chairman Mao who rescued me."

LI WEIGUO, too, remembers the ascension to power by the Communists as liberation from poverty and despair. Li Weiguo's mother had died of illness when he was only seven, and he was thirteen years old at the time of Liberation in 1949. His father—an educated man who had once served as a minor clerk in a government office—had lost his position when the Japanese invaded and took control of his native town. Li Weiguo's father found himself unable to support his small son, and so sent him at the age of nine to live with an uncle in Tianjin. Several years later, Li Weiguo's father died. How and why, Weiguo has never known. There is no grave to mark his remains. His body was never recovered. Weiguo simply assumes that his father died of hunger. Weiguo's uncle had a job mixing herbs at a pharmacy specializing in traditional Chinese medicine, but his wages were not sufficient to support his young nephew. So Li Weiguo was forced to quit school and was sent to work as an apprentice in a small factory that made socks.

"I was just a small potato, the youngest, the lowest on the ladder, and everyone could give me orders. The head of the workers asked me to do everything for him—make his bed, make tea for him—and if I did it too slowly, he beat me, and I would cry. They only gave me food in the factory, no wages. And I slept there in the factory. I had no home. It was a small factory. They sold the socks on the first floor. There was a small backyard where the socks were dyed. And on the second floor were the small machines that they used to make the socks. At night, we just slept on the floor next to the machines. I had only one day off a month, when I got to go to visit my uncle."

Li Weiguo, too, remembers Liberation. "Before Liberation, I was so poor I couldn't even go to school. I had to work. If I didn't work, where was I to get food? Then after Liberation, I got into middle school, and the government paid me money. They knew the families of young kids were poor. So I got a scholarship, and every month they gave me an extra five dollars. I could eat. They gave me books. If there were no new China, no Communist Party, maybe I would have died. Maybe there would be no Weiguo today. New China gave me new life. For poor people like me, our whole life turned over. Liberation established a new China."

CHEN QUANHONG, as a young adolescent, supported the Communists out of patriotism, because the Communist Party was concentrating its attention on organizing the Chinese people to fight the Japanese while Chiang Kai-shek and the Nationalists continued to direct their efforts toward the destruction of the Communist Party "bandits." Chen Quanhong is in his mid-fifties now, a strikingly, memorably handsome man. A professor at a major Chinese university, he dresses humbly, in the heavy blue cotton padded jacket of a worker. His face is etched in wrinkles, chiseled in character, and from his eyes shine a light that is part intelligence, part tragedy, and part certainty that no foreigner could possibly ever comprehend the story he is able to tell. With the vividness and depth of emotion reserved for the memories of childhood, Chen Quanhong remembers the incident that transformed him from a happy-go-lucky schoolboy into a fledgling Chinese patriot. It was when, as a student in junior middle school, he read a story by Alphonse Daudet.

"I lived in a Japanese-occupied area during the War of Resistance against Japan," recalls Chen Quanhong, "and some of my earliest and most vivid childhood memories are of the Japanese and the occupation. I still remember reading 'The Last Lesson.' "

Told in the first person by a not-always-so-serious Alsatian schoolboy, "The Last Lesson" is the story of the final class conducted in French after the Prussian takeover of Alsace and Lorraine. The teacher, Monsieur Hamel, arrives for the occasion dressed in his Sunday finest, and the villagers, too, have come to observe. "Monsieur Hamel began to speak of the French language, saying it was the strongest, clearest, most beautiful language in the world, which we must keep as our heritage, never allowing it to be forgotten, telling us that when a nation has become enslaved, she holds the key which shall unlock her prison as long as she preserves her native tongue." At the end of the class, Monsieur Hamel, choked with emotion, scrawls "Vive la France" in huge letters across the blackboard and dismisses the class for the last time. The young schoolboy, who has arrived late for the class, is overcome with regret that he has not taken the study of his language and culture more seriously, that now the opportunity is forever lost.

"I read 'The Last Lesson' just before our school was taken over by the Japanese," recounts Chen Quanhong, "and I knew that it wasn't just a story but was about my own life, my own school, as well. Indeed, the Japanese did occupy our school, and we had Japanese teachers who made us study Japanese. I remember that every time a Japanese would come into the schoolroom, we all had to stand up and bow, remember wondering why it was that we Chinese children had to bow before the Japanese.

"But at the same time the Japanese had occupied our school and were making us study Japanese, they still had to depend on Chinese teachers as well. The teacher who had the greatest influence on me, whom I remember to this day, is the one who taught me classical Chinese. He told us that maybe China will lose its own traditions, its own culture, by and by, but he said, 'I want to teach you our old traditions, our culture, our ancient language.' It was no doubt under his influence that I ultimately became a student of medieval Chinese history and learned my devotion to the study of China's traditional past.

"But even so, the influence of the Japanese in my town was very strong, and we Chinese were slaves to the Japanese, doing their bidding, without ever being conscious of or recognizing our own enslavement. We simply lived as the Japanese ordered us to live. So at that time, even though I was very young, I had begun to develop a certain sense of Chinese patriotism, based both on my dislike of the Japanese and my study of traditional China.

"At the conclusion of the Japanese war, I had hopes for a native revival in China, for a renewed commitment to Chinese tradition and culture, and I believed Chiang Kai-shek shared this commitment. Like many other young people at the time, I had misunderstood Chiang. I thought he was the country's great leader, the salvation of China.

"Education in my school became more eclectic after the war—influenced by the West and particularly by the United States and the Soviet Union. At first, I was very much influenced by American education, very sympathetic to what I learned about the United States. I started reading *Life* magazine and going to American cowboy films and listening to American jazz. The American information bureau used to hold dancing parties, and I went to them, too. But the same thing began happening to Chinese youth then that I fear is happening today—some of them began accepting all of Western culture, good and bad, indiscriminately. I remember in particular one of my schoolmates. He told me that he wished he were an American instead of a Chinese. That pained me. It hurt me to think that my good friend wanted to be an American.

"And I gradually began to lose faith in the ability of Chiang Kai-shek to lead China. I had a music teacher at the time who directed us students in staging some plays that were critical of the Guomindang—*The Anti-Japanese War Couple* and *Ten Thousand Yuan of Paper Money,* which was about the rampant inflation then plaguing the country. I liked to read a lot, too—literature, both Chinese and foreign, particularly Russian literature and such authors as Gorky.

"At that time, the Russian and American embassies seemed to be competing in their efforts to supply propaganda to Chinese youths, with the Soviet Union providing one form of propaganda and the United States providing a completely different kind. I couldn't understand why there should be such different kinds of lives among human beings. It was really very confusing.

"In 1947, though, I obtained some revolutionary books through the Soviet embassy—a short biography of Lenin and some selections of the writings of Mao Zedong. I had to read Mao's works secretly and would sit on my bed at night reading them by candlelight. Mao's thought was very new, very different, and I was not at all clear what it was about, but under this kind of influence, I began to hate American culture and in particular the American soldiers who lived in my town. To this day, when I think of American soldiers, all I can picture is them walking through China's streets arm in arm with young Chinese prostitutes.

"I was still not politically conscious, certainly, but I began to develop a sense of justice, or at least a sense that there was little justice in China. I participated in the Anti-Hunger Anti-Civil War Movement in Nanjing. Shortly thereafter, my teacher—the one who had taught me my love of Chinese history—was assassinated by the Guomindang, and my loyalties began shifting decisively in the direction of the Communist Party."

IT is not only the poor who look back upon Liberation with favor or those who had become politically active in movements against Chiang Kai-shek and the Guomindang. The rich, like Li Meirong, are less effusive, perhaps, less prone to nostalgia, but their memory of Liberation is nonetheless positive. Li Meirong was the daughter of a wealthy Tianjin merchant. She had grown up, waited upon by servants, in a huge forty-two-room house built in the traditional style around courtyards and gardens. The pictures in her childhood scrapbook show Li Meirong in elaborate silk brocade, mandarin-style, and little slippers with turned-up toes, her mother in opulent fur. Li Meirong still remembers the sumptuous banquets, the lavish entertainment, the music and dancing that were frequent events in her grandparents' home. Her parents fled to Hong Kong in advance of the conquering Communist armies, but Li Meirong and her grandmother remained in Tianjin. "When the new government first came in, I was happy," she remembers. "Everyone was happy. There was a period of great hope, great expectation. Because the old government had been overthrown and a new one was about to begin. We welcomed the new government."

The poor were certainly its most enthusiastic supporters, but the new government was welcomed not just because it promised the poor a relief from their misery. It was welcomed because it promised safety and security, because China was united once more, and because there was peace. For China had been splintered, atomized, destitute, at war, for how long? Since the Opium War of 1839, when the country had suffered crushing defeat at the hands of Great Britain and the way had thus been opened for the establishment of the foreign treaty ports that gnawed away at China's national sovereignty? Since the bloody and devastating Taiping Rebellion of 1850–64 that had shaken the Qing Dynasty to its very foundations and left some thirty million people dead in its wake? Since the Sino-Japanese War of 1894–95? The collapse of the Qing dynasty in 1911? The disintegration of the country into competing, marauding warlord satrapies after 1916? The invasion by Japan in 1937? No one alive at the time of Liberation could remember any sustained period of peace, stability, continuity, security. Of course they welcomed the new government.

And for a while, at least, the new government delivered on its promises.

"The 1950s?" It is Li Weiguo speaking again. "Those were the golden years. After Liberation, there were no beggars, no prostitutes. The government organized the prostitutes and trained them to do other work. They wouldn't allow them to be prostitutes. The law was very strict. They would put you in jail if you were a prostitute.

"I saw the whole society change a lot, the whole country. The government paid factory owners interest, and slowly, very slowly, the ownership of the factories became ownership by the whole country. So working conditions in the factories improved. The party organized the workers to have unions. So most students, most people, felt hopeful for the whole country. We could see the changes with our own eyes.

"The whole society was very safe. You could open your door when you went to sleep at night. If you lost something on the street, you could always find it at the Public Security Bureau. If someone found something in school, you would always want to try to find the person who had lost it. It was no longer difficult to find a place to live. The government built very simple new houses for the workers. They called them 'new workers' villages.'

"Relations between people were much, much better then. People could trust each other. People did their work conscientiously. People studied harder. The prices were much lower. The policies were very stable. Everybody thought of the bright future, everyone wanted to serve the people, serve the country. In middle school, most people were in high spirits. We talked about our own idealism, our idealism for the whole country, about what we wanted to do in the future. We felt very hopeful. We thought the Communist Party and Chairman Mao were very good compared to the Guomindang and Chiang Kai-shek. They had changed the whole country. They were respected.

"And lots of Communist Party members really did a good job for the people. The peasants came to the big city, but they really restricted themselves. Whenever they did something, they thought it over, thought about whether it was right for the whole country. So I thought I wanted to be a member of the Communist Party. That was my ideal. Every young kid thought like that."

It is Milan Kundera, writing of the same time, the same events, and a different country, who best understands the mood and the metaphor of the Chinese nostalgia for the '50s.

I too once danced in a ring. It was in the spring of 1948. The Communists had just taken power in my country . . . and I took other Communist students by the hand, I put my arms around their shoulders, and we took two steps in place, one step forward, lifted first one leg and then the other, and we did it just about every month, there being always something to celebrate, an anniversary here, a special event there, old wrongs were righted, new wrongs perpetrated, factories were nationalized, thousands of people went to jail, medical care became free of charge, small shopkeepers lost their shops, aged workers took their first vacations ever in confiscated country houses, and we smiled the smile of happiness. Then one day I said something I would better have left unsaid. I was expelled from the Party and had to leave the circle.

That is when I became aware of the magic qualities of the circle. Leave a row and you can always go back to it. The row is an open formation. But once a circle closes, there is no return. It is no accident that the planets move in a circle and when a stone breaks loose from one of them it is drawn inexorably away by centrifugal force. Like a meteorite broken loose from a planet, I too fell from the circle and have been falling ever since. Some people remain in the circle until they die, others smash to pieces at the end of a long fall. The latter (my group) always retain a muted nostalgia for the circle dance. After all, we are every one of us inhabitants of a universe where everything turns in circles.

Beyond their love of China and the initial enthusiasm with which they greeted the establishment of a government that promised to introduce socialism into China, the group whose lives form the basis for this book have another thing in common. They are all aware of the magic qualities of the circle. Some had even danced in the ring. You Xiaoli, after trekking for two weeks by train and donkey and foot, after being officially cleaned and deloused, coiffed, permanent-waved, and dressed, had danced in a circle from which she got to shake hands with Mao Zedong and listen to Liu Shaoqi deliver a three-hour, twenty-seven-cigarette speech. And when she returned to her university, so many people shook the hand that had shaken the hand of Mao that her hand became swollen and bruised. And in Li Meirong's scrapbook are pictures of her, arms linked with her schoolmates, all dressed in neat dark skirts and clean white blouses, banners unfurled, marching, kicking, chanting, celebrating what exactly is a little murky but something about opposing U.S. aggression and supporting the Soviet comrades. And in 1954, You Xiaoli and her schoolmates had again all dressed in their finest and been bused to Sun Yat-sen Park to form a circle around Zhou Enlai and some visiting comrade from the Soviet Union, and they had all linked arms and taken two steps in place, and lifted first one leg and then the other, kick, kick. Zhou Enlai had stood in the middle and gracefully, rhythmically, had imitated their dance, taking two steps in place, lifting first one leg and then the other, kick, kick. And Bai Meihua, daughter of a high-ranking party cadre and believing herself special thereby, was often, when growing up, dressed in white, red scarf of the Young Pioneers around her neck, and whisked to the airport to present bouquets of flowers to visiting foreign dignitaries. And during the Cultural Revolution, those who still remained in the circle, young and old, graceful and awkward alike, had often linked arms and taken two steps in place, one step forward, kick, kick, doing the loyalty dance to the man they all agreed was the red, red sun in their hearts, Party Chairman Mao Zedong. "Old ladies with bound feet and small boys and girls all danced together," recalls You Xiaoli. "They held hands and there were special songs. The special songs came over the loudspeaker. Every day, every morning, afternoon and night, at least two times a day, they danced the loyalty dance. The bound feet of the old ladies were especially ugly. Those old, poor women with bound feet were forced to dance. I can still remember their faces. They were frightened and uncomfortable. And it was difficult for them to sing. Old ladies in China had never even spoken loudly, let alone sung."

"Can you imagine what it was like to be eight years old and to see all the adults in the country, millions and millions of people, joining hands together and doing exactly the same dance and only one dance and singing the same songs and only two songs?" Xiao Liang had asked. "Even then I knew something was terribly wrong."

OTHERS had stood at the edge of the circle, trying to get in. Li Weiguo continued to dream of joining the party and took Liu Shaoqi as his model, reading and rereading Liu's *How to Be a Good Communist*, underlining, memorizing, starring, writing marginal notes. But he was never permitted into the circle. His father had died most likely of starvation born of poverty, but before the Japanese invasion, he had been a petty official for the Guomindang government and hence a member of the exploiting class and an enemy of the new state. His son, no matter how well he emulated Liu Shaoqi, was not worthy of party membership.

You Xiaoli, too, had tried countless times to join the party. But even though she had grown up in desperate poverty, even though her mother had died of starvation, even though she had fled to the liberated areas and devoted her life to the Communist Party of China, she was nonetheless, illegitimate or not, the daughter of a wealthy landlord. That her father had refused to recognize You Xiaoli's existence, that the family of the landlord had turned his maidservant, You Xiaoli's mother, out on the street together with her children, did not change the fact that You Xiaoli was the daughter of an enemy.

Song Erli, too, had tried to join the circle, the Communist Youth League. But Song Erli was the son of a rightist, and so his grades had to be better, his politics more revolutionary than those of his schoolmates before grudgingly, provisionally, the circle admitted him. Children of bad class background, so the saying went, had to work ten times harder than those whose families were "good." Erli grew up hating not the circle but his father, the rightist.

Song Wuhao, too, had grown up standing on the outside longing to be in. With his Guomindang connections and his Western education, Song Wuhao's father was always suspect, and so, therefore, was his son. Song Wuhao had hoped that through his revolutionary participation in the Cultural Revolution, the circle would open to him at last. And for a few brief, exhilarating, exuberant months, it did.

It is because of what happened to them during the Great Proletarian Cultural Revolution that they are all aware of the magic qualities of the circle. For during the course of the Cultural Revolution, all were decisively, decidedly, and violently excluded from the circle. As the rest of China was linking arms and taking two steps in place, lifting first one leg and then the other, kick, kick, doing the loyalty dance to Chairman Mao, these people were being accused of one form or another of counterrevolutionary crime.

What is more, all of them were innocent. Not completely innocent, of course. They were human. They were flawed. And they lived in a society where innocence was not rewarded. It is the lotus that emerges from the muddy water bright, beautiful, innocent, and clean. But they were innocent of the crimes of which they were accused. Or the crimes of which they were accused would not, under normal circumstances, in sane societies, be considered crimes— crimes like having relatives overseas, or having been educated abroad, or being the "offspring of a counterrevolutionary."

You Xiaoli was the exception. You Xiaoli really was innocent, a saint, a lotus blossom in the form of a person. True, she still loved Song-dynasty paintings. She had learned to love them wandering secretly, quietly, on tiptoe, around her father's opulent, antique-filled house before she and her mother were forcibly expelled. Loving Song-dynasty paintings was probably a crime during the Cultural Revolution, a mark of the bourgeoisie. But it was not one of the crimes of which You Xiaoli was accused. She was accused of a multitude of sins, from being a spy to having opposed Chairman Mao. But You Xiaoli had never been a spy and had never opposed Chairman Mao. "I loved Chairman Mao," she protests even today. "I believed that Chairman Mao was our Messiah. Even locked up in the university prison, I still loved Chairman Mao. I kept thinking that if only he knew what we intellectuals were suffering, he wouldn't like it, he would stop it. If only Chairman Mao knew. Outside, on the campus, there was a huge plaster statue of Chairman Mao. It was uncovered, open to the sky. When it rained, I used to feel so sorry for Chairman Mao because he was getting wet. There was nothing to keep him dry." As a counterrevolutionary and a spy, You Xiaoli was forbidden to wear the Mao button that was yet another symbol the Chinese populace had enthusiastically accepted as evidence of their loyalty to the party chairman.

But in the darkness of night, loving him faithfully and incarcerated for having opposed him, You Xiaoli surreptitiously pinned a Mao button next to her heart.

Li Meirong was not a saint, but she was also innocent. She really did dress more stylishly than the other teachers in her middle school, really was more beautiful, with her finely honed, aristocratic features, her pale skin, her eyes. The pictures in her scrapbook make that clear. "Li Meirong," they demanded at one of the struggle sessions against her, "why are your clothes so pretty? Why do you always dress so fashionably?" Li Meirong told them that she made all her clothes by hand and offered to teach them how to sew. Then they made Li Meirong take off her glasses and said, "Li Meirong, what is wrong with your eyes? Your eyes are foreign, Western. You don't have Chinese eyes. What is wrong with your eyes, Li Meirong?" And then they seared her forehead, her cheeks, and her arms with lighted cigarettes.

But even during the Cultural Revolution, it was not, officially at least, a crime to be pretty. Li Meirong's real crime, the official accusation brought against her, was that she was a landlord and a spy. Li Meirong's father had indeed been rich. She did have relatives who lived outside China. Those relatives had even sent her letters. There had been occasional correspondence. "How is your health?" Li Meirong had written. "Xiao Li has just started school, is doing well. We are all doing fine." That was the evidence against her. It did not make Li Meirong a landlord and a spy.

Li Weiguo really had taken Liu Shaoqi as his model to emulate. He did regard Liu's *How to Be a Good Communist* as his Bible. But he was not on that account opposed to Chairman Mao. Perhaps he had admired Mao Zedong a little less than Liu Shaoqi. But he had never known there were differences between them. And Mao had never written a primer on how to be a good Communist.

Qiu Yehuang, Li Weiguo, Wu Gengsheng, and Gao Cuixia had learned to swim in muddy waters—Wu Gengsheng and Gao Cuixia to get ahead, Qiu Yehuang and Li Weiguo merely to stay afloat. During the antirightist campaign, all had participated in attacks against people they knew to be innocent. Mao Zedong had a theory about the circle, a theory about enemies and friends. He said that at any given point in history, 5 percent of the population were to be considered the enemy, outside the circle, the legitimate object of attack, while 95 percent of the population were to be considered friends, upon whom the Communist Party might rely. And periodically, such as during the antirightist campaign of 1957, Mao and associates had choreographed the 95 percent to link arms dancing, taking two steps in place, one step forward, kicking the 5 percent in unison from the circle. So fearful were people of being kicked from the circle that they linked arms with their countrymen and danced the dance, kicking to avoid being kicked.

But it was not for their attacks on innocent people that Wu Gengsheng and

Gao Cuixia, Qiu Yehuang and Li Weiguo were accused during the Cultural Revolution. To the contrary, the system rewarded people for attacking the innocent. They were attacked, rather, for their close connections with superiors who had come under attack; or for a chance misstatement; or for their family background; or because the political orthodoxy of yesterday had become the political heterodoxy of today.

THAT some are capable, even in the worst of times, not only of making moral choices but of acting on them, is exemplified here by You Xiaoli. What is remarkable about You Xiaoli is not the nature or extent of her torture but the fact that she remained as innocent at the end of the Cultural Revolution as when it began. Subjected to many forms of torture, to torture that for most would be beyond the limits of human endurance, she never confessed to crimes of which she was not guilty. She never lied. She never betrayed a relative, or a colleague, or a friend. Given the situation in which most victims found themselves during the Cultural Revolution, hers is a most remarkable achievement indeed.

But You Xiaoli is the exception. Most chose to try to stay in the circle at the price of their own integrity. Most chose survival over morality. For if they were victims, they were survivors, too, and survival in the worst of times is not always conducive to innocence. Satan was right when he challenged God in the Book of Job: Most men will sacrifice integrity in order to survive. Suffering is rarely ennobling. Most of those who were victims of the Cultural Revolution emerged from the episode considerably less innocent than when they had entered it.

They confessed to crimes of which they were not guilty. They lied. They betrayed colleagues, relatives, and friends.

WHY did they talk? Not usually for the same reasons that I listened—not to bear witness. Or at any rate, not to bear witness for the same reasons that survivors of the Holocaust bear witness. Not because they saw China as part of a larger humanity, not out of a sense of moral obligation to humanity, not to transmit the lessons of their experiences to generations to come. Not so we would not forget. For they are Chinese and China is an inward-looking society, a society of secrets, a society that has little sense of itself as something more than Chinese, as part of a larger human community. *Zhongwai you bie*— "Chinese and foreigners are different"—is the catchword the faithful use to warn against sharing secrets with outsiders. The stuff of which the Cultural Revolution was made is still not officially deemed entirely appropriate for revelation to the outside world.

But it is also that they were self-absorbed, so caught up in the telling of their own stories that they were unable to sense the larger significance of which they were a part.

Song Wuhao was an exception.

"Why do I talk to you? Why am I willing to tell you my story?" he asked. "Because I represent the youth of China, and because I want to speak for them. I think my case is typical of many people my age, even classic. When the Cultural Revolution began, I not only supported it, I was a *zaofan pai,* a revolutionary rebel. I was a fanatic. Later, as you will see, it was different. The Gang of Four took the springtime of my youth and smashed it to the ground. I can never recover those years. I want the world to know and to understand our experiences, the experiences of youth like me."

And Huang Chaoqun, too, had a sense of bearing witness, a sense of the necessity of exposing evil in order to prevent its recurrence. "Why did Solzhenitsyn write *A Day in the Life of Ivan Denisovitch?"* he asks. "There are many literary works like that in Chinese history, in classical Chinese literature. They are not about political persecution like the Cultural Revolution, but still many good works of classical Chinese literature are the result of the torture of the writer himself. Take a novel like *The Dream of the Red Chamber. The Dream of the Red Chamber* is the author's, Cao Xueqin's, life, his true experiences, even though it is fiction. Today, people are still afraid of being criticized for exploring the dark side of our country, our party. Many people are still afraid of being criticized for not keeping secrets from others, like foreigners. They talk about burying, not about exposing, the dark side—'hide the evil, praise the good.' Today in literature it is like that. You can't write too much about the evil. You are criticized for exploring the dark side. But if we do not expose the evil, maybe there will be another Cultural Revolution. If we expose the dark side, point out who did the evil things, maybe it won't happen again."

But if few spoke for posterity, to people beyond their borders, many were propelled by the same private emotions that have led other people from other cultures, survivors of other extremities, to bear witness. Like pain. The motivating compulsion for most, I think, was pain, and the belief that by talking that pain might in some measure be diminished.

"For myself," said You Xiaoli, "there are a lot of things I want to say. I want people to know that I was a victim. I think that must be a common, normal psychological state. Human beings like to talk about their sufferings. It's a kind of . . . not a healing of the wound, but still to some extent it reduces the pain. The most terrible thing during the Cultural Revolution was that it was such a long time with nobody to talk to, no one to listen."

Some talked not only out of pain but out of guilt, as a means of confession, of expiation. Jiang Xinren, for instance, was twenty-one years old when the Cultural Revolution began. He had taken up guns and used them during the Cultural Revolution's bloodiest, most violent phase. One morning he awoke and asked himself what he had been doing and why. In answering, his whole conception of himself, and of man and society, was changed. It is not Chinese —Confucian, Buddhist, or Maoist—to conceive of man as inherently evil. But Jiang Xinren, in his guilt for what he did during the Cultural Revolution, came to conceive of himself, his generation, his nation—man in general—as evil. Upon his shoulders he has taken the burden of guilt not merely for his own actions but for those of his generation and for the whole Chinese intellectual class. "I want to confess," he told me, "for myself, for my generation, for the Chinese nation."

And some talked simply because they knew their stories were interesting.

ARE they telling the truth? How can one know for certain? It is not just that memory is fallible but that it is painful, too. Wu Weidong was racked with guilt. That, at least, was clear. But he never told me that he had been a revolutionary rebel in the early days of the Cultural Revolution, that he had participated in the persecution of his teachers. I lived on his campus, and his colleagues made sure I knew. So I have used Wu Weidong only as background, for the insights he gave. And Wang Hongbao, even after scores of hours of interviews, did not tell me that he had turned against his father. It was only when I saw the gap in his story and asked about it that he admitted his shame. And it was Li Shimei's wife, not Li Shimei himself, who told me that Li Shimei had been married previously—to a peasant girl he had met after his parents had been incarcerated and he had been sent to live and work in the country-side. These weren't lies exactly, simply a reluctance to tell.

It can be argued that the private circumstances in which the interviews took place were more conducive to truth than the formal brief introductions and tea through which information, but not necessarily the truth, is generally transmitted to foreigners. The stories and the manner of telling ring differently from that of the professor on film.

CERTAINLY trust was a basic precondition to revelation, trust that I would be a sympathetic, supportive, and nonjudgmental listener, and trust that I could and would maintain their anonymity. That I was an outsider and foreign may well have meant that it took longer to establish trust, but once it was estab-lished, my foreignness counted in my favor. Governed as so many were by residual fears that the Cultural Revolution might someday come again, and knowing the attacks against them had been launched by friends and colleagues within their own work units, those who spoke to me saw an outsider as the only safe outlet for unburdening. "You are safe to talk to," said one. "I know you won't tell the government what I've said."

Sometimes the first interview would begin with a recitation of the prevailing orthodoxy on the Cultural Revolution, but both tone and substance changed dramatically when individuals began to recount their own personal stories. For many, the Cultural Revolution had been a profoundly lonely and isolating experience which still weighed heavily on their minds. None had ever had an opportunity to talk about himself and his experience in such sustained detail. The exquisiteness with which they remembered, their ability to lose themselves in those memories, was akin to psychotherapy, in which painful memories of the past sometimes replay themselves as in a film. Distant memories often forced their way to consciousness with a clarity so sharp that it seemed the individual was actually reliving his experiences, able in the telling to imbue them with the proper and painful emotions that the exigencies of the actual experience had prohibited. And indeed, while remembering was often an intensely painful experience, while the insomnia that ordinarily plagued them worsened after our sessions and the number of pills it took to induce sleep increased, the experience of talking was usually therapeutic. In the best of the interviews, what they said is true in the way that memories in therapy are true.

It is Studs Terkel, father of oral history and master of the art, who best answers the question of whether they are telling the truth. He writes:

> This is a memory book, rather than one of hard fact and precise statistic. In recalling an epoch, some thirty, forty years ago, my colleagues experienced pain, in some instances; exhilaration, in others. Often it was a fusing of both. . . .
>
> Are they telling the truth? The question is as academic as the day Pilate asked it, his philosophy not quite washing out his guilt. . . .
>
> In their rememberings are their truths. The precise fact or the precise date is of small consequence. This is not a lawyer's brief nor an annotated sociological treatise. It is simply an attempt to get the story . . . from an improvised battalion of survivors.
>
> That there were some who were untouched, or indeed, did rather well isn't exactly news. This has been true of all disasters. The great many were wounded, in one manner or another. It left upon them an "invisible scar." . . .

It is upon the invisible scars, the invisible wounds, that this testimony focuses. What you have to listen for, what you have to hear, are the slow, silent screams.

Because the wounds, by and large, really are invisible. The screams really are silent. Everyone I interviewed was a functioning member of Chinese society. Some, like You Xiaoli, were still suffering from the physical wounds inflicted upon them during the Cultural Revolution, but none has had to stop work completely. This was not always true of their family members, some of whom had been so psychologically or physically damaged by the Cultural Revolution that they have been unable to resume work. Song Wuhao's father will never work again, or Huan Xing's wife. And many of the families with whom I spoke had lost one or more of their members, whether through beatings, suicide, factional violence, or the refusal to grant medical aid to the so-called counterrevolutionaries. All had lost friends. Their memories are cluttered with the deaths, the suicides, the insanities. It is little wonder that the traumas, the scars, are a dominant legacy of the Cultural Revolution. What is most remarkable really is not the wounds but the tremendous resilience of those who have been through so much.

THREE

NIE YUANZI'S BIG CHARACTER POSTER: THE SPARK THAT LIT THE PRAIRIE FIRE

Most remember the day it began, and most agree on the date: June 2, 1966.

It was on that day that the *People's Daily*, the nationally circulated official daily newspaper of the Chinese Communist Party, published Nie Yuanzi's "big character poster,"* together with an editorial of enthusiastic support.

Nie Yuanzi was a middle-aged member of the Philosophy Department at Peking University. She was not a scholar or even an educated woman. But the position she held was one of considerable power. Nie Yuanzi was a member of the Chinese Communist Party and head of the Philosophy Department's party branch.

"Beida," as Peking University is colloquially known, had long been China's most prestigious—and politically progressive—institution of higher learning. During the wave of intellectual and political ferment that surrounded the May Fourth

*A privately written but publicly posted political proclamation or statement of opinion.

Movement of 1919, the prestigious faculty and elite students of Beida had stood at its progressive core, leading the movement forward. In 1918, even Mao Zedong himself, then twenty-five years old and freshly graduated from Hunan's First Normal School, had worked there. As a lowly assistant librarian speaking the thick, barely intelligible accent of rural Hunan, Mao had brushed shoulders with (and, he would later claim, been shunned by) China's intellectual giants. Some believe it was at Beida that the seeds of Mao's later antagonism toward his country's intellectuals were sown. "To most of them," he told the journalist Edgar Snow years later, referring to the university's intellectual elite, "I didn't exist as a human being."

But it was also at Beida that Mao had met and been befriended by the university librarian, Li Dazhao. Li Dazhao was not with Mao Zedong in Shanghai in 1921 when the Chinese Communist Party was formed, but both of them are counted as founding members.

IN 1952, some three years after Mao's peasant guerrilla forces had taken over the country, Beida moved from its original cluster of red brick buildings close to Beihai Park in the heart of Peking to the northwest suburbs some forty-five minutes by bicycle away, incorporating under its aegis and occupying the grounds of the formerly Rockefeller-supported, American-run, and Christian-rooted Yenching University. With its green lawns, its sloping roofs of gleaming gray tiles, its water tower in the style of a pagoda, its focal point a peaceful lake (Weiming Hu—"Lake Without a Name") lined by acacias and drooping weeping willows, the campus of Yenching University was redolent with the Chinese past—a sharp contrast to the utilitarian, drab gray buildings, the stunted trees, the dusty, clay-baked grounds of Chinese universities constructed after the Liberation of 1949.

But the traditional architecture and placid setting of the Yenching University campus belied the reality within. The meaning and import of Nie Yuanzi's big character poster can best be understood in the context of the changes introduced to Beida, indeed to all of China's universities, with the Communist ascension to power.

FOLLOWING Liberation, the Communist Party of China had moved cautiously but inexorably to take control of the country's universities. In the early years, the years when the party's primary urban focus was on the sheer consolidation of power, its efforts within the universities were directed on the one hand toward instilling everyone within them with a basic foundation in the Marxist-Leninist ideology that would guide the new government's policies and on the other toward "reforming the thought" of the older, more senior university faculty. With the outbreak of the Korean War in June 1950, thought reform was directed particularly toward faculty—men among the most renowned and widely respected of China's intellectual elite—who were known to have had ties with the United States, the country with which China was then at war.

Li Weiguo's memory of the early 1950s as "the golden years" is widespread among Chinese, but hardly universal. The experiences of many of China's senior and Western-educated university faculty, a tiny but elite core of prominent intellectuals, were different. In the face of the Japanese invasion of 1937 and Chiang Kai-shek's lack of enthusiasm in getting his armies to fight, many of China's patriotic intellectuals had withdrawn their support from the government, which they believed had not mounted a sufficiently vigorous defense of their motherland. Some had formed the China Democratic League, trying to steer a third, more moderate and democratic course between the two extremes of the Nationalist and Communist parties. When the middle road proved impossible, most had conceded to the inevitable and placed their faith and their hope in the victorious but still relatively little-understood and little-tested Communist Party of Mao Zedong. Most were prepared to offer public professions of loyalty to the new government. Some, after periods of soul-searching that varied in length and intensity, even returned to China from secure positions abroad—in the United States, England, Japan, and Southeast Asia—in order to profess their faith in the new Communist regime and to offer their services in the building of a new China. Many seemed willing enough to participate in thought reform, honestly endeavoring to purge themselves of their bourgeois pasts and to imbue themselves with the proletarian world outlook. For some, the opportunity to participate in thought reform was even part of the appeal of the Chinese Communist Party. "One of Mao's notions that was so important, so attractive," recalls Yao Baoding, "was the notion of ideological remolding—that people could change, that they could remold their thoughts, transform their thinking, become new people. I underwent ideological remolding, and those sessions were really very, very useful."

But others were horrified at the spectacle of the country's senior intellectuals prostituting themselves in public, castigating themselves before colleagues, students, and friends. For their shameless and apparently abject self-confessions, their heartfelt denunciations of themselves and their friends, their chest-pounding *mea culpa*'s for their previous collusion with American "reactionaries," "secret agents," and "cultural imperialists," some earned from their less effusive colleagues the label *feng pai*—the "wind faction," people who blow with the prevailing political wind, no matter how frequently it shifts, how far from course it veers.

Zhou Peiyuan, trained in physics at the California Institute of Technology, was regarded by some as a *feng pai*. During the thought reform movement of the early 1950s, Zhou confessed both that when he returned to China from the United States in 1929 his "whole body had been saturated with the pernicious germs of the bourgeoisie" and that while on a return visit to do research in 1943 he had cast his lot with the imperialists and taken part in "military research work supported by the American imperialists and designed to murder the peace-loving people of the world."

The rewards of blowing with the wind were substantial. Decades later, during the Cultural Revolution, Zhou Peiyuan became president of Peking University.

"The way to get ahead," Huang Chaoqun asserts, "was to curse yourself, to claim that you were dirty, polluted, to attack other people—your family, parents, the foreigners—say you were polluted by them. Then you could be considered to be okay, reeducated." Huang Chaoqun was in his early forties during the thought reform campaign. Like Yao Baoding, he had as a young man fled from his home to a liberated area to throw in his lot with the struggling forces of the Communist guerrillas. He was part of a team of youthful intellectuals who participated in the liberation of the university where he was ultimately to be made a professor. As a liberator, he was not compelled to undergo thought reform himself. But he did not like much of what he saw during the movement, viewing the self-criticisms demanded by thought reform as a way for those who had jumped on the bandwagon late to get ahead, ingratiating themselves with the new regime. But despite his distaste for this, the first of the movements the Communist Party led on university campuses, he remained an ardent supporter of the new regime.

Troubled loyalists, torn between the dictates of conscience on the one hand and a patriotic commitment to their country and its newly founded government on the other, had a more difficult time. Lu Zhiwei, president of Yenching University in the early days after Liberation and before its takeover by Beida, was forced to resign that post after writing an apparently unsatisfactory self-confession admitting that he was as incapable of hating American imperialists as he was of hating anybody of any class.

Revolutionary enthusiasts, often young, were sometimes so deeply enamored of their cause that they seemed blinded to the implications of their acts. Lu Zhiwei's daughter, Lu Yaohua, was one such revolutionary enthusiast. At a mass rally at Peking University, she publicly denounced her father as a "100 percent collaborator with imperialism." Her action in "drawing a clear line of demarcation" from her father presaged a new age in Chinese family relations, as children were called upon so frequently to denounce their elders that many parents feared to discuss politics with their children, yielding the task of political socialization almost entirely to school and state.

THE thought reform campaign of the early 1950s was a small-scale movement, confined to a select group of highly unusual intellectual elite. "It's true that some people weren't getting benefits from Liberation," Li Weiguo admits. But

Li Weiguo's confidence that the vast majority were benefiting remains unshaken. "If people recognized the Communist Party and said they supported the new government, then the party united with those people. So most of the people at that time were for the Communist Party, for Chairman Mao. The number of the people who didn't benefit was very small."

Nonetheless, the thought reform campaign stood as a harbinger of the politics that would become increasingly frequent in the decade and more to come: the politics of persecution and slander, the politics, alas, of hate.

Efforts at thought reform were quickly followed by structural changes designed to consolidate further the party's role on university campuses. Early in 1952, Chinese universities underwent the first in a series of reorganizations designed to transform a system of higher education that had once been profoundly influenced by the West to one that would replicate in substance and organization the educational system of the Soviet Union.

The liberal arts education disappeared, as did the liberal arts university itself. A few comprehensive universities teaching both science and the humanities remained, Beida in Peking and Fudan in Shanghai among them, but in general both universities and the students within them became increasingly narrowly specialized. Students of the sciences were no longer permitted to take courses in the humanities, and students in the humanities and social sciences had no exposure to the sciences. Undergraduates were assigned their majors upon acceptance by the university, and virtually all their coursework, political study excepted, took place within a single department. Many of the social sciences that had long enriched the curricula of major Chinese liberal arts colleges— disciplines such as sociology, anthropology, and political science—were abolished altogether. The teaching of English was confined to a very few students in a handful of elite universities and prestigious institutes of foreign languages, as Russian became the required foreign language for all who sought higher degrees. Texts from the Soviet Union came to predominate, and politically cautious faculty lectured without deviation directly from the books Big Brother supplied, as students faithfully copied the material that was later to be learned and regurgitated by rote. Political study meetings, convened several times a week, became required courses of study; world history, Western philosophy, and logic were dropped from college catalogues.

Members of the Chinese Communist Party came to occupy positions of considerable power within the newly reorganized universities. In the initial phases, it is true, many were intellectuals themselves—intellectuals of the type who had become early supporters of the Communist Party, joining Mao Zedong and his guerrilla bands in Yenan and other liberated base areas in the late 1930s and 1940s. But others who came to exercise power were political cadres, not merely unacquainted with the codes and mores of academic life but frankly uneducated. Inevitably, there were strains.

It would be difficult to exaggerate the educational and psychological distance that separated the cosmopolitan, Western-educated university professor of China in the early 1950s from the peasants who made up 80 percent of the Chinese population and provided the Communist Party with some 70 percent of its membership—the Communist Party peasants who, in 1949, had triumphantly marched into China's cities and then attempted to govern. It is difficult to imagine how peasants might be capable of governing the most populous nation on earth, let alone of leading that nation into modernity. For Chinese peasants were inhabitants of a countryside the greater portion of which by 1949 had yet to see the light of the twentieth century—a countryside rooted in poverty, where life was lived at the margin of subsistence, where superstition still governed and ghosts walked the land, where evil spirits were credited with causing sickness and disease. It was a place where justice, when meted out, was harsh, and the severed heads of executed criminals were put on public display and their blood was sold to be drunk for strength. It was a countryside where the vast majority of the population was illiterate, where 70 percent of the men and 99 percent of the women were unable even to read a simple letter, where most, in their entire lives, would never travel farther than the nearby market town, where the wooden wheeled carts which served as a primary means of conveyance had not been improved upon in tens of centuries. But it was these peasants who came to hold positions of considerable power in China's universities shortly after the Communist Party came to power. And if it was not the most backward and unsophisticated of the party's peasant cadres who came to staff the reorganized universities, the political cadre were in any case more like their peasant brethren than they were like the intellectuals they had been sent to govern. They were what Huang Chaoqun, then recently appointed an assistant professor, describes as the "urban peasants."

Huang Chaoqun had fought for the liberation of China, sacrificing everything. Leaving his position as a junior faculty member at a major university in an area controlled by the Guomindang, he had trekked by foot for days, weeks, months, over hazardous terrain, through hostile territory, to reach a liberated area controlled by the Communists and to devote his whole energies to bringing liberation to others. But Huang Chaoqun has difficulty speaking well of the urban peasants. It is not merely their lack of education and their rural roots that he believes renders them questionable leaders of his country's universities. It is also their lack of revolutionary commitment. For most of the urban peasants, Huang Chaoqun argues, were first liberated by the Communist Party and then encouraged to join their ranks. They sacrificed nothing to join the revolutionary cause. Huang Chaoqun and his comrades had given up everything. "I think I am a true revolutionary," he says. "I wasn't concerned about status and privilege. I wanted to free the poor and oppressed. For the urban peasants, their home villages were in the liberated areas. They were liberated by the party in their own home villages, and then those people got power, position, control over us. But we are the ones who gave up our well-to-do life for the revolution. Even me, the poor, poorest boy in the world, I was already an assistant professor, but I gave up the city life and went to the liberated area. I walked through the countryside, and through city after city and town after town, village after village, to go to the liberated area. And we read. Marxism-Leninism. We read *Capital*. But they didn't do that. They didn't read. They don't know about Marxism—the urban peasants, the ones who are now the high-ranking cadres and the middle-ranking cadres. They joined the revolution early from their own hometowns, when their hometowns were liberated. They are the donkeys, the mules of the revolution. Why did they join? They were hankering after family fortune. We gave up everything, but they have the power." The urban peasants, once assigned to universities, did not aspire to teach courses that were part of the substantive curriculum. They did what they were best able to do, which was to convene political meetings, to mobilize their charges in the cause of socialism, to foster participation in the series of political campaigns that began sweeping the country like waves, one following inexorably upon the other.

Students—youthful rebels, enthusiasts in the cause of socialism—were enlisted in criticism sessions against their professors, undermining thereby the traditional teacher-student relationship that had been predicated upon deferential respect for knowledge and age. "Students were taught to be rough, tough," recalls Huang Chaoqun. "They were taught to be antihumanistic, without emotions, without any sympathy toward other people. All emotions were considered to be bourgeois, capitalist, as though the proletariat were emotionless people. I hated that time."

The thought reform campaign and the reorganization of universities were not the only movements in the early 1950s to mar the golden years. There was the "three-anti" campaign of 1951 against corruption, waste, and bureaucratism, and the "five-anti" campaign of 1952 against bribery, tax evasion, fraud, theft of state assets, and leakage of state economic secrets. There was the movement for the suppression of counterrevolutionaries in 1955. These campaigns were directed less against intellectuals than against the urban merchants, industrialists, and businessmen who had not fled to Taiwan. Men of the church were also singled out during the 1955 campaign. Ignatius Gong Pinmei, the Roman Catholic bishop of Shanghai, was arrested then. He had steadfastly advocated independence of the Church from the government and refused to break his ties with the Vatican. He was arrested for having formed a counterrevolutionary clique which colluded with the imperialists against the motherland under the cloak of religion. He was finally released after thirty years, at age eighty-three, in July 1985.

In 1957, Mao Zedong said that during the period between Liberation and

1954, government security forces had "liquidated" 800,000 enemies of the people. Lin Xiling argued in the same year that during the movement against counterrevolutionaries in 1955, 720,000 people had been wronged. It was one of the many statements Lin Xiling made that year that contributed to her arrest. She spent fifteen years in jail and labor reform camps. Not everyone was as sanguine about the golden years as Li Weiguo.

By early 1956, the party had come publicly to recognize that the effectiveness of thought reform was limited, that the new government was having difficulty winning the hearts and minds of China's intellectuals. Zhou Enlai estimated that only about 40 percent of China's higher intellectuals actively supported the Chinese Communist Party and its government, that another 40 or so percent formed an intermediate group who offered their support but were not active politically. Ten percent of the intellectuals, he said, were "backward" and opposed socialism, and another 10 percent were downright counterrevolutionary.

In mid-1956, cautiously at first, more emphatically by the beginning of the following year, leaders of the Chinese Communist Party began urging intellectuals to speak their minds freely, to put forth their criticisms of the governing Communist Party and the faults of its socialist government. A slogan was attached to the encouragement: "Let a hundred flowers bloom, let a hundred schools of thought contend." It was the first time in history that a ruling Communist Party had so directly solicited the real views of its citizens. Precisely why Party Chairman Mao Zedong fostered such debate and what exactly he expected to hear remain, even now, a mystery. Some believe that he encouraged public dissension as a means of allowing steam to escape without blowing off the lid. Some feel that Mao was nonetheless shocked by the unexpected vehemence of the criticisms the movement unleashed.

China's intellectuals hesitated initially to express themselves. With the multiple, cross-cutting, simmering tensions engendered by the thought reform campaign and the reorganization of China's universities, with the abuse that the transfer of academic power from intellectuals to the party had entailed, their hesitation was not without reason. Li Xiaotian was afraid that such encouragement was a ruse, like coaxing a snake out of its hole only to lop it in two. Like others, he feared that those who dared to offer criticisms would ultimately be called to task.

The criticisms were mild at first, formulaic and stereotypical, calculated repetitions of statements already publicly made by the country's highest leaders. But in May 1957, with continued prodding, the floodgates opened and the pent-up silence of nearly eight years of Communist Party rule came pouring through in bitter words.

There were those who expressed dissatisfaction with the domineering role of the party cadre on university campuses—with the folly of the unschooled presuming to exert so much control over education and the educators, with the absurdity of what, in the eyes of those in power, constituted sins against the party—like remarks that the three-hour speeches of the party cadre were excessively long. There was one who said that the cultural standard of one of the leaders in his university was so low that his speeches were virtually incoherent. There were complaints that too much time was spent in political study meetings and at the obligatory, celebratory mass rallies—that after all the meetings and all the rallies there was little time left for teachers to prepare their classes or researchers to conduct research. There were accusations of arrogance and complacency on the part of certain members of the party, allegations that because the talents and training of many party men were not commensurate with their duties, many had bungled their jobs—that the party leadership was assigning square pegs to round holes. "Some of those who have become principals," Chen Yangzhi pointed out, "know absolutely nothing about education. Quite a few ignoramuses who cannot even read simple documents without difficulty have been appointed to positions of leadership." At Shenyang Normal College, it was said that the head of the Russian Language Department, a party member, knew not a single Russian letter. There were allegations that Communist Party members did nothing all day but eat, that they were arrogant and conceited.

Concern was openly expressed that too much had been copied, too uncritically, too closely, from the Soviet Union, that the West, for all its capitalist faults, had lessons to teach as well, particularly in the realm of science. There were remonstrations that science, at least, was classless. There were complaints about the idealization of the Soviet Union and allegations that China's own traditions were being neglected, that China's own scientists, some of them equal in training, intellect, and accomplishment to the finest in the world, were being ignored in the turn toward the Soviet Big Brother. Long Yun, onetime governor of Yunnan province and then an official in Peking, wondered aloud why China was being asked to bear all the expenses for its role in the Korean War and why China had to pay back, with interest, the loans from the Soviet Union. He pointed to the fact that after the Second World War, the United States had released its allies from the obligation to repay their debts. He wondered why the Soviet Union had never paid China for the factories in Manchuria it had dismantled and shipped away at the conclusion of the Second World War.

There were pleas for a restitution of the defunct social sciences and arguments that the social sciences had a role to play in socialist construction. There were laments about the state of student-faculty relations, questions as to how teachers could be expected to perform knowing that for any chance remark, some inchoate thought, the students might pounce, accusing the careless teacher of being a "class enemy." There were allegations of discrimination against deserving nonparty faculty, of favoritism to unqualified party and Youth League members, of neglecting talent, intellect, and hard work in determining promotions. There were allegations that party members responsible for assessing academic salaries and determining promotions had never even read the academic works of the faculty. Some even suggested that Communist Party control over universities should be brought to an end.

One man pointed to a shortage of consumer goods and wondered who exactly in China was enjoying the higher standard of living that socialism allegedly had brought. "They are the party members and cadres who wore worn-out shoes in the past," he responded to his own musings, "but who travel in saloon cars and put on woolen uniforms now."

There were laments about what was happening to relations among friends. "Since 1952, campaign has succeeded campaign, each one leaving a great wall in its wake," said Xu Yiguan, "a wall which estranges one man from another. In such circumstances, no one dares to let off steam even privately in the company of friends, let alone speak his mind in public. Everyone has now learned the technique of double-talk—what one says is one thing, what one thinks is another."

There were allegations of injustice in the several political campaigns since 1949—the "three-anti" and "five-anti" campaigns, the campaign for the suppression of counterrevolutionaries—and proposals for the establishment of a commission to correct those injustices. Some pointed out that during those campaigns many under attack had been unable to endure the mental torture and humiliation and had chosen suicide by jumping from tall buildings, or drowning in rivers, or swallowing poison, or cutting their throats. "When the party organization finds a person useful," said another, "it treasures him even though he has committed the crime of murdering its friends, comrades, and other people belonging to the party. When it has no more need of him, it nonchalantly excludes him even though he has sweated and shed his blood for the party. Some party members disown their relatives and are estranged even from their fathers. When a party member writes to his mother, he addresses her as 'comrade.'"

And in the end, there were accusations against the Communist Party itself, predictions that without sorely needed reform the people would ultimately rebel against it. Some proposed the institution of a genuine multiparty system, arguing that if the Communist Party were to compete in free elections, it would at least have to work harder to overcome its faults. There were assertions that intellectuals were worse off under the Communists than under either the Japanese or the Guomindang. Lin Xiling, fiery female leader of the democratic movement at People's University and a party member herself, argued that true socialism is highly democratic but that China's socialism was not. She concluded that neither China nor the Soviet Union was genuinely socialist. There were attacks on even the highest-ranking of party leaders, allegations that they were the source of the present evil.

THE snakes had come out of their holes.

And their heads were lopped off.

The flowers had been allowed to blossom a mere six weeks.

China's politics of persecution entered a new stage. In the antirightist campaign that began in June 1957 as the party's response to the criticisms unleashed during the blooming of the Hundred Flowers, the number of participants—persecutors and persecuted alike—was larger. Hundreds of thousands of intellectuals, artists, and writers—party and nonparty alike—were declared rightists and kicked out of the circle, their punishment ranging from exile in labor reform camps to mere demotion in rank, reduction in salary, and ostracism by friends and peers.

For many individual Chinese, many whose stories are included here, the antirightist campaign of 1957 was a watershed, the end of innocence, the eclipse of the golden years.

Li Xiaotian, himself a member of the Communist Party and one who had sacrificed for the Liberation of China, had spoken out in criticism, for what he believed was the good of the party and the state, during the blooming of the Hundred Flowers. During the crackdown that followed, he was labeled a rightist and exiled to China's northeast to do labor reform. Li Xiaotian believed himself innocent of the charges against him. He knew that he was not a rightist but a revolutionary who had had the good of the country and the party at heart. Nonetheless, he accepted the false judgment against him. "Many people labeled rightists accepted these campaigns sincerely," he said. "Because they believed. They thought that they themselves as individuals were wronged, but they believed that the party stood for a just cause and that therefore their personal misfortune didn't mean much. If the people and the party could benefit from the campaign, then it was worthwhile to make personal sacrifices." And yet, it was precisely upon accepting the false accusation against him that Li Xiaotian's faith in the Communist Party and socialism first began to waver.

Both of Song Erli's parents were declared rightists, and Song Erli's life was irrevocably changed. So as not to be excluded from the circle, he had to study harder to get the same good grades, had to shout slogans louder to demonstrate the same revolutionary zeal. Song Erli came to see his mother as the tragic heroine unjustly accused by colleagues jealous of her beauty and her skill. His father he came to hate. "He really was a rightist," says Song Erli.

Wu Jiang's father, too, was labeled a rightist. Wu Jiang first was angry and then grew to hate his father, believing the label, and shamed and humiliated by the burden that label meant for himself. It was not until his father was dying, some two and a half decades later, that the son came finally to love, understand, and forgive.

Li Meirong and You Xiaoli "escaped through the net" during the antirightist campaign, but only through luck. Both knew that in the next campaign, they too would be attacked.

During the period of blooming and contending, Li Meirong had signed a number of big character posters criticizing the principal of her middle school, a party member, accusing him of being undemocratic and authoritarian, of failing to concern himself with the interests of the teachers and students. Because of her political activities, she was certain when the crackdown began that she would be labeled a rightist. The colleague who had actually written the big character poster was labeled, but Li Meirong was not. "But after that," she recalls, "things changed.

"Through all of Chinese history, there have been many dynasties. Dynasties have come and gone; governments have always changed. Always the new governments are welcomed by the people, but always the new government has come eventually to oppress the Chinese people. Always the governments have made freedom difficult. It was the same with this new government. When the new government first came in, everyone was happy. There was a period of great hope, great expectation.

"The antirightist campaign was the first signal that things were going to change. After that, no one felt he could speak freely again. We all knew that it could happen again, and that the next time we would be attacked. So we began not to trust the new government. After the antirightist campaign, people were more careful about what they said, whom they talked to. That was hard on me. It was difficult being so careful always about what I said. I talk too much. I like to speak my mind without thinking. I say what I am thinking at the time and then forget about it."

You Xiaoli, too, had spoken out. At one of the many political study meetings that she and her colleagues had frequently to attend, one of the leading party cadres, a man whom Huang Chaoqun would surely describe as an urban peasant, had made a speech condemning "some of our friends" who liked to dress in clean clothes, who liked to listen to bourgeois music and look at bourgeois paintings, who washed their hands before they ate. You Xiaoli was quite an enthusiast of Beethoven, Tchaikovsky, and Chopin. She liked Rembrandt and the French impressionists. She dressed neatly. Sometimes, even in the winter, she wore skirts. She was in the habit of washing her hands before eating. She was outraged by the outlandish talk of the urban peasant. "Why did we join the revolution in the first place?" she stood up to ask. "To improve people's life, to give everyone a chance to be educated, to allow everyone to become civilized. Why does the capitalist class have all these things—good music, fine paintings, nice clothes? Because they are more civilized, more educated. Why should we dress so tastelessly? We don't have to wear expensive, fancy clothes. But for the same price, we could still have a sense of color. That's civilization. That's culture. At the same price.

"Feudalism—we launched the revolution against feudalism, to get rid of feudalism. But we're missing the stage of capitalism. Capitalism is more progressive than feudalism. That's Marxism, that's what Marx says. That's progressive. All those dirty things, all those ugly things, those backward things— why are they proletarian? If we want all those ugly things, why did we need a revolution at all? We should struggle to get the beautiful things, to make the proletarian class richer and richer, more and more beautiful, to make life better and better."

You Xiaoli was fortunate during the antirightist campaign. She was in the hospital with appendicitis and developed complications following the operation. She was sick for the entire campaign. One's presence was necessary to be attacked. "But it isn't by chance that during the Cultural Revolution I was criticized so bitterly," she says.

HAD the crackdown that followed the blooming of the hundred flowers been confined merely to those who had stuck their heads out of the hole, the lesson would have been painful, yes, but nonetheless simple, unambiguous, and clear: the Party, in all circumstances and at all times and all costs is to remain scrupulously and unquestioningly beyond criticism or reproof. In the absence of a tradition of civil liberties, in the absence even of a tradition of loyal opposition, without the expectation that speech will be free, many accepted the formal terms of the antirightist campaign and decided that those who had dared so vociferously to criticize really did deserve the label of "rightist." Had not Lin Xiling, after all, really said that China was neither socialist nor democratic? Had not the British-trained and internationally known anthropologist Fei Xiaotong pointed out that agricultural collectivization had contributed to the decline both of income-producing subsidiary enterprises and of the variety of available food? Had not some of the attacks on the party been nothing short of scurrilous? Was it not true, as the party said, that the accomplishments and achievements of the party since Liberation were predominant, that its mistakes had been minor and few? And if the punishments meted out to rightists had somehow not quite fitted the crime, if there was in fact no small grain of truth behind many of the criticisms, if many of those labeled rightists had not really, in their criticisms, stepped beyond the Party-defined bounds of permissible debate, still it could be argued—as it was during thought reform and land reform and the campaign for the suppression of counterrevolutionaries—that the number of those unjustly punished was small, that the vast majority of

Chinese were still reaping the copious fruits of socialism. At least, so some reasoned, the numbers of those excluded from the circle were thankfully, mercifully, small.

BUT it was not merely the heads of the snakes that were lopped off. Educational institutions, from primary and middle schools to technical schools, and up to the level of the university, were assigned quotas—between 5 and 10 percent of their staffs—to be delivered to the state as "rightists." And because the quotas for rightists were often higher than institutions had legitimately qualified rightists to fill, rightists had to be invented. What is more, in a society in which accomplishment was measured by quotas fulfilled and units vied for the status of having not only met but surpassed their obligations to the state, some institutions not only fulfilled their quotas but enthusiastically overfulfilled them.

Indeed, some institutions exercised considerable imagination and ingenuity in handing over the requisite number of rightists. Huang Chaoqun's school, for instance, boasted among its staff a man convicted in 1952 of robbery and rape. In the spirit of leniency toward criminals that had prevailed in the early 1950s, the man had been given only a three-year sentence. By the time the Hundred Flowers began to blossom, the rapist had returned to the school. He had not yet resumed work, but his job was being held for him subject to his continued demonstration of good behavior. When intellectuals were encouraged to speak out, the convicted criminal had spoken out too, publicly decrying the injustice, severity, and harshness of his three-year sentence and accusing the party which had meted out his punishment of being as cruel as Qin Shi Huang—the first emperor of the ancient Qin dynasty, the consolidator of the Great Wall, the burner of the books and enemy of the intellectuals. To the relief of many female comrades on campus, unconcerned with fine distinctions between criminal and political misbehavior, the rapist's tirade was rewarded, when the crackdown began, with the label of rightist. He was sent to the farthest reaches of the country to do labor reform.

Another woman, during the period of blooming and contending, had criticized Khrushchev because she understood that at the Soviet Union's Twentieth Party Congress in February 1956, Khrushchev had attacked Stalin. Indeed, Mao himself would soon attack Khrushchev. In 1960, the Soviet technicians assisting in key industrial projects throughout China would be withdrawn, taking the blueprints for factories then under construction with them and plunging Chinese industry into chaos. Within years, the Sino-Soviet rift would first mushroom and become public and then degenerate into mass anti-Soviet hysteria. By 1966, the Soviet Union would officially be regarded as hopelessly and unremittingly "revisionist," and to be considered a "China's

Khrushchev" would be the ultimate crime. "China's Khrushchevs" would be said to exist at every level of Chinese society, from the president of the People's Republic, Liu Shaoqi, the "number-one China's Khrushchev," down to the no doubt bewildered and confused China's Khrushchevs in the smallest rural production brigades.

But in May 1957, the Sino-Soviet split was still not public knowledge, nor was Mao's disgruntlement with Khrushchev. Khrushchev's image was still untarnished. Far from being permitted to engage in criticisms of the Soviet Union, Chinese citizens were allowed to sing only its praises. The creative and honest woman named Chen Yide who had concluded that Stalin and Khrushchev could not both be right, and who had decided that it must be Khrushchev who was bad, was declared a rightist and sent to do labor reform. Her life did not change when Mao's own critique of Khrushchev became public. She remained in labor reform on Hainan Island for twenty-two years, until 1979.

Even the ebullient and ever optimistic Li Weiguo was sobered by the antirightist campaign and the effect on individuals of the quotas. "One of my good friends got arrested during the antirightist campaign," he remembers. "All she had done during the Hundred Flowers movement was to say that the leader of the school should attend the group meetings where the policies were being criticized, to listen to the criticisms. She said that the political movement wasn't sufficiently developed yet in our school. We should let the movement really develop and the party members should listen to what the masses were saying.

"Then, during the antirightist campaign in 1957, she was criticized for this —because the school had its quota of rightists to fill. If she had recognized her guilt and said, 'Yes, I am guilty,' her punishment would have been lighter. But she wouldn't recognize her guilt, so it got worse and worse for her. She was so stubborn. So finally they put her in jail.

"This left a very deep impression on me. That's why when the Cultural Revolution began, I was a conservative. I didn't want to criticize the party and become a rightist."

THERE is another sense in which the antirightist campaign in the summer of 1957 was a turning point for many individual Chinese—because of the choices the movement compelled. The antirightist campaign was a mass movement, demanding near-universal participation. In the work units where meetings were held to denounce those alleged to be rightists, attendance was mandatory. To fail to participate in the denunciations, to refuse to stand up and say a few words in attack, was, or so some people believed, to risk being attacked oneself.

For Li Weiguo and Qiu Yehuang, the antirightist campaign represented their own fall from innocence, their first move toward complicity with the new regime in acts that violated their conscience, the first sacrifice of their integrity in the interest of staying in the circle.

Li Weiguo was then still a student at one of China's leading scientific universities. His senior professor and mentor, then already in his sixties, had been singled out as a rightist for scathing, if accurate, criticisms leveled against the party cadre who had come to power within the university following its "liberation." As the antirightist campaign unfolded, Li Weiguo, as a student of one of the university's leading rightists, was put under considerable pressure to attack the man he so respected and admired. Li Weiguo protested his ignorance of the professor's past, but he was ordered nonetheless to prepare a public attack. "Not everyone was able to remain very clean," Li Weiguo confesses. "People's hands got dirty. I criticized my professor. I said, 'You only believed in theory. You didn't believe in practice. Marxism-Leninism emphasizes practice, not theory.' Afterward, when he was rehabilitated, he treated me in very friendly fashion. What I had said didn't really hurt his heart. The sentence I used was what he really had said. Even so, what I said was too serious, was more than I should have said. But it wasn't a lie."

Qiu Yehuang, too, kicked to avoid being kicked. He was a junior editor, then in his early thirties, at one of China's major publishing houses.

"There was an order that every place had to uncover a certain percentage of rightists," Qiu Yehuang explains. "Well, people were scared. I was forced to criticize one of my colleagues, a young man, against my conscience. Oh, everybody had been criticizing him. But they had to get someone who hadn't criticized him yet. That was me. It was against my conscience. He was innocent. Almost innocent. He had translated Hemingway. At the time he had translated Hemingway, it was okay to translate Hemingway. Then it wasn't okay to translate Hemingway. Even now, I feel sorry that I criticized him. But I did it, I know, to survive myself. Lots of Chinese had to do that. If I had the chance, I would apologize to him. I was forced to do it. Because you didn't know who was going to be the next rightist. If you wanted to stand on the correct side, you had to criticize a rightist element. Everybody was criticizing. If it were now, I wouldn't do it. I was young. But that's no excuse. I don't think my speech made his situation worse. No, I don't think so. But even so, I shouldn't have done that. That's what made me disillusioned. The policy. The policy of pushing people out of society."

The goal of Li Weiguo and Qiu Yehuang had been to survive the movement without being attacked themselves. They pride themselves both for having held out for so long and for refusing to deviate from the truth. But for attacking people they knew to be innocent, they have been burdened ever after by a residue of guilt.

"They should feel guilty," asserts Huang Chaoqun. "How could they attack other people? Look at me," he continues. "I attended those antirightist meetings every day. I just sat there. I didn't say anything. I didn't say anything in the blooming part either. So when the antirightist campaign came, I couldn't be attacked as a rightist or praised as an activist. If you said something during the blooming, when the party called you to say something—suggestions, advice—you could be attacked as a rightist. But if you didn't say anything, they couldn't get you. If you keep quiet, there isn't any danger.

"Of course, during the Cultural Revolution I was attacked for that. They said that I was there every day and didn't say anything. At the antirightist meetings, at all meetings, there is a person in charge of taking notes on everyone's words, and afterwards it's put in the files for thousands of years so when any movement is launched, they can look over the files and see what you said. So when the Cultural Revolution came, they looked over my file, and there were no words from Huang Chaoqun. I had attended all the meetings but never said a word. I said, 'No, I'm not a person to speak much.' They said, 'You mustn't have liked the antirightist movement.' There were many people like that. They didn't attack people. And they weren't attacked. That was me. So those people should feel guilty. Many people like to climb into a higher position, to be given more of a chance, more advantage."

To be sure, as Huang Chaoqun suggests, for those who wanted not just to survive but to get ahead in the new system of politics by persecution, the antirightist campaign was not a burden but an opportunity. For politically ambitious activists, a different lesson was there to be learned: attack first, not merely to be safe but to climb the ladder of political success. And while the attacks of Li Weiguo and Qiu Yehuang had not deviated from fact—Li Weiguo's professor really had emphasized theory over practice and there was no question but that Qiu Yehuang's colleague had translated Hemingway—the attacks of the politically ambitious were not always grounded in truth. At their worst, charges were often hyberbolic, vituperative, and *ad hominem,* the statements of those under attack distorted and taken out of context. That Fei Xiaotong was a major figure in the blooming of the Hundred Flowers was true. He had indeed called for the reintroduction of sociology into Chinese universities and had criticized certain unintended consequences of agricultural collectivization. But the attacks by his former friend and colleague Lin Yuehua—accusing Fei of attempting to incite a Hungarian-type incident in China and alleging that within a week of the death of his first wife Fei had fallen in love with another woman, putting his wife completely out of his mind—were beyond the bounds of reality.

So were the attacks of Gao Cuixia on his student. Gao was a leading member of the Communist Youth League at his university when the Hundred Flowers movement began. He had never distinguished himself academically; his accomplishments had been more in the political realm. As an enthusiastic participant in the several political movements that took place on his campus during his student days, he had earned for himself the appellation of "activist." Shortly before the Hundred Flowers movement began, he had been rewarded by admission into the party and appointment to a junior faculty position in the university from which he had graduated. In the antirightist campaign, Gao Cuixia became one of the first to rise in accusation, singling out one of his own students—young, naïve, frightened, and confused—as a rightist. What Gao had not realized was how utterly and unabashedly he himself had been admired by the object of his attack, how fully the accused had attempted to imitate and emulate him at every turn, how thoroughly his student had taken Gao Cuixia as the model upon which to conduct his own life. When, in desperation and despair, betrayed by the very man he had so admired, the youthful admirer *cum* rightist committed suicide and his diary was seized for the evidence it might contain of his political crimes, his efforts at emulation were revealed. The strategy of attack first for political reward was hardly fail-safe. Far from exonerating the deceased, the public revelations from the diary of Gao Cuixia's student led to the addition of Gao himself to the ranks of the rightists.

But on the whole, the strategy of preemptive attack was politically wise. A whole generation of leadership, from the grass-roots levels to the most exalted halls of national power, rose and prospered on the foundation of the persecution of enemies both imagined and real. Even Gao Cuixia was rehabilitated far earlier than most: while others were still doing labor reform, he returned to his position of power within the Communist Youth League.

But as Li Weiguo, sobered but still optimistic, points out, "Even though bad things happened in the antirightist campaign, still, compared to the whole country, the whole people, it was a very small thing. It was the intellectuals, the people who had studied in universities, who were affected, and their numbers were small. And just some of the intellectuals were affected. Ten percent, five percent of them were in trouble—not everybody. So there were changes in 1957, yes, but it still wasn't so bad. The whole country wasn't in trouble."

It would be another two years before the whole country was in trouble.

JUST as the thought reform movement of the early 1950s had been followed by major organizational changes within Chinese universities, so the antirightist campaign of 1957 was followed by a second reorganization of the universities. By 1957, the party had come to exercise considerable power within Chinese universities. Indeed, the extent and nature of party control was one of the major, recurring complaints of university faculty during the blooming of the Hundred Flowers. But that power nonetheless remained informal, irregular, without clear-cut definition in the universities' organizational chain of command. But with the reorganization following the antirightist campaign, branches of the Chinese Communist Party were established in all academic departments, and party committees were set up at the level of central university administration. Full power over all aspects of university life, academic and administrative alike, was vested in the central party committee, and academic departments in turn were controlled by their branch party secretaries, who stood as direct links in the chain of command from center to department. Both academically and administratively, Chinese universities came frankly and fully under direct party control.

Staffing the new party branches and committees proved problematic. There were, to be sure, scholars and faculty who were also members of the party, and the ranks of party intellectuals had grown through the party recruitment drives of the mid-1950s. These individuals were given responsible political positions. But the number of party intellectuals was still not sufficient to fill the positions that party control of the universities required. Thus there was an influx of outside party members into the universities. Many who came to take control were uneducated, indeed sometimes nearly illiterate, their roots not in urban China but in the countryside, their party memberships tracing to the peasant movement that had brought the Communist Party to power.

Nie Yuanzi owed her position in Peking University's Philosophy Department to the changes wrought by the second reorganization.

This second major university reorganization since the socialists had come to power was accompanied by yet another campaign—the campaign to "pull out the white flags" within the university faculty. "White flags" were intellectuals opposed to socialism. The banner of the Chinese Communist Party was red, the traditional Chinese color for joy. Students were called into service once more in the campaign against the university's white flags.

Ma Yinqu, one of China's leading, most highly respected intellectuals, was one of those declared a white flag during the course of the second reorganization. Ma Yinqu was a specialist on population problems. He had, it was alleged, fallen under the spell of Malthus. He had argued that the population of China was too large and would have to be controlled. Ma Yinqu, until then, had been president of Peking University.

A certain level of demoralization began to set in among many of the faculty in China's universities, a decline of enthusiasm, an underlying strain in their relations with students. "When you have been attacked once, twice, three times, many times, in your life, how can you be as energetic as before?" asked You Xiaoli. "In the old society, professors were very much respected by their students. But if you go before your class and students don't respect you at all, if they think you are the class enemy, that you are bourgeois and capitalist, how can you be that enthusiastic about your teaching? So the relations between professors and students weren't good."

But these strains were still confined to the nation's universities. By 1959, the entire country was in trouble.

In November 1957, in Moscow, Mao Zedong announced to the leaders of the international communist movement that China's dream of nearly a century, the dream of wealth and power, of economic parity with the West, could in the short span of only fifteen years at last become a reality. Through the miracle not of science but of concerted hard work, with hundreds of millions of people laboring together, China would be transformed from one of the poorest, most economically backward nations of the world to one that would first equal and then surpass Great Britain in industrial product. It was the policy—ambitious, optimistic, utopian, and doomed—that he called the "Great Leap Forward." It was greeted with outpourings of enthusiasm.

Within less than a year, in the countryside of China, gongs were pounded and peasants cheered as the agricultural collectives that had been formed in the mid-1950s were amalgamated in a few short weeks into gigantic communes of tens and sometimes even hundreds of thousands of people. Officials, even those ordinarily committed to hard facts and sober analysis, predicted that the average output of grain would shortly increase from a nationwide high of more than 6,000 pounds per acre to 60,000, even 300,000 pounds per acre—yields that defied even the wildest imagination and increases that would have made those of the green revolution seem meager by comparison. Those gains were to be achieved not through application of modern, scientific, and tested farming techniques but through the backbreaking, primitive labor of plowing the soil deep and planting the seeds deep and close. By the fall of 1958, as the harvest approached, many areas claimed already to have produced yields of tens of thousands of pounds per acre. As the harvest was gathered, food suddenly became free and was offered plentifully to all. In order to spare peasant women from the labors of cooking, to free them for work in the fields, and because communism, after all, seemed just around the corner, meals were to be cooked and eaten communally in gigantic dining halls.

For a few brief and exciting months, China's dream of so many decades seemed indeed to be approaching reality. The harvest of 1958 was a bumper one, the largest in China's history. It was so large that the peasants lacked sufficient manpower to bring it in, and cityfolk had to be sent to the countryside to help. Li Weiguo, then in his last year at the university, was one of the urban dwellers to participate in gathering the gigantic harvest. In the fall of 1958, his classes were canceled and he and his classmates were sent to work in a commune several hours by bus from the city. Li Weiguo was too much the scientist to accept at face value the dramatic claims then being publicized throughout the land. "In its details, when the Great Leap Forward started, I didn't believe so much of it," he says. "What you read in the newspapers strayed so far from the truth. One acre can't produce so much. One date on a tree can't weigh half a pound. So I didn't believe that. I'm a scientist."

Nevertheless, Li Weiguo supported the Great Leap Forward. For him and his classmates, it was a great adventure: "It was fun." Li Weiguo is ever jovial, ever charming and endearing, ever the optimist. There is an irrepressible twinkle in his eye. "It was like camp. We all got together. Classes were canceled. We built a tent and all lived there. There were lots of programs for us, entertainment—singing, dancing. What we were doing seemed significant for the whole country, plus a lot of fun. So for youth, you can imagine, it was a very exciting time for us. We thought we could eat all the food we wanted and not pay any money. That was so exciting."

Li Weiguo supported the Great Leap Forward not just because it was exciting but out of patriotism, too, because of its promises of a wealthy and powerful China. "We listened to lectures in the countryside," he recalls. "One of the leaders of the Communist Party said we would catch up with and surpass Great Britain in fifteen years. So those were very exciting words. I liked to listen to them. We students were full of passion to do everything; we wanted to change the country quickly. If you are patriotic, then this is what you want. There were some things I couldn't believe. But most of the things I believed. Mao's influence was great. I believed him."

But in the frenzied enthusiasm of the Great Leap Forward, in the attempt not just to fulfill but to overfulfill the already optimistic quotas, output figures calculated by local rural cadre were inflated upward, so that when the inflated figures were totaled at the national level, the harvest as officially reported far exceeded the actual output. What is more, the national government behaved as though the inflated output figures were true, taxing peasant communes in kind at a fixed percentage of their reported output. In the communal dining halls, before the peasants realized that their harvest was being taxed away, they gorged themselves for free in grateful celebration of the Great Leap Forward as lesser-quality food that would ordinarily have been eaten by humans was thrown to the fattening pigs. "For a while," recalls You Xiaoli, "we were eating six meals a day. We were told that we were entering the stage of communism immediately."

When time came to plant the next crop, knowing that they had just produced the largest harvest in history and believing that the problem of food that had plagued the country for centuries had been solved, the Chinese completely removed from cultivation a large amount of arable land—one-third the arable land in Guangdong province alone and 12 percent of the area sown to grain nationwide. Within months, peasants who had just produced the largest crop in their country's history were reduced to a famine level. What the government had not taxed away, the peasants had eaten.

In 1959, the weather—so perfect the year before—changed, plunging parts of China into drought and inundating others in flood. The policies of "deep plowing" and "close planting" took their toll as well. Seeds planted too deep never sprouted from the soil, and when the seeds planted too close together did sprout, the growing plants sometimes smothered each other. Agricultural output declined precipitously.

Industrial output plummeted, too. Then in 1960, the Sino-Soviet split became public, and the Soviet Big Brothers, advisers and technicians who had been guiding the industrialization of China, left for home en masse, taking their blueprints with them. The country, painfully poor and backward in the best of times, was in a depression. There it would remain for "three bad years" —1959, 1960, and 1961.

NOT every part of China was equally affected. The situation was worse in the countryside than in the cities, worse in the north than in the south. Shanghai, the country's largest city, was little affected, and Nanjing, the capital of Jiangsu province in the rich and fertile Yangtze River delta, was barely affected at all. In those cities that were affected, the most privileged were able to minimize privation. Wang Hongbao's father was a high-ranking city official, a leading party member in Peking. Frequent visits to local restaurants, established especially to deal with the crisis, kept his family relatively well fed throughout the worst of the famine. Housed in unmarked buildings, such restaurants served food only to holders of special coupons distributed exclusively to the party elite.

Most residents of Peking were hungry. Li Meirong's family attempted, like millions of others, to raise chickens in their Peking apartment, letting the fowl outdoors to forage in the dark of night. But her family went hungry, and the chickens starved to death. Many saw colleagues and friends suffering, and some saw them die. Infants, especially, perished when their mothers' milk ran dry; the thin rice gruel that was the only available substitute failed to supply the minimum nutrients necessary to support a growing life. The leader of the Communist Youth League in Song Erli's middle school died. A young idealist devoted to the well-being of others, she had frequently given those in need her rice coupons. She died of hepatitis.

Huang Chaoqun led his students to plant a field of sweet potatoes, hoping that with a reasonable harvest his class could become self-sufficient in food. In the spring of 1960, they planted an entire plot with little pieces of sprouted sweet potatoes. When the buds, deprived of both water and fertilizer, failed to send up shoots, he led his students back to dig out what they had planted. Salvaging the long since rotten pieces, they cleaned, boiled, and ate them.

You Xiaoli, slim at 115 pounds, dropped to 82 pounds during the three bad years. She still recalls what she ate.

"In our school, we had only half a pound of grain a day—corn flour, not rice flour. And no vegetables. Now I think that half a pound would be plenty of rice to eat a day. But then we had nothing else. Nothing. Everyone was hungry. Do you know what my mother-in-law did during those three years? She cooked one pound of noodles at three in the afternoon and said we'd eat at six—so during that three hours, the noodles could soak up so much water that there would be a lot of them. But, of course, after a while you became hungry again.

"Sometimes my mother-in-law and I would go to one of the villages nearby and scrape the bark off the trees. That's what the peasants were doing, scraping bark off trees, so we dared not take too much. We were afraid they would be angry with us for stealing their bark. Then we would boil the bark all day to make it soft enough to eat. We had coal. There was no shortage of fuel, of inorganic things. And sometimes we boiled the leaves from trees or wild herbs.

"We didn't have salt even. I remember seeing my sister in Nanjing during that time. She had salt, so I drank three glasses of salt water. The salt water made me feel so good. Without salt, I felt so weak. For three years, I just had water, grain, and a little, little, little bit of salt. For three years. I had much more white hair then than I have now. Afterward, it became black again."

In 1960, in the midst of the crisis, You Xiaoli was invited to a conference, at the conclusion of which was a huge banquet, attended by several hundred people and presided over by Premier Zhou Enlai. The speech by Zhou Enlai began nearly simultaneously with the arrival of food on the tables, and You Xiaoli, who assumed her adulation of Premier Zhou would be shared by all assembled, stood, listening attentively to his every word. She can still recite from memory much of what he said that night. When the speech was over and she returned to her table, the food was gone. "It was full of empty dishes, an empty table," she recalls. "I didn't get a bite from that feast. I thought everyone would stand there to listen to Premier Zhou's speech. But at the feast, everyone was hungry. No one listened to him. All the food disappeared. So when people are hungry, that's a big test."

How many in the countryside were dying, few in the cities could have known. As the crisis deepened, the party was repeatedly congratulated, and congratulated itself, for having avoided the potential catastrophe of famine. Anna Louise Strong, an American long resident in China, quoted Rewi Alley, another foreigner long resident in China, comparing the three bad years of 1959–61 to the famine of 1926–29, which had brought an estimated twenty million deaths. But in the early 1960s, Strong reported, even as people were subsisting on a mixture of ground corn stalks, sorghum stalks, leaves, and bark, with edible roots and a little grain added, no one was calling the situation a famine. Tao Zhu, then the dominant party leader for the south-central region of China and a man of national repute, went on record, when the crisis was drawing to an end, as saying, "What we are proud of is that under such backward production conditions we have succeeded in enabling everyone to have enough food, though the food may not be very good. This seems very 'ordinary' . . . but it is something which China could not accomplish in the past several thousand years."

But disasters do not have to be labeled as famine for people to die of hunger. Reports of malnutrition and death filtered to universities from students who had visited their rural relatives during school vacations. Soldiers, too, spread word of what they had witnessed on furlough, and shared with friends the contents of letters from their rural homes. Many university students and staff were sent to rural areas to participate in the myriad new tasks the Great Leap Forward had compelled—deep plowing, the building of backyard steel furnaces, the construction of dams, and more ordinary harvesting. Some saw for themselves the privations of the countryside. Some lived with peasants on the verge of starvation. And some of those who had earlier believed that the Communist Party of China was the country's savior began for the first time to doubt.

"I can remember exactly where I was and what I was doing when I began to doubt," Zhao Wenhao begins. He speaks quietly, cautiously. He rarely shares his doubts, and even now is uncomfortable with his confession. Zhao Wenhao is in the process of reevaluating his past, reconsidering his previous enthusiastic support for the Communist Party. It is a painful, tormenting process. Even now his break with the past is far from complete. "It was the fall of 1959, in a commune on the outskirts of Peking. I had been sent there to do manual labor. The press was reporting on the excellent situation, how good and glorious things were. The catchword was 'The situation is very good and becoming better and better.' There was no food to eat in the village. The peasants were eating the leaves of trees, boiling leaves in water, mixing them with a little corn flour to make the leaves stick together, making *wotou*. But the peasants' *wotou* didn't even hold together because there wasn't enough corn flour. Actually, we intellectuals were lucky. We were eating sweet potato leaves. The best are the leaves of the sweet potato. Then the leaves of the plum. The worst are willow leaves. The peasants were eating willow."

Zhao Wenhao did not share his doubts at the time. "Most of us who had doubts remained silent. If you had doubts, you were scared. You thought, 'How could I dare to doubt?' Besides, for most people, the doubt wasn't over the whole regime but over whether the party had made serious mistakes. The degree of doubt the people had shouldn't be exaggerated."

Intelligent people, educated people, people who recognized the party's utopian policies as sorely ill advised, people who knew the party press was laden with falsehoods, nonetheless either suspended judgment or failed to speak out as the crisis unfolded. "I didn't believe in digging deep," recalls You Xiaoli, "because I used to dig in the countryside myself. I knew that if you dug that deep, raw earth without fertilizer would come up. My poor husband. He went to the countryside to dig deep—deeper than he was tall. He jumped into the hole he was digging and still had to dig deep. But we couldn't say anything about it. That was the policy."

And when the crisis deepened, they accepted the party's explanation that the disaster had been caused by bad weather, by the perfidious and sudden withdrawal of the Soviet technicians, by mismanagement by local-level cadres —all of which was true, but only a partial explanation for the difficulties racking the country. They were patriots, often ardent patriots, committed to the goals of the Great Leap Forward. However obviously ill advised the particular policies mistakenly designed to achieve those goals may have been, people wanted to believe Chairman Mao, wanted to believe that their country could catch up with and overtake Great Britain economically within fifteen years. The authority of Chairman Mao, as so many have repeated, was very, very great.

And they remembered the antirightist campaign and what had happened to those who had responded to the party's encouragement to air their views. And lest they should forget, there was another reminder when the crisis began. In the summer of 1959, as the dislocations of the Great Leap Forward were becoming apparent but before the situation had reached its nadir, one of China's leading officials, Minister of Defense Peng Dehuai, had, at a closed party meeting, written to Mao of his grave misgivings. He labeled the Great Leap both a leftist misadventure and an example of petty bourgeois fanaticism, and offered a largely accurate critique of the many difficulties the policies were beginning to engender. Peng Dehuai was purged. If the antirightist campaign was a turning point for many individual Chinese, the case of Peng Dehuai was a turning point for the Chinese Communist Party, as the party itself grew increasingly split.

Peng Dehuai's downfall was followed by a nationwide campaign denouncing him and anyone who had supported his views. Party members at all levels of Chinese society were attacked as "right deviationists" for any doubts they had expressed over the policies of the Great Leap Forward. The campaign was smaller, more confined, less turbulent than the antirightist campaign of 1957. Fewer people had dared to speak out.

The purge of Peng Dehuai and the campaign against right deviationists delayed the corrective measures the party might have taken to minimize the disaster. It was not until 1960 that policies designed to bring the country out of the crisis, policies that would later be attacked as "capitalist," were finally introduced.

What the people of China did not know then, what no one could have known, was that the famine of the three bad years had actually been worse than that of 1926–29, which Rewi Alley believes killed twenty million people. It was worse even than the Chinese famine of 1876–79, which is widely believed to have been the worst in human history. Based on figures recently released by the Chinese themselves, leading demographers in the West have estimated that between twenty-seven and thirty million people beyond the norm, most of them under ten and over forty, died during the three bad years. With the precipitous drop in fertility as well, the number of expected births during that same period declined by thirty-three million. The famine of the three bad years ranks as the worst in recorded history. Millions had died with a minimum of disruption to either faith or public order.

"We didn't have enough food and we started starving," recalls You Xiaoli, "and then we heard from our students and colleagues whose families were in the countryside that so-and-so had died and so-and-so had died. Although it was so hard during the three bad years, I never heard either in the countryside or in the cities complaints against the party or the government. No. The complaining was about the bad weather and the Soviet experts. Why? Because people still believed that it was the Communist government, the new government, that had improved people's lives. In 1960, I went to the countryside to help plow and plant, and we had so little to eat. Peasants were starving and we were starving too. We ate the chaff of the grain—not rice—wheat, barley—left over for so many years. Even the animals wouldn't have eaten it in a normal year. We ground it together with insects to make flour, mixed it with wild grass, and then steamed it into—what? You couldn't call it bread.

"I heard sometimes the young people complaining, but the old peasants would immediately tell how it had been in the old China—'There wouldn't be any you anymore,' they would say. We would all have died together. I heard them tell their children, because we lived in their house, that in old China the children would have been killed by someone to be eaten. People ate people in old China, you know.

"That's why I say that no matter how bad the three bad years were, still they weren't as bad as in old China. In old China, we didn't have so many old people or so many young. People didn't live that long, and there was so much infant mortality. There were more people around to die during the three bad years. And also it was only three bad years. Three bad years out of how many good ones?"

There is a fundamental sense in which You Xiaoli is right. Life expectancy has risen dramatically in post-Liberation China, just as the incidence of infant mortality has dropped dramatically. From 1949 to 1981, average life expectancy increased from thirty-five to sixty-eight years, and infant mortality dropped from 250 to 40 per 1,000 live births. Those trends had begun before the three bad years. You Xiaoli is right that one of the reasons so many died during the three bad years is simply that there were more children and old people to die. She is right, too, that in post-Liberation China there have been only three years of famine. The starvation years of 1959–61 have never been repeated.

ONE of the universal tragedies of famine is that those with power are often able to turn disaster to their own advantage. In the rural areas of China, the onus for what had gone wrong during the three bad years was often placed on the shoulders of local-level cadres, who had not only been instrumental in carrying the policies of the Great Leap Forward to extremes but who, in the famine that followed, had often claimed for themselves and their families more than their fair share of the collective's meager supply of food.

Late in 1962, after the country had begun to recover from the period of natural disaster, at a time when peasants were impoverished but no longer starving, the party instituted a "Socialist Education Campaign," designed to investigate and correct instances of corruption on the part of local rural cadres —cadres who, when their fellow villagers were hungry, had allocated to themselves and their families an excessive share of collective output, cadres whose power over the local populace was unchecked. To implement the Socialist Education Campaign, many intellectuals, including university students, were sent to the countryside in teams, where they lived with local peasant families, investigated instances of corruption and abuse within the villages, and sought means to rectify the continuing injustices they found. Many university students were still in the countryside in June 1966, when Nie Yuanzi's big character poster was published and the Cultural Revolution began.

Song Erli, then graduated from middle school and a student at one of China's most respected and prestigious universities, was one of those sent to the countryside. He had never been there before, and what he saw unnerved him. The extent of cadre corruption, the unbridled power of the rural leaders, and the helplessness of the peasants disillusioned him. "I was in charge of one production team," Song recalls, "and worked with that team from the time my group entered the village until the final auditing of accounts. We from the universities played the role of savior in those villages. We were there to reform the system in the countryside. We investigated complaints against the production team leaders and the accountants. The accountants in the countryside were very powerful, far more powerful than city intellectuals could ever imagine. The effect of intellectuals in education is on paper, in writing, in what people read. The effect of accountants is in the mouth, in how much food people eat.

"As an intellectual going to the countryside for the first time, I saw reality a lot more clearly. The Socialist Education Campaign made me see how terrible the unlimited power of the grass-roots cadres could be. The leaders in the countryside had a lot of power, and nearly every one of them had been corrupted by that power, and the majority of them had been corrupted very easily, very early. True, their crimes couldn't be so terrible, since the number of people they controlled was so small, but the complaints against them were many. The peasants were simple people, and they had suffered during the three bad years. The corruption had started with the movement to establish people's communes in 1958, and one of the reasons they are getting rid of the commune system now is that that corruption has never been put right; it is impossible to wipe out corruption when cadres have so much power. In rich areas, even when the cadres distributed the lion's share to themselves the peasants still had something to eat. But in the poorer areas, with corrupt cadres, the peasants just got less. The cadres became the local emperors of their small teams. Peasants in a feudal society had to give others the power to manipulate their fate and decide whether they would live or die. It was the same power that the team- and brigade-level cadres and the accountants got."

By the mid-1960s, gradually replacing the euphoria with which the Communist liberation of China had been greeted and the optimistic idealism that had characterized the "golden years," beyond the fear and malaise that were, for some, the legacy of the antirightist campaign of 1957, intensified by the disasters of the Great Leap Forward, was a sense of disillusionment with the Chinese Communist Party itself, a feeling among some that the Communist Party—or some members of it—had come to betray the ideals they publicly espoused, the ideals of asceticism and unselfish service, of unquestioning sacrifice for the people. An impression was growing that some members of the Communist Party were claiming special privileges for themselves at the expense of the very people they were supposed to serve. Some intellectuals, revolutionary but committed to the modernization of their country, believed that the lack of education, the peasant roots, of a large percentage of the party was a major cause of both the incompetence and the corruption in which the party was mired. Among others, there was a sense that the promises of socialism had failed to materialize, that the standard of living was stagnating, that the cumbersome bureaucracy the party had built was slowing the country down.

Yao Baoding had for thirty years been an admirer of the Chinese Communist Party, one of those intellectuals who, as a young and idealistic man in his early twenties, had made the long and dangerous trek from Shanghai to the Communist Party guerrilla base in Yenan late in the 1930s. But by the mid-1960s, Yao Baoding thought that something had gone awry. "Something happens when a party goes from being the party fighting for liberation to become the party in power," he said. "Something changes. During the struggle for power, the party bore every hardship. The party was supposed to bear hardship. And that continued after Liberation. For a while, at least.

"In Peking, for instance, it makes a big difference whether your apartment faces north or south. Everyone wants to face south. In the winter, the sun shines in from the south and warms the rooms, and since the cold wind comes from the north in the winter, a southern exposure keeps out the north wind. But if you face north, in the winter you get the wind and in the summer the cooling air comes from the south. So with a northern exposure, you are cold in the winter and hot and stifling in the summer.

"After Liberation, when housing was assigned, all the party members got northern exposure. It was considered natural. Of course the party would be the last to accept special privileges, the first to accept hardship.

"There was a Soviet comrade here at the time, just after Liberation, a marvelous woman, who admired the Chinese and the revolution tremendously. But she warned us. She said this was the honeymoon period, that it would change, that China would eventually become another Soviet Union. We didn't believe her. The fifties were such a period of hope and expectation. In China, with such a revolution, how could that happen? But it did."

There was a sense, particularly among intellectuals, that when the peasants of the Communist Party had come to the cities, they had been corrupted by their power, had succumbed to the lure of luxury, had become a new class.

The lineage from which Sun Heren is descended, far back into the Qing dynasty, is liberally and proudly sprinkled with intellectuals. Many of his forefathers had been teachers, and others, successful aspirants at the imperial civil service exams, held important government posts throughout the last of China's dynasties. It is a tradition of which Sun Heren is proud. Sun Heren himself is now an associate professor at one of China's leading universities. As a young assistant professor in the mid-1950s, he had joined the Chinese Communist Party, following thereby his family tradition, becoming an intellectual in the service of the state. But by the mid-1960s, he had become disillusioned with the party of which he was a member. Like many intellectuals of similar background, Sun Heren has a certain disdain for China's peasantry, a sense that while peasants and the unschooled may be useful as the fighting force for the destruction of one dynasty and the establishment of a new, China can best be governed, as it always has been, by educated men.

"There is a Yugoslav, Milovan Djilas," Sun Heren says, "who has argued that in every case where the Communist Party has taken over, the party begins to establish itself as a new class. It has happened everywhere—in the Soviet Union, in Yugoslavia, and I think Mao Zedong saw it happening in China. Many—most—members of the Communist Party at the time of liberation were uneducated men, peasants, with only a few years of schooling, if any. Many of them had joined the party very young, when they were only children.

"There were exceptions, of course. Zhou Enlai and Deng Xiaoping had been educated in France. Mao Zedong, even though he had never graduated from college, was still an educated man. When the Communist Party took power and moved into the cities, those uneducated people began to be corrupted—by power, by luxury.

"I think one of China's greatest problems has to do with the position of intellectuals. The party realizes that it needs intellectuals, that we are absolutely necessary for carrying out the revolution, for carrying out modernization. They must give us some freedom to do our own work. The best time for intellectuals was 1956, 1957, before the antirightist campaign. There was a positive atmosphere, an atmosphere of hope and freedom. But it was never the same after the antirightist campaign."

Jiang Xinren was a university student in Shanghai in the mid-1960s. The factory that Jiang's grandfather owned and his father had managed had been nationalized in the mid-1950s, and the family's standard of living had declined. Jiang Xinren's disillusionment with the party stemmed less from the party's claim to special privileges than the failure of the party to foster economic growth and improve the standard of living.

"By 1966," recalls Jiang Xinren, " 'New China' was already almost twenty years old. But it seemed as though something was wrong. Everyone, really, felt that something was wrong. China was supposed to be socialist, and socialism was supposed to cause economic growth, increased production, to raise the people's standard of living. But those things didn't seem to be happening. People's standard of living was staying the same. It wasn't going up.

"At the time, we attributed many of the problems to bureaucratism. The problems of bureaucratism were everywhere in China—in the universities, in the government, in the factories, in every work unit, every organization. And bureaucratism was inevitably associated with the party, because most of the bureaucrats, all the leading bureaucrats, were members of the party. In China, the party controls everything, even the schools and the universities. The party controls from the top down."

By the spring of 1966, the strains engendered by nearly twenty years of Chinese Communist Party rule—by the thought reform campaign of the early 1950s; by the three-anti and five-anti campaigns against the bourgeoisie; by the movement to round up counterrevolutionaries; by the antirightist campaign of 1957; by the Great Leap Forward and the famine of the three bad years; by the purge of Peng Dehuai and the campaign against right deviationists; by the Socialist Education Campaign and the "four cleans" campaign—were multiple, complex, and cross-cutting. Something, as Jiang Xinren said, had gone wrong.

But those strains were largely hidden. The voices of complaint were largely silent. The most articulate critics of the new regime had been silenced by the antirightist campaign, and dissent within the party had been stifled by the purge of Peng Dehuai and the campaign against right deviationists. But as

Chairman Mao himself had pointed out in 1957, "You may ban the expression of wrong ideas, but the ideas will still be there."

MAO's government was hardly the first in China to ban the expression of "wrong" ideas. The legacy of Qin Shi Huang and the burning of the books, the persecution of intellectuals, is as vivid today as though the first emperor had ruled only yesterday. For such persecution has often been repeated through the centuries.

In the most recent past, it had been the government of Chiang Kai-shek and the Guomindang that had suppressed freedom of speech. But some of the country's intellectuals had found ways to evade that suppression. The way employed by Lu Xun, China's greatest and most brilliant twentieth-century writer, was both the best and the most widely admired. It was the *zawen*, meaning literally "miscellaneous [or "random"] essays." Lu Xun's essays were in fact bitingly satirical critiques of the Guomindang government and of Chinese society in the 1920s, part of a much longer literary tradition in China of "pointing at the mulberry and reviling the ash." Pointing at the mulberry while reviling the ash was a form of attack even the Chinese Communist government had employed. In the early stages of the Sino-Soviet dispute, for example, Yugoslavia had served as the mulberry to the Soviet Union's ash. To determine China's current view of the Soviet Union, it was necessary to read what the government had to say about Yugoslavia.

For his scathing denunciations of Guomindang rule, Lu Xun remains to this day banned in Taiwan, and the most publicly and officially adulated author on the Chinese mainland—in spite, or perhaps because, of the fact that he died in 1936 and was never a party member. But as early as 1942, after so many left-wing writers and admirers of Lu Xun had trekked to Yenan to join forces with the Communist guerrillas there, Mao Zedong had cautioned them that "there was no need of *zawen* critical of the Communist Party." And for many years, China was without *zawen*.

In the summer of 1959, only a month before Peng Dehuai wrote his "letter of opinion" to Chairman Mao criticizing the Great Leap Forward—and at a time when others, too, were expressing veiled misgivings about both the Great Leap Forward and the man who had initiated it—*zawen* began to stage a limited comeback.

WU HAN was a well-known and highly respected historian specializing in the study of the Ming dynasty, a teacher, colleague, or friend to several whose stories are included here. Like many Chinese intellectuals who fled to Kunming following the Japanese occupation of Peking in 1937, Wu Han had early become disillusioned with the Guomindang and had hoped, in the late 1930s and 1940s, that China might find a third, democratic road that was neither Communist nor Nationalist. He became one of the leading members of the Democratic League. Wu himself had written *zawen* critical of the Guomindang. When the third road proved impossible, Wu, like so many of his intellectual contemporaries, had thrown his support to the Communist government. Indeed, one of his students in Kunming remembers his bravery in praising the Communists and expressing doubts over the Guomindang even as he taught in a Guomindang-controlled area. During the thought reform campaign of the early 1950s, Wu greeted the advent of Communist rule in China with a series of essays professing his faith—albeit with qualifications and from a critical stance—in the new government. His friends and students believe that his endorsement of the new government was sincere, and that he came through the movement with his integrity intact.

In the mid-1950s, Wu Han underwent a change. In a move that was not public but that surprised many of his old friends who learned of it, he became a member of the Chinese Communist Party. During the antirightist campaign of 1957, in an ugly and vicious voice, a voice that seemed unlike him and that belied the scholar he was, he publicly attacked two of his former friends and colleagues in the Democratic League who had been most active during the blooming period in speaking out. It was around that time also that Wu was appointed vice-mayor of Peking—further proof to the disenchanted that the price of political success in "New China" was participation in the persecution of one's colleagues and friends.

In 1959, however, Wu Han may possibly have changed again; even those who knew him do not agree about this. In any event, after a relative scholarly silence that dated from the Liberation of 1949, Wu Han began publishing once more. Many of his new pieces were devoted to an examination of a historical figure named Hai Rui—a Ming-dynasty official extolled by Wu Han for his unbending personal integrity and refusal to kowtow before authority, for his single-minded pursuit of justice and his insistence on speaking out. Mao himself had praised Hai Rui, calling him a man to be studied, a man from whom to learn. There are those who believe that Wu Han's extolling of Hai Rui was merely an attempt, in true Maoist spirit, to render Ming-dynasty history accessible to China's masses; and it is certainly possible to read these pieces in that way. There are those who believe that Wu was kowtowing before the party chairman by choosing to write about Hai Rui. "Hai Rui was praised by Mao Zedong," asserts Huang Chaoqun. "That's why Wu Han wrote that play. He thought he was following Mao." (Huang believes that the attacks against Wu Han that followed were in the old tradition of "pointing at the mulberry and reviling the ash": in Huang's view, it was not really Wu Han who was the object of attack but his senior colleague and friend, the mayor of Peking, Peng Zhen.)

There are still others, however, who believe that in writing about Hai Rui, Wu Han was reviving the tradition of *zawen*. The beauty of satire, of course, is that it allows for a multitude of interpretations, interpretations that those with vivid imaginations can carry far beyond the original intentions of the author and interpretations which the author himself can often convincingly deny. This is why it remains a vehicle of expression in times when speech is not free.

Once one is apprised of the possibility of satirical intent, warned that Wu Han may have been using his pen as a sword and pointing at the ash while attacking the mulberry, Wu Han's Ming-dynasty morality tales take on a rather different meaning. It is possible, in Wu's condemnation of the Ming emperor —pompous, vainglorious, self-righteous, deluded, and dogmatic—to read a condemnation of Mao himself. In Hai Rui—the upright, moral, incorruptible, and unbending official, the official who, unlike the bamboo, clung steadfastly to his own beliefs without ever bending or giving in, the man who was the antithesis of what so many believed so many Communist Party officials had become—it is possible to read a rebuke to the governing party of China. In Hai Rui's insistence that a school is a place for professors to teach their students, in his refusal to kowtow before high officials, in his denunciation of hypocrites, in his incredulousness at the extent to which people can suffer without complaint, in his encouragement to the oppressed to dare to speak out, it is easy to read a critique of Wu Han's academic colleagues who were suffering but remained silent, kowtowing before Communist Party authority, allowing the universities in which they worked to become prostitutes to politics. In the Ming emperor's dismissal of Hai Rui, it is easy to see Mao Zedong's dismissal of Peng Dehuai. "There is a tradition among Chinese writers of using the past to attack the present," says Zhao Wenhao. "Wu Han was a famous historian of the Ming dynasty. He wasn't ignorant of that tradition. He had used it to attack Chiang Kai-shek."

Wu Han's opera *The Dismissal of Hai Rui* opened in Peking to generally good reviews in February 1961, during the depth of the depression of the three bad years, as people in Peking were still hungry, while many were no doubt wondering what had gone wrong. It was staged only a few times before being banned. But Wu continued to write, with impunity, until September 1962. At that time the political climate in China changed.

IT was in September 1962, at a meeting of the Tenth Plenum of the Eighth Central Committee of the Chinese Communist Party, that Mao Zedong refined his personal interpretation of Marxist dogma, offering the analysis that would later serve as the theoretical underpinning for the period that would in retrospect be labeled the "ten years of great disaster."

To understand the implications of what Mao said in 1962, it is necessary to go back a few years.

In 1956, with the completion of major changes in China's economic system —with ownership of industry transferred to the state and ownership of land and major farm tools vested in agricultural collectives—Mao had announced that the transformation of China from capitalism to socialism was, in the main, complete. With that transformation, orthodox Marxist theory would have taught that classes, being defined materially in terms of man's relationship to the means of production, had consequently disappeared. With ownership of industries in the urban areas in the hands of the state (the whole people) and ownership of land owned jointly by those who tilled it (the collective), everyone stood equal before the means of production. Gone were the exploiting capital-ist oppressors of the working-class proletariat, abolished was the system of private ownership of land that led so inexorably to a system of exploitation by landlords of their tenants. And with the end of classes, so too, according to orthodox theory, should class struggle have come to an end.

Yet Mao increasingly came to see class not merely materially, as one's relationship to the means of production, but as a state of mind as well, and one's state of mind, Mao recognized correctly, could persist long after the means of production had been socialized. What is worse, Mao eventually concluded that the capitalist state of mind was somehow contagious, that it had taken hold even in the ranks of the very Communist Party that had led the socialist revolution. And as long as the capitalist state of mind persisted, so then too did classes.

And so too, argued Mao at the Tenth Plenum in September 1962, did class struggle. It was the need to carry on the class struggle, to bring the class struggle to its logical conclusion, that had stood as the ultimate justification for each of the many campaigns that had swept China since the Liberation of 1949. There was reason to presume, from Mao's 1962 speech, emphasizing as it did the persistence and inevitability of class struggle, that another campaign was about to erupt. Wu Han was wise to stop publishing. The signals suggested that another wave of persecution was about to begin.

But the campaign that followed was confined largely to the countryside, to the Socialist Education Campaign in which Song Erli and so many other college students participated. It did not spread to the cities for another three years. Song Erli was still in the countryside on November 30, 1965, when the *People's Daily* published an article by Yao Wenyuan entitled "On the New Historical Play *The Dismissal of Hai Rui.*"

An astute Shanghai-based left-wing radical, Yao Wenyuan was a party theoretician and close, and soon to become closer, friend of Mao's wife, Jiang Qing. His article appeared first not in the *People's Daily* but in the Shanghai *Wen Hui Bao.* Mao was in Shanghai at the time of its publication there. He had tried, to no avail, to get such a piece written and published in Peking and had gone to Shanghai to press his case. Yao Wenyuan had complied. The article was an attack on Wu Han and his play, labeling it a "poisonous weed."

Between the publication of Yao Wenyuan's article by the *People's Daily* in November 1965 and early May of the following year, the Peking newspaper published more than a hundred articles on Wu Han. Some, to be sure, came to his defense, but the majority were attacks. It was, to most appearances at least, an academic debate, a debate on literary criticism. "But there was the smell of gunpowder in the air," recalls Zhao Wenhao. "Something serious was going to happen. Everyone had that feeling."

Liu Zhiping, Jiang Xinren, Wang Hongbao, and Bai Meihua—students at the time—remember the period well. The articles about Wu Han were required reading in their classes. "There were signs that something was happening months before I realized the Cultural Revolution had begun," said Liu Zhiping, nineteen years old at the time and a student at a leading Tianjin university. "There were the criticisms of *The Dismissal of Hai Rui*, the article by Yao Wenyuan. We could all see this. We had to see it. We read those articles, studied them. But we really didn't know what was happening, what was to come.

"Then Nie Yuanzi wrote her big character poster. . . ."

On May 25, 1966, Nie Yuanzi and six of her colleagues had composed a big character poster and pasted it on the east wall of one of the dining halls on the campus of Peking University, the same wall that had come during the blooming of the Hundred Flowers to be known as Democracy Wall. That Nie Yuanzi's big character poster was not entirely spontaneous, that it had been solicited by the wife of Kang Sheng, in turn a close friend of Mao's wife, Jiang Qing, and that other party members on the university campus had refused the suggestion that they write a similar attack, would not be publicly known until more than a decade later.

The big character poster contained a political attack, in a militantly revolutionary style, on a man named Lu Ping. It charged Lu Ping, and his closest associates, with stifling the revolutionary demands of the teachers and students at Peking University, with fostering mere "academic" discussions of China's "great cultural revolution." According to the poster, the university contained strongholds of opposition both to the Communist Party and to socialism while, on the other hand, there were revolutionaries in the university who wished to engage in struggle against these antisocialist, antiparty strongholds. The poster described the struggle as one of life and death, and accused Lu Ping himself of acting to suppress that revolutionary struggle.

Lu Ping, considerably senior to Nie Yuanzi, was, like her, a member of the Communist Party. Unlike her, he was a highly educated man, an intellectual. In May 1966, Lu Ping was not only head of the party's central committee responsible for overall governance of Peking University, he was also president of the university. He had replaced Ma Yinqu after Ma was dismissed as a "white flag."

Nie Yuanzi's big character poster concluded with a clarion call:

All revolutionary intellectuals, now is the time to fight! Let us be united, hold high the great red banner of the thought of Mao Zedong, rally ourselves around the Party Central Committee and Chairman Mao, break the controls of revisionism and all its plots and tricks, so as to resolutely wipe out, lock, stock, and barrel, all the ox ghosts and snake spirits* and all the Khrushchev-type counterrevolutionary revisionists and carry the socialist revolution through to the end.

When the *People's Daily* published Nie Yuanzi's big character poster on June 2, the paper's editorial of support concurred unequivocally with her assertion that Peking University was a fortress of opposition to the Communist Party and to socialism. It enthusiastically and confidently predicted that within a very short while the people of the whole country would rise up to "oppose, beat, and thoroughly destroy" the likes of Lu Ping and his colleagues everywhere.

"Nie Yuanzi was a scapegoat," asserts Zhao Wenhao. "Mao needed someone to start it."

WHY exactly Mao launched the Cultural Revolution, what he thought would happen, what he hoped to accomplish, will remain forever obscure. He feared, certainly, that China was becoming another Soviet Union, that the Communist Party of China was becoming a "new class," saturated with "bourgeois" values of privilege, status, and comfort rather than the asceticism of self-sacrifice and devotion to the common good. He was worried that the country's intellectuals, steeped as they were in Western and bourgeois values, were transmitting those values to the generation too young to have participated in the revolution or to have known the old society. He saw the gap between urban and rural China and believed that little was being done to close it, that peasant youth had little opportunity for education. Mao himself came from a peasant background and had no direct knowledge of the West, no firsthand experience with modern, industrial, or democratic countries. As a longtime revolutionary, he was not opposed to the use of violence. He was seventy-two years old when the Cultural Revolution began and probably feared he had little time left. He turned to the country's young because there was nowhere else to turn. It was

---

*The phrase "ox ghosts and snake spirits" is usually translated as "freaks and monsters." It is translated literally here because of the strong visual images the label conjures up in the Chinese mind (see p. 223). During the Cultural Revolution, the term was widely and freely applied to people under attack.

the Communist Party, the bureaucracy, and the intellectuals, after all, who were now to be the objects of attack.

Chairman Mao had once noted that a single spark could light a prairie fire. Nie Yuanzi's big character poster, published on his orders, was the spark that ignited the conflagration which went by the name of the Great Proletarian Cultural Revolution. But it was hardly the cause.

FOUR

THE INFECTIOUS REVOLT: HOUSE SEARCHES, CATTLE PENS, STREET PARADES, STRUGGLE SESSIONS, AND CADRE SCHOOLS

In the days and weeks that followed, educational institutions in most of urban China succumbed to the infectious student revolt that had begun in Peking and then spread throughout the country. Universities, middle schools, and primary schools canceled classes as students launched attacks, analogous in target and tone to those leveled by Nie Yuanzi, against high-ranking party and academic leaders within their own educational institutions.

"Shortly after Nie Yuanzi's big character poster," explains Song Wuhao of those first exhilarating, exuberant weeks, "all our classes were suspended and we began attacking the authorities in our school—the director of the school and the leading party secretary. We took them away and locked them up and forced them to write their self-confessions. After that, we began attacking other leaders in the school, overthrowing them and locking them up one by one." Fifteen years old at the time, Song

Wuhao was a student in the prestigious middle school attached to Qinghua University in Peking. Noted for its academic excellence and the high percentage of its students who excelled in the rigorously competitive college entrance exams, many students at Qinghua Middle School, like Song Wuhao himself, were the sons and daughters of China's leading intellectuals, the faculty at Qinghua University.

Lu Ping was removed as president of Beida the day after Nie Yuanzi's big character poster was published, and the overthrow of Jiang Nanxiang, president of Qinghua University and simultaneously minister of education, was not far behind. Kuang Yaming, president of Nanjing University and one of the country's leading scholars of the ancient sage Confucius, was also dismissed. As to how targets were selected, "The first boss of any unit was the capitalist roader," explains Bai Meihua, merely a junior middle school student at the time, "then the vice-director, and then his immediate subordinate, and so on down the line, according to his position."

Still, university presidents and principals of middle schools were hardly, in those heady first few weeks, toppling like the proverbial dominoes. The free-floating revolutionary fervor of Song Wuhao and other youth aside, the earliest stage of the movement, immediately following the publication of Nie Yuanzi's big character poster, was characterized by widespread confusion over precisely whom this Great Proletarian Cultural Revolution was against. Among those old enough to remember, everyone knew that when in 1957 the snakes had come out of their holes to criticize the party their heads had been lopped off. One legacy of the antirightist campaign was a finely honed sense of the locus of political power and of the penalties for presuming to challenge it, a profound reluctance to evince any sort of dissatisfaction with the Communist Party or its members. If this was a revolution, then those to be attacked were surely the traditional enemies of the Chinese Communist Party and not the party itself.

The man in whose name the Great Proletarian Cultural Revolution was launched was not at the helm in those first few confusing weeks. The party chairman had yet to return to Peking from sojourns in Shanghai and Hangzhan. Mao's deputy, the president of the People's Republic, Liu Shaoqi, was forced to assume responsibility for a movement he had not initiated and did not understand, a movement that quickly proved at fundamental odds with the values of order, stability, and predictability that he held dear.

In June, just after the publication of Nie Yuanzi's big character poster, Liu had ordered work teams sent into universities to provide adult and party leadership to the student revolt, which threatened to get out of hand. The one sent to Qinghua University was headed by his own wife, Wang Guangmei, an intelligent and well-educated woman who in 1946 had served as the Communist Party interpreter in the three-way peace negotiations between the

Nationalists, the Communists, and the United States. In many cases, the work teams opposed the most rebellious of the students and acted to keep the structural legitimacy of the party intact, protecting responsible party members who only later would be deemed to be "following the capitalist road." In many universities and middle schools, with the party leadership still intact, it was the intellectuals, rightists, and those who leaned toward the right, those who had "escaped through the net" in earlier political campaigns, those Song Erli describes as the "natural victims," who were paraded out like moving targets in a shooting gallery to be struggled against once more.

"Shortly after the big character posters began appearing," recalls Liu Zhiping of her university campus, "the chairman of my department called a meeting. He said that this was a movement to criticize the rightists, that those people who turned the criticisms against the party leadership on campus would end up being declared counterrevolutionaries. So we were encouraged to put up big character posters attacking the rightists, defending the leadership of the university."

"Many of those ranking cadres, members of the party committees, were nothing but hypocrites," insists Song Erli of the early response of party members on college campuses to Nie Yuanzi's big character poster. "At the beginning of the Cultural Revolution, they plotted among themselves, deciding which of the intellectuals should be thrown out. They wanted to divert the spearhead of the movement away from themselves, so they threw out some intellectuals as butts of the Cultural Revolution—like meat to hungry dogs, to satisfy their hunger. And then, when they decided who they wanted to throw out, they instigated the Red Guards, with the sons and daughters of high-ranking cadres as the core, and told them to persecute those people, to ransack their houses. The party committees backed the early Red Guards as fathers behind their sons. And now they pose as victims of the Cultural Revolution and want to see revenge. Isn't that hypocritical?"

Li Meirong, who in 1957 had signed big character posters criticizing the principal of her middle school and had therefore barely escaped through the net during the antirightist campaign, was one who was thrown like meat to hungry dogs during this earliest phase. "I knew my own background. I knew my own past," recalls this woman who grew up dressed in silk brocade and living in a forty-two-room house. "So I knew from the very beginning that I would be attacked." Li Meirong is still elegant and aristocratic in bearing, dignified. Some might describe her as beautiful. Her permanent-waved hair, her long-sleeved blouse, cover the scars left by lighted cigarettes. "Perhaps it was a premonition, perhaps because I had already begun steeling myself for it, but I had a sense of foreboding even before I walked into school on the day the attacks began. One day I walked into the entrance hall to the school, and there were big character posters everywhere. Someone came up to me as soon as I crossed the threshold and said, 'Li Meirong, there are some big character posters attacking you. Don't you want to read them?' I said, 'Yes, of course I want to read them.' "

BUT at the Eleventh Plenum of the Eighth Central Committee of the Chinese Communist Party held in August 1966, a meeting controlled by Mao and allegedly packed with his youthful supporters, a sixteen-point resolution made clear that the revolutionary targets were not merely the "natural victims" of earlier campaigns, or even just the intellectuals who had recently been declared "bourgeois academic authorities," but "party persons in authority taking the capitalist road." One of the Sixteen Points read, "At present, our aim is to knock down those party persons in authority taking the capitalist road, criticize the bourgeois academic 'authorities,' criticize the ideologies of the bourgeoisie and all the exploiting classes, reform education and literature and the arts, and reform all superstructure which is incompatible with the socialist economic base."

It was also at this plenum that Liu Shaoqi—until then second-ranking member of the Chinese Communist Party hierarchy, president of the People's Republic of China, and, since 1935, Mao's heir apparent—was demoted to eighth in the party line.

THE most enthusiastically revolutionary of Peking's young—those at least whose parents had not been objects of previous political campaigns—began constituting themselves as Red Guard representatives of Mao Zedong's thought. The students of Song Wuhao's Qinghua Middle School were among the first to form such groups. On August 1, Mao Zedong himself had blessed the Red Flag Red Guard comrades at Song Wuhao's middle school with a letter enthusiastically supporting them and their "right to rebel against reactionaries," instilling in them thereby the belief that the Red Flag Red Guards at Qinghua Middle School were the most revolutionary students of all. *Zaofan you li*—"To rebel is justified"—became the watchword, the legitimating slogan, for the entire Cultural Revolution.

Soon, having overthrown the authorities within their own schools, the Red Guards of Qinghua Middle School fanned out into other schools to organize their comrades there. As Song Wuhao describes it, "Whenever we went out, wherever we went, everyone listened to us, everyone followed us when we said who was good and who was bad." By uniting with students from other schools and sharing their experiences with them, they spread the movement rapidly throughout the city, from school to school.

On August 18, 1966, Mao Zedong honored the newly formed Red Guards with a spectacular rally, a million participants strong, in Tiananmen Square, the first of eight such rallies to be held between then and the end of November.

Their precision impeccable, their timing perfect, the crowds of university and middle school students in Tiananmen Square, in a display that all the world now recognizes as the quintessential scene of the Great Proletarian Cultural Revolution, raised gaily colored pieces of cardboard over their heads that, viewed from the air or from the height of the Gate of Heavenly Peace where Mao and his lieutenants stood in regal splendor, spelled in gigantic characters larger than the average Peking apartment, "Long live Chairman Mao." Holding high their little red books of Chairman Mao's quotations, tears of joy and adulation streaming down their cheeks, the youthful successors to the Chinese revolution chanted over and over until their vocal cords gave way, "Long live Chairman Mao," streamers from balloons overhead repeating the message, leaving little doubt that both the young Red Guards and the Cultural Revolution were Mao's.

Inexorably, with the publication of the Sixteen Points, the movement spread from the schools into society as the young began to attack "party persons in authority" in a wide variety of governmental institutions who were deemed to be "following the capitalist road." "There was a contradiction in just overthrowing the school authorities and in confining the movement to the schools," explains Song Wuhao. Caught up in the telling of his story, reliving those days some fifteen years after the event, Wuhao's explanation still retains the certainty of his youthful convictions. "A school is part of society, and leaders within the school also had their leaders outside the school, in society. So we had to go beyond the confines of the school to determine who were the leaders of the leaders. It was here that the problems started. We continually had to ask, 'Who are the good people? Who are the bad? How can we know who is good and who is bad?' We were young. We were fanatics. We believed that Chairman Mao was great, that he held the truth, that he was the truth. I believed in everything Mao said. And I believed that there were reasons for the Cultural Revolution. We thought that we were revolutionaries, and that because we were revolutionaries following Chairman Mao, we could solve any problem, solve all of society's problems."

By the fall, the Red Guards of Peking began leaving their own city to carry the torch of revolution throughout the land, and hundreds of thousands of Red Guards from around the country converged on Peking to learn from the experiences of their Peking comrades and in hopes of seeing with their own eyes the man they described as the red, red sun in their hearts.

Tens of thousands took off on foot, replicating in spirit if not in distance, discomfort, danger, or hazardous territory traversed the Communist Party's epic six-thousand-mile Long March, which had begun in October 1934 from the Jiangxi Soviet in China's south and ended a year later in Shanxi province in the north. Made necessary by Chiang Kai-shek's military encirclement and bombardment of the party's Jiangxi Soviet base, the march began with some 100,000 men and lost 80 percent of them en route. "Its route covered a total of 18,088 *li*, or 6,000 miles," writes Edgar Snow, who interviewed some of the survivors, Mao Zedong included, shortly after their arrival in the northern town of Yenan, "about twice the width of the American continent. The journey took them across some of the world's most difficult trails, unfit for wheeled traffic, and across the high snow mountains and the great rivers of Asia. It was one long battle from beginning to end."

A remarkable odyssey that ranks as one of the great exploits of military history, the reality of the Long March is no less heroic than the myth it has become. It was during the course of the Long March, in 1935, that Mao Zedong succeeded in establishing himself as the party's preeminent leader, and it was from the party's base in Yenan, where the Long March finally ended, that the revolution that brought the Communists to power was launched.

Liu Zhiping, nineteen years old in 1966 and a student at one of Tianjin's elite universities, was one of tens of thousands of China's young who attempted during the Cultural Revolution to emulate the Long March. Imitation of the epic flight of the Communist Party was one way of proving oneself revolutionary without attacking one's teachers or engaging in the destruction that the rowdier of the young chose as a means of demonstrating their revolutionary zeal. "Chairman Mao had said that young people should understand society, and I decided that I did not yet understand Chinese society well enough," Liu Zhiping explains, "that in order to understand the Cultural Revolution I first had to understand my own society. And Chairman Mao had said that intellectuals should not be separate from the common people, that they should make investigations of society. I felt that I was one of the common people but that I still didn't know Chinese society. I had always lived in the cities and had never really known the Chinese peasants, so I decided to make an investigation. Some of my friends and I—thirteen of us altogether—decided to go to Yenan, the cradle of the Chinese revolution, and to try to begin to trace the party's history from its origins in Yenan.

"All we took with us were our quilts, a blanket, some clothes, and some books—less than five pounds for each person. And we had some money.

"We first went from Tianjin to Peking so we could start out from Tiananmen Square. We took a picture of ourselves there, all ready to set out. We carried a big red flag inscribed with the name of our group, and we all wore army uniforms. Since we were revolutionaries and this was our Long March, we didn't take trains or buses or even walk along the highways. We just took little dirt paths through the countryside to get to Yenan. We used a compass to tell us what direction we were going. Along the way, we visited with the poor peasants, worked with them in their fields. In the evenings we talked with them—about the history of their village, about their family histories, about what the landlords had been like, about oppression. We wanted to learn what oppression had been like.

"The poverty in the villages was surprising, yes. But at the time we explained the poverty to ourselves by saying that life in the countryside was so much better than it had been before Liberation. And I thought that the poor peasants were so much better than the intellectuals. They lived in such simple houses made of mud and straw. They worked so hard. They got so little. The poor peasants supported us, and we learned from them. Often we would stop and spend a few days in a village, working with the peasants. When we would leave, they would cry. They could tell that we were different from them, but still they liked us.

"For almost two months during our Long March, I didn't have a single drop of oil and no meat at all. We ate only two meals a day, and usually our meals were just bread made of corn. Only occasionally did we eat bread made from wheat. And there were very few vegetables. In the countryside, the only time the peasants would ever kill a pig—eat meat—is during the Spring Festival.

"I remember one day on the Long March—it was in Taiyuan, Shanxi province. I was so hungry. We had already walked almost seven miles that day, and there was a small restaurant in Taiyuan. It was so small that it was hardly a restaurant at all. I went in with my friend, and I ate a small bowl of rice and some bean-curd soup. It cost two cents. Then afterward I felt so bad. I was supposed to be a revolutionary. Why can't a revolutionary stand hunger? Revolutionaries shouldn't eat in restaurants. So I made a self-criticism. I was so idealistic, so eager to be a revolutionary. But even today, I can still eat a lot. I can easily eat two big bowls of noodles.

"It took us forty days of walking to reach Yenan. When we started out, we could only walk about twenty miles a day, because our feet got so blistered and we weren't used to so much exercise. Later, we could go as much as forty miles. But we averaged twenty-five. We had started in late October 1966, and arrived there in December. When we got there, we had our pictures taken in front of the pagoda. We had seen it so many times in pictures and in the movies, and we were so proud of our Long March. We visited the museum and saw all the caves where Chairman Mao had lived."

OTHER Red Guards traveled faster by far, though in scarcely greater comfort. In an encouragement both to spread the revolution and to permit young people to "exchange revolutionary experiences," trains could be boarded for free, and China's young took to the rails by the millions in the "great revolutionary linkups." Those less politically inclined seized the opportunity to visit distant relatives and friends and to sight-see at numerous scenic, cultural, and historic spots, being minimally sheltered and fed at each stop by local middle schools and universities, sleeping in dormitory rooms vacated by students who had similarly taken off for parts of China unknown or in classrooms on desks pushed together to form makeshift beds. "The food was very simple, noodles or rice and one dish at each meal—not bad, not good," recalls Bai Meihua of her experience. "We didn't care about food at the time. We thought that this was a revolution." Bai Meihua spent two months with several of her friends visiting the coastal cities of eastern China. It is the two-day train ride, and hard berth, from Peking to Canton she still remembers best. "You can't imagine how crowded the trains were," she says. "The train was packed, absolutely packed, with people sitting on the overhead luggage racks and lying under the seats. There was no way, once you were on, even to move. Sometimes I stood when other people were standing, and sometimes I was able to slide down and sit. Since it was impossible to move, it was impossible to go to the bathroom, either, so I didn't use the bathroom the whole time. We had no water on the train, either, only steamed bread. I felt so thirsty. I thought I was going to die on that train. Really. I thought I would die. When we finally got off in Canton, I couldn't walk. My legs were all big and swollen, and I just stood on the train platform for forty-five minutes, maybe even an hour, before I could begin to walk."

THE more politically raucous (and doubtlessly more so the farther away from home) seized the opportunity of the revolutionary linkups to expand the campaign against the "four olds"—old ideas, old customs, old culture, old habits—with a reckless, joyous, exuberant abandon. For this was a *cultural* revolution, and many interpreted it as a revolution *against* culture, a revolution against all that was old.

It was still summertime when Ma Aidong arrived back in Shanghai from a stint in the countryside assisting in implementation of the Socialist Education Movement, unaware of the decree that the pigtails she had never cut and that hung nearly to her waist were now classified as "four olds." She managed to break loose from the Red Guards who assaulted her with scissors as she left the Shanghai train station with one pigtail still intact. But she then felt so humiliated over her appearance that the bus ride home seemed interminably long, and she ran to her room to cut off the other pigtail before even saying hello to the mother she had not seen in nearly a year. "Frankly," recalls this woman who has never been anything but loyal to the Communist Party and Chairman Mao, "I was indignant."

The charming wooden signs that had stood above the multitude of tiny city shops, carved with graceful characters and designating in quaint and felicitous Chinese the function of the shops within, were ripped from their mountings and burned. So were the more modern, garish, and "bourgeois" neon signs. Display windows no longer tantalized buyers with samples of the products to be bought within, but were filled instead with posters of Mao and handwritten reproductions of quotations from his poems and selected works. The behavior of the shop clerks changed, too. Qiu Yehuang was a *xiaoyaopai* during the Cultural Revolution—literally a member of the "free-floating faction," meaning those who were able to avoid participation in the upheaval. *Xiaoyaopai* were rare. It was not easy to avoid participation. Usually, *xiaoyaopai*, like Qiu Yehuang himself, were apolitical, often in their late twenties or early to middle thirties—too old still to be students and too young to have clouded their records with behavior others might consider counterrevolutionary. Qiu Yehuang had spent most of the opening weeks and months of the Cultural Revolution at home, indulging in his love of reading. When he emerged into the new world of the Cultural Revolution, he discovered a new code of etiquette. "At first, I had just stayed at home so much that when I finally went out, I didn't know the new way of behaving," he says. "Once I went into a store to buy a new shirt. The salesperson was standing there, and when I walked in, he said, 'Long live Chairman Mao.' Long live Chairman Mao? Not 'Hello, good morning.' 'Long live Chairman Mao.' So I said, 'Long live Chairman Mao. I would like to buy a shirt.' So he sold me a shirt.

"It was the same with the telephone. The receptionist at the work unit would always answer, 'Long live Chairman Mao.' Then I would say, 'Long live Chairman Mao, extension 456.'"

Big character posters came to fill every available inch of public wall space; and decoration everywhere, homes included, was limited to the posters of Mao that poured by the hundreds of millions from the presses of New China Bookstore, distributed first, by New China Books, to work units, and from there by each work unit's office of administrative affairs. There was another poster, too, less widely distributed but nonetheless particularly popular with admirers of Premier Zhou Enlai. It was a picture of Mao Zedong, Zhou Enlai, and Zhu De in the mid-1950s greeting an unseen foreign dignitary at the airport in Peking. The poster had had to go into its second printing with the Cultural Revolution. The original had shown Liu Shaoqi there, too. The pictography of the Cultural Revolution excluded China's head of state from history. In the reprint, the image of Liu Shaoqi had been brushed out of the scene.

New China Bookstore was also responsible for distributing the tens of thousands of huge statues of a benevolent, sometimes almost smiling, Chairman Mao that sprang up, as the Chinese would say, like bamboo shoots after a spring rain, one to each unit and surrounded by a bed of flowers, arriving in pieces on several trucks, erected piece by piece behind bamboo scaffolding. In work and residential areas where identical two- or three-story buildings were often lined up in a row, it could often require several buildings before the leading slogans of the day, in huge red characters, were finally spelled out. Long life was wished to a variety of people, organizations, and ideologies—Mao Zedong, the great, glorious, and correct Chinese Communist Party, Marxism-Leninism/Mao Zedong Thought. In agriculture, people were encouraged to learn from the model Dazhai and in industry from Daqing. The names of streets were revolutionized, from Prosperity Lane and Boulevard of Eternal

Peace to Liberation Way, Red Flag Road, and Antirevisionist Boulevard. In some places, the ceaselessly revolutionary Red Guards decreed green to mean stop and red, the color of revolution and joy, to mean go. But after incomplete acceptance of the decree by railway crews led to several accidents, official intervention laid the controversy to rest in favor of tradition. The few shrubs and flowering plants which added rare color and life to cities dominated by browns and grays, plants whose existence in a place where water is scarce and fertilizer precious had always been tenuous at best, were uprooted and allowed to rot.

Huang Chaoqun's university had long run an experimental dairy farm with cows originally imported from the Netherlands, supplying the university with high-quality fresh milk and butter. During the Cultural Revolution the revolutionaries killed all the cows, ate the meat, and turned the stables into warehouses where the "revolutionaries" stored property seized from the "bourgeoisie." Dairy cows from Holland were regarded as bourgeois. So was the experimental farm that had grown apples, peaches, pears, strawberries, grapes, and pecans. The fruit trees were all chopped down, the strawberry plants uprooted. The herb gardens for traditional Chinese medicine were also destroyed. They were considered "four old." "The Red Guards did harm to everything living," laments Huang Chaoqun, "not just human beings but plants, trees, cows." "Our campus was so much more beautiful before the Cultural Revolution," apologized You Xiaoli on a tour of its pocked and barren grounds, "but the Red Guards destroyed all the flowers and plants."

Librarians and friends of libraries, those who believed in a people's right to read, often took great personal risks in protecting books the Red Guards had targeted for destruction. Books were secreted away box by box, to be hidden in homes and buried underground. As young Yang De lay bedridden with a prolonged illness, her Communist Party member father surreptitiously stole books slated for destruction to bring to his daughter to read. Much that could have been destroyed was preserved. But the contents of entire sections of libraries—the Chinese, Western, and Russian classics—were often put to the torch in huge outdoor bonfires. Jiang Xinren remembers participating in several such rallies at his university in Shanghai. When libraries were saved, card catalogues were sometimes destroyed. "If they had been allowed, they would have burned the libraries to the ground," insists Huang Chaoqun, "but they didn't because there were revolutionary books there too. Mao was there, and Marxist-Leninist books."

But libraries were burned. In Zhongshan University in Canton, first the Red Guards burned all the books from the collection of Western classics, then they burned all the books that were not obviously Marxist-Leninist/Mao Zedong Thought, and then they burned the library to the ground.

The free trains and revolutionary linkups provided the opportunity for a campaign against the four olds truly national in scale. Throughout the length and breadth of the land, thousands upon tens of thousands of religious edifices, artifacts, and shrines—Buddhist, Moslem, Christian, and Confucian—often hundreds, sometimes thousands of years old, the essence of the country's heritage from the past, were savaged. Mercifully, much that was magnificent, grand, national in symbol and massive in scale was preserved. The People's Liberation Army was sent to safeguard the priceless Forbidden City and the Summer Palace in Peking. The army similarly guarded the vast imperial grounds, dotted with numerous houses of religion, in the sleepy provincial town of Chengde to the north of the capital city. Zhou Enlai moved to protect the edifice that houses two of the most beautiful and valuable carvings of Buddha in Han China, the magnificent Jade Buddha Temple in Shanghai. Mao's wife, Jiang Qing, took over for her own use the sprawling grounds of Beihai Park in Peking, and revolutionary rebels throughout the country, in imitation of the very behavior they had criticized in those they were seeking to overthrow, took up residence or established their headquarters in elegant traditional gardens that had once served as homes to high-ranking imperial officials, inadvertently thereby preserving historic sites from rampage. The rambling, elegant Ping-shan Garden in Yangzhou remained intact because a revolutionary opera troupe established residence there. In Dunhuang, many temples and ancient buildings were destroyed. But the Dunhuang caves, priceless repositories of the world's finest Tang-dynasty Buddhist art and sculpture, located just before the Silk Road reaches the treacherous Taklamakan Desert, survived the Cultural Revolution without a scar. When Langdon Warner had defaced the caves early in the twentieth century by removing a number of murals for Harvard's Fogg Museum, Dunhuang and environs had plunged into three years of famine. If Dunhuang's rebels were divided politically, they at least agreed on the danger of offending the spirits. Damage to the caves would bring famine to all.

Not everything of national significance was protected. In Qufu, Shandong province, birthplace of Confucius—the sage whose philosophy had served as China's state ideology for two millennia, whose thought and morals were quintessentially "old," who stood as the repository of traditional Chinese culture—the local inhabitants, many of them descendants of Confucius in the seventy-sixth and seventy-seventh generations (Kong is their surname in Chinese), were unable fully to protect the vast Kong family estates from attack. At Kong Woods—the cemetery in Qufu where some 100,000 of the philosopher's descendants are said to be buried, the size of the burial mounds a rough indication of the status of the deceased in life—the Red Guards, many of them from Peking, toppled numerous stone tablets and destroyed a statue of Confucius that had stood on the grounds for centuries.

The Kong family cemetery was not the only burial ground in China to suffer defilement during the Cultural Revolution. On Hainan Island, the grave of the upright Ming-dynasty official Hai Rui, so highly praised by Wu Han, was defiled. In some parts of China, when cremation became mandatory, filial children nonetheless had acceded to their parents' most fervent and insistent wishes. Secretly, in the darkness of early morning, they had buried their parents in coffins underground. During the Cultural Revolution, when their crimes were made public, the sons themselves were forced to dig up the coffin, open it, pour gasoline on their parent's decaying body, and light it with a match.

In traditional China, bodies of officials posthumously found guilty of crime were sometimes disinterred and decapitated, their rotting heads displayed to public view. Lü Liuliang, a Confucian scholar who refused to transfer his loyalties when the Ming dynasty was replaced by the Qing, was found guilty almost a century after his death of offending the imperial court. His body was so disinterred, decapitated, and publicly displayed. In 1967, the Red Guards tried to dig up the body of Ma Jinglan's father, who had died in 1952 of natural causes and been buried in Babaoshan before cremation was made mandatory. For his lifelong cooperation with American missionary educators, Ma Jinglan's father was determined during the Cultural Revolution to have been a counter-revolutionary and American spy. The Red Guards desisted in their efforts at disinterment after finding his coffin intact but succeeded in exhuming the remains of other counterrevolutionaries buried nearby. In the Shanghai ceme-tery for foreigners that now holds the remains of Song Qingling, widow of Sun Yat-sen, the man credited with the revolution that led to the downfall of the last of China's imperial dynasties, a Red Guard attack left no tombstones standing. In the xenophobia of the Cultural Revolution, foreigners, almost by definition, could safely be assumed to be counterrevolutionary, their remains unfit to be covered by Chinese soil.

"Many Red Guards became rich because they dug up coffins," asserts Huang Chaoqun. "Rich people in the old days sometimes buried jewelry, gold, relics, with the body. Gold never spoils. Jade, precious stones, never deterio-rate. There were many such tombs."

In Confucius's home village of Qufu, the young outsiders from Peking sacked the grandest of the country's Confucian temples, allegedly built two hundred years before the Great Wall, smashing priceless, centuries-old sacri-ficial vessels, writing tablets, and other historic artifacts. It is said by one of Confucius's descendants that the Red Guards from Peking Normal University, under the leadership of the fiery female Tan Houlan, were the most insistently destructive. It was they, after failing in numerous attempts to topple the twenty-foot-high stone tablets that stood in the courtyard of the temple, who wrapped thick rope around the tablets and felled them in a tug-of-war of some twenty students against the stone. In Xian, the heads of the great stone creatures guarding the imperial tombs were lopped off and sold.

Much that was destroyed was more prosaic, local in meaning, provincial in charm. In the alleyways of larger cities and in lesser towns and villages, every-where is testimony to the Red Guard rampages. The magnificent pipe organ of the Nantang Catholic Cathedral in the Xuanwu Men section of Peking was destroyed, replaced now by a dilapidated, squeaky foot-pedaled instrument. The interior of the Catholic church in Jinan was defaced and dismantled, and churches throughout the country are naked of the crucifixes, statues, artifacts, and stained glass that once graced their interiors. In the Moslem areas of cities, the worshippers themselves are nowadays hard at work, in those mosques that have been returned to those for whom they were originally built, painstakingly restoring the damage. Many temples, mosques, and churches, official protestations of China's new freedom of religion aside, have yet to be returned; they are used for warehouses, cottage industries, and schools. At the Thousand Buddha Mountain, a Buddhist shrine on a hillside outside Jinan, used during the Cultural Revolution as a public exhibit for "comparing the bitterness of the past to the sweetness of the present," the heads of the countless stone statues of the Buddha have been cemented back in place, but others, where the damage was from scraping rather than felling, remain defaced. In many Buddhist temples, the damage is irreparable. When Red Guards in Changzhou removed the entire contents of the interior of the Temple of Heavenly Tranquillity, it took a week for the bonfire to reduce itself to ashes. There is a sameness to the interiors of Buddhist temples open to foreigners now, leading to a suspicion that somewhere in China is a Buddha idol factory whose workers labor dispiritedly replacing the images destroyed during the Cultural Revolution with cheap, shiny, gold-painted, fat plaster idols even less distinguishable one from the other than blue Mao jackets from gray.

In most of China proper, there was still something tempered, measured, tenuous about the marauding Red Guards. They could have destroyed the buildings in which the country's historic, cultural, and religious relics were housed. But for the most part, the buildings themselves were left standing. In Tibet, where the traditional Dalai Lama was both religious and secular leader of his people, who are ethnically and religiously distinct from the Han Chinese, where until 1950 there were 6,254 monasteries and prayer flags continuously fluttered and prayer wheels incessantly turned, where religion is so deeply embedded into the pattern of life that matters of state were decided only upon consultation with the oracle and few tasks are performed without propitiation of the gods, where Chinese rule was imposed only through subjugation and where the inhabitants nonetheless rebelled in 1959 against Chinese Communist rule, the story is different. It is not just that the practice of religion was officially outlawed, folk festivals banned, and traditional dances and song, incense-burning, and all Tibetan art forms and customs prohibited, that prayer flags were ripped down and replaced with revolutionary red banners, the *mani* stones and mantras demolished and replaced by colossal slogans of Mao, the second floors of homes razed as "bourgeois" and residents forced to live with their animals in the ground-floor stables. Writes John Avedon, the most comprehensive chronicler of the fate of post-"liberation" Tibet:

By September 1967 . . . widespread destruction began in earnest. Older Red Guards supervised the operation equipped with booklets in which each article's designation, either to be saved or destroyed, was noted. Images of gold, silver and bronze, expensive brocades and ancient *thankas* were packed and sealed. Intricately carved pillars and beams were dismantled for use in the construction of Chinese compounds. Then, under red flags—with drums, trumpets and cymbals providing a fanfare—local Tibetans were forced to demolish each monastery. Giant bonfires were lit to burn thousands of scriptures, while those not incinerated were desecrated—used as wrapping in Chinese shops, as toilet paper or as padding in shoes. The wooden blocks in which they were bound were made into floorboards, chairs and handles for farm tools. Clay images were ground to dust, thrown into the street for people to walk on and mixed with fertilizer. Others were remade into bricks for the specific purpose of building public lavatories. *Mani* stones, once among the most common expressions of prayer, were turned into pavement. Frescoes were defaced, the eyes of their images gouged out in a manner reminiscent of the twelfth-century Moslem destruction of Buddhist monasteries in India. Bronze and gold pinnacles crowning every temple's roof were pulled down and—along with other metals—resmelted.

When the pillaging was done, dynamite was placed in the gutted buildings and their walls blown up. Field artillery was also used, so that within a three-year period the entire landscape of Tibet stood scarred by ruins resembling bombed cities. Because the buildings' walls were so thick, virtually none . . . could be completely razed, but stood as ghostly ever-present reminders of what had been.

When, in the late summer of 1979, the first delegation representing the Dalai Lama to visit Tibet since the flight of the Tibetan spiritual leader in 1959 was taken to the Norbulingka palace outside Llasa that had once served as the Dalai Lama's summer home, they found an edifice once used for state occasions locked. Peering through broken windows, they saw the temple filled to a height of twenty-five feet "with a mass of shattered heads, limbs and pedestals, the mangled remains of centuries-old statues." "Unfortunately," a cadre explained of the destruction in Tibet, "under the left-deviationist policies of the Gang of Four, some excesses occurred."

While most of China had witnessed the mass murder of the country's heritage, Tibet had witnessed its genocide.

SONG WUHAO was too deeply immersed in the fervor of rebelling against the reactionaries to take advantage of the opportunity for tourism or to participate in the destruction of the four olds. "Because we Red Flag Red Guards believed that we were the most revolutionary, and because we believed that the problems weren't just in the schools but in society as well," explains Song, "we decided we should leave Peking and go to other places to make revolution there. So we went to Shanghai, Harbin, Changchun, Wuhan, Tianjin, and everyone listened to us, because we were the most revolutionary. We were the students of Qinghua Middle School.

"I left in October for Shanghai as part of a group of Red Flag Red Guards. When we got there, we went to the offices of the city government, and we told them that we were from Peking, that Mao Zedong supported us, that we were real revolutionaries, so they had to support us, too. They did. They gave us cars, money, the right to broadcast our views over the radio, offices, personnel support. We lived in the best quarters the city government could provide. So we had lots of authority. We could demand all sorts of things, because they knew that if they didn't support us, we would overthrow them, because we were the most revolutionary.

"We told the Shanghai city government that we were there to make revolution, that just as the central government had revisionists in it, so the Shanghai municipal government had revisionists in it. We told them that we had the power to make the decisions about who was revisionist and who was revolutionary. We said we would grab the revisionists in the name of revolution. Under those circumstances, they supported us. No matter who they were, they supported us. Even if they didn't really believe us, they had to support us, unite with us, help us, provide for us, because they knew that if they didn't support us, we would overthrow them."

Government ground to a halt. "They couldn't move," says Song Wuhao. "They were paralyzed. The whole city government was paralyzed. We united with people who supported us and opposed people who didn't support us, overthrew them, because we were revolutionaries."

IT was in October 1966, the month that Song Wuhao and his comrades left for Shanghai, in a meeting of a Communist Party work conference, that Liu Shaoqi submitted his first "self-criticism," balanced and measured in tone, apologizing for failing to understand the Cultural Revolution during its initial, earliest phase. The self-criticism, apparently, was accepted by the party members present. But beginning in October and increasingly forthrightly by November, Liu Shaoqi came under sustained and public attack. "We kept attacking, spreading the attacks from the small leaders to the big leaders, all the way up to Liu Shaoqi," reports Song Wuhao. "Every stratum of society was subject to examination, attack, overthrow. It was a mass movement."

Taciturn, serious, careful, stern, and thoughtful, Liu Shaoqi was hardly a civil libertarian. He had joined the Communist Party as a student in the Soviet

Union in the winter of 1921–22. It was he, in Yenan, who had first begun elevating Mao Zedong to the theoretical ranks of a Marx or an Engels, he who had first begun speaking of "the Thought of Mao Zedong." It was Liu Shaoqi, some would say, who first started the cult of Mao.

But in contrast to Mao, who changed the rules to suit his own ends, Liu Shaoqi was a bureaucrat, an organization man, even, one might say, a strict constitutionalist. Where Mao emphasized class struggle and mobilization of the masses and hence was both divisive and antibureaucratic, Liu emphasized procedure and unity. He played by the rules. "Liu's life," writes Lowell Dittmer, his American biographer, "may be viewed as an attempt to combine order with revolution and equality with economic efficiency and technocratic values. Over a period of more than a quarter century, he served as a constructive and stabilizing force within the party and the regime." "Mankind," Liu told his children, "includes the landlords, rich peasants, counterrevolutionaries, and bad elements. The proletariat are not at all selfish. They have a broad heart. The proletariat cannot emancipate itself without reforming those elements into good people, without changing all the negative factors into positive factors."

Mao's definition of the "people" had been different. Mao had excluded the landlords, rich peasants, counterrevolutionaries, and bad elements from the ranks of the "people." It was against these "nonpeople," Mao insisted, that the proletariat and all revolutionaries should struggle.

When Liu Shaoqi's own children, early in the Cultural Revolution, succumbed to the fervor of the campaign against the "four olds" and began participating in house searches of the former capitalists and members of the bourgeoisie, Liu Shaoqi stopped them. Taking out a copy of the constitution of the People's Republic of China, he had said, "If you want to destroy the four olds, I don't oppose you. But you can't go to search people's houses and beat people. I am the head of state. I am responsible for implementation of the constitution. Many democrats cooperated with our party for dozens of years, and that is the important fruit of our work with the United Front. It was not easily won, and we can't let it be destroyed in one day. . . . I am responsible for your actions."

"At the time," recalls Song Wuhao, "some people defended Liu Shaoqi and said he was good while others said he was bad. So society was divided into two parts, those defending Liu Shaoqi and those who wanted to overthrow him. And because there were people who defended Liu Shaoqi, there were fights, battles. It became a civil war. Mao Zedong, Jiang Qing, and Lin Biao all said that Liu Shaoqi was China's biggest capitalist, biggest revisionist, whereas others opposed Mao, Lin Biao, and Jiang Qing with respect to their judgment on Liu Shaoqi. So there were two factions. At our school there were two factions. From the top to the bottom of society there were two factions. Because I believed in Mao and the Red Flag Red Guards believed we listened best to Chairman Mao's words, I and my faction opposed Liu Shaoqi. That is the background to my story."

IN the months and years that followed, countless Chinese—from Liu Shaoqi, Deng Xiaoping, Tao Zhu, and others at the pinnacle of the Communist Party hierarchy down to the befuddled team leader in the rural people's commune, from presidents of universities, leading party secretaries, and heads of departments down to ordinary faculty, from middle and primary school principals and teachers to factory managers, writers, artists, religious figures, members of the former landlord and bourgeois classes, people who had studied abroad, those who had relatives in the United States, Hong Kong, or Taiwan—came under attack. By 1969, seven of the seventeen members of the Politburo had been deprived of office and declared enemies of the party. Fifty-three of the ninety-seven members of the Chinese Communist Party Central Committee had been purged, as had four of the six regional first party secretaries and twenty-three of the twenty-nine provincial first party secretaries. Two years later, Lin Biao, the man who had replaced Peng Dehuai as head of the military and Liu Shaoqi as the party chairman's heir apparent and closest comrade-in-arms, had turned against the very Mao he had once so slavishly, obsequiously flattered, the man one of whose words he had once said was worth ten thousand of anyone else's. Lin Biao was revealed to have been plotting a coup d'état. His plane crashed in Outer Mongolia, in flight to the Soviet Union.

People were accused of being opponents of Chairman Mao and followers of the capitalist road, of being China's Khrushchev and followers of China's Khrushchev, followers of Wu Han, followers of Liu Shaoqi, and followers of Lin Biao, rightists, ultraleftists, "May sixteenth elements," and "stinking ninth elements."* They were labeled counterrevolutionaries, traitors, renegades, and spies, bourgeois academic authorities, "ox ghosts and snake spirits," stinking wives, rotten eggs, sons of bitches, and worthy progeny of counterrevolutionaries.

As the movement progressed, it began somersaulting, flipping this way and flopping that, like a fish out of water, as the revolutionaries of one stage of the movement became the counterrevolutionaries of the next, the persecutors during one phase the persecuted of the next.

"During the Cultural Revolution, the central Cultural Revolution Group of the Party issued so many contradictory instructions," said Song Erli. Song Erli's father, a rightist, came under attack almost immediately after the

---

*"May sixteenth elements" were individuals falsely accused of having belonged to a probably nonexistent ultra-leftist group advocating the overthrow of Zhou Enlai. "Stinking ninth elements" was the term of opprobrium applied to intellectuals, the lowest in the hierarchy of outcast elements.

publication of Nie Yuanzi's big character poster. He spent most of the duration of the Cultural Revolution in incarceration. "My father was locked in the 'cattle pen'* the whole time. He used to say that at the same time there were five generations of 'ox ghosts and snake spirits' living in the cattle pen together," recalls Song Erli. "First, the old intellectuals were locked up. Then the former Communist Party secretaries. Before the Cultural Revolution, intellectuals had never been on an equal par with the Communist Party secretaries, the veteran revolutionaries who founded the new republic. But during the Cultural Revolution, they were equally humiliated. The people who had attacked the intellectuals so severely during the antirightist movement were revealed during the Cultural Revolution as utter hypocrites. The person who criticized my mother in one movement was criticized himself in the Cultural Revolution. Then the early Red Guards were put in the cattle pens, the ones who had opposed only the grass-roots party leaders but had become the top conservatives and defended the municipal party committee. And then after a while a second wave of revolutionary rebels went into the cattle pens —those who had not only accused the municipal party committee but accused the military as well. Many professors, many bourgeois academic authorities laughed at this ridiculous state of affairs. They were delighted to see what was happening to the party cadres, because the cadres had never treated them well. The intellectuals had constantly been the objects of all sorts of political movements, criticized for this and criticized for that. But then, after all the party cadres got pulled down, the intellectuals got to laugh secretly. They all lived together in the same cow pens. They were equal now, equally humiliated."

ONCE one member of a family came under attack, so too did all its other members, spouse and children alike. A Chinese proverb has it that a calamity that strikes one member of a family will reverberate to nine of its branches *(huo yan jiu zu)*, whereas good fortune will smile even on the household chickens. Traditional Chinese law held not just the perpetrator himself but family members too accountable and punishable for crime. In capital offenses, it was not the criminal alone but members of his family as well who were subject to execution.

The proverb governing the Cultural Revolution was modern in composition and ostensibly Marxian in reference, but its effect was hardly new. "If the father is a revolutionary," the governing saying went, "the son is a good fellow, too. If the father is a counterrevolutionary, the son is a rotten egg." Class became caste during the Cultural Revolution, and children were considered guilty for the sins of their fathers. "Rotten egg," "son of a bitch," and "worthy

*A makeshift jail.

progeny of a counterrevolutionary" were epithets pinned on children of the accused.

Wang Ping still remembers the humiliation and the pain of learning as a little girl of eight, when the Cultural Revolution began, that she was a member of the exploiting class. Both her parents had been members of the Communist Party, revolutionary cadres proud of their roles in liberating China. But Wang Ping's grandfather had been a landlord, and in the climate of the Cultural Revolution, both of Wang Ping's parents were labeled, by virtue of their background, the "class enemy." Throughout her childhood, Wang Ping dreaded the forms she had to fill out at the beginning of each term on which she had to identify her class. She is still haunted by the cruelty of her teachers, who forced her to stand in front of her classmates, publicly identifying herself as a member of the exploiting class. She still drives herself harder than her fellow teachers, because she grew up, like Song Erli, being told that only if she worked harder could she reform herself into the equal of her peers. The psychological price of her success has been high.

Li Meirong's son was only seven years old when the Cultural Revolution began, in his second year of primary school. Classes in his school were canceled, but students still met for political study and struggle sessions. Some of those struggle sessions were directed against Li Meirong's son, who was accused of being a rotten egg, a son of a bitch, and the worthy progeny of a counterrevolutionary. On the way to and from school, he was similarly taunted. Li Meirong's son did not understand what was happening to him, why he had been singled out for attack, and Li Meirong found herself powerless either to protect him or to explain.

Young people who came from "bad class backgrounds"—whose parents had been labeled landlords or capitalists or rightists—were prohibited from joining the Red Guards, and those whose parents came under attack during the course of the Cultural Revolution were similarly excluded. That both his parents had been declared rightists in 1957, and were singled out for attack immediately after the Cultural Revolution began, prohibited Song Erli from ever joining the Red Guards. "I was never allowed to be a Red Guard," he says. "It wasn't even a dream. My background was wrong." And because Wang Hongbao's father, longtime revolutionary cadre and member of the Peking party elite, was attacked shortly after the downfall of the Peking party committee in late May 1966, even before the first group of students had declared themselves Red Guards, Wang Hongbao was excluded from participation as a rebel. "I wasn't even allowed to go to Tiananmen to see Chairman Mao," he remembers with a twinge, fifteen years later, of regret. Bai Meihua, Song Wuhao, and Liu Zhiping, early participants in the Cultural Revolution, came under attack immediately after their parents.

Theoretically, it was possible to "draw a clear line of demarcation from" the family member under attack and thus to avoid implication in his crimes of counterrevolution. Spouses and children alike were often put under considerable pressure to separate themselves from the offending relative. Young middle school and university students, prohibited otherwise from joining their peers in the exuberantly contagious adolescent rebellion, often succumbed to the pressure. For China's young, the Cultural Revolution was a difficult event to miss. One of Liu Shaoqi's daughters, Liu Tao, attacked her father, and Wang Hongbao attempted to draw a clear line of demarcation from his. He was still prevented from participation in the Cultural Revolution. Song Erli, too, turned against the father with whom he had never gotten along and whom he genuinely believed to be counterrevolutionary. Liu Zhiping finally tried to draw a clear line of demarcation from her father but ran away rather than attack him directly. Song Wuhao was publicly tortured in an effort to turn him against his father.

Yu Luoke, whose parents had both been labeled rightists, tried to offer a reasoned refutation of the so-called "theory of the blood line" that decreed him, because his parents were counterrevolutionaries, a rotten egg. Yu Luoke had suffered from his parents' label, twice excelling at the college entrance exams academically only to be denied entrance for political reasons, because of his parents' past. Yu Luoke argued that the connection between the class from which an individual was descended and an individual's political behavior was minimal, that the influence exerted on young people by the social environment far outweighed the influence of the family. Yu Luoke thought that children of rightists should be treated the same as children of parents from "good" class backgrounds.

In the summer of 1967, Yu Luoke was arrested for those views. During the nearly three years he spent in prison, Yu Luoke was given the opportunity to repudiate the opinions he had earlier expressed, offered a chance to confess that the argument he had made was a crime. But Yu Luoke refused.

On March 5, 1970, at the age of twenty-eight, because he continued to refuse to recant, Yu Luoke became one of the rare genuine martyrs of China's Great Proletarian Cultural Revolution, executed for the tenacity with which he clung to his beliefs. In Peking's Workers' Stadium, before a crowd of tens of thousands, little red books waving, revolutionary slogans filling the air, Yu Luoke was shot.

THE divorce rate went up during the Cultural Revolution as women, in particular, attempted to draw a clear line of demarcation from their husbands. Many women hoped that by so doing they could protect their children from attack. Maomei's mother in Xu Huaizhong's story "Anecdote from the Western

Front" and Tang Lin in Lu Wenfu's "Dedication" both divorced their husbands in order to protect their children.

Some women not only divorced their husbands but participated in the attacks against them.

"Let me tell you the story of my best friend, my classmate, and what happened to his family during the Cultural Revolution," Zong Fuxian began one drizzly, overcast afternoon in Shanghai.

"We had been best friends for years, and since I had been a small child I had gone to his house frequently and also knew his parents quite well. We had become very close, and his parents were like an aunt and uncle to me. His father was an engineer in a research institute, and his mother, also an intellectual, worked in the same unit. During the Cultural Revolution, a tragedy struck the family. The father was labeled a Japanese spy because he had worked in the northeast during the period of the Japanese occupation. Upon being labeled a Japanese spy, he was confined, locked up, and isolated from his family. He was tortured in the hope that he would confess.

"But the father could not stand the torture that was brought to bear against him, and so eventually he confessed that he was guilty of being an agent, a spy for Japan. The father's confession was read at a big meeting, and the paper on which it was written was held up for everyone to see.

"The mother had been put under great pressure to draw a clear line of demarcation from her husband, and during the period she was being subjected to such great pressure, she learned that her husband had confessed, that he had said that he was a Japanese agent, a spy. So at the meeting that was held to denounce him, the meeting where his confession was read, it was she who stood up and took the lead in shouting the slogans against him—down with her husband."

When women refused to draw a clear line of demarcation from their husbands, they were often given mandatory front-row seats in the struggle sessions against them. Liu Zhiping's mother was forced to witness the struggle session against her husband. "There was a big struggle session," she recalls, "and people came from all over the city to attend the struggle session against the party persons in authority who were taking the capitalist road. My father was one of the people on the stage being struggled against. They made my mother sit in the audience, in the front row. There were twenty or thirty people on the stage being struggled against, and they were all made to kneel down on the floor. All the relatives of the people being struggled against were sitting in the audience, in the front. The people who were running the struggle session said that this was a revolution and that relatives should draw a clear line of demarcation from those being attacked. The relatives weren't allowed to show any sign of sympathy. They used whips to beat those people on the stage, and one person used his foot to kick my father, and my father fell right off the stage, into the audience, right in front of my mother. But my mother couldn't go to help him stand up again. Two friends of my family who were there in the audience helped him stand up again."

YUNYUN'S father turned his own child out of his home.

Huang Chaoqun's son is adopted. He and his wife were unable to have children. But, in time-honored Chinese custom, Huang Chaoqun's brother—an ordinary worker in Shenyang and thereby a member of the proletariat and hence revolutionary—gave his infant fifth son to Huang Chaoqun and his wife. Yunyun, as the son was familiarly called, was never told of his adoption. Mr. and Mrs. Huang intended to tell him when Yunyun reached adulthood.

Huang Chaoqun came under attack with the opening salvoes of the Cultural Revolution and was sent to the countryside to labor as a peasant. Mrs. Huang was attacked shortly thereafter and was locked in a cattle pen in her work unit. The Huang family salary, once a combined monthly total of $250, was reduced to a mere $15, and of that, $5 had to be sent to aging Grandfather Huang in the countryside. Until shortly before the Cultural Revolution, Grandfather Huang had lived with the family. But as his strength began to wane and his health to deteriorate, Grandfather Huang noted that the dead of the city were invariably cremated. Fearful that his request for a proper burial would not be honored, Grandfather Huang had returned to his native village to live out his remaining days, assured that with his death he would be buried next to his wife.

With Mr. Huang in the countryside and Mrs. Huang incarcerated, there was no one to care for the eight-year-old child. Mr. and Mrs. Huang arranged for Yunyun to go to Shenyang to live with his natural father, and Yunyun's natural father, initially at least, agreed. But after Yunyun had been there a few weeks, the anxiety surrounding his presence began to build. Mr. Huang's brother was afraid not that Yunyun's real parentage would be discovered but that others would learn that Yunyun's adopted parents were "ox ghosts and snake spirits," bourgeois academic authorities, accused of being counterrevolutionaries and spies. He was afraid that his humble family might also be attacked. Yunyun's natural father forced the child to return to his own home to fend for himself alone.

The apartment to which Yunyun returned was occupied by two revolutionary rebel families. Yunyun was allotted a single room, stripped bare of all furnishings, and a corner in the outdoor corridor to cook his and his mother's meals. Locked as she was in the cattle pen, Mrs. Huang was unable to prepare her own meals, and buying them, now that her son had returned, was prohibitively expensive. Mrs. Huang came to depend on her son for sustenance.

Yunyun was a resourceful and independent young child. The parents of his best friend faced fates similar to those of his own, and the two friends learned to shop and cook together. Too poor even to purchase the matches necessary to light the pressed-coal-dust balls they used for fuel, the two children used to light a coal ball in a friendly neighbor's stove, carrying the glowing charcoal to start their own fire. But sometimes toward the end of the month, Yunyun would run out of both money and food. He still remembers one evening, after three days without eating, going to the home of Xu Li in the hope of being given some food. Yunyun did not know that at the earliest struggle sessions against his father, it had been Xu Li, their longtime family friend, who, in a speech saturated with the hyperbolic rhetoric of the day, had stood at the podium pointing a finger at Huang Chaoqun, leading the attacks against him.

What Yunyun remembers today is Xu Li's face in the window, peering out from behind a curtain, to see who was knocking. Xu Li never opened the door.

For all his precocious independence and resourcefulness, for all the support he received from his little friend, eight-year-old Yunyun could not survive alone. A few months after Yunyun's natural father had turned him out, his parents were able to place their adopted son in the care of another of Mr. Huang's relatives. There he stayed for ten years, until his parents were rehabilitated in 1977. Mrs. Huang, during that time, was given permission to see her son only once, spending two weeks with the child in 1972. Mr. Huang did not see the child at all.

Yunyun is married now and has a child of his own. He is bitter about the Cultural Revolution, unforgiving, unyielding. But Yunyun has never been told that it was his natural father who during the Cultural Revolution forced him to independence at such an early age. Ashamed now of having turned away his own son, Yunyun's father has pleaded with the young man's adopted parents to shield the son from the truth.

"There are hundreds of such stories," Huang Chaoqun asserts. "People just stopped being human beings at that time. They were just crazy. They were wilder than wild beasts. They were subhuman beings."

IT was not only members of the immediate family who attempted to avoid association with the accused. A specter of fear hung over more distant relatives, too. "It was family members you trusted least," Li Meirong insists. Li Meirong's brother-in-law, an upwardly mobile party official with much to lose should the Cultural Revolution turn against him, had informed his superiors shortly after the attacks on Li Meirong began of his longtime suspicions that his sister-in-law was a spy.

Bai Meihua's aunt, called upon to aid the family as their period of tribulation approached, did so with only the gravest reluctance. Bai Meihua's family knew well in advance that Mr. Bai would ultimately be singled out for attack and that their house, when he was, would be searched. As a government official, Mr. Bai had a number of official documents in his home. In an effort to protect them, Mrs. Bai had her daughter take the most important and valuable of the documents to the home of Mrs. Bai's sister. But Bai Meihua's aunt was reluctant to take the documents, nervous that Bai Meihua had been seen bringing them in, afraid that if the delivery had been witnessed her house, too, would be searched. She insisted that nothing else be brought for protection. "Even now," says Bai Meihua, "my mother's relations with that aunt still aren't that good. Because she remembers that in those most difficult times, my aunt did not want to help. We see my aunt only once a year now, at Spring Festival, but my mother would never go to her house. My mother says that a friend in need is a friend indeed, but that my aunt isn't that kind of person."

THE homes of those under attack during the Cultural Revolution were raided and often occupied by the "revolutionary rebels," their possessions removed, stolen, or destroyed. Li Meirong's apartment, decorated with irreplaceable Ming and Qing antiques collected over the years by her parents, grandparents, and their parents too, was searched numerous times, the furniture removed piece by piece, first by one faction of the young Red Guards from Li Meirong's middle school and then by another, never to be seen again. When their apartment was stripped nearly bare, the doors of all rooms but one were sealed shut with *fengtiao*—two long, narrow paper strips pasted in an X over the door and bearing the date and time of closure, the name of the revolutionary organization responsible for ordering the room secured, and the revolution- aries' official seal. In traditional times, *fengtiao* were applied only on highest authority, signaling both that the government had ordered the property sealed and that only authority could legitimately enter. In more modern times, re- sponsibility for *fengtiao* was delegated to Communist Party secretaries. When universities closed for the summer, *fengtiao* were pasted over offices, dormitory rooms, and classrooms as a precaution against the possibility of unauthorized intrusion. Similarly, books rendered obsolete and removed from circulation by the ever-changing political line are safely stored in rooms sealed by *fengtiao*.

Li Meirong, her husband, and their two children spent much of the Cultural Revolution living squeezed into their tiny kitchen, the only room from which *fengtiao* had not excluded them, taking turns sleeping at night because there was no room for all to lie down. They never dreamed of breaking a seal to gain more space. "This group of Red Guards would come and put up their *fengtiao* and then another group would come and pull down the *fengtiao* and do their own search and put up their own *fengtiao*," Li Meirong said, "but an 'ox ghost and snake spirit' would never touch a *fengtiao*."

Huang Chaoqun and his family had moved into their own apartment only two years before the Cultural Revolution began, after spending their post- Liberation life living in two small rooms in an older, not very well maintained four-room apartment, sharing kitchen and bath with the family that occupied the other half of the dwelling. Housing was a problem socialist and growing China had yet to solve. During the Cultural Revolution, Huang Chaoqun's new apartment was searched, its entire contents—furniture, books, clothes, photograph albums, jewelry, everything—removed. Huang Chaoqun was left with only the clothes on his back and not even a change of underwear. After six years, his underwear and shirt had long since disintegrated, and the padding of his jacket was seeping through numerous holes. Three of his family's four rooms were occupied by two revolutionary rebel families, who quarreled among themselves about how to divide the space. When Huang Chaoqun was not at work on the farm, and after his wife had been released from the cattle pen, they spent the duration of the Cultural Revolution in a single barren room, sleeping on the concrete floor without so much as bedsheet or quilt. Their circumstances were bettered with the addition, after several years, of a straw mattress which they placed on the floor.

Song Wuhao's house was searched four times. "They searched in everything," he remembers. "In all the drawers, under the mattresses, under the rugs. We had to stand aside. We didn't dare to move or to say anything the whole time they were there. They took my parents' wedding pictures, my father's graduate degree, his thesis. In the United States, my father had collected stamps, so he had a rather nice stamp collection. They took that away too. They took everything that my parents had from before Liberation—my parents' wedding clothes, all the presents they had gotten when they got married, my mother's necklace, her ring. They took the clothes that my father had worn in the United States, when he was a student. My father had a painting, a Chinese painting, by a very famous artist. He loved that painting. They took it, too. And they took his bankbook with all his savings. They said they wanted to use these things as evidence of his crimes. After our house had been searched, the revolutionary rebels came in and occupied it."

The house search (chaojia) was not new to China's Cultural Revolution. In traditional times, under dynastic rule, the homes of accused and discredited officials about to be arrested, exiled, or executed were also subject to search and to seizure. The house search was used to provide evidence against the accused, and when it was complete, the personal property of the accused was either sealed with fengtiao or stored in official warehouses. The family holdings became property of the state and were ordinarily held as a hedge against the possibility that with a future exoneration the outcast official or his family might legitimately reclaim their possessions. Surviving catalogues of property officially seized provide contemporary historians with a record of the immense luxury in which traditional Chinese officialdom basked.

That traditional house searches were often less orderly in practice than in theory, that the police who conducted them often used their official duties as a means of collecting booty, is exemplified by the most famous of China's traditional house searches, the scene in the most widely read and extensively researched of all of China's novels, the Dream of the Red Chamber, in which the magnificent, rambling, Chinese-style palace of the Chia family is subjected to an ignominious search of the premises and confiscation of property. In traditional times, however, authority, even when grossly abused, would never have been vested in the young. It was the young Red Guards of China's middle schools and universities who conducted the house searches of the Cultural Revolution. *Lord of the Flies* may be a universal statement of what the unguided, unsupervised young can become , but China is one of the few places where the nightmare has become true in fact.

In particularly noteworthy cases during the Cultural Revolution, when the property of the accused was peculiarly varied and vast, or when the accused was particularly famous, homes of the "bourgeoisie" were transformed into public exhibits, "living museums," that the revolutionary masses could visit and inspect at will. Mei Li'an's home in Zong Pu's novel *The Stone of the Three Reincarnations* was turned into such an exhibit.

Ma Weidong actually visited one such living museum. "In Shanghai, after the searches of some of the bourgeois families," Ma Weidong explains, "they would turn their houses into public exhibits, like museums, where you saw how the bourgeoisie lived." Ma Weidong's parents are both working-class members of the Chinese Communist Party and longtime supporters of the Chinese revolution. They were beneficiaries of Liberation and grateful for it. But benefit had come primarily in the form of decent housing and job security, modest but certain wages. The family, in contrast to other members of the party, had never claimed special privilege or become well-to-do. Their daughter, a college student at the time, was incredulous at the wealth of the old bourgeoisie. "I went to one of those houses," she remembers. "They had the porcelain displayed everywhere—the old, antique porcelain. And the books. Rows and rows of books, many of them in foreign languages. And the furniture. Old, antique, wooden furniture. But mostly I remember the clothes. Most Chinese people don't have very many clothes. We just have enough to wear one set while the other is being washed, and they don't have a lot of variety or different colors. But in the house I visited, they had taken all the clothes out of the wardrobes and trunks and had them displayed all over the room. There were so many of them. I couldn't imagine that one family could have so many different clothes and in so many different styles and colors. We didn't envy them their riches, though. We were proud to be poor."

People were put on public exhibit, too. Chen Quanhong, his handsome, wrinkled face now a study in character, was taken from town to town and paraded through the streets, a rope around his neck, "like a dog," he says. An auditorium at Huang Chaoqun's university was turned into a "museum of living people," where the "ox ghosts and snake spirits," counterrevolutionaries, traitors, and spies were put on public display. Visitors to the museum of living people could spit at and beat the living examples at will. A favorite game of those who had come to attack was to force the people on display to lick from the floor the spittle that had missed its mark. "I could hear the screams of others being beaten," remembers Huang Chaoqun. Some did not survive.

Many were paraded through city streets with dunce caps on their heads and accusatory placards around their necks. Sometimes the Red Guards who had organized the event beat gongs and sometimes the accused struck spoons against metal basins signaling the arrival of a *youjie*, a street parade. Differentiations of status persisting even among the defamed, those formerly of rank were paraded on the back of open trucks while more ordinary citizens were forced to walk. Often, particularly when the parades were by foot, the "ox ghosts and snake spirits" were herded along by whip. Peng Kang, the president of Jiaotong University in Xian, died one hot summer day from the beatings administered during such a parade.

Chinese criminals condemned to execution, both traditionally and today, are paraded around the streets, as public examples to those who might be similarly tempted to err, on the way to the execution ground. Traditionally, the condemned were expected to entertain the curious and wide-eyed crowds, following the carts for the spectacle they made, by singing verse from Peking opera. Lu Xun, whose satires were sometimes directed at his countrymen's fascination with spectacle and gore, decided to give up medicine and turn to writing when he saw on film a scene of the Japanese military that had invaded China executing by decapitation a Chinese declared a spy for working with the Russians. The scene was being witnessed by a group of apathetic but healthy Chinese, "come to enjoy the spectacle." In "The True Story of Ah Q," Lu Xun describes the final street parade of the confused and hapless Ah Q, about to be shot for a crime he did not commit all the while believing he has been condemned for being the revolutionary he has tried but failed to become.

But the immediate justification for the street parade of the Cultural Revolution was less Ah Q or tradition than Party Chairman Mao. In his 1927 "Investigation into the Peasant Movement in Hunan," Mao had written about the rebellious peasants forcing landlords to don dunce caps and taking them on street parades. "To put it bluntly," Mao had written, "it is necessary to create terror for a while. . . . Proper limits have to be exceeded in order to right a wrong or else the wrong cannot be righted."

You Xiaoli was often during the Cultural Revolution taken on *youjie*. "First they started taking my husband out and parading him around the streets," she remembers, "and I was very worried and frightened. They made these people wear hats made of cardboard, and on the hats they would write the person's name. In the 1920s, when the peasants overthrew the landlords, the landlords were given tall hats to wear. During the Cultural Revolution, they treated us like landlords. My husband especially was paraded through the streets of the city. I was mostly paraded on the road near the campus. But they would put my husband on a truck and take him around the whole city. The first time he was taken out, I was afraid he would be killed. I went and waited for him at the gate of the campus until he came back. I thought he was dead. Then I saw him coming back, holding his hat in his hand. Later, it happened so often that I stopped being worried. When I was treated that way, paraded through the streets, it had already happened so many times that I wasn't really afraid. I used to take my *fanghe,* my box to buy food, with me because after the parade I would go to the dining hall to buy dinner."

But there is one street parade that You Xiaoli remembers better than others, one that was the worst.

Despite the grinding poverty in which her children were raised, You Xiaoli's mother was a proud and intelligent woman. In the face of adversity, she had little to give her children but courage. From as early as You Xiaoli can remember, her mother had taught her never to bend before misfortune. Her mother's teachings had been epitomized for You Xiaoli in a saying: In cold so intense that you are on the verge of freezing, still you should turn toward the icy wind; with hunger so great you face death by starvation, still you should stand straight and tall. And if you must grit your teeth so hard they break into pieces, then swallow your teeth without spitting them out.

As a tribute to her mother, who had died of starvation, You Xiaoli had pasted that saying on her office wall. During the Cultural Revolution, its evocation of deprivation from hunger and cold was taken as You Xiaoli's assessment of what socialism had wrought for her country. She was paraded through the streets with the "counterrevolutionary" saying pasted to her chest and back. "Look how You Xiaoli hates our socialist society!" the Red Guards shouted to the ogling crowds. "She says we can die of cold, die of hunger in our socialist society! She says she'd rather die of hunger and cold and grit her teeth until they break!" As the Red Guards beat her on the head with bamboo sticks, trying to make her bow in humiliation before the crowds, the throngs of gawking onlookers spat and jeered, joining the Red Guards in chanting "Down with You Xiaoli."

OTHER "living exhibits" were less intentional. "There was an actor, a very famous actor at a film studio in Shanghai, who came under attack," remembers Ma Weidong. "His job during the Cultural Revolution was to serve as a parking attendant for the bicycles that were parked in front of the film studio. You would give him a penny and he would give you a little slip of paper with a number on it and put another slip of paper with the same number on it on your bike. Then you would give him your slip of paper when you came back to get your bicycle. My office at that time wasn't really anywhere near the film studio. It was a long walk, in fact. But sometimes I would go to park my bike there just for the opportunity to see him and say a few words to him. Before the Cultural Revolution, he must have worn Western business suits and had a Western-style haircut, but during the Cultural Revolution, he just wore ordinary clothes like everyone else and short hair. But he was still very handsome. When I paid him, I would always say a few words to him, like 'How are you? How are things going?' He was always very kind. Then again when I picked up my bicycle, I would always say something kind. Probably he wouldn't remember me now."

But the actor would remember Ma Weidong. He would, in fact, remember her well. Not everyone in China succumbed to the infectious cruelty that characterized the movement. Some people, despite the hysteria, remained kind. Victims of the Cultural Revolution, isolated from their friends and ostracized by all, found in the rare words of kindness, from wherever they came, the courage to carry, stumbling, on.

You Xiaoli still vividly remembers how sometimes when she was being paraded on the streets, elderly people, at the sight of the parade, would turn their backs to the spectacle, refusing to grant the show legitimacy by even so much as a glance. Once the Red Guards delivered You Xiaoli to a factory to participate in manual labor. She was supposed to pull carts laden with heavy steel rods. Seeing her emaciated and weak, the shop foreman, an old-model worker, sat You Xiaoli down in his office. "Are you really a spy?" he asked, offering her a cup of tea. "No, of course not," You Xiaoli replied. "I didn't think so," the old worker responded. "Then, come, let's get you something to eat." At the factory cafeteria, You Xiaoli spent the afternoon eating dumplings —forbidden food to "ox ghosts and snake spirits"—to her heart's, but not her stomach's, content. She was sick with diarrhea for two days after.

Huang Chaoqun was once taken to a factory where the workers were supposed to participate in a struggle session against him. But the workers refused to attend. The struggle session, for lack of participation, was canceled. One winter, the Red Guards took Huang Chaoqun to a rural commune where the poor peasants were supposed to organize a struggle session against him and where Huang Chaoqun was supposed to receive reeducation from the rural poor. Seeing Huang Chaoqun shivering visibly, his padded jacket scant protection against the cold, one of the peasants removed his own greatcoat and gave it to Huang Chaoqun. Another brought him tea.

And toothless Lao Zhang, senile now and sometimes less than coherent, can still ramble on forever about the white-coated policeman from the Public Security Bureau who saved him from certain death. Walking down the street one afternoon, old even then, Lao Zhang accidentally bumped into two young and militant Red Guards. One had pulled out a knife and the other was brandishing a whip when the policeman interfered. "Can't you see where you're going?" the policeman demanded of the old man in carefully feigned anger. "It's your fault for running into these young warriors. Why don't you get on your way?" Lao Zhang was able to escape.

THE street parades and house searches were special events in the lives of China's "ox ghosts and snake spirits." Struggle sessions, always dehumanizing, sometimes violent, were the primary and most frequent means through which the accused were attacked. They were usually held in the work unit of the accused—in classrooms, offices, or auditoriums—and it was colleagues, students, friends, and sometimes even relatives, people one knew and saw every day, who participated in the attacks. Subordinates were pitted against superiors, students against teachers, friends against friends, colleagues against colleagues, and, often, children against parents and spouse against spouse, rending the very fabric of Chinese society. When spouse and children refused to join as persecutors, they were often, like Liu Zhiping's mother, forced nonetheless to accompany the accused, reluctant witnesses to the humiliation of the relative they refused to betray. Liu Shaoqi's six-year-old daughter only momentarily stopped the proceedings when, forced to watch the Red Guards humiliating her parents—pushing down their heads, twisting their arms, poking their bodies, jabbing their knees, bending them first in one direction and then in another, hitting with their fists, kicking with their feet, dragging Liu Shaoqi by his thinning white hair, forcing him to raise his head to be photographed and forcing it down again—she screamed out in terror and struggled to crawl out of the crowd.

In some work units, the struggle sessions and various other political meetings were so numerous and lasted so far into the night that those who lived any distance away often could not return home in the evenings. Buses stop running at ten-thirty from the city outskirts in China and eleven at night within. In one work unit, it was only when a seven-year-old child, too young and inexperienced to manage the propane stove he was attempting to light to cook his evening meal, had set himself and the kitchen on fire that women with young children were excused from participation in the nightly political struggles.

It was at struggle sessions against her that You Xiaoli was on several occasions knocked unconscious, at a struggle session that her back was broken, at struggle sessions that the young Red Guards seared Li Meirong's arms and cheeks with lighted cigarettes. It was at a struggle session in Liu Libuo's middle school on a hot afternoon in August that seven teachers were first given the *yinyang* haircut, half their heads shaved, and then covered with a mixture of urine and feces fetched from the nearby latrine, and forced to stand, bent over from the waist, hands behind their back, elbows straight, in the position known as "doing the airplane" as the afternoon sun made its scorching journey across the summer sky. "And even afterward," Liu Libuo says, "they wouldn't let them wash it off."

It was at a struggle session that Song Erli lost control of his bladder. "The physical torture was terrible," he recalls. "I can still remember the first time I was brought out in public to be beaten. Spiritually, I was not afraid. But physically, something happened. Even before the beating. I felt a quiver. Then my legs began to tremble, and there was something cold along my spine. I felt ashamed of myself, because I felt I shouldn't act in that way. I trembled so apparently that the people standing around me who were going to beat me laughed. I who had seen so much. I shouldn't have been afraid of that. The beatings were done by my fellow students. I didn't feel so much pain. I don't even remember the beatings. It is beforehand that I remember.

"Then once they made me put my head in a classroom desk. The desks in the school had shelves, not drawers, just a top and a bottom, and the bottom serves as a shelf. They made me put my head inside the shelf, and then they began beating on the outside, on the top and bottom of the shelf, beating my head that was inside the shelf, from above and below. It only frightens you. It doesn't really hurt you. They tried not to kill people when they wanted a false confession. But when they were hitting me like that, I peed. Involuntarily. My physical response was out of my control. Ordinarily, I retained my composure. But during the actual process of being tortured, during particular processes of torture, it wasn't so much pain as that I couldn't control my own physical response. That humiliated me."

Wan Xiaotang, the first secretary of the Communist Party in one of China's largest cities, Tianjin, was one of the first to die as a result of the violence to which he was subjected during a struggle session against him. He was hardly the last.

If the accused was famous enough, important enough, the struggle sessions were spectacles, public events, convened in huge, open sports stadiums. The crowds could number in the tens, even hundreds, of thousands. Ba Jin, one of China's leading novelists, was forced to kneel for hours on broken glass before a crowd of some ten thousand people in Shanghai. Wang Hongbao's father was taken, together with numerous other of the city's ranking leaders, before a huge crowd at the Workers' Stadium in Peking, the crowd spitting and jeering at the men before whom they had once been so ostentatiously deferential.

On April 10, 1967, Liu Shaoqi's wife, Wang Guangmei, was brought before a crowd of some 100,000 rowdy, unruly, hooting young people on the campus of Qinghua University, the same campus where several months earlier she had headed the work team that attempted to lead the students in the earliest stage of the movement. Wang Guangmei's crimes were numerous and diverse. Most recently, as head of the work team, she was alleged to have stifled the

revolutionary movement of the Qinghua students, deliberately but falsely labeling the revolutionaries "counterrevolutionary." It was one such revolutionary
falsely labeled by Wang Guangmei who led the struggle session against her.
Kuai Dafu was his name, and he was the most charismatic of all the revolutionary rebels. Wang Hongbao still speaks with awe and with pride of having once
been in his company, and Jiang Xinren traveled all the way from Shanghai to
"learn from Kuai Dafu."

Of the many crimes of Wang Guangmei, the one that most fascinated the
crowd that day was the one she had committed in 1963, in Indonesia, at a state
banquet held in honor of her husband and hosted by President Sukarno
himself. There Wang Guangmei had worn a long silk traditional-style *qipao*,
with a mandarin collar and a slit up the side, decorating herself with earrings
and pearls. She had even danced, chest to chest (and flirtatiously, the accusations asserted), with the Indonesian head of state. She had shaken hands with
the nearly naked, and thereby scandalous, folk dancers who had performed for
the visiting Chinese head of state. The crowd strained, pushing forward for a
closer look, young girls vied for the opportunity to perch on the shoulders of
their male classmates, thousands jumped repeatedly into the air, sometimes
losing their shoes, to see over the heads of those in front, as Wang Guangmei
was forced, at the outdoor struggle meeting at Qinghua University, to don
another *qipao*, a string of Ping-Pong balls around her neck in mock imitation
of the pearls she once had worn, her captors repeatedly forcing her to climb
atop a table in the center of the stage to provide the gawking audience a better
view, and Wang Guangmei just as insistently jumping off each time she was
forcibly hoisted up.

The struggle session at Qinghua was not the only one to which Wang
Guangmei was subjected. On July 18, 1967, the crowd outside the red-walled
compound of Zhongnanhai west of the Forbidden City, where China's central
leadership resides shielded ordinarily from curious crowds, had already been
camped for days. It numbered in the hundreds of thousands. Banners and
streamers fluttered from tops of tents and makeshift huts; slogans and big
character posters were plastered on every available inch of wall; cooking fires
from makeshift kitchens sent forth wafts of aromatic smoke. Balloons overhead
urged that Liu Shaoqi be driven out of Zhongnanhai, that his "new counter-
attack"—his second "self-confession"—be smashed. More than a hundred
loudspeakers blared forth revolutionary slogans and spewed forth revolutionary
speeches, demanding, among other things, that Liu Shaoqi and his wife be
brought to a struggle session to receive the judgment of the revolutionary
masses.

That evening, Liu Shaoqi and Wang Guangmei were led separately to
struggle sessions against them in two of Zhongnanhai's dining halls. Then in
his late sixties, the Chinese chief of state was forced to stand for two hours

bent forward from the waist, head bowed, prohibited from responding to the accusations hurled against him. When he took out a handkerchief to mop the sweat from his brow, the handkerchief was struck from his hand.

Two and a half weeks later, on August 5, Liu Shaoqi's family was the object of another struggle session, this time in the courtyard of their home—the children in the audience, each guarded by a soldier, mother and father together the focus of attack. A movie camera had been sent by the revolutionaries to record the historic occasion.

By the end of the struggle session, Liu Shaoqi's face was swollen and bruised. Many of the beatings had been administered with Chairman Mao's little red book of revolutionary quotations. He had lost his shoes. He could no longer stand upright. His right leg dragged limply behind him. He needed support to walk at all.

As husband and wife were being led back to captivity, Wang Guangmei stopped only a few paces from where their children were watching. She broke loose from her captors, turned and faced her husband, her hands reaching out. Husband and wife grabbed each other's hands and held on, a circle of two. Hands in each other's hands, they looked into each other's eyes, trying to straighten their bent and broken bodies. Liu Shaoqi was kicked and beaten, but still husband and wife clung to each other, hand in hand. Rudely, they were pulled apart. Wang Guangmei struggled loose from her captors again, grabbed on to her husband, and refused to let go. Only by violence were they separated.

It was their final farewell.

"I THINK it is because their lives are so boring," says Wang Hongbao, attempting to explain the seamy spectacle the Cultural Revolution became. What Wang Hongbao remembers is the curiosity, the fascination with which the spectacles were watched. "When they were the leaders, everyone was very respectful to them," he says. "But when they came under attack, everyone wanted to come and see the leaders. Not necessarily to attack them themselves but to see them being attacked. There is a strain in the Chinese national character that loves *renao*, loves excitement. It is a strain that Lu Xun has written about, a strain that has existed traditionally and that continues to exist even now. When people fight on the street, everyone comes to gather around, to stare, to watch. Or if there is an accident. Sometimes there are public executions on television, and people turn on to watch. When the trial of the Gang of Four was televised in China, everyone who had access to a television watched. Everyone.

"Most people don't find their work very interesting. At night, you can see on the street, people come out just to sit. If there is a game of chess, a small crowd will gather around. I don't find chess very interesting, but some people seem to find it interesting just to watch. At some of the small shops where you go to eat dumplings, people will wait for two hours to buy some dumplings. They just stand in line for two hours and chat with their friends and smoke and wait for the dumplings. The cook will stand there with all the people waiting and slowly, casually wrap the dumplings, pinch the skins together until there are enough to fill the steamer. Then after they are in the steamer, it takes half an hour for the dumplings to cook. After half an hour, maybe some people will buy three pounds, some five pounds, and after ten people are served, there are no more dumplings. But there are still thirty people waiting. So it takes two hours, and people just wait patiently."

Life in China without the spectacle of the Cultural Revolution would indeed have been boring. Alternative forms of entertainment were sparse. With the campaign against the "four olds" prohibiting any traditional Chinese forms of entertainment, Peking opera and other forms of local, traditional opera—time-honored sources of relaxation for workers, peasants, and intellectuals alike—were banned. The attack on bourgeois capitalism excluded anything from the West, and Western music and films, considered decadent and bourgeois, were silenced. Official revulsion against Soviet revisionism forbade imports from the former Big Brother, so Soviet ballet was no longer performed. Teahouses, where old men used to spend their days in reminiscence of times gone by, playing cards and listening to storytellers recount the legends of the past, were closed. Chess and cards were forbidden. Mahjong, noisy and boisterous, had long since been declared illegal. For entertainment, the people of China had their choice of the eight model operas sanctioned by Mao's wife, Jiang Qing, in which the heroes were perfect and the villains despicable and there were no characters in between, and which, nearly everyone agreed, were "boring." Or they could join in the carnival that was the Great Proletarian Cultural Revolution, the carnival that was entertainment indeed. The young could tour the country in the great revolutionary linkups, participating with joyous abandon in the destruction of the "four olds" and engaging in the wanton attacks against the ox ghosts and snake spirits. The adults could cheer and shout as the ox ghosts and snake spirits were herded through the streets like cattle, or visit the "living museums" in the homes of the bourgeoisie, or join the crowd come to watch and spit and jeer at the struggle sessions the public was encouraged to attend.

COUNTLESS numbers of people were incarcerated. The jails quickly filled, and office buildings, classroom buildings, and dormitories became primary places of detention. The generic name for such makeshift jails was "cattle pens," and they ranged in fact from pens that had once housed pigs to small, dank closets without furniture or light to college dormitory rooms. The appellation "cattle pen" referred more to the status accorded the prisoners—the "ox ghosts"—than to the physical space they occupied. Just as one's previous status determined whether the accused would walk or ride during the street parade, so one's previous status often had a bearing on the quality of cattle pen to which those under attack were confined. At Qincheng prison not far from Peking, near a famous hot-springs spa once frequented by the Qing dynasty's empress dowager, garden apartments were built amid groves of walnut and fruit trees to house the high-ranking prisoners of the Cultural Revolution. Some of rank were permitted to remain at home, under house arrest. After the July 18 struggle session against him, Liu Shaoqi was held, together with his family, under house arrest in Zhongnanhai. They were separated from one another—the four children in one part of the house, Liu Shaoqi in his office, and Wang Guangmei in the back courtyard—and meetings and communication among the family members were forbidden. Party leader Tao Zhu and his family were similarly held, but they at least were permitted to communicate.

In mid-September, Liu Shaoqi's wife was taken away and put in solitary confinement in Qincheng prison, where she spent the next twelve years under a suspended sentence of death. Not everyone of rank retained trappings of status. Some of the country's highest-ranking and once most privileged leaders were so ill treated that they died.

Sent to a May Seventh Cadre School to perform manual labor, gathering animal manure to be used as fertilizer, Huang Xing spent his first six months in the countryside in a pen that had earlier been home to the local pigs. Accused, when the work teams arrived on his campus, of being a counterrevolutionary, Jiang Xinren spent two months locked in a darkened room, five feet by five feet, without furniture or light. "The dormitory room you live in," said a faculty member, referring to the foreign students' residence at Peking Normal University, where the rooms were twelve feet by six with concrete floors and cinder-block walls, "was a cattle pen, a special cattle pen for relatively important people. All the rooms were cattle pens. The reason it was such a good cattle pen is its location. It is quite a distance away from any of the university gates, so if someone were to try to escape, it would have taken quite a while to get to any of the gates, and the probability is that they would have been caught. Your building is also the one from which there were the most suicides. Many people jumped from your building."

Yao Baoding spent six years in jail, in solitary confinement, and his wife spent three in one of the university's cattle pens. The rhythm of Yao Baoding's day was determined by the interrogators whose task it was to extract Yao's confession that he was a spy—four hours of interrogation in the morning, a break from noon to two for lunch and rest, and three hours more of questioning in the afternoon. Ironically, even during the Cultural Revolution, the two-hour rest break at noon remained, for many of the revolutionaries, inviolable.

Sun Heren spent thirty-five days in jail, most of them in a room twelve feet by eight, with twelve other people, most of whom were criminals in fact. There were no beds in the room, only six lice-infested blankets, one for every two people with one group of three forced to share. The prisoners slept on the floor. At one corner of the room was the bucket that served as a urinal. Prison life was boring, and Sun Heren became friendly with one of the inmates who took particular pride in his skill as a master pickpocket. Sun Heren challenged the master thief to demonstrate his skill, promising the thief one roll of steamed bread—half his daily allotment of food—if, within half a day, the thief could steal the professor's little red book of Chairman Mao's quotations without being caught. "This was really a big deal," explains Sun Heren. "There was nothing else to eat, so agreeing to give him one of my *wotou* was really a big deal. But I completely forgot and let down my guard, and he stole my little red book. But then he wouldn't take my *wotou*."

During the period of his captivity, Sun Heren came to serve as the pick-pocket's champion. The pickpocket was often beaten and kicked by the prison guards. "They beat him as a warning to us," says Sun Heren. "If we didn't behave, they would beat us, too." With great formality, Sun Heren read to the guards from Chairman Mao's little red book, choosing as his passage the "three main rules of discipline and eight points for attention." He focused particularly on point number five, which forbade hitting or swearing at people, and point number eight, which prohibited ill treatment of captives. "So they didn't dare beat him after that," says Sun Heren, "because Chairman Mao had said it." Instead, they put Sun Heren in solitary confinement.

Sun Heren did not remain long in jail, because jails, even during the Cultural Revolution, were used primarily to detain genuine criminals. Sun Heren's crimes were political rather than criminal. Upon his release, he was incarcerated for two years in a cattle pen.

Chen Quanhong, too, began his period of tribulation as a prisoner in jail. What was most humiliating to this dignified professor and avid student of Chinese history and classical literature was that he was placed in a cell with a group of common criminals and treated as though he, too, were a thief. But he benefited from his association with the local thieves. One of the robbers had managed to hide on his person a set of fingernail clippers. In return for a daily cigarette from Professor Chen, the robber nightly used the fingernail clippers to open the manacles in which Professor Chen's hands were locked behind his back. Upon his release from prison, after forty-five days in captivity, Chen Quanhong too spent several years in a cattle pen. When released, he had neither job nor income. Living in a single room with his wife and young child, Professor Chen was able to eke out only the barest existence, transporting building materials in the district where he lived. For fifty cents a day, he pulled like a beast of burden a two-wheeled cart that sometimes held more than 2,500 pounds of steel rods.

The fathers of both Song Erli and Song Wuhao spent most of the Cultural Revolution in cattle pens, and their mothers several years. Bai Meihua's father spent six years in a cattle pen, and You Xiaoli nearly one. You Xiaoli's cattle pen was a small room in an office building that she shared with five other women. As befit the animals they were deemed to be, there was no furniture in the room—only straw on which to sleep. The day began early for the accused, with all of them standing before a portrait of Chairman Mao, the red, red sun in their hearts, the man become god, to whom they daily wished a long, long, long life. Heads bowed, they asked their great leader for the day's instructions. A criticism meeting against them, led by the revolutionary rebels, followed. "Then, during the day," says You Xiaoli, "we all had to do manual labor to reform ourselves." You Xiaoli's job was to clean the toilets. Often while You Xiaoli was working the revolutionaries would come to beat her. "Because I was an ox ghost and snake spirit, anyone could come and beat me," she said. When I did manual labor, anyone, everyone could come and say that I was doing something wrong. They could come and kick me, beat me, throw stones at me while I was working."

Food during the Cultural Revolution was a matter of politics, too. Not only were their salaries reduced but the rice coupons of the ox ghosts and snake spirits were withdrawn. Rice, until recently, has been strictly rationed in China, its cost heavily subsidized by the state. The primary staple for the ox ghosts and snake spirits was *wotou*—steamed bread made from coarse and gritty grain or sweet-potato flour. For almost ten years, You Xiaoli was allowed each day only one salty, salty pickle, "the size of half my thumb," and three pieces of *wotou* made from coarse, old sweet-potato flour. "It was so old the bread was the color of chocolate," she recalls. Huang Chaoqun, tall and thin at 150 pounds, emerged from the Cultural Revolution weighing 93. It was not until the end of the Cultural Revolution that he learned that his friend Lao Wang, a fellow teacher, had died. "How did he die?" Huang Chaoqun had asked. "Did they beat him bitterly?" No, the beatings hadn't been so bad. "Was it a terrible struggle meeting?" No, not that either. He just became thinner and thinner and then he stopped breathing. That's all. He just disappeared. "The lack of food and the physical labor made us very weak," said You Xiaoli. "And of course the beatings made us even weaker."

RELEASE from prison or a cattle pen was rarely during the Cultural Revolution a return to freedom. Beginning in 1969, adults by the millions were shipped from the city to the countryside, most of them to what were euphemistically called May Seventh Cadre Schools, all of which were thinly disguised labor reform camps. Many of the May Seventh Cadre Schools were actually located on the grounds of former labor reform camps. Others were situated on barren wasteland, on which those who had come to be "reeducated" had to construct their own barracks and break land for the production of crops. In some cases, but more rarely, the "students" were actually integrated into village life, living under the same roof with the poor peasants whose task it was to reeducate the intellectuals.

One did not have to be a victim of the Cultural Revolution, labeled with one of the various epithets applied to the class enemy, to be sent to a May Seventh Cadre School. As the hysteria of the Cultural Revolution continued, it was not merely intellectuals deemed "bourgeois" for whom reeducation was considered necessary but anyone with any education at all. Whole schools and research institutes were transferred to the countryside. When the camps were not large enough to accommodate the entire force of a work unit—or when the continued functioning of a particular organization was considered vital—employees went to the countryside in shifts, spending by rotation a year or two.

Both Song Wuhao's and Bai Meihua's fathers remained incarcerated throughout most of the Cultural Revolution, but their mothers were sent to May Seventh Cadre Schools. Wang Hongbao's parents went together. Qiu Yehuang, too, spent several years at a May Seventh Cadre School, not because he was ever accused of a political crime but because he was an intellectual. Li Meirong and Huang Chaoqun consider themselves lucky for the time they spent in the countryside. Laboring as ordinary peasants was a respite from attack.

WITH so many adults either incarcerated or sent to the countryside, the problem of the unsupervised young became acute. Very young children could often be delivered into the care of an elderly relative, and some actually accompanied their mothers to the May Seventh Cadre Schools. Some children, like Bai Meihua, were lucky. With her father incarcerated and her mother working so far away that she was able to visit the children only once a week, with her home occupied by the revolutionary rebels, Bai Meihua was able to find help from an older, retired woman who lived nearby. "She had worked with my father in the past, so she knew that he was a good man," says Bai Meihua. "She herself did not come under attack during the Cultural Revolution. Her family didn't suffer, so there was no reason really for her to help me, to take the risks that she did. But she let me go to her house to eat, even during the daytime. I often ate there—breakfast, lunch, and dinner, and my whole family was welcome there." The woman is very elderly now, senile and crotchety. Bai Meihua's husband does not like her. But Bai Meihua continues to visit her once a week.

But even some of the youngest children were unable to find anyone to care for them. Historian Wu Han's daughter was ten and his son two at the beginning of the Cultural Revolution, when he and his wife were jailed. Their home was occupied by the revolutionary rebels and the children were driven out. For a while, a senior party official took the children into his own home.

Then he, too, came under attack. After that, no one, not even Wu Han's own relatives, dared to see or care for his children. On $10 a month, the two children lived alone in a run-down room on the outskirts of Peking. When they dared to go out, the Red Guards surrounded them, beat them, stoned them, and called them sons of bitches.

When her children were allowed their first visit, after Liu Shaoqi's wife, Wang Guangmei, had been imprisoned for five years, they found their mother, still in solitary confinement, emaciated and weak, dressed in an old military uniform that had been dyed prison-black. Her hair had turned white, and she was unable to straighten at the waist. Upon seeing her children, Wang Guangmei looked at them without speaking. Her face was blank and without expression. "I never dreamed you would live," she finally managed to say. Wang Guangmei was not the only mother during the Cultural Revolution who feared for the lives of her children.

Many of the "sons of bitches" found no one to care for them. Bands of children began wandering the streets, stealing for food and sleeping by night in railway stations, corridors, or huts. Song Wuhao came to such a fate. His parents were both incarcerated and his home was occupied by the revolutionary rebels. "I couldn't go home, and I didn't have any money or any food or any work," he recalls. "All I could do was wander by myself from place to place, sometimes on the streets of Peking and sometimes I would sneak on board trains. I went to Tianjin, Jinan, Nanjing, and Shanghai. I left the cities and went into the countryside. To stay alive, all I could do was drink water from the rivers and steal sweet potatoes from the peasants' fields. This lasted from January to May of 1968. During much of that time, I was cold, freezing. I sometimes thought I would die from the cold."

Young boys in particular, often the sons of high-level cadres then incarcerated and under attack, formed gangs. They were often at war, one gang against another. Wang Hongbao was on the fringes of such a gang. "They were corrupted," he says. "I mean they smoked and stole things. They were corrupted because their parents had come under attack, and they opposed the Cultural Revolution, opposed Jiang Qing, opposed Chairman Mao. They called Mao the *lao touzi*—the old man. They drank beer, fought, stole things. They chased girls in the street, listened to Western music at home, fought with each other—not just with other factions, but with other gangs."

By the end of 1967, the problem of unsupervised children became too acute to ignore, and bands of youngsters were rounded up by the thousands and placed in "study classes" which, in the level of discipline imposed and of freedom denied, bore a remarkable resemblance to prisons. "I was put in a small room and not allowed to go out," recalls Wang Hongbao. "I was confined there as though in prison. The food was terrible in the study class. Every morning a bell sounded and we had to get up, form a line, and march out to the study class like prisoners. We studied Mao Zedong together, studied Mao's thoughts in order to be reeducated. But we weren't treated as badly, really, as prisoners in a real jail." Song Wuhao, too, was repeatedly locked up, sometimes in prisons, finally in a study class. The "graduates" of such study classes were shipped summarily to the countryside.

As the children of the counterrevolutionaries struggled to find food to eat and places to sleep, as they degenerated into lawless, roving gangs, those people who had managed to stay in the ranks of the Red Guards and revolutionary rebels, active participants in the revolutionary cause, had disintegrated first into feuding, then violently warring factions. They took up guns and used them against each other. Photographs reaching Hong Kong from the neighboring province of Guangdong showed young female Red Guards carrying baskets filled with the severed noses and ears of males from the opposing faction. In June of 1967 alone, at least fifty cities witnessed major outbreaks of violence. Qian Mao, fifteen years old at the time, remembers the street fights in her home city of Chungking—the tanks, the guns, and the faces of the participants in the fighting blackened with coal dust to avoid recognition.

JIANG XINREN was one of those who used guns. Jiang Xinren may have killed.

FIVE

THE SPECTER OF DEATH: MURDER, SUICIDE, AND THE REFUSAL TO GRANT MEDICAL AID

HAUNTING the Cultural Revolution, hanging over it like a cloud, was the ever-present specter of death. Many who spent those years of tribulation in incarceration were spared from looking at death directly, but for those who managed to escape captivity, death was difficult to avoid. Bai Meihua, You Xiaoli, Jiang Xinren, Song Erli, Sun Heren, and Qiu Yehuang were firsthand witnesses to death. They remain haunted by what they saw, remembering the incidents in vivid detail, needing still to bear witness, to share that painful, jarring, grotesque detail—the splattered brains, the rope still swinging, the absence of blood, the writhing of the body, the color of the face, the swollen bodies of the drowned.

Those who did not witness death directly all knew people—relatives, friends, and colleagues—who died. Everyone lost someone during the Cultural Revolution. "Of people with whom I have shaken hands, twenty people died," one writer said, "and many more with whom I am less well acquainted." Some thirty people died at You Xiaoli's university and a similar number at Huang Chaoqun's. Song Erli, in one period alone, witnessed ten suicides at his. Jiang Xinren, twenty-one years old when the Cultural Revolution began, lost four of his close friends to factional fighting, one while they were fighting together. At the Fourth Congress of Writers and Artists, held in the fall of 1979, Yang Hansheng read the names of over a hundred writers and artists who had died during the ten years of turmoil. At Hunan Medical College, a third of the senior faculty of the department of psychiatry committed suicide. At Qilu Medical School in Shandong, formerly Christian-run, nine of the best-trained and most competent senior faculty died. At Zhongshan University, the faculty and students who had not been sent to the countryside awoke one morning to find the entire senior faculty of the history department murdered, hanging from the trees that line the university entrance. The Gang of Four alone have been shouldered with the deaths of nearly thirty-five thousand people.

At Shandong University in Jinan, they found the dead body of a student, stabbed to death, stuffed into an incinerator. Halfway between Jinan and Nanjing, in a field of sorghum, they found the bodies of more than a hundred young students, fatalities of a battle between rival Red Guard factions. The Lake Without a Name at Peking University was awash with lifeless, bloated bodies. In June 1968, thirty-five bodies washed from the Pearl River into the Hong Kong–Macao estuary. Experts at the American consulate in Hong Kong, extrapolating from the flow of the river, estimated that there were at least another thousand bodies that never made it down. They found Wang Zhi-guan's body hanging from a tree in the hills outside of Nanjing, and in Peking many went to Coal Hill, the highest spot in the city, to hang themselves there. Wen Fengliang cut his throat with a knife.

At the height of the violence in Peking, trucks patrolled the streets, picking up the dead. "They didn't want people to see too many dead bodies lying around," says Qiu Yehuang, "so they tried to pick them up as soon as possible. The crematorium was so busy they had to stack the bodies like bricks, all around outside the crematorium, waiting to be burned." Ma Jinglan's mother died during that period. The trucks that serve as transport for the dead and that generally arrive immediately upon being summoned were so busy that it was three days before the mother's remains could be taken to the crematorium at Babaoshan. Then the crematorium was so busy that Ma and her husband had to wait in line. They waited in line from early in the morning until late in the afternoon before the body of Ma Jinglan's mother was burned. Many of those waiting in line with them were parents of young Red Guards.

THEY died by murder, beating, and torture.

Wu Han, the vice-mayor of Peking and author of the play about Hai Rui that served as the excuse for launching the movement, died, we must presume, of murder, of the wounds he suffered from being beaten. He was brought one day in October 1969 from prison to a hospital, his hands in manacles behind his back, covered with blood, vomiting blood, his hair all pulled out. He died shortly thereafter.

Qiu Yehuang, like many of his countrymen, became a firsthand but silent witness to murder. As a *xiaoyaopai*, a member of the "free-floating faction," Qiu Yehuang says, "I was very lucky during the Cultural Revolution. Nothing much happened to me.

"But even though I didn't participate," he continues, "I saw many things, heard many things, learned many things."

One of the things Qiu Yehuang saw during the Cultural Revolution was the murder, on a bus, of a capitalist. The lives of capitalists were cheap during that time. "Once I was riding on a bus in Peking," he says. "All of a sudden I heard people yelling, 'Capitalist, capitalist,' and I saw a man being beaten. He was very frightened and didn't know what to do. He was an older man, and they just kept beating him. No one did anything to stop the beating. No one would do anything to stop that, because if you tried to help, you could be called a capitalist and be beaten too. They beat this man until he died, and then they just threw him off the bus onto the ground. It was awful, but I couldn't do anything."

Often, because of what he saw and heard and learned, Qiu Yehuang could not sleep at night. When he did, he had a recurring dream. He dreamed he was on a magic carpet, escaping to peace. "Sometimes I would dream that I was on a magic carpet, floating over Europe—over Italy, Germany, France. Those countries looked so green, so fresh, so clean. So peaceful. The sky was so blue. The magic carpet would swoop down, getting ready to land in one of those countries. But just as it would get ready to land, it would swoop up again into the clouds, and I would float over another country, swoop down, and swoop up, over and over again. I would be so close, but the magic carpet would never let me off. And always I woke up in China. In the middle of the Cultural Revolution."

Wang Shuchang witnessed an incident on a train similar to the one Qiu Yehuang saw on a bus. "In the fall of 1966," he recalls, "I was on a train on a revolutionary linkup, and I saw some other Red Guards accuse an old lady. She was very old and very frail. The Red Guards accused her of being a capitalist. Then they started beating her. They beat her to death. At the next train stop, they just put her body on the platform and told someone at the station that she was a capitalist. Then they got back on the train to continue their revolutionary linkup." Wang Shuchang had been an excited Red Guard until then, but he withdrew from politics after what he saw on the train.

"I can sort of understand how it happened," says Yao Baoding. Yao Baoding is speaking slowly, matter-of-factly, puffing on a cigarette. "The landlords were the enemies then. They weren't people really. You could use violence against them. It was acceptable. There is a young man here on campus who was just a student at the time of the Cultural Revolution. He participated in the beating of a landlord—the beating of a landlord to death. He is only one of many such young people. I don't really think he knew what he was doing. They didn't know he would die. But I have often wondered how he feels now."

Bai Meihua's uncle was murdered during the Cultural Revolution. He was an officer in the People's Liberation Army and the only relative of the Bai family who, during the period of their disgrace, continued to maintain contact. He came to visit every Sunday.

Then one Sunday he failed to come. "My mother was worried," recalls Bai Meihua. "High-ranking military cadres were having a relatively easy time during the Cultural Revolution, but still, my mother was worried, so she asked me to go to his house to find out what had happened. He lived a long distance away, in the Peking Military District, so it took me a long time by bus to get there.

"My uncle wasn't there. Only my aunt. She just said, 'On Wednesday your uncle was taken away and put into prison.' So I returned home to tell my mother.

"My mother was very worried, and since my father was in jail and we weren't allowed to communicate with him there was no way to tell him what had happened. My uncle was very tall, very strong, in very good health. But just two weeks after he had been put into prison, my aunt received a phone call saying that my uncle had become seriously ill, had been hospitalized, and had died. We were so surprised that he should become so ill so quickly and die. He had never been ill before. He had been in such good health. It was just so hard to believe. They said they wanted us to come to see him. We agreed. We asked for permission from the military unit to examine the body.

"He was in the 301 Hospital, the best military hospital in Peking, and my aunt, my mother, my little sister, and I all went together to see the body. But when we arrived, the army soldiers stopped us. They said we couldn't all go in, that only one person could go in to see the body. My aunt was very upset, and my mother was afraid she was about to faint, so she, my mother, was the one to go in. She was in the room for less than a minute before they asked her to leave. They had cleaned his body and put on a clean new uniform with a cap with a star on it and the military insignia. He was my father's favorite brother.

"When my mother came from the room, she simply said, 'Your uncle has really died. I saw his body. But I do not believe that he died of illness.' At that time she was afraid to say what was really in her heart, afraid to say that he had been beaten to death."

In 1975, eight years after his death, an investigation was made and the truth of the death of Bai Meihua's uncle was revealed. "My uncle had been beaten to death with steel bars," Bai Meihua says. "He was beaten to death by soldiers.

He was first beaten black and blue. Then his kidneys were hit and he got blood in the kidneys. He died from blood in his kidneys."

THERE are rumors of atrocities from China, of bloodcurdling, hair-raising atrocities, of castrations and crucifixions. Qiu Yehuang insists that he has heard that at a major research institute in Peking, the bodies of a scientist and his wife who had committed suicide were chopped by the revolutionaries into pieces, the ligaments of the couple put on public display as a demonstration that they were counterrevolutionary down to their very bones. Qiu Yehuang believes the story is true. But again it is from Tibet that stories of the most gruesome atrocities come—stories of mutilations and dismemberments, of severed genitals and gouged-out eyes. It was in Tibet that crucifixions occurred, in Tibet that boiling water was poured on victims in an effort to extract confessions. Chinese women remain reluctant to talk about the rapes of the Cultural Revolution, but sexual mores disintegrated during that time and rape of female victims was common. In Tibet, not only was rape common but monks were forced to copulate publicly with nuns. Near the Tibetan border with Nepal, monks were forced to stand on pedestals and read Mao's little red book aloud for three consecutive days. Those who refused were shot, their corpses dragged through the street as people were forced to spit and throw dirt on them. The bodies of the dead were publicly displayed as a warning of the inevitable end of all reactionaries.

Many deaths attributed during the Cultural Revolution to illness or suicide were in fact murder. In some cases, when attempts at suicide were at first not successful, the revolutionaries ensured they became so. In the courtyard in front of Yang De's home, a neighbor accused of being counterrevolutinary publicly cut his throat. He was bleeding to death, breathing from the incision in his neck, when discovered by the neighborhood Red Guards. A young revolutionary held a handkerchief over the man's throat, preventing him from breathing. He smothered to death. Yang De believes that with medical treatment he could have been saved. Many suicides were engineered. Sometimes the accused would be kept awake, under the glare of lights, for several days, constantly interrogated by rotating teams. The accused—disoriented, confused, weak, and teetering as he walked—would then be taken to the roof of a building and led to the edge. If, in his disorientation and confusion, the accused fell to his death, the death was reported as suicide. So were deaths where the fall had been preceded by a push.

You Xiaoli was encouraged to commit suicide during the Cultural Revolution. One of the tasks she was asked to perform during her period of captivity was window-washing—standing on a narrow ledge three stories high washing windows from the outside without anything to hold onto. When she tried to attach herself to the window frame by a belt, she was criticized. One night, on the second floor of a classroom building, there was a struggle session against her held to accuse her of being a spy and a capitalist roader and a counterrevolutionary academic authority. You Xiaoli was beaten during the meeting, and when it was over, as she was being allowed to leave, someone kicked her from behind just as she reached the top of the stairs. She tumbled down the flight of stairs and in a state of semiconsciousness was pulled into the darkness outside. People she could not see began jumping on her back, and You Xiaoli lost consciousness. When she woke, a rope, already tied with a noose at one end, was lying beside her. At night, in the crowded cattle pen that You Xiaoli shared with several other women, sometimes people would come in as they lay sleeping on the floor and jump up and down on the "ox ghosts and snake spirits." One morning You Xiaoli woke up in her cattle pen to find that a bottle of sleeping pills had been placed beside her.

"I knew they wanted me to commit suicide," You Xiaoli says, "so when I got to see my son the next time—he was only seven years old then—I told him that if he ever heard that his mother had committed suicide, he should not believe them. I would never commit suicide. It would be murder if I were to die. If I had committed suicide, my son would always be considered the child of a reactionary, which is very bad for children. He would never have been able to get a good job."

So often were murders during the Cultural Revolution officially registered as suicide that some are still not persuaded that the real cause of death has ever been revealed. "Often when I hear that people committed suicide, I don't believe it," You Xiaoli says. You Xiaoli still remembers when she and other ox ghosts and snake spirits were marched quickly past the body of Huang Jiaoshou as an ostensible warning to them against the suicide Huang Jiaoshou was alleged to have committed. But the twine around Huang's neck was no thicker than a shoestring and he was hanging not from the ceiling but a doorknob. You Xiaoli thinks he was murdered.

"I think perhaps Lao She is like that, too," she says. "They say he committed suicide by drowning. But it was just a mud puddle with only very little water. I think perhaps someone pushed him."

Lao She is the most famous case of a possible murder officially recorded for history as suicide. A novelist best known in the West as author of *Rickshaw Boy*, Lao She was educated in England and was in the United States at the time of Liberation in 1949. When Zhou Enlai encouraged Lao She to return to China, he did. Lao She was sixty-seven years old when the Cultural Revolution began and in failing health. He came under attack immediately, suffering humiliation, abuse, and beatings at the hands of the young Red Guards. Officially, it is said that Lao She was persecuted to death by Lin Biao, the Gang of Four, and their counterrevolutionary line. But the actual cause of his death is nonetheless attributed to suicide by drowning. It is said that when under attack, accused of being antiparty and antisocialist, Lao She responded by protesting, "No! I love the party! I love Chairman Mao! I love socialism! I love!" It is said that his last words were "I believe Chairman Mao and Premier Zhou understand me. The people understand me." It is said that Lao She was studying Chairman Mao to the end, that he had copied Chairman Mao's poems by hand and bound them together in a book, that the book of Chairman Mao's poems was floating beside him in the pond.

"But everyone knows he was murdered," says Huang Chaoqun. "Everyone. That morning, my friend went for a walk to the lake. He always takes a walk very, very early in the morning. He saw Lao She. The water was so shallow. He was lying at the edge of the pond, his face down, his body out of the water. I believe he was killed and thrown into the water. They just put his mouth and nose into that little bit of water. Do you think people could commit suicide that way?"

Lao She's wife has said that her husband disappeared one day on the way to his office. Four days went by without a sign. At one o'clock on the fourth night, she received a telephone call from a stranger telling her to come to a pond outside the west gate. When she got there, she could see nobody. She walked around the pond and came upon his body, covered by a mattress. There was no water in his lungs, and his shoes were dry.

BUT people did die by their own hands during the Cultural Revolution. The suicide rate increased dramatically. People jumped from buildings and drank insecticide. They hanged themselves from the exposed radiator pipes that run along the ceilings in northern China or tied ropes to the branches of trees. They drowned themselves in rivers, lakes, and ponds. They lay across the tracks in front of oncoming trains or threw themselves in front of cars. They electrocuted themselves.

To commit suicide during the Cultural Revolution was officially regarded as a betrayal of the revolution, of which the suicide itself constituted proof. "To commit suicide," wrote former first party secretary of Guangdong province Tao Zhu during his period of captivity, a period when the struggle sessions against him were frequent, "means that the person has something to hide and doesn't want to have his problems cleared up." The stigma of having betrayed the revolution was passed on to the descendants and relatives of the suicide victim himself. Many refrained from suicide during the Cultural Revolution not because they wanted to live but in order not to bring shame to their families. "I never thought of giving up during the Cultural Revolution," Li Meirong asserts. "Never. Not once. I thought of my children. Things were bad for my children during that period. Very bad. But they would have been worse had I given up, had I died, had I committed suicide. I would never have done that to my children. I had to stay alive, to keep going, for them."

So often was the adage of suicide as betrayal repeated that even those who had confronted the question of suicide themselves only to decide against it retain the lingering belief that some of those who took their own lives did so as an admission of guilt. Huang Chaoqun is one of those who retains the nagging, troubling thought that one of his good friends who committed suicide during the Cultural Revolution, a man Huang Chaoqun knows to have been innocent of the crimes of which he was accused, may have been guilty in fact.

Indeed, some during the Cultural Revolution may have committed suicide out of guilt. But this was not the reason most people took their own lives.

Some killed themselves in anger, out of protest over the humiliation to which they had so unfairly and unjustly been subjected. "An intellectual may be killed," an old saying went, "but he cannot be insulted." Some, though they were rare, preferred death to the insults they had received.

Some killed themselves in fear, as the only means of escape. To become a victim of the Cultural Revolution was a terrifying experience, and death by one's own hand appeared to some as the only acceptable route.

But most killed themselves out of despair, in the hopelessness born of depression. "People committed suicide because they were not optimistic enough," You Xiaoli tried to explain. "There was no bright future." Indeed, many who adjusted to the Cultural Revolution did so in the belief that it could not last, that someday it would have to end. Many of those who committed suicide could see no end.

Qiu Yehuang was a witness not just to murder but to suicides, too. "Once, I like to swim," he says, "and I decided to go swimming. It was in August of 1966. Usually I went to a particular lake to go swimming, but this time, I don't know why, I decided to go to another one. It was usually very crowded at this time of year, and as I was riding my bicycle from my home to the lake, I was wondering if it would be crowded. But as I approached the lake on my bicycle, it was very quiet and still, and I didn't know why. Then I understood. There by the side of the lake were three dead bodies. Suicides. They had killed themselves by jumping in the lake. Someone had pulled them out and they were waiting for the truck to come to take the bodies away. I couldn't tell you what those people looked like. It was awful, just terrible to see.

"I kept riding my bicycle to see my brother. I was very shaken. I told him what I had seen. He said that this was normal. He said that on that very day, at his university, seven people had killed themselves by jumping from buildings. Seven people. In just one day."

"Suicides?" Song Erli said. "I have many suicide stories. I could talk about suicides for hours on end." And he did.

"As a young man, I experienced many suicides," he continued. "During those years people took their lives so easily. I still recall so vividly her face— the face of a young girl who committed suicide—her face when she was wriggling on the ground with her eyes half opened and a drop of blood on her mouth. It was quite calm, her face."

It was a life taken out of terror, as a means of escape, that Song Erli describes.

"There was a group at the school who were under a lot of pressure for having opposed the army," he says, "and they were trying to shift the blame to others by putting up big character posters on the door of the dormitory where she lived. It said all sorts of things—'You female ox ghost and snake spirit, you betrayer of our country, you who lost the face of our great nation, you must confess in three days or otherwise revolutionary action will be taken.' Lots of people got such ultimatums. But this was the first for her, and she jumped out of the window just a few minutes after those boys left. I rushed to the spot just one or two minutes after she leaped. I saw her wriggling on the ground with one leg just broken. No blood. Just one or two drops out of her mouth. She died a half-hour later in the hospital. The doctor said her heart had been shaken out of position.

"There were three upsurges of suicides, from different sections of the population," Song Erli tries to explain. "First, at the very beginning, in 1966 and 1967, there were those who were very important people. Like Lao She." Song Erli apparently has not heard that Lao She may have been murdered. "And Jian Bocan, the historian; Fu Lei, the translator. And some top-ranking cadres, like Yan Hongyan. Quite famous cases."

Jian Bocan, more so even than Wu Han, was one of China's most famous and widely respected historians, the chairman of the Department of History at Peking University. Like Wu Han, he believed the past held lessons for the present. Like Wu Han, Jian Bocan came under attack in 1965 for his "historicism," and even Mao Zedong himself singled Jian Bocan out for comment, saying that intellectuals like Wu Han and Jian Bocan were "going from bad to worse."

Jian Bocan was also, however, rehabilitated far earlier than others.

It was in 1968, on the evening of the very day that he was rehabilitated, his name publicly and officially cleared, that Jian Bocan and his wife bathed and dressed in their finest clothes, drank a bottle of poison, and lay down on their bed together to die. It was a suicide of protest, an act of defiance against the insults to which they had been subjected.

It was not uncommon for people to delay suicide until they had been rehabilitated. Some waited out the Cultural Revolution in disgrace, until their name was finally cleared, only to commit suicide in protest when word of their rehabilitation was finally made official. When Lao Pan, declared a rightist in 1957, heard that he was about to be cleared, after more than twenty years in disgrace, he told his family, "Now, at last I can die." The family organized a two-week vigil, calling in relatives from distant cities, to persuade him not to take his own life, trying to convince him that after twenty years of suffering he had to live another twenty years in happiness. They persuaded him to live.

Fu Lei, the erudite Chinese translator of Balzac, was a Renaissance man, flamboyantly conversant with music, literature, and art. He had been declared a rightist in 1957, and his son, Fu Cong, while studying piano in Eastern Europe, had defected to Great Britain. The dual suicide of Fu Lei and his wife, in September 1968, must also be seen as a suicide of defiance, an act of protest.

So must the suicide of Yan Hongyan.

Yan Hongyan, the first party secretary in Yunnan province, was probably the highest-ranking political figure to commit suicide during the early stages of the Cultural Revolution. When the building housing the offices of the provincial party committee was surrounded by Red Guards demanding that Yan Hongyan come out in person to answer their charges, an angry Secretary Yan called Premier Zhou Enlai to protest his innocence and express his displeasure at the demands that he answer to the young. Zhou Enlai assured the provincial secretary that there was nothing to fear from the young warriors. Yan Hongyan hung up the receiver, picked up a gun, and shot himself in the head.

"THE second wave of suicides," continues Song Erli, "was from 1968 through 1970, during the first 'clearing of the class ranks' movement."

In mid-1967, when the army had moved to reestablish order in China, many of the young rebels had opposed attempts by the military to assert control. The factionalism that had long divided the young took new form as the rebels split into "oppose the military" and "support the military" factions. The military were ruthless, however, moving onto university campuses not just to establish order but to persecute the young who had opposed them, a persecution carried out in the name of "clearing" or "purifying" the "class ranks." It was during this period that Song Erli personally witnessed ten suicides on his campus. "I saw the most suicides then," says Song Erli, "because then the students suffered. Early in the Cultural Revolution, only the professors suffered. Now students and young teachers suffered."

Song Erli describes the suicide of a young teacher—a man with the temperament of a poet, a man who found politics boring. "There was a young teacher who was somewhat active during the Cultural Revolution as a revolutionary rebel. He had defended the army in 1967, so he was appointed part of the revolutionary committee in his department. He was a party member. In fact, even before the Cultural Revolution he had been on the party committee in his department. Anyway, he was quite trusted. During the Cultural Revolution, he became eminent. There was nothing wrong with him. But there were lots of factional disputes in his department, so members of other factions were jealous of his appointment. They said that during the most critical months, when there were discussions about whether to defend the army, he had wavered. Some members in the department were jealous, so they put up an ultimatum saying, 'You aren't worthy of being a member of the revolutionary committee because you wavered at a critical moment. So we are having a meeting today at two o'clock. You have to be responsible for your actions, you have to come to answer our questions.'

"At two o'clock, he failed to come. They waited for half an hour. Then they went to his home to find him. But they couldn't find him in his dormitory. He was a good young teacher, so he had a small apartment to himself, with a closet behind the door, and as they left, someone opened the door casually and found him hanging there. Word spread, and we all went to see. I went and saw him. But his tongue wasn't hanging out. I've heard that when you hang yourself, your tongue comes out. But not him. His face was a little purple, but it looked calm.

"We all read his diary to criticize him for betraying the revolution. I read it and found a psychological reason for his committing suicide. He was getting tired of politics. He thought everything was so dull. He had the temperament of a poet. He found even the most exciting factional fight boring. The forced invitation to answer questions at the meeting was just the last straw. He shouldn't have taken it so seriously. The demand came from people who were in the same organization. They had all fought in the same ditch. They wouldn't have done anything serious to him. We were surprised at his response. But at that time suicide was in the air. People had no patience with their lives.

"Then," continues Song Erli, "came the third upsurge of suicides—during the second purging of the class ranks, the 'movement to ferret out the May Sixteenth elements.' I personally think the third wave was the most serious. But maybe the second one, in 1968–70, was bigger."

Song Erli was one of those revolutionary rebels who had opposed the military in 1967. For his opposition, he had spent two and a half years, from the spring of 1968 to December 1970, on a military farm, writing and rewriting and rewriting again his confession—painstaking descriptions of how he had come to oppose the military and what forms his opposition had taken. At the end of 1970, Song Erli and most of his comrades on the military farm were sent back to their university, imprisoned in a "study class," for the "movement to ferret out the May Sixteenth elements." Song Erli was one of those accused of being a May Sixteenth element.

The original movement against the "May Sixteenth elements" can be traced to 1967. May Sixteenth elements (May 16, 1966 was the day the Central Committee issued the circular that launched the Cultural Revolution), were said to be ultraleftists, and at the time of the original accusations against them, they were said to have opposed Premier Zhou Enlai—both to have put up big character posters denouncing the premier and to have established a clandestine organization against him. Today there is a strong doubt that there ever was a May Sixteenth organization, and most Chinese believe that if the group did exist, its members numbered fewer than a hundred people in Peking. Yet in 1970 and 1971, in the second movement to ferret out the May Sixteenth elements, hundreds of thousands of people were accused of belonging to the clandestine group. Tens of thousands so confessed. Conducted by the worker-peasant-soldier propaganda teams which had taken over the universities in 1969–70, many of their members barely literate and completely unacquainted with conditions in the universities, the movement was mired in ignorance, hypocrisy, and lies. "The members of the worker-peasant-soldier propaganda team were young soldiers from the People's Liberation Army," remembers Qiu Yehuang. "They were very young, from the countryside, ignorant. All they knew was that Chairman Mao was the great, glorious, and correct leader of the Chinese Communist Party."

What was new about the movement to ferret out the May Sixteenth elements was that the accused—incarcerated, interrogated, and tortured—were asked to supply the names of others who were also members of May Sixteenth. As thousands succumbed to torture, they began supplying fabricated lists of others in the secret movement, and the numbers of those falsely accused consequently mushroomed. Those who feared that they themselves might be attacked, or those with grudges to settle, often accused people they knew to be innocent. Many falsely accused committed suicide.

Yang Jiang's son-in-law, Deyi, was falsely accused of being a member of the May Sixteenth elements. Repeatedly he was "struggled against" in an effort to force him to supply the worker-peasant-soldier propaganda team with a list of other members. Rather than fabricate a list, he committed suicide—as a means of escape. "My son-in-law had been the first to admit that he was somewhat of a 'right-leaner,'" writes Yang Jiang, "but he simply could not abide that bunch of ultra-leftists. When the campaign to root out the 'May Sixteenth' elements began at the university, several ultra-leftists who were suspected of having 'May Sixteenth' tendencies got together to accuse Deyi of being their 'organizer,' saying that the 'May Sixteenth' roster was in his possession. As he was leaving me for what turned out to be the last time, he said: 'Mama, I can't have a bad attitude toward the masses, nor can I talk back to the Propaganda Team, but that doesn't mean that I'm prepared to fabricate a roster and get other people in trouble. I'm not about to start lying!'"

When Deyi returned to his university, he was placed in detention. He was struggled against three times a day, in an effort to force him to produce a list of other May Sixteenth elements. It was then that Deyi took his own life.

"He hanged himself from a radiator pipe," reports one of Deyi's university colleagues. "In the history building—a small room, one that wasn't used often, a classroom. He put a rope around his neck. The news traveled quickly that he was dead, but everyone was afraid to cut him down. First, all sides had to make certain that he really had committed suicide, that he had not been murdered. He was one of the first, maybe the very first, person to commit suicide at my university during that period. The worker propaganda teams were there controlling the university then, and the faction that I belonged to resented their presence. We were afraid they wanted people to die, whether by murder or suicide. I was part of the team that was to go to investigate his death. We went to the room. The door was closed, but there was a small glass window in the door. We looked through it and could see him there. The rope was still swinging."

"There was a girl in my study class who committed suicide during that time by hanging out the window," Song Erli recalls. "Someone had said she was a May Sixteenth element. So she tied her sheet to something on the window and tied the sheet around her neck and jumped out of the window to strangle herself. After such a death, they had a meeting to accuse her of the betrayal of committing suicide. People had to go on stage to say, 'She introduced me to the May Sixteenth on such-and-such a day.' It was shameful.

"And then there was the young man who served as a guard while I was locked up in the study class." Song Erli describes a suicide born of depression and despair. "He was a very intelligent young man who refused to take part in political movements. He was fond of studying mathematics and was the best student of mathematics in my entire school, a top student. Since he was so reluctant to take an active part in political movements, he became a guard. But the whole time he was supposed to be a guard, he just sat at a desk and worked on his mathematics, writing formulas and studying. He took sympathy on the people he was guarding and let them have an easy time. He let them go to bed earlier than the appointed time, which was one o'clock in the morning. We all had to get up at six o'clock in the morning, and one of the problems with the movement, one of the reasons so many people confessed, was that they were allowed so little sleep.

"One day an army officer suddenly broke into the door of the room where one of my friends was being kept and the mathematician was guarding him. He asked the boy, 'You there studying your mathematics, do you know who you are supposed to be guarding?' 'Of course, he is Wang,' the boy answered. He was trying to evade the question. The army officer smacked his hand against the table and said, 'Damn you, he's the class enemy. By taking such an attitude toward the movement, you are destroying the movement.' But the boy stood up to quarrel. He wasn't afraid.

"When I was escorted to the dining hall for lunch that day I saw lots of big character posters saying that the guard's attitude toward the revolution should be criticized. Otherwise the revolution couldn't be carried out. They confiscated all his belongings, including his several volumes of diary, and in his diaries they found enough to incriminate him as a counterrevolutionary.

"In the big character posters against him, the guard was taken as an example to persuade others to be active. He had never taken a part in the revolution, never taken a single action. Action was too much for him. Finally, the leading group decided to stop the criticisms of him, to shift back to the class enemy. But by that time, he had already gone somewhat insane. He just sat there with his notebook and his mathematics book all day. But he didn't really read or calculate formulas. He just looked at his notebook without moving. He was so seriously ill that he asked for permission to return to his family in Suzhou. The leaders of the movement knew it was dangerous to continue to make an example of him anymore, but the army officers couldn't let anyone leave. They thought that if anyone left, the movement couldn't go on. He was really dangerously ill, but still they wouldn't let him return to Suzhou. One day at six o'clock in the morning, he jumped out of a third-story window. He wasn't discovered immediately because it was too early in the morning. When he was discovered, he was sitting on the ground, vomiting blood. But people wouldn't help him because he was a dubious person. By the time the ambulance came, he was already lying on the ground. Then he died, whether in the ambulance on the way to the hospital or right after he got to the hospital, I'm not sure. But just as he was dying, or just after he had died, his father came, because he had written a letter to his father. So people said that if his father had arrived a little earlier, he wouldn't have died. His father asked for compensation for the death of his son, but the army officer said no, that he had committed suicide, that the cause of his death had not been illness. But the father said no, his son was mentally ill. Then it was discovered in his diary that he had said that he was going to die but that it wasn't the fault of anyone else. So he was considered a man who had betrayed the revolution by committing suicide.

"So that ended the life of a brilliant young man, such a good mathematician, a man who had been so good to so many students during their time of difficulty. Now most people have forgotten him. I saw some of my classmates recently, and they had almost forgotten him."

Even after the Cultural Revolution had progressed from tumultuous upheaval to routinized oppression, suicides still occurred. Born usually of hopelessness and despair, such suicides were often the end result of a long period of depression. Historian Wu Han's daughter, Wu Xiaoyan, who had been only ten years old in 1966 when both her parents were imprisoned and she was forced to assume responsibility for her two-year-old brother, did not commit suicide until 1975. It was sometime in 1974, after she had buried the ashes of her mother, that Wu Han's daughter is said to have gone mad. She was first put in prison and then in a mental hospital and then sent home. In the winter of 1975, she killed herself by drinking poison.

THEY died during the Cultural Revolution not only from murder and suicide but, unnecessarily, from illness—from the refusal to grant medical aid to the so-called counterrevolutionaries, because the counterrevolutionaries could not afford to see doctors, even—in some cases—because doctors did deliberate harm to their patients. Doctors during the Cultural Revolution were frequently singled out as counterrevolutionaries themselves, reduced to the status of orderlies, changing bedpans, cleaning toilets, and mopping floors. In one hospital in Guangdong province, one of the medical unit's Red Guard factions surrounded the hospital, patients and staff still inside, and burned it to the ground. Patients in some psychiatric hospitals were said to have been electrocuted because the nurses and orderlies did not know how to apply electric shock therapy. Nurses and orderlies often assumed the functions of doctors. Those labeled enemies of the people were often denied admission to hospitals controlled by the rebels. Some, when they were admitted, nonetheless became the object of struggle sessions as they lay ill in their beds. Doctors in adversity proved human, too. They participated in the cover-ups when the revolutionaries dictated that murders be labeled suicide or illness. They participated in struggle sessions against "counterrevolutionary" patients.

When doctors were called to treat Liu Shaoqi, his sickroom copiously decorated with big character posters denouncing him, the doctors and nurses combined their ministrations with loud denunciations of China's Khrushchev, beating him with their stethoscopes. Injections were administered with intent to cause pain.

Wu Han's seriously ill wife was sent back to Peking from a labor reform camp but could not get medical treatment. Her children took her to the hospital, but when her identity was revealed, no doctor would minister to her needs. They refused even to give her food. Wu Han's wife died there, in the hospital, with her children still trying to find someone to help.

When Li Weiguo found his roommate, accused during the Cultural Revolution of being a counterrevolutionary, unconscious from a self-administered overdose of drugs, he had to obtain special permission before getting the young man admitted to the hospital.

You Xiaoli, despite the broken back and numerous other internal injuries she suffered during the Cultural Revolution, never received medical care.

Huang Chaoqun, too, was beaten during the Cultural Revolution and suffered from internal bleeding. Both politics and finances prevented him from receiving care.

But when victims of the Cultural Revolution were seriously, persistently ill, when their lives were imminently in danger, the problem was less the inaccessibility of medical care than a delay in receiving it. The disease which most frequently proved fatal was cancer. What is more, most Chinese believe that the Cultural Revolution and death by cancer are linked. The mind-body dichotomy that has dominated Western conceptions of illness is alien to most Chinese. "We believe in China that one's emotional state and one's physical health are interrelated," explains Zhao Wenhao, whose mother died of cancer during the Cultural Revolution. His mother, like Zhao Wenhao himself, had been attacked, becoming anxious and depressed. "We say that disease can be caused by seven types of emotions—by too much joy or anger, by worry or too much inner contemplation, by sadness, fear, or shock. So I believe that it was my mother's emotional state, her fear, her anxiety, her worry, that led to her death." Song Erli's mother died of cancer, too. "I believe my mother died of cancer because she suffered so much spiritually," he says.

Many Chinese doctors, though their interpretation is more sophisticated than simple cause and effect, share that view. Said one, "Anxiety can be considered one of the factors leading to cancer. If a person already has the factors that produce cancer but that patient is psychologically healthy, then that could prevent the cancer. If not, this can quicken the onset and development of the cancer."

Writer Ba Jin's wife, Xiao Shan, died of cancer during the Cultural Revolution. Thirteen years her senior, Ba Jin was one of China's greatest living novelists, author of the famous and largely autobiographical *The Family*—the story of a large and wealthy Chinese family facing the turbulent era of China in the 1920s, the disintegration, decay, and corruption of the old order, the seeds of the revolutionary new.

Ba Jin came under attack shortly after the Cultural Revolution began, in August 1966, and with him, his wife—the "stinking wife" of a capitalist. Plumbing is rare in the homes of Shanghai, where Ba Jin and his wife resided. Instead of toilets, or the public privies of Peking, people use wooden buckets. Every morning early a wagon comes through the streets and the contents of the buckets are emptied into a large, cylindrical metal container to be taken to the countryside. The relationship between countryside and city in this part of China is intimate. As early as the tenth century, the area around Shanghai began producing new forms of rice that permitted double- and even triple-cropping, requiring applications of large amounts of fertilizer and leading in turn to an enormous biological revolution and the establishment of gigantic cities. The countryside then and now could not produce the food necessary to feed the cities without being supplied in turn with the tons of night soil the metropolis daily yields. When the Cultural Revolution began, Ba Jin and Xiao Shan were locked together in their *matong jian*, the room that held their bucket. Their home was searched repeatedly, then turned into a public exhibit, and Ba Jin was on call day and night as a "living example" to be displayed before the revolutionary masses. Xiao Shan, wearing around her neck a placard identifying her as an "ox ghost," was assigned the task of sweeping the streets in the area around their home, an area covered by big character posters attacking her husband, his "stinking wife," and their "sons of bitches" children. So humiliated was she by her duties and by the placard that damned her that Xiao Shan tried to complete her chores early, before the night soil was collected and the rest of the city had wakened. Often, when there were struggle sessions against Ba Jin, his wife was forced to accompany him, again wearing a placard that identified her as "ox ghost and snake spirit Xiao Shan." Once when young Red Guards from Peking broke into their home late at night, Xiao Shan fled to the local police station to implore the guardians of public security to protect them and their home. The police did not come. When Xiao Shan returned home, the Red Guards beat her with a brass-buckled belt. "The blue mark on her left eye remained for several days," says Ba Jin.

Xiao Shan's health deteriorated. "I saw her becoming thinner and sadder every day," says Ba Jin. "I saw the fire of life in her gradually going out."

Xiao Shan was no longer able to sweep the streets. But she was unable to get medical care. "She was sick, but she couldn't get medical treatment," says Ba Jin. "That was also because she was my wife. We tried everything we could until three weeks before she died we sent her to the hospital through the back door. But the cancer cells had spread, and the cancer of the intestines had become the cancer of the liver."

When Xiao Shan was finally admitted to the hospital, Ba Jin had been forcibly separated from her, sent to work in a May Seventh Cadre School. He was refused leave to be by her side. It was only because he was ordered to be the object of a struggle session in the city that he was able finally to be near her during those last few days.

When Xiao Shan died, not a single one of her friends came to the private ceremony in Long Hua Cemetery where Ba Jin and his children said their final goodbyes, "because first," says Ba Jin, "we didn't inform them and second because I was a person who had been under investigation for nearly seven years. There was no memorial speech. There were no guests who came to pay their tribute. There was only the sorrowful weeping. I felt grateful to those relatives who came to take part in the ceremony and to a few of my daughter's classmates who volunteered to come and help."

At the crematorium, before her body was burned, Ba Jin had one last picture taken of him together with his wife. "The image it will leave will not be a very good one to look at," he says, "but I will treasure this last picture.

"So everything ended."

TAO ZHU, once the first party secretary for Guangdong province and then the first party secretary for all of central south China, also died of cancer during the Cultural Revolution. He, too, was denied medical care until it was too late. It was Zhou Enlai who finally ordered medical treatment and who gave permission for the belated operation that diagnosed the former provincial leader's condition. Tao Zhu, when the Cultural Revolution began, was promoted to the directorship of the Propaganda Department of the Party Central Committee and was one of China's few key leaders. But he quickly came under attack. His operation took place in April 1969.

Six months later, in mid-October, when Tao Zhu was on the verge of death, he was ordered evacuated immediately from Peking to Hefei, Anhui province. It was Lin Biao's "Number One Order" that compelled the evacuation. In October 1969, Lin Biao was still Chairman Mao's closest comrade-in-arms and claimed to be afraid of an imminent Soviet invasion. As most of the residents left in Peking were "digging tunnels deep," spending their days building subterranean air-raid shelters that crisscrossed the city like a net and moving whole work units underground, some of the most famous of China's disgraced and incarcerated officialdom were being surreptitiously relocated.

Tao Zhu's wife was offered a choice. If she accompanied her dying husband to Hefei, she would be forced permanently to sever all contact with her daughter. No one beyond husband and wife was ever to know where Tao Zhu had been sent. If Mrs. Tao chose to maintain contact with her daughter, she was to be allowed no more contact with her husband. Mrs. Tao and her husband consulted. The decision was Tao Zhu's. "I can't live long," he had said. "You can't help me much, even if you go with me. You'd better try to be with Liang Liang." Mrs. Tao stayed with their daughter.

Mother and daughter were sent to live in a dark, dank, insect-infested hut in the countryside of Guangdong, the province in the southern part of China bordering Hong Kong where Tao Zhu had gone in the early 1950s and where he had spent most of his post-Liberation political career. His deputy during the time Tao Zhu spent in Guangdong, the man who replaced him as provincial first party secretary, was Zhao Ziyang. Zhao, too, was purged during the Cultural Revolution. But at its conclusion, he was made the first party secretary of Sichuan province, the rice bowl of China. The reforms he introduced there, based in many ways on the successful reforms he and Tao Zhu had introduced into Guangdong after the "three bad years," became in the late 1970s the model for all of China to emulate, the basis for China's celebrated agricultural reforms. In 1980, Zhao Ziyang became premier of the People's Republic of China, assuming the position once occupied by Zhou Enlai.

Tao Zhu died in Hefei on November 30, 1969, forty-three days after he arrived. His family has never received his ashes.

WHEN Li Laoshi's father knew that the end was not far away, he first refused food and then stopped drinking liquid. He wanted his system clear when he finally breathed his last. He asked to be bathed and dressed in the suit that he long before had chosen for the occasion. Then he was moved from his bedroom to the tiny living room of their Peking apartment. He positioned himself, legs together and straight, his hands crossed over his chest, his head looking upward, waiting to die. His family took turns sitting with him. No doctors were called, no extraordinary measures taken. It was time for Mr. Li to die.

When he did, his body was wrapped in a cotton-padded quilt and placed in the back of a truck that transported his remains to the crematorium at Babaoshan. Li Laoshi, her mother, and her brother rode to Babaoshan by bus. They all wore black armbands. After the cremation, the family brought the ashes home, and Li Laoshi sat down to open the box and look. Taking some of the ashes out and placing them in her hand, she looked at them, felt them, with a mixture of wonder, curiosity, and sadness that her father's life had so quickly come to that.

Death is a part of life in China. The elderly often die at home, with minimal medical intervention. It is important to Chinese to die at home. Overseas Chinese who have lived abroad for decades often return to their native place to die. In earlier days, in some parts of China, there was even a tradition called *ganshi*—walking the corpse back home. So important was it to die at home that a person who died on the road was actually walked home, as though he were alive, the skill of those whose occupation it was to lead the corpse being measured by how realistic the movements of the corpse appeared. Children, however far away they might live, however important their work, are expected to return home to be with a dying parent. Offices unquestioningly grant leave to any of their employees with a parent who is ill. Without the children by his side, it is said, the parent cannot close his eyes when death approaches, cannot leave the world in peace.

Nor is the corpse a thing to be avoided. It is customary to take pictures of the deceased, both at the moment of death and dressed for burial. Li Meirong's scrapbook begins with several pages of photographs of her mother both on her deathbed and just before burial, wearing a black silk skullcap, garbed in traditional robes of silk brocade, and surrounded by flowers. Mourning, too, is an integral part of life in China.

In post-Liberation China, the rituals of mourning were greatly simplified, particularly in the cities. First, the body would be displayed—in the hospital, an auditorium, or, for high-ranking officials, in the Great Hall of the People —and mourners would come to say goodbye. Only the family and closest friends would accompany the body to the crematorium. But after the remains were cremated, a memorial service would be held. With the box of ashes placed on a table, a black-bordered picture of the deceased hanging above it, and recorded funeral music playing in the background, the mourners would file in to hear speeches of final farewell. "The politicians make use of the memorial service to propagandize things," complains You Xiaoli. " 'Let's all turn our grief into strength and make achievements in the four modernizations,' they say now. Before it was 'Make achievements in the Cultural Revolution,' or whatever the current policy was." But still, the dead were mourned.

Compounding the deaths of the Cultural Revolution, the deaths by murder, torture, and suicide, the deaths because counterrevolutionaries found medical care so difficult to obtain, was a prohibition, at least for those under attack, of even the minimal rituals of death and dying. Sun Heren was locked in a cattle pen when his mother's life began to ebb. His brother sent a series of urgent telegrams, informing Sun of his mother's deteriorating condition, urging him to return. But the members of the worker-peasant-soldier propaganda team did not give Sun the telegrams. It was not until his mother had died that Sun Heren received them.

For the first time in his adult life, Sun Heren cried—less because his mother had died, for he had known she was suffering from cancer, than because he had failed in his obligations as a son. "So my mother died with her eyes open," he says. "I was depressed for a long time after that, because I could not go home to help." Zhao Wenhao, too, was prohibited from returning home to his dying mother, able to be with her only as she breathed her last. At the time, he remembers feeling only numbness. Today he is burdened by guilt. He, too, failed as a son.

When the dead, like Xiao Shan, had departed before the charges against them had been cleared, they were ostracized in death just as they had been in life. No memorial services were held. No one came to pay their final respects. And when the deceased had died separated from family, the ashes were often never returned.

When the deceased had taken his own life, as so many of the persecuted did, the traditional memorial service for the dead was often replaced by a struggle session against them. For suicide during the Cultural Revolution was taken as proof of guilt, as a betrayal of the revolution, of which the suicide itself constituted proof.

THE most compelling illustration of the abyss of grotesquery into which the Cultural Revolution descended is the death of China's former chief of state, Liu Shaoqi, the man accused of being "China's Khrushchev" and the "number-one party person in authority taking the capitalist road," the man whose image had been brushed out of the record of the country's revolutionary history.

For four years, the children of Liu Shaoqi followed every lead, chasing every shadow, in search of the remains of the father they knew to be dead. In mid-1976, they were told that in a certain room in Babaoshan was an anonymous box that might contain their father's ashes. Through subterfuge and carefully disguised, because the children of Liu Shaoqi remained pariahs in revolutionary China, they gained admittance to the room. Ironically, the box that dominated, placed in its center and covered with the party flag, contained the ashes of Kang Sheng. It had been Kang Sheng's wife, Cao Yi'ou, who had encouraged Nie Yuanzi to write her first big character poster. Kang Sheng and his wife were close friends of Jiang Qing. Kang Sheng was one of those who had led the attacks against Liu Shaoqi.

The anonymous box, which might or might not hold the ashes of Liu Shaoqi, was mottled with cigarette holes, covered with spittle. Not even death spared victims of the Cultural Revolution from attack.

Liu Shaoqi's health had steadily declined following the beatings of the

August 5 struggle session in his courtyard at Zhongnanhai. At first, it took him an hour, even two, simply to put on his clothes, fifty minutes, an hour, sometimes two, to walk the thirty yards from the confinement of his office to the dining hall where he was assigned to eat. He walked unassisted and alone. The soldiers assigned to guard him refused to help.

Then he was unable to walk at all, incapable of making the painful, time-consuming trek. His food had to be delivered directly to him.

Meals came irregularly. No one wanted to be accused of feeding "China's Khrushchev." One meal delivered had to last for several meals. Liu Shaoqi had only seven teeth. He had difficulty chewing the gritty buns and coarse rice. The food that he saved for later turned stale. He got diarrhea. His body grew weak. His hands trembled. He had difficulty bringing food to his mouth. It spilled on his body and face.

Doctors were called. The treatment sessions were struggle sessions. Under medical treatment, Liu Shaoqi's health further deteriorated. Liu Shaoqi was a diabetic; his medication and vitamins were withheld.

In midsummer 1968, Liu Shaoqi developed pneumonia. Medical personnel were dispatched. The meeting that would officially expel the president of the People's Republic of China from the Chinese Communist Party which he had served and led for some forty years was approaching. There were authorities "at the top" who wanted Liu Shaoqi alive, a debased and humiliated witness to his ignominious expulsion. The team of doctors sent to examine Liu Shaoqi recommended that his health could be improved if he was transferred for treatment to a hospital. The recommendation was rejected. The team proposed that the posters attacking the patient that filled his room be removed. That proposal, too, was turned down. Liu Shaoqi was to be kept alive, but only in order to suffer.

Liu Shaoqi lived. He was too weak to get out of bed. His muscles atrophied. His arms and legs were black-and-blue from the frequent injections. No one changed or washed his clothes. No one helped him out of bed to go to the toilet.

It was on his seventieth birthday, November 24, 1968, that Liu Shaoqi, unable any longer to eat, being fed through a tube in his nose, lying in bed in pain, received word that the Twelfth Plenum of the Eighth Central Committee of the Chinese Communist Party, having met some three weeks earlier, had expelled him from their ranks. Liu Shaoqi was finally transferred to a hospital.

Still he lived.

On October 1, 1969, Lin Biao sent out the order to evacuate from Peking to the interior many of the country's former high-ranking officials whose fates were not unlike Liu Shaoqi's. The former president of the People's Republic —feeding tube down his nose, a vacuum suction in his throat, an intravenous feeding tube in his body, naked, and covered only by a quilt—was flown in the cold to a special prison in Kaifeng.

Again Liu Shaoqi contracted pneumonia.

Less than a month later, on November 12, 1969, he was dead.

One of his former guards, called back to Kaifeng from Peking, found the former chief of state of the world's most populous nation lying on the concrete floor of the prison basement, his naked body covered with a sheet. The dead man's hair was over a foot in length.

The guard cut Liu Shaoqi's hair and shaved his wispy beard, put clothes on his body and shoes on his feet. He took a photograph of his former boss, preserving for posterity a visual record of the ravages those years had wrought. At midnight, in the deepest of secrecy, Liu's remains were transported by jeep to a nearby crematorium, the stiffened legs of the deceased protruding out of the vehicle.

Liu Shaoqi was cremated under the pseudonym of Liu Weihuang, and "illness" was listed as the cause of death. The death certificate registered no occupation for the man who had joined the Communist Party in 1921 and risen to its apex, who had made the Long March and led in China's struggle for Liberation, who had become president of the People's Republic of China and was its consummate, most conscientious bureaucrat, who had been transformed almost overnight and for reasons that still defy explanation from Chairman Mao's heir apparent to "China's Khrushchev" and the "number-one party person in authority taking the capitalist road," an alleged "renegade, hidden traitor, and scab," who had died in disgrace completely deserted by all his former comrades, Mao Zedong and Zhou Enlai included. His family was not informed for another three years, the people of China for ten.

The contents of the anonymous box of ashes at Babaoshan have never been identified.

SIX

RASHOMON:
THE STORIES OF BAI MEIHUA, SONG WUHAO, LIU ZHIPING, JIANG XINREN, AND SONG ERLI

"WHEN people tell you that they were always opposed to the Cultural Revolution, that they never supported it," Wang Hongbao warned, "you must not believe them. You must ask them more. Because when the Cultural Revolution began, everyone supported it. Ninety percent of the people, ninety-nine percent of the people, supported it—even those who were accused, even those who came under attack."

Wang Hongbao is the son of a high-ranking party official in Peking, a man who had been a close associate of the historian and vice-mayor of Peking Wu Han. Because of that association, Wang Hongbao's father had been purged shortly after Wu Han. In 1966, Hongbao was a middle school student at one of the boarding schools on the outskirts of the city, a school whose classrooms were filled with the sons and daughters of the country's political elite. On Saturday afternoons, the grounds of the school, dotted with ponds and paddy fields, would become crowded with black Red Flag limousines as the chauffeurs of the Chinese leadership arrived to escort their patrons' children home. When the officials were criticized for using their limousines for unofficial purposes, a special bus was sent to pick up the children and drop them off in the center of town.

There is an edge of bitterness to Wang Hongbao's warning, anger barely suppressed against those whose memories have selectively edited their pasts. There is much about his own behavior during the Cultural Revolution that Wang Hongbao would like to forget, much about which he speaks only with a reticence suffused with tension—his attempt to "draw a clear line of demarcation" from his father, his brief life as a member of a roving, violent gang.

"My father was one of the very first people to come under attack, right after Wu Han, right after the purge of the Peking Party committee," he continues. "And my father believed he was wrong. He believed he had committed serious mistakes. He came home one day and told us that. He said that he had not committed mistakes intentionally, that he had not really realized at the time that they were mistakes, but that still he had made mistakes. But he said that he had always supported Chairman Mao. We must not blame anyone for what was happening to him and for what would happen to him. I came to believe that the attacks against my father were warranted.

"Mao's status was very high; his authority was very great. He was like a god. Nothing he said could be contradicted. Everything he said was right. So when he and others said my father had committed mistakes, I believed them.

"And that's the other thing. *Everyone* believed he had committed mistakes. The old intellectuals believed they had committed mistakes. You should have seen them. They were all confessing to their mistakes. Even Liu Shaoqi believed at first that he had committed mistakes, even Liu Shaoqi wrote his self-confession. So when people tell you they never believed they had committed mistakes, you must not accept it."

To try to determine from those who lived through it the facts of the onset of the Cultural Revolution is to become enmeshed in a *Rashomon* story of gigantic scale and monumental complexity. That everyone is describing the same historical episode there is no question. But the ways in which individuals experienced that episode are remarkably diverse. Guilt, above all, plays remarkable havoc with memory.

Wang Hongbao is right that at the beginning of the Cultural Revolution many, maybe even most, people supported it—or wanted to support it, or thought they should support it, even those who were victims. Most people did examine their own pasts in painstaking, meticulous detail to find out whether and how they might have erred. Many were even prepared to accept their own guilt. For many, it was not until so many others whom they admired and knew to be innocent and good were attacked that their support for the Cultural

Revolution waned and confidence in their own innocence, however haltingly, returned. For some, it was the behavior of the revolutionaries that called the Cultural Revolution into question.

"At the beginning of the Cultural Revolution," recalls You Xiaoli, who had come under attack immediately, "I thought maybe it was right. I thought maybe we intellectuals did have too much privilege. I thought a lot during those days, and I really examined myself to see if I had committed any mistakes. I truly loved Chairman Mao and socialism and communism, and I believed in them. I thought that maybe I was backward, that I should study the Cultural Revolution, because I wanted to be more and more revolutionary. And I thought maybe the revolutionaries were real revolutionaries because Chairman Mao had called them revolutionary. But then I saw the leaders of the revolutionaries beating, robbing, taking money from professors, using that money to buy things for themselves, raping women. They were only 'so-called' revolutionaries. I saw these things only because I was a capitalist roader. They hid their ugly acts from others."

Some people, even those who suffered, continue today to support the Cultural Revolution. "Did I support it?" Yao Baoding, now in his early seventies, asks. "Of course I supported it. Everyone supported it at first. Almost everyone. I still support it. And I say this from the perspective of someone who suffered. Six years in jail. Solitary confinement. And my wife—three years locked up in her office on campus.

"I really believe, I still believe today, that there were two lines prior to the Cultural Revolution, that Mao Zedong and Liu Shaoqi each represented a contending line. Now that Liu has been rehabilitated and his selected works have been republished, the differences between Mao and Liu have been downplayed, at least in the public announcements. But those differences were there. They really were. For me, the Cultural Revolution was a struggle against bureaucratism. Liu Shaoqi represented the bureaucracy and bureaucratism. Something had gone wrong with the party. There was a real fear that China would become a new Soviet Union, that a new elite was developing, a new class.

"Mao was taking a terrible gamble when he launched the Cultural Revolution. I think he knew he was taking a terrible gamble. But I think he felt that he had little time left, that there was no other leader with his vision, no one capable of carrying out his vision after he died. So he took the gamble.

"He lost, to be sure."

IT is less the persecuted who have difficulty admitting their initial support for the Cultural Revolution than those who were the persecutors, those who benefited from the movement and whose careers advanced. For the Cultural Revolution, even more than the antirightist campaign before it, provided an unexpected opportunity for aspirants to upward mobility. By attacking and overthrowing their superiors, the upwardly mobile were often able to assume positions of power themselves. That their power was often obtained both violently and through fraud is not something most who were able to attain it are willing to admit. "Look," says one of the characters in *Rashomon*, "everyone wants to forget unpleasant things, so they make up stories. It's easier that way."

Most did not actually make up stories. They simply refused to talk. Qian Butong was like that. "The Cultural Revolution is a thing of the past," Qian Butong had responded when asked what he had been doing during the Cultural Revolution, faithfully mouthing the official view. Qian Butong was an administrative official in his university—a party cadre, not an intellectual. He had had, at most, a primary school education. Before the Cultural Revolution, Qian Butong had been in charge of the teachers' fund. Each month, a tiny percentage of the faculty's salary was withheld, allegedly to be banked, with interest, as a contingency fund. The fund was for use by the teachers should any of them, faced with a family emergency, need a loan. Party Secretary Qian Butong was in overall charge of the fund, but one of You Xiaoli's former students, the party secretary's assistant, was responsible for the paperwork. In 1965, it was she who came to You Xiaoli in considerable anguish to ask for her advice. Qian Butong had been embezzling from the fund for a long time.

You Xiaoli confronted Qian Butong with the allegation. The party secretary denied that he had embezzled funds, and when the Cultural Revolution began he took a leading role in attacking You Xiaoli. His behavior was not unusual. "He had to be the first to rebel," explains You Xiaoli, "because he was afraid that otherwise people might expose him. So he said that he was persecuted. He said that You Xiaoli was a reactionary, that You Xiaoli was spreading rumors against party leaders. He said you can never trust anything You Xiaoli says because she creates all sorts of rumors. Maybe he was afraid I had told somebody about him. Actually, I never told anybody."

It was Qian Butong who, during the attacks against her, orchestrated and directed many of the beatings of You Xiaoli. He was promoted for his performance as an activist during the Cultural Revolution.

"I wouldn't exactly say I was a victim," Lin Daren had begun, his voice casual, his demeanor nonchalant. "I was a *xiaoyaopai*, someone who was able to stay out of the Cultural Revolution." But everyone on his campus knew, and many were willing to say, that Lin Daren had distinguished himself as an activist in the attacks against his old friend and teacher Huang Chaoqun, and the accusations he hurled had been deliberately and provocatively lies.

Gao Cuixia, who, during the antirightist campaign of 1957, had driven one of his students to suicide, presented himself initially as the hapless and innocent victim. Later he admitted that at the beginning he thought the Cultural Revolution was good, that he had supported it, participated in it, but only after the story he told was so riddled with contradiction that his credibility had been forever destroyed. "He is an evil man," snapped one of his victims. "Don't believe him. Stay away."

Ever doleful, mournful, subdued, and depressed, Wu Weidong had described his experience of the Cultural Revolution as a "living hell." "It is not true that everyone supported the Cultural Revolution at the beginning," he argued. Wu Weidong claimed to have opposed the Cultural Revolution from the beginning, said that his doubts had been simmering years before the Cultural Revolution began, that the Cultural Revolution had brought him nothing but unmitigated disaster. He was rich in information about those years, unceasing in his criticism of Mao and the Gang of Four, strangely understanding of those who had been duped into following the "ultraleft," articulate about the political nature of his present malaise.

But so distrusted and disliked was Wu Weidong by his colleagues that they continued privately to inveigh against him, supplying in ever increasing detail lurid descriptions of his behavior during the Cultural Revolution, his attacks on his colleagues and superiors, the beatings in which he took part, his rise to membership on his department's revolutionary committee as those he had so relentlessly attacked were overthrown. "You know old Professor Zhao?" one demanded, barely able to control his anger. "He still walks with a limp. You know why he walks with a limp? He was beaten during the Cultural Revolution. Wu Weidong beat him. Wu Weidong, yes." "And Chen Shiguang. You've heard of Chen Shiguang. Chen Shiguang is a very famous professor. He still gets headaches and a ringing in his ears. Because he was beaten on the head during the Cultural Revolution. Wu Weidong beat him on the head. Yes, Wu Weidong, who seems so quiet and soft. He was a strong young man in his late twenties then. Maybe he's sorry he did it. Today maybe he's sorry. But he has never apologized. And what about tomorrow? He's an opportunist. I don't trust him. You shouldn't trust him. If there were another Cultural Revolution, he'd do it again. He'd be among the first to attack."

THE *Rashomon* tale that is the Cultural Revolution becomes more manageable when only its younger characters are considered. It was among China's young that Nie Yuanzi's big character poster struck the most resonant chord, the young who provided the movement with its most enthusiastic support. For the Cultural Revolution was for the students in China's middle schools and universities a truly exciting opportunity to demonstrate that they were revolutionary through and through. Everyone wanted to prove himself revolutionary. For if there was any point on which all the young of China agreed, it was that revolution and revolutionaries were good.

But if most of China's young initially supported the movement, and all agreed that revolution was good, the motivations for their support are remarkably diverse. Song Wuhao, the fifteen-year-old student at the middle school attached to Qinghua, whose father was a professor at the university, who had participated with such joyous enthusiasm in the initial stages of the movement, attacking the principal of his school and the leading party secretary, taking them away and locking them up, had until then stood outside, just on the edge, of China's revolutionary tradition. Song Wuhao fervently wanted entrance. His father was a scientist who had received an advanced education abroad. His Western education and orientation, a certain reticence before socialist rule, his former ties to the Guomindang, had not brought particular harm to Song Wuhao's father under the new regime, but neither had his past served him well. Like Li Meirong and You Xiaoli, Professor Song had barely "escaped through the net" during the antirightist campaign of 1957. By 1966, he saw himself as a marked man, biding his time until the next major political movement would cut him down.

Song Wuhao had felt excluded because of his father's background, an outsider in China's socialist society. He wanted to become a revolutionary, to belong. The Cultural Revolution offered him his chance. His response to the publication of Nie Yuanzi's big character poster was immediate, unhesitating, unquestioning. "I was excited when the Cultural Revolution began, happy about it, eager to participate," he recalls. "Because the Cultural Revolution was a revolution, and revolution was good, revolutionaries were good people. My generation had never participated in a revolution. We hadn't participated in the War of Resistance against Japan or in the struggle for Liberation. So we all wanted an opportunity to become real revolutionaries ourselves."

BAI MEIHUA'S support for the Cultural Revolution was no less enthusiastic, immediate, or unquestioning. It was Bai Meihua who, as a young child in primary school, had often been whisked from her classroom to the Peking airport to present flowers to visiting dignitaries from abroad. Her father, the son of a not very prosperous merchant, had graduated from a junior middle school in Shanghai in the late 1930s, after which he left his family and many of his friends to travel to the revolutionary base in Yenan, where the Communist Party made its headquarters following the Long March. There he had joined the Chinese Communist Party and had participated in the Communist takeover of power. In 1966, he was a Communist Party official, a high-ranking cadre. Bai Meihua had grown up steeped in China's revolutionary tradition, nurtured on China's revolutionary myth. Her father was an old revolutionary, and Bai Meihua believed that she was revolutionary too, and special by virtue of that fact.

She was thirteen years old when the Cultural Revolution began, in her first year in a junior middle school whose graduates had every reason to assume that they would be chosen to continue on to the finest of their country's elite universities, even to be sent abroad for a college or graduate education. "When you were accepted into this school," says Bai Meihua, "you knew you were being selected to study abroad." Her middle school was closed shortly after the publication of Nie Yuanzi's big character poster.

"I was the daughter of a high-ranking cadre," Bai Meihua explains. "My father had made the Chinese revolution. He had wanted to wipe out the counterrevolutionaries and to establish a new China. So when I and my friends heard that there were counterrevolutionaries in China, of course we immediately wanted to join the movement to wipe them out. At that time, Mao's personality cult was very strong. All we knew was that socialism was good, capitalism was bad. So we supported Nie Yuanzi. We were revolutionary rebels. For me, the Cultural Revolution began with Nie Yuanzi's big character poster. Mao said that the big character poster was revolutionary, so this was the beginning of the Cultural Revolution.

"We organized the Red Guards to support Nie Yuanzi and to pull down the capitalist roaders. At that time I never thought about what kind of movement the Cultural Revolution would be or what its real purpose was. We didn't even know that much about the capitalist roaders."

As Song Wuhao was locking up the principal of his school and forcing him to write his self-confession, Bai Meihua was acting as the youngest participant in the house search of a high-ranking party official. "Most of the cadres' children supported Nie Yuanzi," she recalls. "We joined the Red Guards, we participated in the house searches, we beat people, we tried to pull down the capitalist roaders. We thought that whoever Mao said was a capitalist roader was a capitalist roader.

"We were told that all things in a capitalist roader's family were capitalist things. The families of the capitalist roaders had to be occupied by the revolutionaries, so we, the revolutionaries, had to occupy their houses. We were told this by the Red Guards in the universities. We were told that we had to use the revolutionary ax against the counterrevolutionaries. The house search was considered one of those acts, one way of using the revolutionary ax against the counterrevolutionaries." Bai Meihua and her friends were told that the head of the ministry where her father worked, a man named Chen, was a counterrevolutionary against whom the revolutionary ax was to be wielded.

"At that time, our Red Guard organization had offices in the main office building of the ministry. So we met there to discuss the house search, to decide which day to perform it, when to go, where to assemble, and how to divide our tasks once the house search had begun. When the day came, we all got together in our offices at the ministry. We were all wearing army uniforms, because it was considered very glorious then to wear army uniforms. All the girls put on caps, like the boys, and we tucked our hair up under our caps so we looked like boys. We rolled up our sleeves. And we all took off our belts and wore them around our waists, on the outside of the uniform. The belts were our weapons. When we wanted to beat someone, all we had to do was to take off our belts. I was the youngest in the group to participate in the house search, a little tag-along, really. I was only thirteen. Most of the others were fourteen or fifteen. We all agreed that we would use the revolutionary ax against Chen, that we would treat him as the enemy, because he opposed Chairman Mao. We knew we would beat him, too.

"We certainly had no trouble finding his house, since he was the minister and lived in the ministry's courtyard where our office was and where many of us also lived. Chen lived with his elder sister. His wife had already divorced him, and immediately after the Cultural Revolution began, after he had been put down, all of his children had left, drawing a clear line of demarcation between themselves and their father. His children wanted to make revolution, but they couldn't unless they drew a clear line of demarcation.

"We arrived at the house and knocked on the door. It was opened by his elder sister, and as soon as she had opened it, we all rushed inside. She was very surprised, and asked us what we wanted. One of the boys said, 'We want to live here. This house doesn't belong to you. It belongs to us, the revolutionaries. Be honest, because if you are not, we will beat you. We will even beat you to death. You are the wife of a landlord.' She really was the wife of a landlord.

"Then we began the house search. We were organized into different groups. Some people were assigned to go through all the documents and papers. Some just went through and threw things on the floor. Some were assigned to question Chen. Some, the boys, were assigned to give Chen's elder sister the *yinyang* haircut. They used scissors to cut all the hair off one side of her head.

"Several women in our courtyard already had *yinyang* haircuts, because they were cadres with the ministry. Such people had to come to the office every day to sweep the courtyard, clean the lavatories, mop the floor, clean the buildings. Some cut their hair really short to cover up the fact that they had *yinyang* haircuts. It was very ugly, and the women with *yinyang* haircuts looked very sad about it, but they dared not say anything.

"Chen was very honest. He just stood in a corner of his house, staring at us, not saying a thing. He pretended to be very cool. We went through his suitcases, his chests of drawers, his wardrobes. Before the Cultural Revolution, Chen had gone abroad several times, and there were many beautiful souvenirs in his house from his travels. And there were lots of clothes, beautiful clothes. And phonograph records. It was very rare at that time for anyone to have a phonograph and records.

"Actually, there were really two main things we wanted during the house search. First, we wanted to find some materials that would have provided evidence that would prove that he was opposed to Chairman Mao and the party. We thought he must be hiding something, so we examined everything. There were many reports, regulations, documents in his house, but they were all official—nothing that could have proved that he was opposed to Chairman Mao and the party. We found no such evidence.

"The second thing we wanted was money. We asked him for money, but he said he didn't have any. We said, 'You certainly do have money. We know you have money, and you have to give us your money or we'll beat you.' We made him kneel on the floor. We said, 'You're not being very honest. You have a high salary. Every month you get a lot of money, but you have only yourself to support.' Then they beat him, slapped him on the face, because he wouldn't tell us where his money was.

"He was beaten another time while we were there, too. One of the boys said, 'You kept so many things given to you by the foreigners. You should give these to the ministry, not keep them for yourself. You're a capitalist roader.' Then he slapped him, beat him. At that time, if the revolutionaries wanted to beat someone, they could. There was nothing to prevent us from doing that.

"Chen didn't say anything when he was being beaten. He just looked at us, just suffered the beating without saying a word. They used their belts to beat him.

"We took lots of things away with us that day. We took most of the beautiful souvenirs from abroad. I don't know where they went or what happened to them. Most of what we took, though, was clothes, their beautiful clothes. The boys wore the clothes. And we took his record player and the phonograph records and used them in our office. We listened to the music a lot. Since we weren't going to school and we weren't studying, and there often wasn't a lot to do, we spent a lot of time in our offices listening to music.

"There was a regulation at that time that all landlords and landlord families had to return to their own villages in the countryside, so we told Chen that his sister couldn't stay there anymore, that she had to return to the countryside. She agreed, and said that she would leave the next day. Some of the boys said they would accompany her, and that we would all go to the station to see her off. So we left, with all the clothes and souvenirs. Later that day, we went back again to confirm that we would be waiting for her the next day to send her back.

"Some of the boys accompanied her to the countryside on the train. They were still after her money. While they were on the train, the boys beat her, demanding her money. They kept asking her where her money was and demanding that she give it to them. At first she said that she didn't have much money and that what she did have was all in her brother's hands. But then, after they kept beating her, she finally said that they could find some money in her pockets. So they searched her pockets, and found a checkbook with more than two thousand dollars, all the money Chen had been able to save since Liberation. Immediately after that, after they had got the checkbook, they left the train at the very next stop and returned to Peking. At that time, it was very easy for anyone to take money out of the bank. They were the young Red

Guards and this was the Cultural Revolution, and the regulations weren't at all strict. Besides, the clerks in the bank were also revolutionary rebels, and they regarded this as a revolutionary action. So we got the money.

"We distributed the money among ourselves. Not equally, though. A few of the boys got most of it. We used it to go out to restaurants together and to buy cigarettes. Since we were young, we didn't have salaries at the time, and we didn't dare ask our parents for money.

"After that, we went back to Chen's a few more times for other house searches, so in the end, there was really nothing left in his house."

LIU ZHIPING's father, like Bai Meihua's, was a longtime member of the Chinese Communist Party. Like Bai Meihua, Liu Zhiping was proud of her father's revolutionary past and believed that she was revolutionary, too. "My father was a revolutionary cadre, and I had been very proud of that," she says, "happy to have come from a revolutionary family. I had always thought that I was a revolutionary, too, that I was working for the Chinese revolution, and I had been very proud of that."

But Liu Zhiping would not have liked Bai Meihua. Liu Zhiping's father was an "ordinary" cadre, not a high-ranking one, and Liu Zhiping, like so many Chinese, had come to resent the special privileges enjoyed by the sons and daughters of the high-ranking party officials. "We didn't like that kind of student," she says. "They had been admitted to the university because their parents were high-ranking party officials."

Until the Cultural Revolution began, Liu Zhiping was happy, content with her lot. The Liberation of China had treated her family well. "We weren't rich, certainly, but we were comfortable," she says. She was the first in her family to be given the opportunity for a college education, and while she was not the best student in her class, Liu Zhiping was still very good. She was respected and well liked by both her classmates and the faculty, an enthusiastic activist in many of the events organized for her class. She liked her university, her fellow students, the faculty, the president. She thought it was a genuinely "proletarian" university.

"Ninety percent of the students on campus were from worker, peasant, and cadre families," she remembers. "Not high-ranking cadre families. Ordinary cadre families. Families of the old revolutionary cadres who had formed the mainstay of the revolution. We thought that our university was a proletarian university—not just because of the composition of the students but also because of the way it was run. The president of the university used to visit us in our dormitory rooms—just come in to talk to us. And the teachers, the teachers would clean the classrooms together with us."

When Nie Yuanzi's big character poster was published and students on Liu Zhiping's campus began putting up big character posters criticizing the president of the university Liu Zhiping believed was proletarian, attacking even the chairman of her department, she was unhappy and confused. "All those students who made these attacks on the president of the university and the head of the campus party branch were the sons and daughters of high-ranking party officials, students whose mothers and fathers worked in the ministries. They knew something from their parents that we other students didn't know. Besides, we didn't like them." They were in the minority, though, and Liu Zhiping and her friends joined readily with the majority, organizing a big parade, painting posters and shouting slogans in defense of the president of the proletarian university and the leading party secretary.

But within weeks it became clear that majority though they were, Liu Zhiping and her friends were not going to carry the day. The arrival of the work team on campus in mid-June made it clear that the president of her university, the leading party secretary, the chairman of her department, all those people she respected as proletarian, were to be the objects of attack. "Classes were suspended so we could criticize these people. But I didn't understand," she remembers. "Why should we criticize these people at all? When the work teams arrived at the school to investigate the Cultural Revolution activity there, they criticized us, the majority of the students, defending the minority who had attacked the president. The rest of us, the majority, were called conservatives, and we were criticized, and I was one of the people suspected of being a conservative. It was very serious. We had a meeting that lasted all night, where the leaders of the university were criticized very severely. It was very strange that the leaders of the university should be so severely criticized and that those who defended them should be considered counterrevolutionary. The atmosphere at that meeting was very tense, and many of the students, my friends, the ones who had supported the president, cried. The whole issue had become one of the revolutionaries against the counterrevolutionaries, and we who considered ourselves so proletarian had become the counterrevolutionaries. The work teams labeled the masses, the majority on the campus, the leaders of the school, as the enemy. The president and the leading party secretary were made to step aside.

"So it was very confusing to me. I had always been a revolutionary. My family was revolutionary. But this was a new kind of revolution. I spent most of my time by myself, in my dormitory room, sitting on my bed, studying. I would read the works of Chairman Mao over and over again, trying to figure out according to which of Chairman Mao's principles the Cultural Revolution had been launched, trying to figure out whether the reality of the Cultural Revolution fitted with the principles of Chairman Mao. I was so confused. But I couldn't talk to anyone about this, because you couldn't really question the Cultural Revolution. I didn't know. I felt I had to learn more."

In the fall of 1966, when young students were encouraged to leave their schools and to spread the Cultural Revolution to other parts of the country in the great revolutionary linkups, Liu Zhiping took advantage of the free train travel to return to her home in Suzhou. She wanted to talk to her father, to see if he, the old revolutionary, could help her understand the Cultural Revolution.

But Liu Zhiping's father was no help. He was already suspicious of what had been happening. Liu Zhiping was frightened. "I told him he was conservative," Liu Zhiping recalls. "In fact, I thought he was dangerous. I could tell that he was against this revolution, the Cultural Revolution. I told him that even though he was an old revolutionary cadre, this revolution would ultimately turn against him. I knew he opposed the Cultural Revolution. I could just sense it."

When Liu Zhiping returned to her university after meeting with her father, she was confronted with a dilemma. She believed herself revolutionary. She had always thought of herself as revolutionary. But in this, China's Great Proletarian Cultural Revolution, she had already been painted as a conservative. If the movement continued in the direction it seemed to be moving, with participants divided between the revolutionaries and the counterrevolutionaries, she was likely to be declared a counterrevolutionary. She was worried about her father and his obvious reservations about the new revolution. Confronted with this dilemma about how to ensure her revolutionary credentials, Liu Zhiping decided to leave the confusion and contradictions of her university and set out in emulation of the Communist Party's Long March. Away from her university and the political activity there, Liu Zhiping could at least avoid attack. Enduring the hardships the Long March would bring, learning from the revolutionary poor-and-lower-middle peasants, sharing their weal and woe, would serve as ample proof of Liu Zhiping's revolutionary commitment. It would not be the last time during the Cultural Revolution that Liu Zhiping would choose to remain revolutionary by leaving the fray.

JIANG XINREN was twenty years old and a university student in Shanghai when the Cultural Revolution began. Jiang's grandfather had owned his own business before Liberation, and Jiang Xinren's father had served as a manager in his grandfather's factory. After Liberation, when the factory had been taken over by the state, Jiang's father had continued to work there—not as the manager, but as an accountant. Jiang Xinren's father was officially considered an intellectual, but he was nonetheless regarded, because of his capitalist background, with a certain measure of suspicion. Jiang Xinren's father lived in fear that in one of the many political campaigns, his own bourgeois background would become the target of attack, and over the years, his son saw him becoming increasingly silent, withdrawn, and tense. Liberation had not brought any particular benefits to the Jiang family. Indeed, their standard of living had declined. Jiang Xinren had worried that the standard of living of China's people did not seem to be rising under socialism. It was a problem he associated with bureaucratism. "So when I read the big character poster by Nie Yuanzi in the *People's Daily,* I was very excited," he says, "and I and some of my friends began writing big character posters ourselves, following Nie's example, attacking bureaucratism, attacking the president of my university. This was a very exciting period for us. It didn't last long, though. It ended very quickly with the arrival on campus of the work teams who were sent to inspect and investigate the Cultural Revolution on the campuses."

In contrast to Liu Zhiping's campus, where the work teams had immediately singled out the president of the university for attack, the president of Jiang Xinren's university was protected. "In Peking," explains Jiang Xinren, "the work teams were controlled by Wang Guangmei, particularly at Qinghua, but in Shanghai they were controlled by the Shanghai municipal-level party authorities." Cao Diqiu, Shanghai's mayor and first party secretary, was in charge of the work teams in that city, and the experienced party bureaucrat acted quickly to preserve order and stability. As a result, Jiang Xinren, for having so enthusiastically written big character posters in emulation of Nie Yuanzi, was declared a counterrevolutionary and locked for two months in a cattle pen. It was only in August, after Chairman Mao's revolutionary line had carried the day at the meeting of the Eleventh Plenum, and following the publication of the Sixteen Points, that Jiang Xinren was released. He returned to the political fracas as an ardent supporter of Mao. "When I was first released from the cattle pen," he remembers, "I attributed my release to Mao Zedong. He was my great savior, and I wanted to do everything I could for Mao Zedong. The other side, the conservatives, were following Liu Shaoqi, so I hated them and hated Liu Shaoqi, because they were the ones who had put me in the cattle pen." From then on, Jiang Xinren devoted full time to revolutionary activity.

SONG Wuhao had grown up on the edge of the Chinese circle, but he had never been entirely excluded. Song Erli, a young primary school student in 1957 when his parents were labeled rightists, faced a constant battle against the ostracism the label of his parents so frequently threatened to bring him. Song Erli grew up believing his father counterrevolutionary and hating him for it. In his first year in college, Song Erli had applied for membership in the Communist Youth League. "Lots of young people in China are Youth League members," Erli explains. "It's a mass organization, similar to the Young Pioneers. But there were some problems with my being admitted. It was really insulting. All the discussions of my qualifications seemed to center on the fact that I appeared to be a little smarter than others."

Song Erli indeed is a little smarter than others. His mind is like a boxer in motion—dancing, thrusting, jabbing, nimble, agile, tough, and quick. "At my university, there were basically two types of students. About a third of them came from urban areas, and many of those were the sons and daughters of intellectuals. But the majority, maybe two-thirds, came from the countryside. I don't mean to suggest that I was a particularly gifted student, but still, what seemed easy for me, what was hardly like studying at all, posed insurmountable difficulties to many of the other students—particularly the students from the countryside. So this made me the butt of many arguments after I had applied for membership in the Youth League. There were some league cadres, party members, who said, 'He's all right. Just because his grades are better than others doesn't mean his ideology is questionable.' But others within the league had been opposed to me. They supported the ideological trend at the time. They believed in 'red and expert'—that you had to be ideologically red first and educated second—and all its sinister implications. And my parents' background came into question. At that time, the term 'son of a bitch' had yet to be introduced, but they could still say that I had been born a member of the bourgeoisie, even though my parents had never owned their own business, even though they were intellectuals. So they said I had a problem of 'shifting my standpoint' from the bourgeoisie to the proletariat. Had I shifted my standpoint? Was I in the process of shifting my standpoint? I was the butt of criticism." Song Erli was finally admitted into the Youth League, but only grudgingly so. He was never fully accepted there.

Song Erli was twenty years old when the Cultural Revolution began, in his third year at a leading university in Shanghai. According to the dominant "theory of the blood line" which decreed that if one's father was a revolutionary, his son was a good fellow, too, that if the father was a counterrevolutionary, his son was a rotten egg, Song Erli was a rotten egg and officially excluded from participation in the movement.

But Song Erli was a rebellious and independent young man. He refused to accept the judgment of the party and society, refused to believe that political propensity was an inherited trait, refused to believe that because his father was a counterrevolutionary he was a counterrevolutionary too. Song Erli believed himself revolutionary. He was no less an enthusiastic supporter of the Cultural Revolution than Song Wuhao, Bai Meihua, or Jiang Xinren. Song Erli did not know a great deal about what democracy is or how it is carried out in practice, but he saw the Cultural Revolution as a revolution for democracy and against feudalism and ignorance.

"Perhaps I am just a natural rebel," he says. "My personal propensity is individualistic. I am not given to agreeing with others so readily, so easily. This has been true since I was very young, just a schoolboy. I remember once in junior middle school, the secretary of the Youth League was a professional cadre, a party member. Every few weeks, we students were gathered together to listen to him give a speech. I once made the comment that this week's speech was worse than the last. For that I was criticized by the class monitor

—a girl, a very dogmatic girl. She said it was impossible for a speech given by the leading comrade to be worse than the last. Every speech had to be better than the last.

"Perhaps I am not really a natural rebel," he continues. "Perhaps it is because my own personal experiences taught me that I suffered under that system, that Chinese feudalist type of communism. By feudalism, I mean power that is unlimited, unbalanced, unchallenged, power that allows no other voice, no discussion, no dissent, no disagreement—an unbelievably centralized totalitarianism which formed the most serious threat to China's economic development and socialist revolution ever since the late 1950s. That was why the Cultural Revolution was inevitable. The tragedy was that it failed to overcome that feudalist totalitarianism. On the contrary, it strengthened it. The word 'bureaucracy' so many use in describing the Cultural Revolution is just a euphemism. What bureaucracy is is a centrally controlled state machine, a machine which stifles people's initiative, a machine which has taken the most hardworking, diligent people on earth and turned them into the laziest. It is not just the party, or necessarily communism, that has so stifled the people's initiative. It's the bureaucratic machine."

Song Erli, because his parents were rightists, was never allowed to become a Red Guard. But despite the official prohibition against his joining the Cultural Revolution, Song Erli was ultimately able to participate. As the Cultural Revolution went into a second phase following the August publication of the Sixteen Points, the "early Red Guards" were superseded by the "revolutionary rebels." Song Erli eventually became an honorary revolutionary rebel. "At first I wasn't allowed to join the revolutionary rebels, either," he says, "but I felt naturally a member of them. I wanted to prove myself revolutionary, and I felt that this Cultural Revolution was mine, even though I often came under attack at that time. At the beginning of the Cultural Revolution, students were made to feel effective. There were all sorts of editorials in the *People's Daily* about how great the students were. So I thought I was great. I thought I could play a part."

Song Erli's first revolutionary action was to prepare and put up, with considerable pride, his own big character poster. "It was quite a good one," Song Erli asserts. "I had done a lot of research.

"I was a revolutionary rebel. But I am an intellectual," he continues. "I wanted a revolution for democracy, not for ignorance. I never attacked intellectuals. I never beat anyone.

"During the second stage, from about October 1966 to March 1967, the revolutionary rebels were the most active participants in the movement and the spearhead was directed against the party bureaucrats. I wouldn't say the revolutionary rebels did nothing against the intellectuals. But attacks by the revolutionary rebels against the intellectuals were exceptional, out of the ordinary. Often they were simply symbolic actions taken by certain revolutionary rebel organizations to show that they were truly revolutionary. But the spearhead of the revolutionary rebel attack was against the party bureaucrats. Generally speaking, the revolutionary rebels were so busy attacking the bureaucrats and in turn being attacked themselves that they just ignored the professors.

"During this stage, the revolutionary rebel stage, the composition of the participants became more complex. Many of the early Red Guards joined the revolutionary rebels, and the heads of the revolutionary rebels all came from good class backgrounds, from 'revolutionary' families. But even those leaders with such good family backgrounds were different from the leaders of the conservative groups because they were nonconformists, activists, individualists, so despite their 'good' class backgrounds, they hadn't been so well liked by the party committees. Kuai Dafu was like that. He could boast that all his relatives, from his parents to his grandparents and so on, had not a single blemish in their personal history. But Kuai Dafu was a nonconformist. There were Kuai Dafus everywhere as heads of local revolutionary rebel groups.

"You must understand that people joined the Cultural Revolution to attack or to be attacked at different times, in different ways, for different reasons," he explains. Song Erli has become something of a political analyst of the Cultural Revolution, and with his sharp and probing mind, his analyses are hard-hitting, jabbing first this way and then that. "Eventually nearly the whole society joined. You were either the persecutor or the persecuted. Eventually, everyone suffered during the Cultural Revolution. Everyone suffered in turns. True, there were the so-called *xiaoyaopai,* but many of them were just cowards or people who cared too much about themselves. You must think of the Cultural Revolution in terms of stages, with different people participating differently at different times.

"The Red Guards led the house searches, for instance, but it wasn't the Red Guards who actually occupied the houses. The Red Guards were young students, without families. They had no concept of family. It was serious housing problems that led to the occupation of other people's houses, and some of the revolutionary rebels had families. So there was a practical reason for occupying other people's houses. Those who did the occupying weren't satisfied with their own housing. But most of those people weren't revolutionary rebels in the true sense. Some called themselves rebels just to frighten the former owner of the houses. Everyone, anyone could say he was a revolutionary rebel at that time, and now the revolutionary rebels have a bad name because people say that their houses were taken over by the revolutionary rebels. But that's not fair. The people who did the occupying were neighbors, workers, younger cadres in the work unit. To say they were revolutionary rebels gives the revolutionary rebels a bad name.

"For me, the Cultural Revolution was a revolution against feudalism, a revolution for democracy. And it *was* a revolution, a socialist revolution, but not necessarily a revolution where the party cadres would retain control. It was more a revolution for a humanistic socialism."

WHATEVER their different perceptions at the beginning of the Cultural Revolution, however diverse their reasons and extent of support, their country's Great Proletarian Cultural Revolution would ultimately betray them all—Bai Meihua and Song Wuhao, Liu Zhiping, Jiang Xinren, and Song Erli alike. All would become victims of the Cultural Revolution. The paths that they and their families had charted would take dramatically unexpected turns. All of their lives would change.

BAI MEIHUA, by virtue of her father's position, was the first to be transformed overnight from a young Red Guard and faithful follower of Chairman Mao into a *gouzaizi* (literally, a "son of a bitch") and the offspring of a counterrevolutionary—a victim of the Cultural Revolution. Her father came under attack in the fall of 1966. As Bai Meihua has already pointed out, "The first boss of any unit was the capitalist roader, then the vice-director, and then his immediate subordinate, and so on down the line, according to his position." Mr. Bai, being relatively high-ranking, was not so far down in the hierarchy of attack.

Mr. Bai was taken into custody immediately after the accusations against him began, and it was months before the family learned for certain where he had been incarcerated. Mrs. Bai, in the meanwhile, was sent to work in a suburb of Peking, too far away to return home in the evenings. Usually, she was able to return home to spend part of Sunday with her children. Beyond that, and except for the help they received from the elderly woman who was an old colleague of her father's, Bai Meihua and her seven-year-old sister were on their own.

Having read the handwriting on the wall well before Mr. Bai was actually accused, the family had time to make preparations. Knowing that their house would be searched, they burned all their books that the Red Guards might think were "four olds," and they broke and threw away all the phonograph records that Mr. Bai had brought back with him from the Soviet Union. Then they stored all their personal belongings and their valuables in the single room they hoped the rebels would allow them to occupy. The furniture supplied to them by the state—one of the privileges accorded high-ranking cadres—they left for the rebels to use.

The Bai family were even warned of the exact day and approximate time the Red Guards would come. "It was a very kind man, a very good-hearted man, who told us," Bai Meihua remembers. "He warned us that he had heard that that evening the Red Guards planned to go to the homes of the old revolutionary cadres for the house search. He said we must prepare."

So well prepared was the family that nothing was taken from their house. Meihua and her sister were confined to a single room, and their apartment was occupied by two revolutionary rebel families. "They were young cadres, younger colleagues of my father," explains Bai Meihua. "They didn't have any power in the ministry. But they wanted to seize power, to overthrow the old revolutionary cadres, so they became revolutionary rebels. Their whole families lived in our house and used our furniture. The houses of the revolutionary cadres, like my father, were better than the houses of the ordinary cadres. For instance, we didn't have to buy our own furniture. It was given to us by the government, and it was nice. We had sofas and easy chairs. But ordinary cadres had to buy their own furniture, and usually it wasn't as nice."

With their home occupied by the revolutionary rebels, Bai Meihua and her younger sister ordinarily returned home only to sleep. "Since my mother was gone so much of the time and was able to return so rarely, it was only my little sister and I who lived in the house. But we dared not go to our house, except very late in the evenings, and even then sometimes we were too frightened to return home. There were two types of people then, the 'red families'—the workers and peasants—and the *gouzaizi*—the sons of bitches. I was a son of a bitch and the revolutionary rebels had occupied my house, so I didn't want to go home. I was afraid to go home. But there was no place to go, no house to return to. During the daytime, I just wandered the streets, went to visit some of my friends, just killing time, talking. At that time, I had only a very few friends, because no one would dare to get in contact with me or my mother. The friends I did have were all like me. Their parents had been taken away.

"Since I couldn't really use my own house and had to stay outside most of the time, I really had nothing, only the clothes I wore, so I never changed clothes and very rarely bathed. I was very dirty. Occasionally, at a friend's, I would have a chance to bathe and wash my clothes. I would just stay there and wear my friend's clothes until my own were dry.

"At night, usually my sister and I would go home to sleep. But we had to wait until very, very late, until at least twelve or one o'clock, after the revolutionary rebels who were occupying our house were asleep. Sometimes we slept in the corridor just outside the front door. Sometimes we locked ourselves in the one crowded room that was still reserved for my family. Then we would wake up very early, at about four or five, and sneak out, before the revolutionary rebels had woken up. We would get up and quietly unlock the door to our room and listen to make certain that they were still asleep. Then we would run out as fast as we could. Sometimes, after we had sneaked inside, they would find us, but fortunately they only ever found us after we had gone into our room and locked ourselves inside. My mother had made my sister and me promise that we would never open the door when they knocked on it. She said that if we opened the door, they would try to drive us out of the house. But usually, since we came back so late and left so early, they didn't even know we had been there.

"Later my mother learned that the revolutionary rebels wanted to occupy even the one room that we still had to ourselves, so my mother returned home and negotiated with them. She said that we had to have that one room, that they couldn't drive us completely out of our house. After some time, the revolutionary rebels relented and agreed that we could occupy the one room. After that, things were much better. An agreement had been reached, and we could even stay in the room during the daytime. We didn't have to be outside all the time. That was in 1967."

Before the Cultural Revolution, the residential complex in which Bai Meihua lived had been reserved largely for senior cadres in the ministry where her father had worked. As the Cultural Revolution moved inexorably forward, pulling more and more leading officials into its wake, those cadres, like Bai Meihua's father, had first come under attack and then been taken away and incarcerated. Their wives, too, were either confined or, like Bai Meihua's mother, working so far away that they were rarely able to return home. Bai Meihua's housing complex came to be peopled by day by the very old, who, by virtue of retirement, had no work unit from which they might be attacked, and the very young, the children of officials whose parents were incarcerated. The revolutionary rebels who occupied the homes of officials by night spent their days in the practice of revolution.

Bai Meihua's father had been in jail for nearly six months before she and her mother found out where he was. "In fact," explains Bai Meihua, "the jail was almost right next to our house, inside the ministry complex. Every time I left our apartment I had to pass right by the building where he was staying. It was an office building, and they had made it into a jail. I can tell you how we found out where he was.

"At that time, during the day, most of the people in the complex were just children. One day, I heard a young girl in my building screaming and shouting. She was yelling, 'Someone has jumped. Someone has jumped. Come quickly.' Within just a few seconds, all the children in the neighborhood were outside, in front of the building where I learned because of what happened that my father was being kept. Word spread very quickly inside the compound.

"A man was lying at the foot of the wall. You couldn't recognize his face at all. All the brains had come out of his head and there was blood everywhere, even on the walls, because he must have hit the wall on the way down. So you couldn't recognize from the face who it was. You had to tell from the clothes. We thought it was one of our fathers. Someone close to the body kept asking, 'Does anyone's father wear white leather shoes? Does anyone's father wear white leather shoes?' He must have visited Russia and brought back white leather shoes. We don't make white leather shoes in China. But no one's father wore white leather shoes. I could tell immediately from looking at the clothes that it wasn't my father.

"At last someone said that he was a former vice-minister, a relative of someone famous. Actually, he had once been a vice-minister but then he had been labeled a rightist in the 1950s and his status had been lowered. But he was still picked out during the Cultural Revolution.

"The body just lay there for four days, and after a while it began to decay and smell. The man's relatives didn't know about it yet, and no one else dared to remove it. Then, after about four days, a car came and some people got out. They put the body in the trunk of the car and drove away.

"I couldn't eat for more than a week after that. Every time I tried to eat, I kept seeing that man with his brains all over the ground and the blood on the wall, and every time I saw him I vomited.

"Even at that time, the man's family didn't believe that their relative had committed suicide. They thought that someone had pushed him out the window. But the revolutionary rebels insisted that it was a suicide. So the man's family quarreled with the revolutionary rebels. The family wanted the Public Security Bureau to examine the body to determine whether it was really a suicide. They said that he had never thought of suicide, that he was incapable of suicide. They said that even when he had come under attack as a rightist in the '50s he was afraid to die. He wanted to live.

"At the time the Public Security Bureau examined the body they said it was a suicide. It was only later, maybe in 1980, that this man was rehabilitated and another investigation was made. He hadn't committed suicide, in fact. He had been pushed. The Public Security Bureau knew that at the time, but the revolutionary rebels had told them that they had to say it was a suicide. Everyone was afraid of the revolutionary rebels, so the Public Security Bureau had to say it was a suicide. During the Cultural Revolution you could say that black is red and red is black, and sometimes you had to say that.

"The second time someone jumped and everyone came rushing out to see, I recognized the person immediately. He was the father of one of my classmates, a girl. She arrived just a little after I did, and I remember watching her. She just looked at the body. Maybe she made a little start, a little sign of recognition, but she didn't cry. She just stared at the body. She didn't say anything. Nothing. Then she just turned away and went home. I remember thinking she was very brave.

"There was no family to take his body away. Her mother was also in prison, in another place, because she had written so many letters criticizing Jiang Qing and the letters had been intercepted by the revolutionary rebels. The letters had been addressed to Premier Zhou Enlai and had said that Jiang Qing was not a real revolutionary, that she had gone to Yenan on purpose, that she had married Mao Zedong on purpose, that what she really wanted was power. So even though she was just an ordinary cadre, they put her in a separate prison. The revolutionary rebels were afraid to put husband and wife together because they were afraid that they might give each other support. They didn't want husband and wife to meet, to talk, because they were afraid that if they met and were able to talk, they might be able to give each other confidence. They thought that if you were alone, isolated, you would commit suicide, thinking there is no way out. So the revolutionary rebels often used this method in dealing with the old cadres, keeping husband and wife and children separated from one another.

"The body was finally removed by the revolutionary rebels.

"The third person to commit suicide didn't die. He broke his back, but he is still alive today. He had been a pilot before Liberation, so he knew how to jump from a building without dying. Some people said he just wanted to make a protest, that he didn't really want to die. I saw him, too. Whenever I went out I had to pass through the alleyway where the building that was being used as a jail was located, so it would have been impossible not to see. We all saw."

In the fall of 1969, three years after he had been incarcerated, Bai Meihua's father was released. He had not seen his family at all during the period of his captivity, nor had he received any word of how they were managing in his absence. Bai Meihua saw her ordinarily stoic father cry for the first time in her life during the meeting that reunited them. It was when he heard of his brother's murder that he cried.

The Bai family reunion was brief. Mr. Bai was still under suspicion, a possible counterrevolutionary opposed to Mao Zedong. He was sent immediately to a distant province to begin work in a May Seventh Cadre School located on the grounds of a labor reform camp. Mrs. Bai was assigned to another May Seventh Cadre School located nearby. She and her husband were able to see each other on Sundays.

Bai Meihua, at age sixteen, before she had even graduated from middle school, was separated from her family and sent to labor on a state farm a thousand miles away from her parents. "I remember still when the train pulled out," says Bai Meihua. "I cried, nearly screaming, and I beat my fists against the seat. I cried again the same way when I arrived at the state farm. The place was so poor. I had a very small room, which I shared, and I didn't want to open my suitcase. I just wanted to take my suitcase and go right back to Peking. But the leaders said I couldn't go back. They said I would have to stay several years at least, my whole life at most. I wouldn't eat for several days. I wouldn't go to the dining hall. I had brought some food with me from Peking, and I ate just that for the first few days. Only when my food from Peking had run out did I venture to the dining hall."

Bai Meihua did not return to Peking for seven years. She never fully adjusted to life on the state farm, but she learned nonetheless to survive. Her tiny frame, the fragility of her features, the femininity of her dress, mask a character that has turned as tough as nails. But she was not always so tough. "I felt very lonely, very alone," she says of life on the state farm, "and I cried a lot, often, especially during the holidays, and most especially during Spring Festival. We all cried, all of us girls. One of us would start, and then one by one all the others would follow, and we would all sit there crying on our beds for hours."

It was the instinct for survival that turned her tough.

Bai Meihua was lucky. She had two advantages. First, she was pretty in a delicate, pale, and fragile sort of way. The cadre who headed the state farm liked her. Often he would surprise her by putting sugar cubes under her pillow, and he arranged for her to have lighter work than other young people on the farm. As others were laboring in misery outside in the cold, Bai Meihua was sitting in a heated office doing paperwork. Second, even though Bai Meihua's father was in disgrace, he had once been a high-ranking cadre, and there were still people willing to help him out and do favors for him and his family. After four years on the state farm, Bai Meihua found herself placed in a university as a "worker-peasant-soldier" student. It was not, to be sure, a very good university, and still it was far from Peking, but it released Bai Meihua from the state farm and gave her something of a college education. After graduating, Bai Meihua was fortunate enough to arrange a transfer back to Peking. She returned to the capital in October 1976, the day before the public announcement that the Gang of Four had been arrested and overthrown.

THE incarceration of Song Wuhao's father, accused of being a bourgeois academic authority, a counterrevolutionary, and a spy, followed by weeks the incarceration of the father of Bai Meihua. Song Wuhao, like Bai Meihua, suffered profoundly when his father came under attack. But the exuberance with which Song Wuhao had initially greeted the Cultural Revolution, the enthusiasm with which he had once seized the chance to overthrow the principal of Qinghua Middle School and to lock him and his close associates up, the excitement he had felt at the opportunity to prove himself revolutionary at last, had already begun to wane. Living in the best quarters the city government of Shanghai could provide, with cars, money, and the right to broadcast his organization's views, Song Wuhao's task had become to conduct "intelligence research" on two senior municipal officials who had been singled out for attack—the same city officials who had sent the work teams to Jiang Xinren's campus when Jiang Xinren was declared a counterrevolutionary and imprisoned for two months in a cattle pen. It was Song Wuhao's task, as part of a much larger team, to gather the evidence that would convict Chen Peixian, first party secretary for all of east China, and Shanghai Mayor Cao Diqiu, of a wide variety of crimes.

But as Song Wuhao carried out his intelligence research, reading the files of Chen Peixian and Cao Diqiu and interviewing numerous people who had been associated with them, Song Wuhao became convinced that they were not bad men after all. Not only, he came to believe, were they not counterrevolutionaries but they were genuine revolutionaries. They had been good revolutionaries all along.

"At the time I began participating in the investigation, I believed that Cao and Chen were bad people, that they should be overthrown," Song Wuhao recalls. "So far as I was concerned, they hadn't supported Chairman Mao's line, and the real question for me was just how to go about overthrowing them, how to gather the evidence that would lead to their downfall. I thought that they had stolen money from the people and that they were part of bad organizations.

"But gradually, as I carried out the investigation, not only did I not think they were bad people, I thought they were good. Everyone I interviewed about them said they were good people, good revolutionaries, that they had never done anything wrong. And none of the files that I read contained any information of wrongdoing."

But as Song Wuhao continued his investigation, increasingly convinced of the innocence of Chen and Cao, he remained silent. He shared his doubts with no one. He thought that he was young, that he had no experience participating in a revolution, and that this, the Cultural Revolution, was a revolution after all. Such was his youth and such the hysterical tenor of the times that the fifteen-year-old would-be revolutionary could not trust his own honest instincts. "As I was carrying out the investigation and began to think that Cao and Chen were good people after all, I didn't tell anyone what I thought," he says. "I didn't say anything about it to anyone. I was a revolutionary. I was Chairman Mao's Red Guard and Chairman Mao was the truth. I didn't really know that my own thoughts, my own doubts could be correct. I was still a child. I didn't have any self-confidence. I had doubts, yes, but I didn't dare trust those doubts. I kept thinking I was still only a child. I was just fifteen years old at the time. But even though I didn't say anything about it, even though I couldn't trust my own thoughts, this did begin to produce a change in my thinking."

Song Wuhao returned to his home in Peking in February 1967. It seemed to him as though the whole country was paralyzed. "Lots of good people were being overthrown and bad people were gaining positions of power," he said. Song Wuhao read the official accusations against Cao Diqiu and Chen Peixian after his return to Peking. "The facts were distorted," he claims. "They weren't true." Then Song Wuhao's own parents were attacked, taken away, and incarcerated.

"Why were my parents overthrown?" he asks today with the same incredulity he must have felt at the time. "More than any other people, surely I understood my own parents. But were they bad people? And the parents of my fellow students were also being overthrown. It seemed as though all the parents of my fellow students were being overthrown, the parents of all my friends. But how could I believe that all my friends' parents were bad people? It was at this point, in February 1967, that my doubts really began, that they could no longer be ignored."

Professor Song was accused of being a spy for the United States because he had studied there, receiving an advanced degree from the University of Minnesota. When the Red Guards came to search his apartment, his degree and the thesis he had written to receive it were seized as evidence of his crime. He was also accused of being a counterrevolutionary, a capitalist, and a "counterrevolutionary academic authority." "The reason he was accused of being a 'counterrevolutionary academic authority,' " explains Song Wuhao, "is that his status at Qinghua University was so high—a full professor." Mrs. Song was accused of having aided and abetted her husband. Husband and wife were taken away and imprisoned in separate cattle pens.

"From that time on," relates Song Wuhao, "I never saw my parents. I didn't know their circumstances, and they didn't know mine. They were never allowed to come home, and most of the time I didn't dare to go home either. People kept coming to our house to question me and my brothers. And the house was searched four times. I was there twice during the search. My parents were never there. This happened after they had been taken away. After the house had been searched, the revolutionary rebels came in and occupied it."

Song Wuhao's own status changed decisively with his parents' change of status. He was transformed overnight from an exultant Red Guard and one of Chairman Mao's trusted young revolutionaries to a son of a bitch and the object himself of tormenting, persistent attack. "When my parents came under attack, I also came under attack. I had to return to my school, and they said I was a 'five black element,'* the son of a spy, the 'worthy progeny of a counterrevolutionary.' Just a few days before, I had been a revolutionary Red Guard, one of Chairman Mao's little revolutionaries, but then . . . they attacked me. They asked me if I knew my parents' crimes. They wanted me to confess my parents' crimes. They said that if I didn't confess, they would beat me, and because I didn't confess, they did beat me, the same Red Guards who just a few days earlier had been working for me, working together with me. Then they locked me up in a tiny little room, just me, all alone.

"I believed I understood my parents. I didn't think they were bad people, spies, counterrevolutionaries, reactionary academic authorities. I thought that they loved their country, their people, China. So when I was attacked, I could only say good about my parents, nothing bad. I respected my parents. So they thought I was a five black element, the son of a spy, the worthy progeny of a counterrevolutionary. They thought I was the lowest person on earth.

"But I believed I was right, and I persisted in saying my parents were good.

*The "five black elements" were landlords, rich peasants, counterrevolutionaries, rightists, and "bad people"—generally meaning those who opposed the Cultural Revolution.

So they struggled against me some more. They made me wear a placard around my neck saying 'Worthy progeny of a counterrevolutionary,' and then my name, Song Wuhao. But they crossed out my name with three X's. That meant they thought I shouldn't even be allowed to live. This lasted from April to December 1967. Finally they gave up. I persisted in my viewpoint, and they didn't know what to do about me, so they finally just let me go."

Unable to go home and without food, work, or money, Song Wuhao left the cities for the countryside. There he kept himself alive by drinking water from the rivers and stealing sweet potatoes from peasants' fields.

"I kept wondering why this was happening. This was a revolution and this is what the revolution is giving me. I thought about the future, about my own future, about my life. I wondered whether my whole life would be like this, wandering through the countryside of China like a vagrant, stealing sweet potatoes from peasants' fields. This was my doubt.

"I thought I had to have an answer, that I had to find out. So in June, I went back to Peking to search for an answer. No one paid any attention to me. At first, I just roamed around the streets. Then, finally, I went to my father's work unit. I asked them why they had locked my father up. I told them that my father is a good person. 'He loves his country. Why have you locked him up? There is no reason to lock him up.'

"They said I was a troublemaker and a nuisance. They took me and put me in jail. Not a cattle pen or an office building. They put me in a real jail, for real prisoners. They said I was a vagrant, that I opposed the revolution, that I was making trouble and creating a disturbance. They said I did bad things.

"But while I was in prison, they never questioned me, never interrogated me. Twice they took me to a big struggle session against me. They put a placard around my neck saying that I was a vagrant and a public nuisance and that I opposed the revolution. They made me do the jet airplane with a placard around my neck. But they never asked me anything, never wanted me to say anything.

"In August 1968, they took me out of prison and sent me to a study class organized by the Public Security Bureau, a class consisting of other people like me, the young vagrants, the public nuisances, the children who opposed the revolution. But shortly after that, they moved me to a study class in my father's work unit, again a class of young people like me. They wanted me to confess my crimes, to recognize that I was a vagrant, a public nuisance, a creator of disorder, the son of a spy, the worthy progeny of a counterrevolutionary, the lowest of the low. When I refused to recognize my crimes and confess, I had to stand in front of a portrait of Chairman Mao and do the jet airplane, and admit my errors, and ask him—Chairman Mao—to punish me, and I was supposed to apologize for my crimes. They beat me. They wouldn't let me eat. But I persisted in my point of view. Then they got the other children in the class to surround me, assault me, besiege me. I couldn't stand it. I escaped. I ran away.

"I sneaked on a train again and first went to Nanjing, then to Chengzhou. I still didn't have any money or any food, and my clothes had become tattered. But in Chengzhou, I was put into prison again. I told them I was a peasant, but they didn't believe me, so after a while, I had no other choice but to admit that I was from Peking. So they took me back on the train to Peking, as though I were a common criminal. They made me beg Chairman Mao's forgiveness.

"When I got back to Peking, I was taken back to the study class at my father's work unit and locked up again. Then they held a big struggle meeting against both me and my father. They put my father and me next to each other on the stage, and they made us do the jet airplane together. Then they began beating my father. With their belts.

"I was miserable, so depressed. What crime had I committed? Was this really China's revolution? I had gone from one of Chairman Mao's trusted Red Guards from the Qinghua Middle School, from a young Red Guard whom everyone respected, with so much power, from a fanatic young revolutionary, to the lowest, most detested person in Chinese society. This Cultural Revolution brought misery to my generation, suffering, difficulty, and misery. From this time on, I doubted history, I doubted society. I began to recognize that there were evil people governing our country, evil people oppressing the Chinese people I loved. I think my experience is representative of the experience of many other youths of my generation. We were the most miserable, most unfortunate generation in China's history. True, the older generation had had its misfortunes, but this was different. We had no future, no ideals. Our ideals had been destroyed."

The story of the joint struggle session against them is one that father and son tell separately. Each breaks down at exactly the same point, unable to continue.

It was deep into the night when Song Wuhao reached this point in his tale, and for many minutes, the only sounds to be heard in the dimly lit room were Wuhao's muffled sobs and tortured breath and the ticking of the clock. There were no words that might have provided comfort.

"Then they began beating me."

Song Wuhao is crying now. His voice comes out a wail.

"They told me they wouldn't stop beating me until I beat my own father. I couldn't believe it. They wanted me to beat my own father."

"It was not the pain," his father had gasped when his composure had returned sufficiently to continue. "It was the humiliation. He is my son."

In the dynastic code, a son who struck his own father was executed. Filial piety was the strongest of Confucian virtues.

Song Wuhao had begged. He had pleaded. He had cried. He had fallen on his knees in anger and cried out for mercy. But his persecutors had continued beating Song Wuhao until Song Wuhao beat his father.

It was eleven years before Song Wuhao saw his father again.

AFTER the joint struggle session with father and son, Wuhao was released from the Mao Zedong study class that had kept him imprisoned and given $100 and a week to leave Peking. It was late December 1968. Chairman Mao had just issued a proclamation calling on the country's educated and urban youth to go up to the mountains and down to the villages to participate in the struggle for production and be reeducated by the poor-and-lower-middle peasants. Other young people, like Song Erli, who had participated as a college student in the Socialist Education Campaign, had been sent to the countryside prior to the Cultural Revolution. But this movement, which saw some twelve million urban youth sent to the countryside between 1968 and 1975 in what was surely the largest forced migration in human history, was different. Most of the urban young believed they were being transferred permanently. It is said by Thomas Bernstein, the scholar who has investigated these transfers most thoroughly, that the dominant motivation in forcing so many young people to leave the cities was related to problems of employment. There were simply more young people graduating from urban middle schools each year than there were jobs in the cities to absorb them. Reports during the Cultural Revolution indicated that between 1966 and 1970 eleven million young people would enter the urban job market, of whom only five million could be provided jobs. The remaining six million roughly corresponds to the number actually sent to the countryside between 1968, when Chairman Mao's call went out, and 1970.

Many young people responded to Chairman Mao's call voluntarily and enthusiastically, desiring nothing more than selflessly to serve the revolution with all their hearts. Photographs from the time show smiling young people leaving by open truck and train, cheered on by audiences lining the roads with red flags flying and gongs and cymbals clanging.

That is not how Song Wuhao went. Song Wuhao fled to the countryside secretly and in terror, taking his twelve-year-old brother with him. "We wanted to go somewhere where no one would know where we were, a secret place," he says. An uncle, a man who had been declared a rightist in 1957 and had fled to the countryside himself, found a village willing to accept two young and frightened children of an alleged spy and counterrevolutionary and made the arrangements to get them there. Song Wuhao and his brother arrived in the countryside by train at about three o'clock one afternoon and set off on foot with their uncle toward their new home.

"By six o'clock in the evening, we were still walking, and it was already dark," remembers Song Wuhao. "We couldn't even see the road. No one said anything. Nothing. No talking. No laughing. We just walked slowly along the road. Why was our country doing this to us?

"Finally, we came to a building and went inside. There was no light and no windows. The walls were completely black, filthy, dirty, covered with spiderwebs. It was already winter and very cold, but the temperatures inside the building and outside were just the same, equally cold. No one lived in the house. It was a shed where the peasants stored their tools, and the door was broken. The floors were dirt, just like the ground outside the house. The peasants had known we were coming, so they had made us beds. They had given us some rice stalks that served as our beds. There was a small jar filled with kerosene, which we lit. It made hardly any light at all, but after we had lit it and could see the shadows around the room, we were more frightened than ever. The only furniture was a broken table. Outside, a big north wind was blowing, which just made everything worse. We were very depressed. We were still children, and we had never known that life could be like this. We didn't know what to do.

"The three of us just sat there on the rice stalks, all huddled together in our coats, talking. My brother and I were afraid to go to sleep, so we talked almost the whole night.

"My uncle tried to advise us, tried to cheer us up and give us courage. He said that we should not lower our heads or bow before adversity. He said we should hold ourselves high, be proud. He told us not to be depressed, to look toward the future. He pointed to himself, to his own case, and said that he had been labeled a rightist when he was only in his twenties, but he hadn't bowed because he didn't believe the label, because he thought it was wrong. He said that as long as we refused to bow our heads and refused to believe the accusations against us, there was hope and we could lead a happy life. If not, if we bowed our heads and believed what was being said against us, we would suffer. He encouraged us to stand up and to overcome our present difficulties.

"We listened to him, but still we felt depressed. We talked about how to live, how to survive in that place. We talked about my parents and about how dangerous it must be for them, how dangerous we really didn't know. We, my brother and I, had planned to go to the university. I wanted to become a scientist. But now, what could we do? Our plans had been destroyed. We couldn't see the road in front of us, didn't know where it would lead, but we knew it would be a hard road to walk. We talked like this until daylight.

"On the second day, in the morning, we were about to begin to make our first meal. Suddenly the door opened and in walked five or six peasants, varying in age from an older woman to a youth. They brought us things that peasants eat. The old lady said to us, 'Children, we hear you have come here to join the production team. We are very happy. We know that you feel that you have been wronged. But we still welcome you, because you have come from Peking, from Chairman Mao's side. We know you aren't used to this kind of life, but we can help you.' When we heard this, we understood how the peasants felt about us, and we were very touched. Our life seemed so difficult, but they treated us honestly, like friends. They told us we could live there. So we were glad and thankful to hear the kind words from the peasant woman.

"We ate breakfast. There were sweet potatoes, which in China are considered one of the lowest forms of food. But the other things were even worse than that. There were some rolls made of corn, and others, black rolls, made of buckwheat. There were little rocks inside the bread, and everything we ate seemed like the type of food you would give the pigs to eat. I couldn't digest it. It was just awful. But the peasants were there, so we had to eat it. We didn't want to embarrass them, so we kept telling them that it was very good, really very good to eat. Afterward, though, when they were gone, I threw it up. The sweet potato was okay, but the corn and the buckwheat were simply indigestible. These peasants had no contact with the outside world, and their methods were terribly primitive. They didn't even know how to make bread. It was just big thick lumps with tough skin on the outside. I was actually afraid when I ate it.

"After breakfast, my uncle took us on a walk through the village and some of the area surrounding the village. He told us that this production brigade was an old revolutionary base area and that the peasants were all very good, very honest, very frank. He said that if they believed you were a good person, regardless of your past, then they would treat you like a good person. It didn't matter what your label was, whether you were a rightist or the son of a counterrevolutionary or whatever. My uncle really knew how to talk, and what he said made me very happy. Had we been anyplace else, we would have been locked up, put in jail. In Peking, we had already suffered a lot, so much bullying. We were considered the lowest of the low. Here the peasants were poor, backward, their clothes all tattered and torn, but their hearts were good.

"First, we walked to the village. The houses were all old and very poor, made of pressed earth with roofs of straw. The children, no matter what age, didn't go to school. We saw the peasants eating a corn porridge in huge bowls. There was no running water in the village, so peasants had to fetch water in buckets from one of the streams on the outskirts of the village. As I looked, I became depressed again. The area was so backward, so poor. My uncle told me that this was the result of the Cultural Revolution, that before the lives of the peasants here had been good but now they had become poor. This, he said, was due to the revolutionary rebels. 'The Cultural Revolution has brought nothing but trouble and poverty. People have nothing to eat, nothing to wear. Because during this Cultural Revolution, all the peasants can do is hold meetings, struggle, criticize, write big character posters attacking everything. No one goes to school anymore. No one works. No one manages the fields. Look at the benefits of our Great Proletarian Cultural Revolution! Nothing to eat! Nothing to wear! Houses that are falling apart!' And he cursed the revolutionary rebels.

"At that time, we didn't really understand, and we dared not agree with what he was saying about the revolution. But he understood. He did understand.

"Afterward, my uncle and I walked around the outskirts of the village. The scenery was beautiful, magnificent, with beautiful mountains and streams. The mountains were covered with green forests, and even though it was still winter, there were flowers everywhere, and all the trees were green. The air was good and fresh and clear. When I looked at that beautiful scenery, I felt uplifted, happy. I had always thought Peking was the most beautiful place in the world. Peking then wasn't like Peking now, so crowded and dirty. Here was a place even more beautiful than Peking. But so magnificent a place, yet the peasants' life was so poor. Why? Even though I was young, I was beginning to understand that our society was wounded. I had to understand that society. But I didn't know what to do or how to understand.

"In the evening, the peasants again brought us our meal—long noodles with a bit of meat mixed in. This was their customary way of entertaining honored guests, and because we were from Peking, they thought we were rather amazing.

"After we ate, the production brigade, some twenty-two families and about a hundred people, held a meeting to welcome us. The leader of the production brigade was a man of around fifty, and while the meeting was very casual and people spoke in no particular order, he was the first to speak. He said, 'Today, Song Wuhao and his little brother arrived in our village, and this makes us very happy. Why? Because they are still very young and they had to leave their parents behind, but they came here to work with us, to participate in the work of the production brigade, and to set up a household. They aren't used to life in this remote area of the countryside, so we must help them. We must treat them as our own relatives, our own children. If they have any problems, we will help them. Chairman Mao said that the movement of up to the mountains and down to the villages is a great movement, and our two new friends are part of that great movement.'

"After he had spoken these words, many other peasants followed with their words of welcome, all of them telling us to relax, that they would help us and treat us as relatives and friends. After they all finished speaking, we also had to speak. I said, 'We are very moved by what you have said. Why? Because you spoke from the heart. Because the poor-and-lower-middle peasants have given us such a warm welcome, we feel as though we are your relatives. We welcome and appreciate your help, and we accept the call of Chairman Mao to go up to the mountains and down to the villages to learn from you, to learn your good thought, your good character. Most important, we hope that after a while, we can become people who can be of use to society.' The reason I said the last sentence, about being of use to society, is that at that time, I still felt I was the lowest, most despised and useless member of society, without any place, any position as a human being. Then I said that I would accept the peasants' education, learn from the poor-and-lower-middle peasants.

"There was still a barrier between us and the peasants. They spoke very casually, very freely. But we, after all, were the lowest elements of society and not able to speak freely and openly. There was no respect for us from Chinese society. But I began to feel a small glimmer of hope that we would be able to live there, to survive, and perhaps to make some contributions.

"I will always remember when I first arrived in the countryside. Those were my darkest hours. I had no hope, only grief and despair. I had always wanted to become a scientist, to contribute to my fatherland, but all those hopes were dashed. But after going to the countryside, I came to love the peasants. Because when I lived with them, they saw my pain, and they tried to help and comfort me. I will always love them."

WHEN Liu Zhiping, the daughter of an ordinary cadre, set out on her Long March to Yenan in the fall of 1966, she already had reservations about the Cultural Revolution. Her fellow university students had already come to regard her as a conservative. Her situation was serious, but her world had yet to crumble. Her sense of identity had yet to come under full-scale attack.

In the late fall of 1967, a year after she had left for her Long March, Liu Zhiping received a telegram from her mother. Her father was seriously ill, the telegram said, and Liu Zhiping was urged to return home immediately.

When Liu Zhiping walked into her family courtyard, she was greeted by a sea of big character posters attacking her father. It had taken time for the revolution to work its way down from the leading cadres like Bai Meihua's father to the ordinary cadres like Mr. Liu. Liu Zhiping's father was accused of having been a traitor, because in the years before the civil war between the Nationalists and the Communists, during the Communist struggle for power, he had done underground party work in an area controlled by the Guomindang. As a member of the party underground, he was arrested, then later released, by the Guomindang. Many party members so arrested and released during the underground struggle were branded traitors during the Cultural Revolution. The assumption was that the price of their release had been the betrayal of their Communist Party comrades.

Liu Zhiping's family was in a state of disintegration. Her mother was distraught and frightened. Her elder sister was at the edge of hysteria, her fiancé having just broken up with her because he refused out of revolutionary conscience to marry the daughter of a traitor. Her younger sister, seventeen years old, had disappeared completely, running away from home in order to avoid the attacks that she was receiving at school as a *gouzaizi*, a son of a bitch. The elderly grandmother who lived with the family had tried to commit suicide by throwing herself into a nearby pond, only to be rescued by passersby. The neighbors, once so friendly, had not only stopped visiting but refused even to say hello, "not necessarily because they thought my father and my family were bad," explains Liu Zhiping, "but because they were afraid that they too would be criticized if they were seen talking to my family." Mrs. Liu was beginning to say that she couldn't stand it any longer. She was beginning to contemplate suicide.

"All I could say was that this was a revolution, that we must support this revolution, because it was Chairman Mao's revolution, and Chairman Mao was always right," recalls Liu Zhiping.

Liu Zhiping describes the dilemma she faced, the dilemma faced by so many young people whose parents came under attack during the Cultural Revolution, young people torn between loyalty to the revolution and Chairman Mao on the one hand and loyalty to their families on the other. "I didn't know what my father had done," Liu Zhiping says. "What he was accused of doing had happened before Liberation, before I was even born. Liberation was in 1949, when I was only three years old. How could I have known what my father had done? I told my mother that she must continue to trust in the party, trust in the people. I said that it wasn't right to struggle against my father this way, to use violence. But I said that this was a revolution, that however bad the violence, it was still a revolution. I told her that she should be able to stand it, that my father should be able to stand it, that my father could stand it just as the others were standing it. I said that if my father were to die, to commit suicide, then he would become the real enemy.

"The rebels asked me to go to my father's office to read all the big character posters there that had been written against him. They wanted me to draw a clear line of demarcation. I said that I didn't know what my father had done before I was born, but that I did know that the education I had received from my parents was a good one. I told them to go check my files, to look at my record, and they would see that my parents had educated me well. I quarreled with them. I told them that I believed in the masses, but I said that beating people wasn't revolution, that it was wrong to beat people. Then I had to go back to school."

When Liu Zhiping returned to her university, she reported the attacks against her father, told her friends and her teachers that her father had been accused of being a traitor. After that, her whole life changed.

"From that day on," she reports, "my own status changed. Because of the attacks against my father, my own position changed. I became a young person who 'could be educated.' Every day, I had to make a public self-criticism. I had to draw a clear line of demarcation. I did draw a clear line of demarcation. I said that I would trust the masses and wait. I said that I didn't know my father's case, that what he was accused of doing had happened before I was born, that I could not know.

"I was ostracized. There were many events in the school then, but I wasn't allowed to take part. If there was an important meeting, I had to stay away. I wasn't allowed to go. I was very depressed. Before, I had been someone special, a good student, active, well liked and well respected. Now everyone knew me only as the daughter of a bad man, a renegade, a traitor to his people.

"I just couldn't stand it. It isn't that I was lonely. There were people to talk to, and I did stay friends with some people. But I couldn't really talk to them about what I was really thinking, about the problems I was having. You see, until then I had believed in everything. When I read the newspaper, I believed what it said in the newspaper. When the party made a statement, I believed what it said. When I read Chairman Mao, I believed what he said. The radio. Everything. And I believed in socialism. I thought I was socialist, and that I was working for socialism.

"But when my father came under attack, I would read the newspapers, and I didn't know what to believe. I didn't know whether my father was a traitor. How could I know? But I decided to separate myself from my family and to become independent. I knew that I wasn't bad regardless of what was true about my father.

"So I decided to leave school again."

Liu Zhiping could never bring herself to "draw a clear line of demarcation" from her father by attacking him directly. Her means of separating herself from her father and from the odium he was bringing to her was to run away again and to plunge herself selflessly into revolutionary work.

Liu Zhiping ran away to the Chinese countryside. "This time there were fifteen of us, three girls and twelve boys. We decided we wanted to establish a school. When we got to the countryside, we scattered and lived in different villages. I and one other girl lived in a peasant's house together. Actually, we lived with an old grandmother and her granddaughter. The mother had died, and when we came, the father moved out. The house was very dirty, so we helped to clean it. There were lice in the bed, and they would bite you all over when you slept. So we found a plastic cover for the straw mat and covered it with plastic so the lice couldn't get out.

"The peasants wanted the school we tried to establish for them. They liked it. They knew that education was important. But still, the school failed. The children were needed at home. If the children left home to go to school, there was no one to help with the housework, and especially during the harvest time, they were needed in the fields. So it didn't work.

"But we were still happy to stay in the countryside, and the peasants were happy to have us. They treated us like human beings, like their own people. I began to feel that there wasn't anything wrong with me after all. It didn't matter to them who my father was or what he had done. They admired us for working so hard, even though we weren't so good in the fields. They told us to stay and start a family there. So I came to feel like one of the common people, like a Chinese, not 'someone who could be educated.' "

But Liu Zhiping and her classmates had left school without permission. Periodically, they received messages from the school urging, then ordering, them to return. Over time, the messages became ever more frequent, urgent, insistent. The students met and debated whether to return. Liu Zhiping, who had voted to stay, lost. The group decided to respond to the urgings from their school. Revolutionaries that they were, they decided to return in Long March style, by foot.

After two days on the Long March that would bring them back to the world they had earlier tried to escape, the girl who had lived with Liu Zhiping in the peasant household became too ill to continue. After more discussion and further debate, it was decided that Liu Zhiping would stay with her friend and the other eleven would continue on by train. "It was at a mining village that we stopped," Liu Zhiping relates, "and the doctors in the mine and the miners themselves were very good to us. They found us a cave—people live in caves in that part of the country—our very own cave just for the two of us. Half of the room was the *kang,* a sleeping loft, and the stove, and in the other half they put a table and some chairs. It was very nice. The miners were concerned about our safety and were afraid that the lock on the door wouldn't hold. So they brought us a big tree trunk to put against the door at night to keep out the bad people—robbers and thieves and other kinds of people. We were just two young girls, so we were very vulnerable.

"A doctor at the mine took care of my friend and gave her medicine and other kinds of treatment, so she gradually got well. I wasn't so bad off as she, but I did have some problems, too. Even to this day, this leg still bothers me."

Liu Zhiping and her friend decided not to return to their university. They would stay and work in the mining community. "The mining people welcomed us," she says. "The miners, most of them, were illiterate, and they wanted us to teach them to read. So we began teaching them to read the newspapers and to write a few characters. After teaching them for a while, I asked if they would show me the mine. They refused at first. They said it was a living coffin, that there were many accidents, that no women ever went into the mine. But eventually, we did get to see it. You went down into the mine through a shaft. It was very leaky underneath, and the pillars were all very loose. And it was very dark. Underneath, along the main tunnel where the tracks ran, there was electricity, but in the small tunnels that went out from each side of the main tunnel, there was none. The miners who worked in those side tunnels had to wear oil-burning lamps on their heads to see, and those tunnels were so narrow the miners had to crawl on the ground when they worked.

"When my girlfriend recovered, we both agreed that we wanted to work in the mine. We worked in the main tunnel, pushing the carts of coal. Each cart held almost fifteen hundred pounds, and you pushed it along a track. It made a terrible sound when you pushed it. At the same time you were pushing a cart forward, someone else was close behind you pushing another cart. So you could never stop or even slow down, because if you did there was always the danger of being crushed by the other cart. My friend and I worked like that for eight hours a day without eating. Later, after work, we would eat hot noodles with the workers. The only vegetables we ate were cabbage and potatoes, because those were the only types of vegetables that would grow in that cold place with that kind of soil. We ate two meals like that a day. I loved working there and living there."

But the calls for students to return to their schools kept getting stronger and stronger. Finally, Liu Zhiping and her friend could ignore the calls no longer. Their university sent someone to the mining town to force them to return to school.

"On the day we left," remembers Liu Zhiping, "everyone in the mine came to say goodbye to us. The whole town escorted us to the train that would take us back to school. They beat gongs and drums and waved flags and we all walked together to the train station. And they gave us each their farewell presents. Everyone who worked in the mine, some two hundred people, had gone together to buy us each a notebook, because a notebook is the symbol of an intellectual, and in each notebook each person had written his name because we had taught them all how to write their names. They said that this was a small token for us to remember them by. In the farewell speech, they said they knew that the work we had to do was important, that it was right for us to return to school, that education was important for the revolution. But they said that in the future, when we were wearing fancy clothes and living in the cities, we should not forget that place, where water is still drawn from wells and where people don't have so much to eat or such good clothes to wear. That was November 1968.

"I still have the notebook. And I could never forget those people."

AFTER having been confined for two months to a darkened cattle pen at the onset of the Cultural Revolution, it took Jiang Xinren about two weeks after his release to recover. "I went home and tried to catch up on what had been happening in those two months," he says. "I felt as if I had been out of the world. I stayed at home and read the newspapers, and talked to my friends. Then I was ready to participate in the Cultural Revolution again." It was late August 1966.

Because of Jiang Xinren's "bad class background," he was prohibited from assuming positions of leadership in the revolutionary rebel organization in which he so enthusiastically participated. "I was always the 'vice' and never the chief in everything I did," he says. His primary responsibilities at first were writing—"mostly attacking the conservative Red Guards and explaining the situation in Shanghai."

Three months after his release from the cattle pen, Jiang Xinren's participation in the Cultural Revolution took a more aggressive turn. "At the time, if you wanted to attack the conservatives," he explains, "it was important to publish a newspaper so people would read what you were saying. Jiang Qing had said, 'Attack with words, defend by force,' so the first thing we had to do was to establish a communications system so we could attack with words. But no one was willing to publish our newspaper. We were only able to make a few handwritten copies, so very few people were able to read it. So we met and decided we had to take over a newspaper."

The newspaper Jiang Xinren and his fellow revolutionary rebels decided to take over was the *Liberation Daily*, the Shanghai city newspaper controlled by the municipal Communist Party committee—the same municipal party committee Song Wuhao had been sent to help overthrow.

"We had it all planned in advance," he says. "The revolutionary rebels—there were a couple thousand of us—formed in various groups at different places outside the building and then we all marched in to take it over. There were only a few people in the building at the time—the chief editor and a few other people. But most of the offices were empty. Some of us—maybe three hundred or so—locked ourselves in and demanded that they publish our newspaper. It wasn't just students involved. It was workers, too, which is really why we were able to do it. While we were locked inside, we got much of our food from our school—we had trucks and they would just go to the school and take rice and vegetables from the dining hall and deliver it to us in trucks. The workers of Shanghai were also divided into two groups, and some of them—many of them—supported us. So they also brought us food and we cooked it in the building."

On November 30, 1966, the city of Shanghai awakened to find itself without its morning newspaper. The next day, December 1, the newsstands were still without the *Liberation Daily*. "We stayed locked inside the building for maybe five or six days," recalls Jiang Xinren. "Then there was a decision from the Shanghai municipal party that both newspapers should be published, both points of view should be aired."

Jiang Xinren remained consistently on the most rebellious side of the Cultural Revolution—so rebellious that he and his faction publicly opposed Zhang Chunqiao, later to be deposed as one of the Gang of Four but then gaining increasing power in both Shanghai and Peking. Jiang Xinren's newspaper printed an article attacking Zhang Chunqiao, accusing him of having collaborated with the Guomindang before Liberation. For such an attack, the leaders of Jiang Xinren's rebel organization were arrested and imprisoned. "They weren't put in cattle pens," explains Jiang Xinren of the seriousness of the accusation, "they were put into real prisons. Since I was only a 'fish' and not a real ringleader, they didn't put me in jail, although they might have had I stayed in Shanghai. But I decided I couldn't stay, that I had to run away.

"I left secretly with some friends, without telling anyone, not even my parents. At that time, all the Red Guards could travel free on the train, and no one could tell from looking that I had been accused of being a counterrevolutionary. Altogether, I was gone from Shanghai for a year."

Jiang Xinren first went to Peking. "It was important to go to Peking," he says, "because that was where the Cultural Revolution had started, and Peking and Qinghua universities were the two most important places to be. That was also where the Cultural Revolution was most idealistic. Kuai Dafu was there, too, and I was something of a follower of Kuai Dafu. There was no violence at Beida and Qinghua then, only lots of arguments. In Peking, the Central Cultural Revolution Group knew exactly what was going on and could control things that were happening in the city. They could always make a quick decision about which side was right and which was wrong, and this way they were able to keep much of the violence under control. In some of the cities farther away, though, it was difficult for the Cultural Revolution Group to know what was going on, so no decisions were made, or it took months to make a decision, and in this situation, the fighting intensified. It just couldn't be stopped."

It was after Jiang Xinren had left Peking that the violence of the Cultural Revolution intensified and the country entered the period of *wudou*—armed struggle. With the country, as Song Wuhao describes it, paralyzed by early 1967, the People's Liberation Army, under the leadership of Lin Biao, its soldiers touted as exemplars of loyalty to the party chairman, were called upon to intervene in the Cultural Revolution "on the side of the left." The military was instructed to aid the revolutionary rebels both in seizing power from entrenched and conservative party bureaucrats deemed to be "following the capitalist road" and in establishing "three-way alliances"—revolutionary committees composed of representatives from the revolutionary rebels, the "revolutionary" party cadre, and the People's Liberation Army. These newly formed revolutionary committees were to replace the party committees as the governing bodies at every level of the country's organizational hierarchy.

But the military, or so the young rebels alleged, intervened more often on the side of order than on the side of the left, often reinstating the very bureaucrats the left had sought to overthrow. The revolutionary rebels themselves became factionalized. Some supported the intervention of the military and cooperated with it in the establishment of revolutionary committees, their members being thereby appointed to the newly formed committees. Dissident factions opposed both the revolutionary rebels who supported the military and the People's Liberation Army itself.

But when commanders of the People's Liberation Army ordered their troops to fire on revolutionary rebels and denounced the rebels as counterrevolutionary, the central military leadership in Peking in turn prohibited the military from further use of weapons against the revolutionaries and ordered them not to label revolutionary rebel organizations as counterrevolutionary or to make mass arrests. The result of the reining in of the military was the eruption and spread of violence and disorder. In the first ten days of May 1967, according to one report, there were well over a hundred incidents of armed struggle. Revolutionary rebel organizations turned against each other and against the People's Liberation Army as well and launched bitter attacks against local military committees, both for having suppressed them in the past and for failing to support them in the present.

With the chaos threatening quickly to degenerate into anarchy, the Cultural Revolution Group in Peking decided to send a number of high-level military delegations to investigate the Cultural Revolution in the provinces. A major objective of the delegations was to put an end to the armed struggle that had broken out between contending factions of revolutionary rebels and between those factions and local military commands. When the delegation sent to investigate the Cultural Revolution in the central China city of Wuhan reversed an earlier decision made by the local Wuhan military command, at least some leaders of the Wuhan command ordered the Peking officials (Xie Fuzhi and Wang Li) seized as the revolutionary masses supporting the local military, including troops from the local garrison, staged a massive demonstration. The military was not so solidly in the Mao Zedong/Lin Biao/Jiang Qing camp as its previously unbroken chain of command might suggest. The detention of officials from Peking by local military commanders came to be known as the Wuhan Incident and signaled the growing power and independence of China's regional military commanders and an increasing split between central and local control.

Now the military itself became the target of criticism as none other than Lin Biao ordered local military units to admit their "mistakes" and carry out public self-criticism. It was at this point that the Cultural Revolution Group zagged left again, ordering some revolutionary rebel organizations armed in order to seize power from the military as China careened further and faster toward anarchy. When, by the end of August, pitched battles had broken out throughout the country, the Cultural Revolution Group zigged right, trying again to reestablish order, but the country continued to hover around anarchy, and the capacity of the center to control the provinces markedly declined.

"The violence was a gradually escalating thing," explains Jiang Xinren, who took up guns and used them during this, the most violent phase. "At first, like when we took over the newspaper in Shanghai, there were no weapons. We just pushed our way in, using our fists if necessary, so no one was hurt. Certainly no one died. Maybe a few people used sticks or clubs at that time, but very few. Later, though, we began to use clubs and pipe swords more and more. And then we began to use knives. Since we were allied with the workers and they had access to the factories, they could make us knives. I used knives. I had knives. Some people died in the knife fights, not immediately but two or three days after the fight. When you know someone is using knives, you are very careful, and I was always very careful to avoid people with knives.

"But the level of violence gradually increased so that people were using guns. At first, the military was supporting the conservatives and began supplying them with guns. This put us at a real disadvantage. Even though we were much stronger in terms of numbers, we still needed weapons in order to defend ourselves. The level of violence really increased after we had guns. I saw many people killed. Many people. Four of my best friends, three boys and a girl, were killed, one when he was standing right next to me.

"It's hard to say what started the violence, really. Nothing sometimes or just an apparently little thing like a big character poster attacking the other side that the other side didn't like. But there was violence, and we did have guns and hand grenades, and I was involved in it. I had a gun.

"At first it just seemed like a game, as though it wasn't real, that it was just something exciting. But then, in August 1967, I was in a big battle with my friends, and we were using guns and one of my friends was shot. He was standing right next to me, just like this, and he was shot. We tried to save him, tried to use emergency measures, but there was no life in him. His eyes had rolled back so all you could see was white, and there was dark blood coming out of his head and the brain tissue because he had been hit in the head. As we tried to save him I could feel that his body was already getting cold, that he was already dead. We pulled him inside, because the battle was still going on outside. I was very angry, and I began to shoot, to fire my gun. I can still see my friend's face after he was dead. Sometimes it still comes back to me in my dreams.

"I don't know whether I killed anyone or not. When you are firing a gun and everyone else around you is firing a gun and people are being killed, you don't know who is doing the killing. It's easy to fire a gun. No one had to teach us then. We all received military training in school, girls and boys alike, and again in college. We knew how to use guns and we knew how to repair them. Besides, it's easy to fire a gun. Anyone could learn."

It was not until the fall of 1968 that Jiang Xinren returned to his university in Shanghai. "There was a call to students to return to their universities. Revolutionary committees were being formed, and everyone was supposed to go back," he explains.

By August 1968, the tide of the Cultural Revolution had decisively turned. The revolutionary rebels who had risen so forcefully to persecute the

"bourgeois intellectuals" and the "party persons in authority taking the capitalist road," who had split into factions fighting each other as well, who had
turned even against the military, were now to be persecuted themselves. On
July 28, at Qinghua University, Mao Zedong himself had presided over a
meeting of five student leaders representing the various factions that had been
involved in the student violence. It is said that Mao had tears in his eyes when
he addressed the young rebels, saying, "You have let me down, and what is
more you have disappointed the workers, peasants, and soldiers of China."
Within forty-eight hours after Mao delivered his remarks, the nation's first
Mao Zedong Thought Propaganda Team was dispatched to Qinghua University with the primary objective of quelling student violence. The People's
Liberation Army directed the propaganda teams as campuses came under
military control.

On August 5, Mao Zedong presented the propaganda team at Qinghua
University with a "treasured gift" of mangoes. As Richard Baum has pointed
out, "The symbolic significance of this act was not lost on anyone: in signaling
his approval of the work of the propaganda team, Mao had signed the death
warrant of the Red Guards."

The movement to "purify the class ranks" began.

"I think that when I went back," Jiang Xinren says of this period, "it was
really the hardest time. There is a difference between physical violence and
spiritual violence, and I think that spiritual violence is really more difficult to
take. At that time, our school was controlled not by the party as before but
by the worker propaganda team. It was very sad.

"It was particularly difficult for the professors. Before I left the university,
as part of the campaign against the four olds, we had gone through the library,
looking for four olds books, and we burned many of the books we thought were
four olds. But those were only physical things, material things.

"For the professors, the worker propaganda teams were the *ding an,* the
final verdict, the final decision, final judgment. When the Cultural Revolution
began and we students began to attack the professors, we didn't have their files.
So what we could do to professors was really only physical. We had tried to
find their dossiers. In China, when you become an adult, you also get a file.
Information is put in your file, and you are never allowed to see it. Your file
follows you wherever you go, but you never know what is in it. That makes
the office that controls the files very powerful. In our school, it was controlled
by a woman, the wife of a high party person in the school. At the beginning
of the Cultural Revolution, we had even broken into offices and looked for our
own files. But we couldn't find them.

"But the worker propaganda teams did have access to the professors' files,
and they used the files to make attacks against the professors. There weren't
very many public meetings then to attack the professors, and when they were
held, they were very short. Mostly the professors were questioned and asked

to confess. They had to write their self-confessions. Over and over they would be questioned and would have to write. But sometimes they couldn't remember. Sometimes they were being accused of things that had happened thirty or forty years before. How could they be expected to remember?

"I think that most of the suicides happened then, not earlier. Professors just gave up hope. That is what I mean when I say it was the *ding an*, the final judgment.

"Many professors then were assigned to do labor on the campus. Since the university was controlled by the worker propaganda teams, the workers didn't have to work anymore, so the professors did all the work. They worked in the kitchens, making the food and serving it. They cleaned the latrines. They swept the campus, cleaned the buildings. You could see them working like that, and it was very sad.

"I also had to write what I had been doing all that time. They would let me write at home and then bring it back to the school." Jiang Xinren avoided persecution during this period by the simple expedient of lying. His participation in the armed struggles, his opposition to the army, had taken place in other parts of the country, away from the watchful eye of either his schoolmates or his superiors. Only his family and very closest friends knew where he had been and what he had been doing since he had left Shanghai after attacking Zhang Chunqiao. "I never told them what I did," he says. "I told them that I had spent most of my time at home, in my house, and that I had been to the countryside, to learn from the peasants, as Chairman Mao had wanted us to do.

"The situation with my family had also become very sad. Of course, they were happy to see me and I told them everything I had done, including the violence and the shooting and that four of my friends had died. But things had changed a lot for my family. Before, my family had always had a servant. We had had the same servant for thirty years, and she was a part of my family. I always considered her my aunt. I never thought of her as a servant. But when the Cultural Revolution came, it was considered capitalist to have a servant, so our servant had to go back to her native village. She never turned against us, never attacked us. But we never heard from her again.

"So my mother had to do all the work in the house. She was very weak. She had always had a problem with her leg, and she wasn't used to doing the housework and all the cooking and shopping. Each day, she would have to go to her job, but she still had to do all the housework. She would go out early sometimes to buy food, and when she came home at night, she would usually have to shop again and to cook and there were many other household chores to do. So she was very tired and weak.

"That year—1968—was the year of going back to class for the revolution. I had had two years of college before the Cultural Revolution began, and while it took me five years to graduate, I only had one additional year of education before I graduated. But the nature of education had changed. Now everything had to be taught according to Mao's thought, and particularly according to Mao's theory of contradictions. Everything had to be based on struggle. So when we were taught physics, the basis of teaching us was contradictions, contradictions among the atoms with all the atoms smashing into each other and one dividing into two. But it wasn't always easy to teach this way. Sometimes nature is harmonious, and it was difficult to use contradictions and struggle to explain all of physics and nature."

It was at this point, in the course of the movement to purify the class ranks, that Jiang Xinren began questioning the Cultural Revolution and asking himself why he had behaved the way he had. His answer, when it finally came, would irrevocably change his life.

"It was during that last year in college that I began to question the Cultural Revolution, that I began to wake up and to ask myself, 'What have I done? Who made us do these things?' Four of my friends had been killed, four of my close friends—the one who was standing next to me and some who had been killed, one by a hand grenade, while fighting in a factory in Shanghai. And one of my very best friends, a girl, had gone insane. During the period of armed struggle, the conservatives had caught her and beat her awfully. They tied her to a tree and beat her stomach and ruined her uterus. She was only sixteen years old then. And now she always smiles all day, twenty-four hours a day. She doesn't think. She can't think. She can't think at all. She just smiles at anyone, everyone, anywhere. When I first saw that girl smiling, I wanted to cry. I just couldn't face the situation.

"And many other people whom I just knew, and still many others whom I didn't know, they had been killed. I had always thought that it was the fault of the conservatives, that the enemy was the conservatives. But then I began to realize that members of the conservatives had been killed too, that they had also lost their friends, that it was just the same for them. When I had first joined the Cultural Revolution, I believed in the ideals of Mao Zedong. I thought I was fighting for Mao and against Liu Shaoqi and I thought that the conservatives represented Liu Shaoqi and were the enemy. But during that year I gradually came to realize that the conservatives weren't the enemy. It was Chairman Mao who made us do that, as part of his own struggle for power. He had used all the Red Guards, both the conservatives and the revolutionary rebels. It was Chairman Mao who was the enemy."

When Jiang Xinren graduated from college in the spring of 1969, his entire class was assigned to work in the countryside. Jiang Xinren was given a choice. Either he could go to Heilongjiang in China's northeast, where he would work on a state farm, or he could go to his family's native village in Guangdong. Jiang Xinren had never been to his family's village. "In China," he explains, "there is the custom that you retain your ancestral village, that that is your home, even though you weren't born there and have never lived there." Jiang Xinren opted to go to the ancestral village he had never seen. He was there for eight years.

FOR Song Erli, the brilliant young university student whose parents both were rightists, the Cultural Revolution provided the opportunity to prove his revolutionary commitment beyond any shadow of a doubt. As rightists, his parents were natural and early victims of the Cultural Revolution. Song Erli was never allowed to join the Red Guards, but by drawing a clear line of demarcation from the father he had come to hate, Song Erli thought he could convince others that he really was the revolutionary he knew himself to be.

"My younger sister was in college in Nanjing when the Cultural Revolution began, and she lived at home," he explains. "She wrote me immediately after the first big character poster had gone up in front of our house saying that my father had collaborated with the Japanese and been a member of the Guomindang. She asked me what to do. Without a second thought, I bought a train ticket for Nanjing. I arrived on the day the Red Guards came to search my family's house. I was there when the Red Guards came. They made a dunce cap for my father, and then they had a struggle session against him in the living room. The Red Guards asked me who I was, and I told them I was a revolutionary rebel. They said, 'Let's see how much of a revolutionary rebel you can be. Do you stand on our side?' So I shouted, 'Down with my father.' And then I wrote a big character poster criticizing my father."

But Song Erli's effort to prove himself revolutionary backfired. Factual reportage was not one of the strong points of the Cultural Revolution. Song Erli, with his counterrevolutionary background, his propensity to individualism, and his mind like a boxer, was a scapegoat luxuriant in possibility. The schoolmates sent to observe Song Erli's behavior during the house search reported that Erli had stood on the side of his father. Despite his personal conviction that he was genuinely revolutionary, Song Erli never proved that to those in power.

But he remains today an ardent defender of the revolutionary rebels, a fervent political analyst of the tribulations they suffered, the injustices they endured. "You read today that the state is still threatened by the revolutionary rebels," he says, "by those with horns on their heads and thorns on their bodies, those who have difficulty being rendered obedient, those who are so ready to resist. They say the revolutionary rebels are the faithful followers of the Gang of Four, that they came to power because of the Gang of Four. But the revolutionary rebels were fighting a revolution against feudalism, and Jiang Qing, Lin Biao, and the military were the biggest feudalists of all. And Mao, too, to some extent. Those feudalists posed as ultraleftists, but they joined in the persecution of the revolutionary rebels. Mao became disgruntled with the revolutionary rebels because many of them were students, intellectuals, whom he hated. The revolutionary rebels, so far as I can judge, were in power at most for no more than a year, and even then their posts were only nominal. Even Kuai Dafu, the luckiest of the revolutionary rebels, was only in power for a year. Then they were all pulled down. Most of them died.

"If there were any revolutionary rebels still in power now, there would be a great hue and cry about how dangerous these people are. 'Beware of the revolutionary rebels. Be careful of the revolutionary rebels.' Those people still in power who are suspected of being revolutionary rebels are in fact just the careerists, the people who know when to curry favor from their superiors and when to push their superiors down, people with personal motivations. The revolutionary rebels were the activists of the Cultural Revolution, but they weren't the careerists. They were mostly college students or young workers who were the nonconformists of the feudalist system.

"The atrocities of the Cultural Revolution shouldn't really be attributed to the revolutionary rebels. But there is a reason for the attacks on them today. They are warnings to young people not to take the same road. In fact, the revolutionary rebels suffered the most during the Cultural Revolution. Let me count. There were at least five or six political persecution movements against the revolutionary rebels. Most of the better-known leaders in revolutionary rebel organizations died. They committed suicide. Or they became insane. It isn't true that most people died during the period of 'armed struggle.' Most died during the movements to persecute the revolutionary rebels. Thousands, tens of thousands, died during those movements, especially during the movement to ferret out the May Sixteenth elements. No one has ever told about the sufferings of the revolutionary rebels."

Song Erli wants to bear witness to the suffering of the revolutionary rebels. It is true that the story of the massive persecutions against them is not well known to the West.

"It was the army that was responsible for the atrocities," he insists. "In the first stage, the atrocities against the intellectuals were committed by the Red Guards. In the last stage, it was the army. Almost all of the revolutionary rebels had lost power by 1967, and after that the whole country was run by the army. The army is different from any other organization. Its orders are carried out perfectly. So the army had unlimited power. Army officers became heads of universities, managers of factories, heads of all sorts of organizations. The Chinese army at that time had more power than any other army has ever had. A regimental commander could become the president of a major university. In Latin America, with so many military juntas, where can you find a regimental commander who is at the same time the president of a major university? The mayors of important cities were military leaders. The army was the greatest perpetrator of atrocities during the Cultural Revolution. Most of the cruelty happened after 1967. Who should be held responsible?

This revolutionary rebel? That revolutionary rebel? At the time, the army was at the head of every unit. These army people came from peasant backgrounds. They had joined the army as peasants in the 1940s or 1950s, even those who became mayors during the Cultural Revolution. And they became intoxicated by their own power. Before such a powerful force, the destiny of the revolutionary rebels was like a fly before an army. That was the common lot of the revolutionary rebels."

When, in the spring of 1967, the People's Liberation Army was called upon to restore order in China and did so by suppressing the rebels, Song Erli had openly opposed the military. He had signed a big character poster opposing Xu Shiyou, the longtime military commander of the east China region. A year later, the military moved in to take control of Song Erli's university, and the army moved to neutralize those who had rebelled against it. Song Erli graduated from college in the spring of 1969, nine months after the military came on campus. "Not that there had been classes since the beginning of the Cultural Revolution," he explains. "They had been called off shortly after Mao's big character poster, 'Bombard the Headquarters,' in August 1966. But still we graduated."

The final exams for Song Erli's class consisted of the students' self-confessions, detailed accounts of what they had done since the beginning of the Cultural Revolution, with particular emphasis on how they had responded to the role of the military. In contrast to Jiang Xinren, who had also opposed the military but who wrote in his self-confession that he had spent the most turbulent period of the movement learning from the poor-and-lower-middle peasants, Song Erli told the truth. He had little choice, because everyone knew what he had done.

"My 'serious mistake,'" explains Song Erli, "had been to oppose the military, particularly Xu Shiyou. I had been associated with the most radical wing of the revolutionary rebels, part of the group that opposed the army, particularly after the incident in Wuhan. Mao had misunderstood the nature of the army in China, and so had Lin Biao. Xu Shiyou was a fierce, old-style general with a dare-to-die spirit who had risen out of sheer bravery from just a rank-and-file soldier to become a general. He had been the bravest general serving under Zhang Guotao, the head of the Fourth Army during the period of the Long March. But Zhang Guotao defected to the Guomindang, so all his generals came into disfavor. Mao wouldn't excuse them. So he sent them to what he thought were less important positions. He appointed them commanders of the military regions. But Mao had misunderstood. He thought that the commanders of the army, navy, and air force at the national level were most important. He didn't understand the relationship between central control and local control. And Lin Biao was the same way. When Lin Biao became minister of defense in 1959, he had placed all his men in central positions, not regional positions. But early in 1967 when the military was called in to participate in the power seizures to overthrow the provincial party committees, the army became an extremely important power force. It was only then that Lin Biao realized that the most important obstacles to his own absolute power were the regional military commanders. The navy and the air force were with Lin Biao, but the army was under control of the regional military commanders.

"When the military were called in to support the rebels in the seizure of power from the party committees, in fact it was the army that brought about the downfall of the local party committees by supporting the revolutionary rebels. But then they turned against the revolutionary rebels, using some groups of revolutionary rebels as their tools to fight other revolutionary rebels. This was the cause of the splits in the revolutionary rebels' organizations in every province, every county, every city. That was the basic pattern no matter how complicated each case may have been.

"So the revolutionary rebels became divided into groups that either opposed the army or supported the army. In some provinces, the most radical elements of the revolutionary rebels supported the army. In other parts of the country, the revolutionary rebels opposed it. In my province, the radical revolutionary rebels opposed the army. We thought the air force was the most revolutionary, the least feudalistic, because the air force was under the direct control of Mao and Lin Biao. Our organization was supported strongly, openly, by the air force. But when Mao showed his support for Xu Shiyou, Xu immediately sent his troops to surround the headquarters of the air force and make them surrender. There was almost an armed conflict. Afterward, the air force that had supported us just disappeared. They were persecuted mercilessly, severely. Even the center knew about it but couldn't do anything. The Gang of Four posed as ultraleftists but in fact they were bureaucrats, feudalists. They joined in the persecution of the revolutionary rebels. They had a hand in it by letting the regional commanders take over everything. Zhang Chunqiao and Xu Shiyou were deadly enemies, but Zhang Chunqiao couldn't do anything about it. Xu Shiyou was the staunchest opponent of the Gang of Four, and his army was the biggest threat to the power of the Shanghai municipal committee and the Gang of Four. The lines of struggle were power lines, not ideological lines. So when the air force fled to Peking, they left those of us who had supported them in the hands of Xu Shiyou.

"The Wuhan Incident in the summer of 1967, when Chen Caidao's troops captured the representatives of the Central Cultural Revolution Group from Peking, was the turning point. Chen Caidao had been the regional military commander in Wuhan for more than twenty years, and his power had become deeply entrenched, much more so than the power of the provincial party committees. It was very difficult to overthrow Chen Caidao, very difficult to overthrow the regional armies. The only power that could maintain order throughout the entire country was the army. The navy and the air force were too small. They couldn't control the whole situation. Mao and Lin acted violently against the Wuhan Incident. But afterward, Mao tried to seek a peaceful settlement in the struggle between Lin Biao and the regional military commanders. He tried to force Lin Biao to shake hands with Xu Shiyou and the other regional military commanders. It was then that Mao realized how dangerous Lin Biao could be if there was no one to balance him, and the only people to balance him were the regional military commanders. Mao was good at playing the balance of power. He knew that if the regional military commanders were overthrown, there would be no obstacles in Lin Biao's march to absolute power. From then on, Lin Biao knew that it would be impossible for him to get absolute power. Lin Biao started going downhill after that, and Zhou Enlai started going up. Previously, the regional commanders had had no one to represent them in Peking. After the Wuhan Incident, Zhou Enlai became their representative.

"So by the end of 1967, the army had become established as a force in every province. Mao recognized it as army control, but the army was the only force capable of exercising control. Perhaps Jiang Qing and her allies had initially seen the revolutionary rebels as potential leaders, but soon she discovered that that was impossible. It was impossible to have Paris communes and locally administered units. And Mao had become disgruntled with the revolutionary rebels because they were mostly students, intellectuals, whom he hated. Most of the revolutionary rebels were students or young teachers. The workers were just figureheads. This was natural, because the whole movement had started in the universities. Perhaps that was one of the reasons Mao decided to let the regional commanders control the whole situation. Mao despised school-educated people.

"But when the army came to power, the first thing it did was to suppress the revolutionary rebels. In the last half of 1967, I had been traveling around as part of the revolutionary rebels that opposed the army, helping some of the leaders of the movement write speeches, doing propaganda work. That was my mistake, my 'serious mistake.'

"In my own personal summary," says Song Erli of the self-confession he wrote as his final exam in order to graduate from college, "I had to admit that during the Great Proletarian Cultural Revolution, the backward side of my ideology had been exposed. At that point, I had no grounds to say that I had done anything good. I had, after all, written a big character poster attacking Xu Shiyou and signed my name to it just before Mao Zedong had called Xu Shiyou to Peking and embraced him at Tiananmen Square in front of millions of people."

The graduation ceremony to which Song Erli was treated following his final examination was organized by the military that controlled his campus. Song Erli's fellow students took part. It was a struggle session against him. Upon graduation through struggle, Song Erli was sent to labor on a state farm controlled by the military. "Every few months, I would receive a special criticism," remembers Song Erli, "and always I would have to write my self-confession. I always kept copies of my self-confessions because I knew that I would have to write them all over again in a couple of months. In my self-confessions, I had to repent everything I had done in the last few months of 1967. I wrote honestly, because I thought that was the best policy. And my activities had been so great. I said that I had written something against Xu Shiyou. Everyone knew that. I had signed the big character poster. I wasn't in the habit of lying. I thought telling the truth was the best policy. It was quite possible for one to become self-contradictory if one wasn't telling the whole truth, since you were required to tell your story again and again. I had to write so many self-confessions, huge piles of self-confessions.

"I was so miserable in those years. I was really at a loss as to what to think. I had become the enemy of the most powerful army in the world and of the army commander who was the most trusted of all of Chairman Mao's military commanders.

"I didn't think it was right for me to write all those self-confessions, but I had to do it because the enemy was so powerful. My destiny was nothing before such a powerful force. I had come right smack against the Great Wall of China. That was the common lot of the revolutionary rebels. I still thought I had been right to challenge the army, the last bastion of Chinese feudal power. But if everything were to start again, if there were another Cultural Revolution, I would avoid such an act. If I had it to do over, I would do it differently, not because of my ideals but because of the power situation.

"Then," continues Song Erli, "came the final act, the most drastic scene in the persecution of the revolutionary rebels, the final, physical liquidation of the revolutionary rebels from the Great Cultural Revolution. It was the movement to ferret out the May Sixteenth elements.

"The movement started at the end of 1969 and was supposed to ferret out those people who had dared to challenge Premier Zhou Enlai. I had never challenged Premier Zhou. Premier Zhou had tried to strike a balance between the two sides, and in fact he had said some fine words about our organization. In the provinces, no one ever opposed Premier Zhou. Even in Peking it is hard to imagine anyone doing so. During the fiercest days of the struggle, a big character poster could stay up at most half a day before another big character poster was pasted over it. No one ever wrote big character posters against Premier Zhou. At most what could have happened is that during the night someone might have used a big brush to write huge characters over a big character poster. Something like that could only have been done at night. We called them 'big slogans.' No one would have written a big character poster opposing Premier Zhou. Maybe a few people in Peking wrote some big slogans, but this didn't happen in the provinces.

"Gradually, the movement to ferret out the May Sixteenth elements spread. The center issued some documents saying that the purpose of this organization

—the organization of the May Sixteenth elements—was to oppose the Communist Party and oppose the army. If you had done anything to oppose the army or a regional military commander, then you had done just what the May Sixteenth group was supposed to have done. Different provinces handled the movement to ferret out the May Sixteenth elements differently. In some cases it just passed without too much fuss. It was just walking across the stage. But in some provinces, especially those where the regional military commanders who had come to power in 1967 were still facing some opposition, the army took the movement as its golden opportunity to wipe out all its enemies.

"Shortly after the movement started, in early 1970, I was transferred from the army farm and sent to what was called a 'study class' administered by the army. In fact, it was a jail. The army officers in charge of it had been given a long list, a supposed roster of the May Sixteenth elements at my university, students and teachers alike. I don't know how they got that list. I still don't know. But I was on it.

"The treatment toward me in fact was light, at least in contrast to that of others. I had to stay in a room guarded over by the revolutionary masses the whole day and night. The whole study class was organized and run by army officers, but most of the people trying to make us confess weren't army officers but my fellow students. It was their task to help criminals like me confess to being May Sixteenth elements. Many of them were engaged to be married, and their families were anxious for them to return home to get married. So they tried hard to get us to confess so they could go home to get married. I was thinking about how to save my neck.

"What you were supposed to do was to confess that you were a member of the May Sixteenth group. You had to say very specifically on what day, in what room, in what building you had taken the vow to join the group and had promised to keep your membership in this group so secret that no friend, no member of your family, would ever know. You had to tell who had introduced you to the group, and sometimes you even had to say whether you faced north or south when you took the vow upon entering the group. Having to say whether you faced north or south is a typical peasant way of thinking.

"They weren't interested only in people who had been opposed to the military. They already had piles of confessions from people who had opposed the military. I had already confessed that I had opposed Xu Shiyou. They were interested in having people confess that they had been admitted into that secret counterrevolutionary group.

"You might think that among the revolutionary rebels those groups that had been part of the support-the-army faction would have been considered loyal supporters of the army, the victors in the struggle. You might think that those on the army's side would have gotten some benefit out of the campaign against the May Sixteenth elements. But in fact, that's not what happened. That's the most interesting part. As the movement developed, some people who really fought heroically for Xu Shiyou were accused of being May Sixteenth elements. Because they were rebels. The army doesn't like rebels. All the leaders of the support-the-army faction were also taken as May Sixteenth members. Not the ordinary members, but the leaders. All of them. Even some who had done almost nothing were labeled. So during the movement to ferret out the May Sixteenth elements, *all* the revolutionary rebel activists were wiped out, no matter what they had done for or against the army. They were put into prison. The army just wanted to identify the activists, to get rid of them. Then the army turned for support to the early conservatives. The conservatives were considered reliable because they had done nothing against anybody, except for having attacked the professors.

"At first I thought this campaign was very strange. I had never heard of this May Sixteenth group. I said I had heard nothing about it. But what was even stranger was that I saw my comrades one after another confess. Every confession had to be made at a mass meeting in front of the whole study class. We criminals would have to sit in the front rows to hear the confessions of our comrades.

"In the beginning, I thought it was ridiculous. But then I thought maybe I had been fooled. Maybe all my comrades *had* joined May Sixteenth and not told me. They were all confessing. They never named the person who had introduced them to the organization, because such information was supposed to be handed over directly to the army officers in private. But by this means the army officers were able to extend the list so that finally it included all the members of the onetime anti-army organizations. So it looked as though everyone in my organization had been a member of May Sixteenth. Some people confessed that they had introduced more than a hundred people to the organization. It was people eating people.

"One day we were called and sent to the largest gymnasium in the city to attend a huge meeting at which several of the most important members of the province were to confess. I can remember it very clearly. One of them was a high-ranking officer who had opposed Xu Shiyou. The other was the highest leader of our organization. Another was a veteran cadre, a member of the provincial party committee. They all confessed in detail, and this time they all named the people who had introduced them to the May Sixteenth organization. The people who had introduced them were Kuan Feng, Wang Li, and Qi Benyu, because by that time those three men had all fallen. They all said exactly when they had gone to Peking, or when Kuan Feng or somebody else had called them to Peking and entrusted them with certain tasks for developing the organization in my province. And after they had confessed, they all had to say how grateful they were to Commander Xu Shiyou for giving them a second life. 'Though I joined the revolution in the War of Resistance against Japan, now I have a second revolutionary life.'

"It was at that meeting that I saw through it all. It was a shameful fraud.

Those gray-haired persons standing on that stage told blatant lies. I knew those people who had confessed. I knew where they had been and what they had said. Their confessions didn't even jibe with one another. They could never have been the members of the same group at the time they were entrusted with the task by 'top May Sixteenth leaders,' let alone this secret May Sixteenth group. They were shameful. These were people who were supposed to be responsible for everything they said. They were the people who had said, 'I am responsible for this organization.' It was so shameful. These were the Communists who had been so staunch in Nationalist jails. Why couldn't they be a little staunch in Xu Shiyou's jail? I really doubted what they had done in the Nationalist jails. By then I saw clearly that the army officers had forced these confessions in order to justify the army's persecution of its former enemies—mostly defenseless students. And it was persecution. Out-and-out persecution. During the Cultural Revolution, the Central Cultural Revolution Group issued so many contradictory instructions that it would be easy to shift the real blame for behaving in all sorts of contradictory ways to Mao or Lin Biao or Jiang Qing or whomever. But if you were a member of a secret group that was something different. That showed that no matter what you had done, right or wrong, you were a member of a secret antiparty group. That is why so much emphasis was put on the forged details of admission. It didn't matter what you had done wrong, as long as you admitted to having been part of a secret group.

"There is something unforgettable to me about that ferreting-out movement. I didn't know how to confess. And what I can be proud of is that I said nothing. I didn't lie. By confessing, people could avoid the most severe punishment. People couldn't stand the torture. By confessing falsely, they at least got temporary relief. Today, they don't feel guilty about the fact that they lied. They don't even feel guilty about falsely naming people who were supposed to have introduced them to the organization. Lots of people said I was an introducer. During such a blatant persecution movement, there was no right or wrong. Everything was upside down, in confusion. So people did the most immediate thing, the thing that at the moment seemed right, excusable.

"It was during that time of ferreting out the May Sixteenth elements that most of the suicides of the Cultural Revolution occurred. And so many young people went insane. When people committed suicide there would always be a big meeting to accuse the dead of betrayal of the revolution by committing suicide. The dead person's former comrades had to go on the stage to say, 'The dead person introduced me to the May Sixteenth group on such and such a day.' It was shameful. I don't think those people felt guilty about this. They had to do it. I asked some people who made these accusations about it later. Some of them said it was just chaotic conflict among comrades. And since there was such chaos, why shouldn't they act to try to avoid bringing trouble to themselves? The person was dead already. It wasn't like the Communist revolutionaries being imprisoned by the Nationalists. In that case, people were facing real counterrevolutionaries. In this case, they were your comrades. You couldn't deny they were your comrades. Why not just confess instead of suffering for an utterly ridiculous cause? It was a way to survive, a way to get through a certain period of time.

"I didn't lie, so I suffered more. The physical torture was terrible."

Song Erli remained in the study class that was really a prison, under army control and being tortured regularly, for eight months. He never confessed. When he was finally released, Song Erli, his studies cut short by the Cultural Revolution but with a college degree in biochemistry nonetheless and a brilliant, dazzling mind that could have served his backward country well, was sent to work in the cold dark pit of a mine in one of the most impoverished areas of his province.

"The army officers had always said openly, without any feeling of shame, that those students who confessed would be assigned to better work places," explains Song Erli. "Jiangsu south of the Yangtze, like Wuxi, is better, very rich. North of the Yangtze is poor, one of the poorest parts of the country. So the army officers said, 'Well, you didn't confess, so we'll assign you to the northern part where the poor peasants who are more revolutionary than students will help you.' But once I got there, the peasants were good to me. The movement was over. But even though I didn't confess, I was still considered a May Sixteenth element because I had been on the magic list compiled by the army men."

Song Erli remained in the mining town for eight years, until 1979.

SEVEN

WHAT WAS THE WORST? THE CULTURAL REVOLUTION AS AN EXTREME SITUATION

WHAT was worst about the Cultural Revolution? The answers of those who tell their stories here are diverse.

You Xiaoli, whose physical torture during the course of the Cultural Revolution would have brought death to many weaker, older, or less healthy than she and who spent several years cleaning her university's latrines, said that what was worst about the Cultural Revolution was not the physical abuse she endured but the burning of the books, the destruction of so many books. You Xiaoli said that the Cultural Revolution was supposed to have been a *cultural* revolution, but instead it had become a revolution against culture, a revolution that destroyed culture.

Jiang Xinren, on the other hand, had participated in the burning of the books on his campus, but he made a distinction between physical violence and spiritual violence. Jiang Xinren thought that spiritual violence was really more difficult to bear. For him what was worst was to return to his university after having participated in the Cultural Revolution in other cities, after the worker-soldier propaganda teams had taken over his campus, and to see university professors like You Xiaoli sweeping the grounds, cleaning the toilets, and preparing and serving food in the campus dining hall.

Song Wuhao, whose enthusiasm for the Cultural Revolution had begun to decline when he saw for himself the invention of false accusations against the two Shanghai officials he helped investigate, said it was the distortion of facts, the absence of truth. For Song Wuhao personally, it was the loss of hope and the betrayal of ideals. Zhao Wenhao said it was the dehumanization.

Song Wuhao's father, who was beaten by his own son and was frequently subjected to other, more impersonal forms of brutality, who still bears the visible physical wounds of the tortures he was forced to endure, said that what was worst was not the torture or the pain connected with it, but the humiliation. Yao Baoding, a superb and devoted teacher, who spent six of the ten years of the Cultural Revolution in jail, said it was the wasted years. So, too, did author Huang Xing.

For Song Erli, who had become a victim during the military's brutal assertion of power, what was worst was the struggle for power, the desire for power, the extent to which people would go to seize and hold on to power, "not only the revolutionary rebels," he said, "but those who had already held power. How ruthlessly they tried to secure it!"

It was Qiu Yehuang, the *xiaoyaopai*, a nonparticipant observer of the Cultural Revolution, who focused first on the deaths, the beatings, the suicides he witnessed from the sidelines. But the deaths, the beatings, the suicides were only the worst that Qiu Yehuang saw. What was really the worst, he thought, and a process he believed had been going on for years, only culminating in the Cultural Revolution, was that "the Communist Party taught the Chinese people to be real hypocrites. They taught people not to say the truth. They were always making up conspiracies, making up big lies. The Cultural Revolution spoiled the spirit of the whole Chinese nation."

Li Meirong agrees. "The system teaches you to lie," she says, and goes on to provide an example. "When I was at the May Seventh Cadre School, particularly at first, my back ached, my shoulders ached, my arms ached, my legs ached. My whole body ached. All over. Everywhere. It hurt so much I couldn't sleep at night. After just a few hours of work each day, I would be exhausted. I would fall into bed, but still I couldn't sleep because of the pain.

"But in our political study classes, we were told that we were supposed to read Chairman Mao's works and all our aches and pains were supposed to go away. So I read the works of Chairman Mao, and after reading him I had to explain that before, my shoulders ached, my arms ached, my back ached, my whole body ached, but now, after reading Chairman Mao, all the aches and pains have gone away. I said all this, but I said it sarcastically, as though I didn't believe it, and the leaders, the cadres, all said, 'Good, good.' But the aches and pains were still there. They don't go away after reading Chairman Mao. You become a liar in order to survive. They know you are lying and they say, 'Good, good.'

"And you had to lie about your leaders, the cadres. Even if you didn't like the leader of your unit, even if you detested him, you still had to say he was good. Those are the ways the system taught you to lie."

Liu Libo, only a junior middle school student at the time of the Cultural Revolution, also sees the decline in honesty as a major outcome of the episode. "During the Cultural Revolution," she says, "people were honest. If someone asked you what your class background was and you were a capitalist, you said you were a capitalist. But people got beaten for being capitalists. Sometimes they were killed. Now, people aren't so honest any more. Even today. We all have to go to political meetings, and we all have to say a few words in support. But we don't believe. Sometimes, afterward, I will ask my friend, 'Did you believe what they were saying?' And she will say, 'No.' But you only say this to your very closest friend, to someone you can trust. We Chinese don't often talk to each other, or talk to each other truthfully. This is particularly true in your own work unit. Why do you think it has been so long and the truth of the Cultural Revolution still hasn't come out? It's because people aren't so honest."

Underlying these diverse assessments of what was worst about the Cultural Revolution is a profound sense of loss—loss of culture and of spiritual values, loss of status and honor, loss of career, loss of dignity, of hope and ideals, of time, integrity, truth, and of life; loss, in short, of nearly everything that gives meaning to life.

But there were other losses, too. Those who were victims lost a sense of trust and predictability in human relations as colleagues, friends, and sometimes even relatives and immediate family turned against them. They lost their homes and many (often all) of their family possessions as repeated house searches resulted in either the destruction or confiscation of private property and books and of intensely personal and valued mementoes. Scholarly manuscripts and research notes were seized and destroyed. Wedding pictures were taken as proof of "bourgeois" proclivities, and diplomas from foreign universities were confiscated as evidence that the recipient was a spy.

Victims lost their incomes and their status. They not only lost their jobs and all hope of pursuing their careers but were forced to perform what, in the cultural context of the Chinese intellectual, was particularly demeaning and humiliating labor—cleaning toilets, making and serving food to university students and staff, pulling grass. And they lost through death—from torture, factional violence, suicide, or the refusal to provide medical care to those labeled "counterrevolutionary"—their relatives and their friends. The depth of these personal losses was only compounded by the prohibition against engaging in the traditional rituals of death and dying and the inability of Chinese under attack to mourn their dead.

In addition to all that victims of the Cultural Revolution actually lost, there was more that the persecutors tried to take away. Much has been made of Mao's efforts to build a "new socialist man," and many outsiders who visited or lived in China during the decade of the 1970s actually believed that he had succeeded. The aim of the assault on self which characterized the Cultural Revolution was precisely the destruction of self, an effort to force those under attack to confess that they were what their labels accused them of being, that they were guilty of the crimes and "mistakes" of which they were accused. Many did come to identify with the labels that publicly defined them. Many confessed to crimes they had never committed. Some did not. But the assault on the self with which victims of the Cultural Revolution were confronted, the clash between their own conceptions of themselves and the accusatory, derogatory labels of the enemy by which they were publicly and socially defined, was for many as profoundly unnerving, unsettling, and debilitating as any of the tortures or physical losses to which they were subjected.

This may have been particularly true for the young, the teenagers, who were still, when the Cultural Revolution began, in the painful adolescent process of finding and defining themselves, their goals, and their roles in society. For Liu Zhiping, there was nothing more shattering than to be transformed overnight from an active, popular, and outstanding student, respected and liked by peers and teachers alike, from a young woman who believed herself revolutionary and was confident she was working for socialism, to "someone who could be educated," the ostracized daughter of a renegade and traitor. For Song Wuhao, exultant in the opportunity the Cultural Revolution provided to prove himself revolutionary at last, there was nothing worse than to tumble in a single day from the most trusted of Chairman Mao's revolutionary Red Guards to what he felt was the lowest of the low, the most despised and detested creature on earth. And when Jiang Xinren, who loved Chairman Mao and believed he had been fighting for Mao's ideals, woke up one morning with the horrifying recognition that in the name of China's great leader, the red, red sun in his heart, he might actually have killed, when he suddenly asked himself who he had become and why, his whole world and sense of self collapsed.

CHINA's Great Proletarian Cultural Revolution, both officially and by those who were its victims, is now often referred to as the *shi nian haojie*—the "ten years of great disaster," even, in some translations, the "ten years of holocaust." Some individual Chinese, without knowing many details of the Nazi concentration camps, have asserted that their own experiences were not unlike the experiences of the Jews in Nazi Germany.

Fundamentally and in its details, the Great Proletarian Cultural Revolution was neither disaster nor holocaust. For a disaster, in ordinary usage, is an " 'event' with a distinct beginning and a distinct end, and it is by definition extraordinary—a freak of nature, a perversion of the natural processes of life," "a furious eruption . . . that splinters the silence for one terrible moment and then goes away." The Cultural Revolution, for those who were its victims, was not really an event with a distinct beginning and a distinct end. Although most victims could describe with relative certainty when the Cultural Revolution began, few could tell you precisely when it ended. It dragged on, through too many twists and turns, too long. And the Cultural Revolution was heralded by those who led it not as a perversion of the natural processes of life but as the way of life its victims justly deserved.

The Nazi Holocaust was a deliberate and systematic act of genocide, resulting in the deaths of some six million Jews. For all the deaths of the Cultural Revolution, the murders were not systematic. The executioners of the Cultural Revolution cannot be accused of genocide. The traumas experienced by victims of the Cultural Revolution did not bear the same horrifying similarity as those experienced by concentration camp inmates, Vietnam veterans, survivors of Hiroshima, or survivors of floods or tornadoes. Victims of the Cultural Revolution came under attack at different times and for different reasons, and the torture to which they were subjected was also highly variable. In contrast to survivors of natural disasters and the Holocaust, whose descriptions of their experiences bear remarkable, uncanny similarities, whose experiences were often nearly identical, no two survivors of the Cultural Revolution tell exactly the same story. And for many, the Cultural Revolution was but the last and not always even the worst in a series of catastrophic events, the number of catastrophic events experienced by a single individual naturally increasing with age. Those who were middle-aged at the start of the Cultural Revolution had already experienced at a minimum the Japanese invasion, the civil war, the antirightist campaign, and the three bad years of 1959–61.

But in a broader sense, the Cultural Revolution, both in actuality and in its long-term individual consequences, bears resemblance to both disaster and to the Holocaust. Both disaster and Holocaust can be considered "extreme situations," a term first used to comprehend the meaning of the Nazi concentration camps and later adopted in studying the experience of Hiroshima. Today, a wide variety of diverse but tragic situations, from flood to war, from Holocaust to Hiroshima, may be labeled extreme situations. To raise comparisons is in no way to suggest that historical events can be equated. What one wants to know is both what about a particular situation renders it extreme and what the long-term personal consequences for those who survive extremity are. For however particular and diverse the details of extreme situations are, however different the cultures in which extremity occurs, those who have survived extremity are often burdened in their survival by remarkably similar psychic wounds.

There are a number of reasons for treating the Cultural Revolution as an extreme situation. The profound sense of loss experienced by its victims, loss of so much that gives meaning to life, is one. Another is the depth of isolation to which so many who were victims were subjected. Of all the tortures to which human beings may be subjected, isolation is the worst.

MOST are not able directly to articulate the sense of isolation they suffered during the Cultural Revolution. Absorbed in the details of their own stories, few were able to engage in even the minimal abstraction necessary to note that isolation was the cause of their pain.

The late Ding Ling, one of China's leading women writers, a Communist Party member who joined Mao's guerrillas in Yenan, a woman who was declared a rightist in 1957 and sent into exile in China's northeast only to be attacked again during the Cultural Revolution, is one of the few to have written explicitly about the experience of intense isolation.

"I had no pen, I had no paper," she wrote of her period in solitary confinement. "If I had something that I wanted to say to someone, there was no one else in the room but myself. It was isolation, complete and absolute isolation. From the day of my birth, I had never experienced isolation like that. Before, during the Cultural Revolution, if during the daytime I had been abused or beaten or was forced to suffer in some other way, still at nighttime I could return to my own shed; and if Chen Ming was there we could share our experiences, offer each other some comfort, and give each other support. The bitter tears could flow out; one didn't have to hold in all the bile. But shut up alone in that room, from daytime to nighttime, from nighttime to daytime, one had the choice of sitting facing the wall or of pacing about between the walls. The loneliness was like a poisonous snake, gnawing away at my heart."

Both the extent of isolation imposed on victims of the Cultural Revolution and the response of individuals to it varied considerably. At its most extreme, isolation took the form of solitary confinement, often accompanied by severe sensory deprivation. But because guilt by association was so decisive a determinant in who would be chosen during the Cultural Revolution as targets for attack, Chinese were stricken en masse by what Robert Jay Lifton would describe as "contagion anxiety," as colleagues, friends, and even relatives maneuvered to distance themselves from the accused. To join the ranks of the accused, it was often quite sufficient merely to have worked for someone already labeled, or to have been his relative or friend. Thus those under attack, even without being incarcerated, were often subjected to profound isolation. For adults like You Xiaoli, Huang Chaoqun, and Li Meirong, the first sign that they were about to be accused was often that friends and colleagues stopped greeting them. For some victims, literally the only people who spoke to them, from the time they first came under attack until they were sent to May Seventh Cadre Schools, except those who attacked them in criticism and struggle sessions, were members of their immediate families. When members of their families had "drawn a clear line of demarcation," as happened with some frequency during the Cultural Revolution, even that contact was denied. Indeed, so total was the isolation that some came to prefer the brutal attacks, both verbal and physical, of the struggle sessions to no human contact at all.

Young students like Wang Hongbao and Bai Meihua, excluded by the attacks against their parents from participating as revolutionaries in the Cultural Revolution, felt unjustly isolated from a political movement which many of them wanted to join. Other young people, like Liu Zhiping, who had a genuine respect for teachers and academic administrators who had come under attack, or Li Weiguo, who had admired Liu Shaoqi and used his *How to Be a Good Communist* as his own guide to moral behavior, often felt isolated because they were in minority, losing factions at the onset of the movement. Some of them ultimately subordinated their own personal political beliefs in order to be a part of the majority, more "revolutionary" factions. The appeal of the circle, of dancing in the ring, was very, very strong.

· For other young people—those who suffered the consequences of having been declared "counterrevolutionaries" or those who, after their parents came under attack, became ostracized as "sons of bitches"—the isolation was far more extreme.

The isolation faced by Jiang Xinren was extreme. Shortly after the work teams came to his campus in June 1966, Jiang Xinren was incarcerated for two months in solitary confinement in a darkened cattle pen. During that time, his only encouragement, his sole benign contact with the outside world, was a single short note smuggled under his door. Suicide and insanity were constant temptations. Jiang Xinren wanted to commit suicide, and often he thought he had gone mad. He came to prefer the brutal human contact of beatings during struggle sessions to the isolation and sensory deprivation of the cattle pen. It is still difficult for Jiang Xinren to talk about those two months, and the words come slowly, painfully, intermittently.

"Since I was considered a ringleader of the counterrevolutionaries," begins Jiang Xinren, "I was put in my own private cattle pen. It was about five feet by five feet. There were no windows, and the door was always locked, with someone always, twenty-four hours a day, standing guard outside. There was no light, either, so it was always dark, and I could never even tell whether it was night or day. I simply assumed that when they gave me food to eat, it must be day. They fed me once, sometimes twice a day.

"There was nothing in the room at all, no bed, no furniture, just a bucket which I used to go to the toilet. The bucket, literally, was the only thing in the room with me. Once a week, I got to empty the bucket, to take it to the latrine to empty. That was the only time I got to see the sunshine. Otherwise, I remained in complete darkness, except that sometimes, at the bottom of the door, in the small gap between the door and the floor, I could see a little bit of light. I was not allowed to take a shower or wash the whole two months I was in the cattle pen, and I was not allowed to change or wash my clothes.

"At first, for the first few days I was locked in the cattle pen, I slept a lot. I was very tired. Then I became angry—angry with the old Red Guards and the work teams. I would yell, shout as loud as I could, at the top of my lungs, cursing the old Red Guards and the work teams. I would think of the dirtiest, filthiest curses that I could and would yell those curses at the old Red Guards and the work teams. Somehow I thought that if I yelled loudly enough, dirty enough, maybe if they wouldn't let me out, at least they would respond.

"For about the first month in the cattle pen, I think I was able to keep track of the days, of how many days I had been in there, maybe not completely accurately, but nearly so. Then it became impossible to tell. I began to think I was going crazy being shut up in that dark room all day, never knowing whether it was night or day. Often I couldn't tell if I was dreaming or awake, and sometimes I thought that I wasn't even alive, that I had already died. In any case, I wanted to die, and certainly I never thought I would be alive today. I thought often of committing suicide. I wanted to commit suicide. I wanted a knife, but I didn't have one, and there was no possibility of finding one. But then I thought about what would happen to my family if I were to commit suicide. Because besides thinking about committing suicide, the other thing I thought about was my family. I thought of myself as a little child, of my father and mother, of how they had raised me. And I dreamed about my family and sometimes couldn't distinguish the dreams from what might be real. Sometimes I dreamed that my father had died and that it was because of me. I dreamed that they had come to my house and beat my parents. I dreamed that they had killed both of my parents, that I was all alone in the world. And when I tried to put the two things together, committing suicide and my family, I knew that it would be terrible trouble for my family if I were to commit suicide. They would be labeled a 'counterrevolutionary family,' and they—all of them —would suffer.

"In all the time I was in the cattle pen, I had only one message from the outside, from one of my friends. The guard at the cattle pen had to be changed according to a regular schedule, and sometimes the changing of the guard must have been a little confusing. Once during the changing of the guard, someone slipped a note under the door—a note written on just a very small, torn piece of paper. I could read it only by holding it to the bottom of the door where the tiny shaft of light came in. There were just a few characters on it. It said, 'We support you. We will continue to support you.' That little note was important to me, very important to me. It was important to know that I was not forgotten, that there were still people outside who continued to support me. But I didn't think I would live. I still thought it would be better to be dead. It was for my family that I lived.

"At first, they took me to struggle sessions two or three times a week, to criticize me for being a counterrevolutionary. Often, during those sessions, I was beaten, but even so I still preferred the struggle sessions and the beatings to being alone in that small dark room all the time. After a few weeks, though, unfortunately, they seemed to forget about me, and the struggle sessions stopped."

SUN HEREN spent most of his time in jail locked in a small, spartan cell with other people. But when he complained about the beatings being administered to his new friend the pickpocket, the man who had demonstrated his prowess by stealing Sun's little red book, Sun Heren was placed for several days in solitary confinement. He preferred the crowded and difficult conditions of thirteen to a cell and the company of what he described as his *nanyou*, his friends in times of difficulty, to the relative peace and luxury of a cell of his own. After being released from prison, Sun spent another two years confined alone in a cattle pen.

Sun Heren is one of the few scholars who were actually able to do productive research during the course of the Cultural Revolution. A mathematician, he needed no books or laboratories to carry out his life's work. At the conclusion of the Cultural Revolution, a number of articles Sun had composed in the solitude of his cattle pen were published. But solitary confinement still took its psychological toll. Sun had never, before being incarcerated, contemplated suicide. He is a warm and outgoing man, the kind who makes friends easily. Growing up learning from the example of the Soviet Big Brother, he had sometimes wondered why, during the Russian revolution, so many comrades in prison had committed suicide. But confined to his solitary cattle pen day after day and month after month, Sun began to contemplate taking his own life and might even have done so had the means been available. The revolutionary rebels had been careful to deprive him of the means.

THE daughter of party leader Tao Zhu, Tao Siliang, in a letter written to her father in December 1978, nine years after his death, describes both the ostracism her family faced during her father's disgrace and the extreme joy her father felt when his isolation was breached. After Tao Zhu had come under attack, he was held under house arrest, together with his wife, in Zhongnanhai, under constant guard and cut off completely from direct contact with anyone besides his immediate family and those who were charged with guarding him. During the period that Tao Zhu's daughter spent with her family—a period when Tao Zhu was being struggled against, sometimes violently—she remembers two times when her father was happy. Once, one evening, under heavy supervision, he was taken out to read the big character posters in Zhongnanhai, and there saw an old friend and colleague, China's foreign minister, then himself under attack, the straight-talking, no-nonsense Chen Yi. They were not allowed to speak, and in fact the only communication from Chen Yi was a slight nod of the head and a look in the eyes, a look which Tao Zhu read as both sympathy and encouragement. Similarly, one day Tao Siliang met briefly with Kang Keqing, Marshal Zhu De's wife and one of only a handful of women to have made, and survived, the Long March, a powerful force in her own right. Kang Keqing asked how Tao Zhu and his wife were doing and encouraged them to persevere. From those tiny cracks in her father's isolation, Tao Siliang reports, he drew tremendous happiness, encouragement, and inspiration.

Everyone who was subjected to similar isolation still remembers vividly today both those brief moments of human contact and who dared to risk them. Many of today's firmest friendships are based on those memories. You Xiaoli still remembers who it was, as she was cleaning the university toilets, who dared to inquire after her health and encourage her and her husband to persevere, who merely turned their heads away in silent embarrassment, and who hurled derogatory epithets. Today, her hierarchy of female friendships is based in large measure upon how women behaved when they confronted her in the university bathrooms. Those like Lao Jin are the closest thing You Xiaoli has today of friends. Lao Jin is a barely literate party cadre, a *tu baozi*—"rural dumpling" —who had become a secretary at the university. But even when the Cultural Revolution was at its worst, Lao Jin dared to encourage You Xiaoli when she saw her, to insist that she and her husband carry on, to assure her that the Cultural Revolution could not last forever. Lao Jin will therefore forever be a friend. Those who remained silent You Xiaoli forgives because she understands the difficulties people faced in having any contact with "ox ghosts and snake spirits." But forgiving those who hurled the derogatory epithets as she carried out her humiliating tasks has been one of the most difficult accomplishments of You Xiaoli's life.

For some individuals isolated from friends and colleagues, the rare occasions of joy were the group struggle sessions that sometimes offered opportunities to meet old friends.

"Not all the struggle sessions had the same effect on him," explains the wife of a leading party member in Peking. "One time there was a really huge struggle session, bigger than all the others, held in the Workers' Stadium. They brought together a number of party leaders and lots of others to be publicly criticized. These were my husband's old friends, and they hadn't seen each other for a long time. Before the meeting began, they put them all together in a room behind the stadium, so they had a chance to talk, to find out what had been happening to each other, how it was. They shared their cigarettes and lighted them for each other. Afterward, they were taken out in front of a huge crowd and there was a massive struggle session against them. At the end, they had to walk in a circle, around the stadium, and the people cursed them and spit at them. But when my husband came home that night, he was happier than he had been in a long time, almost elated. I think you can understand that. He saw his friends whom he had not seen in a long time."

ISOLATED from those who might have given them comfort and support, courage was difficult for many sufferers of the Cultural Revolution to find. Some could not find it.

Li Weiguo is one who succumbed to the isolation to which he was subjected —not through suicide or madness or even by confessing to crimes he had not committed. He turned against the man on whom he had modeled his life, the man he most deeply and profoundly admired, the man who was accused during the Cultural Revolution of being China's Khrushchev and the "number-one party person in authority taking the capitalist road," Liu Shaoqi.

Li Weiguo, a young teacher when the Cultural Revolution began, was known by all to be an ardent admirer of Liu Shaoqi, to have attempted to model his own life on the blend of Confucian ethics and socialist selflessness outlined in Liu's *How to Be a Good Communist.* It is not that Li Weiguo opposed Chairman Mao. "Whatever Chairman Mao said," remembers Li Weiguo, "was right for me. What the Communist Party said was right. What the Communist Party secretary said was right. They represented the Communist Party, and the Communist Party had very, very high authority in my mind. Not only in my mind—among students, the whole society. The Communist Party said something, and we followed. We were very obedient." But it had been Liu Shaoqi rather than Mao Zedong who had provided concrete guidelines, and it was for guidance in how to conduct his life that Li Weiguo turned to Liu Shaoqi.

"I loved Liu's book," Li Weiguo recalls. "It was about how to be a good communist, how to behave toward people, if you had problems how to solve them. Even psychological problems. Like once someone said something bad about me behind my back, and I felt very angry about that. But Liu's book quotes a Chinese philosopher saying that everyone talks behind people's backs, that there is no one who doesn't talk about other people behind their backs, so you should just take it easy about this. Don't be angry. It's human nature. So after reading the book, I felt better.

"And the book told me how to be a good person, a good man—to treat people honestly, to help people if they had some difficulties. It also said that every day you should learn new things, and then at the end of the day you should think about all you have done, what was good for society, what was bad. For me, this was easy to accept, easy to understand. It wasn't the theory of Marxism. In Mao, there are lots of principles, theories. But Liu is more practical, more gentle. His book is about human relations. It isn't just for Communist Party members but for all people. Liu combines the theory of Marxism with lots of ancient philosophers."

Shortly after the Cultural Revolution began, Li Weiguo came under attack —both because he personally had been a follower of Liu Shaoqi and because Li Weiguo had been a close associate of one of the party secretaries in his university who was deposed as a follower of Liu Shaoqi. Li Weiguo was isolated. No one would talk to him. Big character posters denounced him. This went on for more than a year.

"In my mind, I was very confused," remembers Li Weiguo. "Before the Cultural Revolution I respected Liu Shaoqi very much. I thought he was a good man. But Mao said that Liu Shaoqi was wrong, that he was a bad man. The whole society thought he was wrong, bad. This had an influence on me. Maybe Liu Shaoqi *had* done something bad. Maybe he *had* been opposed to Chairman Mao. I couldn't be a member of the revolutionary rebels. No one would talk to me. I was very isolated. People didn't like me. They thought I had done something against the revolution. In my own mind, I thought that Liu wasn't so bad, but I couldn't trust my own belief."

After a year, the revolutionary rebels gave Li Weiguo a choice. He could lead a criticism meeting against Liu Shaoqi and thereafter be allowed to join the revolutionary rebels. Or he could remain isolated and friendless. Li Weiguo chose to draw a clear line of demarcation with Liu Shaoqi. "I didn't want to criticize the book," Li Weiguo says. "I relied on the book. My colleagues knew I still liked the book. But the only way I could join the revolutionary rebels was to draw a clear line of demarcation from Liu Shaoqi. That would show that I stood on the side of revolution."

Li Weiguo tried to keep his faith with Liu Shaoqi by deliberately making his attacks as boring as possible, so boring that the audience would fall asleep. "So I criticized *How to Be a Good Communist,*" he says. "For two hours. Everybody fell asleep. Why did people fall asleep? Nothing I said was very new. I criticized him for not mentioning things. I just slowly worked my way from page one to the end of the book, pointing out what Liu Shaoqi hadn't mentioned. The main point I made was that Liu Shaoqi didn't mention the dictatorship of the proletariat. This was a big mistake because during the Cultural Revolution Mao said that the dictatorship of the proletariat is the most important principle of the theory of Marxism. But Liu didn't mention it. So I did very well in criticizing Liu Shaoqi, because people fell asleep and others read the newspaper."

"After that," concludes Li Weiguo, "I became a revolutionary rebel. I thought then that I was among friends. I wasn't isolated anymore, so I felt better. Sometimes during the Cultural Revolution you had to say things you didn't feel in your heart."

OTHERS, in their isolation, confessed at least to having "committed mistakes," if not to the enormities of which they were accused. Presumption of one's own guilt was particularly prevalent among those inclined to believe in the infallibility of the party and its chairman, for the certainty of infallibility left little room for an objective appraisal either of one's self or of a movement that would leave so many victims in its path.

Self-confessions generally took the form of autobiography, written and rewritten in ever greater detail.

Some people confessed to crimes of which they were not guilty in full knowledge of their own innocence. Such confessions were often extracted not merely through isolation but through torture and deprivation of sleep, and many were promised leniency if they were to admit to the crimes of which they were accused. Such was the case of the "model confessor," a man who was accused of being a spy during the Cultural Revolution and who was promised leniency if he were to confess. He did confess, and not only was he given leniency but he was assigned the task of meeting with other people similarly accused, who had yet to confess, as concrete proof of the leniency that would be accorded them if they followed his lead. But the model confessor was not a spy. He had confessed to a crime he had not committed.

MADNESS was another outcome of the extremity of the isolation to which people were subjected. The pathways to madness are ordinarily complex, but isolation has been regarded by some as the only factor which by itself is capable of inducing mental breakdown. Isolation is even more effective if the isolated individual is also treated as an enemy. Those few survivors of enforced isolation who have written of their experiences, men like Jacobo Timerman and Alfred Dreyfus, have described themselves in the extremity of their aloneness as tottering between the Scylla of madness and the Charybdis of suicide. Both literature on human response to extreme situations and on more prosaic forms of daily stress suggest, moreover, that the amount of social support available plays a major role in how well or ill an individual in those circumstances will contend. Literature on the Nazi concentration camps, most notably Terrence Des Pres's *The Survivor,* shows that for those few able in any way to influence their own survival, group solidarity, the binding together in collective, supportive units, was the most positive force. Scientific sampling of survivors suggests that the "pair was the basic unit of survival in the concentration camp," that a friend was necessary for survival.

Collective, supportive units sprang up in China throughout the Cultural Revolution, particularly among young people whose parents had been incarcerated. Many of those youthful collectivities, like the one of which Wang Hongbao was a part, took the form of roving, and frequently destructive, gangs. But such support systems, however violent, were an important means of survival for otherwise unsupervised youth.

Familial support and solidarity was another important ingredient in survival. And those who were separated from their families or unable to rely on them for help nonetheless note the importance of having just a single friend with whom to share troubles and grievances. Even Li Weiguo was aware of this. For all the isolation to which he was subjected, he did have one good friend. "If you had just one friend, one really good friend, someone you really trusted and someone you could really talk to," he says, "then you could lean on each other. During the Cultural Revolution, I was lucky. My friend, the person I trusted, was my wife." Li Weiguo's wife had been away working in another city during the period of his tribulation.

But when such support systems were unavailable, when isolation was extreme, or when the one remaining source of solace and support available to a victim was finally withdrawn, mental breakdown was a common result.

Bai Meihua describes the onset of madness in one of her friends when the wall of isolation was finally complete.

"One of my friends, a girl a few years older than I, went mad. She is still mad, even though she is now married and has a baby. During the Cultural Revolution, she came under attack from two sides. Her father had been a high-ranking cadre, and during the Cultural Revolution he was in jail for ten years. Her mother had been in charge of the library, and she was also taken away. During the Cultural Revolution, all the other children in her family, all her brothers and sisters, ran away to other places to try to escape from their difficulties. But my friend was the eldest in the family, so she stayed at home to try to help the family. While she was there, the rebels came and searched her house and either destroyed everything or took it away. There was nothing left. Nothing. Not even a quilt. So she came to my family to ask for a quilt. At that time, my family was better off than hers, so of course we gave her a quilt.

"So many people attacked her and called her a son of a bitch that she was afraid even to go outside her house. She was already a university student at the time, and she had a boyfriend.

"Her boyfriend's father was a high-ranking military officer, but he hadn't been persecuted yet. At that time, all the young people were leaving for the countryside, but some young people, especially the children of high-ranking army cadre, were able to get out of going to the countryside by joining the army. Her boyfriend had been told that if he didn't cut off relations with her, he wouldn't be allowed to join the army. So he did.

"This hurt her, hurt her terribly. Her family had already been through so much, and she had been able to bear it. But when faced with the breakup of her romance, she cracked. Immediately. She just went mad."

IF madness was one result of those who succumbed to the isolation and attacks against them, suicide was another. Figures are unavailable in the West, and probably in China, too, but there is general agreement among Chinese that the suicide rate increased dramatically during the most tumultuous years. There are many reasons for those suicides, but surely one was the isolation to which so many were subjected.

Literature on suicide suggests that suicide is more likely if an adverse event also "isolates an individual from significant relationships." Jean Baechler distinguishes between suicide of flight, in which an individual seeks escape from a situation judged to be intolerable, and suicide of grief, following the loss of some central element of one's personality or way of life. While the ultimate influences leading one person in adversity to choose suicide and another to choose survival lie deep in the psyche, the choice of suicide by many who regarded their situation during the Cultural Revolution as intolerable is consistent with the decision that individuals in any culture facing similar adversity might have made. Similarly, the depth of loss suffered by victims of the Cultural Revolution robbed many of what had given meaning to their lives— family, friends, dignity, honor, and work. Grief over what had been lost and the need to escape an intolerable situation must often have combined as motives for ending one's life. Both suicide and insanity are universal patterns of response to the particular form of extremity faced by victims of China's Cultural Revolution.

Repeatedly, in the stories survivors of the Cultural Revolution tell of their acquaintances and friends, and in the short stories about the Cultural Revolution, suicides follow shortly after the wall of isolation becomes complete, after the last remaining source of solace and support is finally withdrawn.

One of Huang Chaoqun's friends, a widower with only one child, committed suicide only minutes after returning from a street parade in which he, Huang Chaoqun's friend, was the principal attraction. The widower's son had drawn a clear line of demarcation from his suffering father, and as proof of how deep and clearly that line had been drawn, the son had taken the lead in his father's street parade, herding his father through town, whip in hand and sometimes in use, like a bullock. When even his son had turned against him, completely isolated and all alone, the widower drank a bottle of insecticide and lay down on his bed to die.

In one short story, "Anecdote from the Western Front," the central figure is a young man named Liu Maomei, whose father had committed suicide during the Cultural Revolution. His father, an old revolutionary cadre, had been accused of being a traitor during the Cultural Revolution because prior to Liberation he had been arrested by the Guomindang and later released. It is a story similar to the one told by Liu Zhiping about her father.

While under attack, Maomei's father had been assigned to tend the boiler in his work unit and his mother had been pressured to draw a clear line of demarcation between herself and her husband. This she ultimately did, putting up a big character poster attacking her husband. Stripped of his only remaining source of solace and support, completely isolated, Maomei's father climbed the chimney of the boiler he was charged with tending and jumped to his death.

A university student in Shanghai, an excellent scholar and brilliant young man, met a similarly tragic death. The young man had become the leader of the revolutionary rebels on his campus, but the faction he had headed was the "oppose the army" faction. When the military moved in to take control of his university, he, of course, was singled out and was placed in solitary confinement in a cattle pen. This young man was already married, but his wife worked in another city, and what with their political activities in the heady days of the Cultural Revolution, they had not seen each other for several years. As happened with some frequency during this period, his wife had fallen in love with someone else. While the man was in solitary confinement in the cattle pen, his wife came to request a divorce—on the dual grounds that she had fallen in love with someone else and that her husband, after all, was the class enemy. Her husband agreed to her request. The next morning his captors discovered him missing from his room, and his severed body was found on the nearby railway tracks. He had committed suicide.

IT was not just the sweeping nature of the losses or the depth of isolation that made the Cultural Revolution extreme. It was the apparent meaninglessness of the movement as well. And the inability of many to find meaning in their suffering led, like the isolation, to false confessions, suicide, and madness. Torture was surely a contributing factor to many false confessions, but the pointlessness of the movement, particularly as it progressed, led many to choose survival through false confession over integrity without purpose. In contrast to an earlier period of Chinese history, when revolutionaries imprisoned by the Guomindang were able to give meaning to their suffering by seeing it as sacrifice for a cause, to the point where actual martyrdom made sense, a case like that of young Yu Luoke* was exceptional indeed. The "cause," for many, was impossible to fathom.

The most chilling and numerous examples of false confessions during the Cultural Revolution arose from the movement to ferret out the May Sixteenth elements, which lasted altogether about a year and a half, from the beginning

*See p. 111.

of 1970 to June or July 1971. Song Erli estimates that at least five thousand people died from torture and suicide during the course of that campaign in Jiangsu province alone. Nearly 800,000 people in Jiangsu were "ferreted out" by the military as members of the May Sixteenth group, and of those 800,000 people a substantial number confessed to having been members. Many informed Chinese believe today that there never was such an organization as the May Sixteenth group, and that if it existed at all it probably consisted of fewer than a hundred people, all of them in Peking. In Jiangsu province, hundreds of thousands confessed to being members of a clandestine organization that never existed.

The psychological toll of forced false confessions was great. Some succumbed to madness. "One of my friends had confessed early in the movement," Song Erli recalls. "He had suffered a lot more than I because he had tried to escape. The army officers were furious with him, and he suffered a very cruel beating. But the most terrible torture was not the beating but not being allowed to sleep. So he decided not just to confess but to hand over a membership list of all those people he had introduced into this clandestine May Sixteenth group. Once, when I was locked in my room, I heard him outside in the corridor when he was being escorted to the lavatory. I heard him shouting, 'Give me back the list I gave you yesterday. Now I recall there are two more people I have to add to the list.' That wasn't forced. He didn't have to add to the list. So he must already have been insane.

"He came to see me later and said, 'Do you know me?' I said, 'Yes, of course, you are so-and-so.' But he said no, he was the liaison officer of the May Sixteenth group. He said, 'I introduced three hundred people into that movement, including you.' He was already crazy at that time. People wouldn't lie in front of their victim. If they told a lie about you, they would never tell you right to your face.

"I saw him again much later, around the time of the downfall of the Gang of Four. He was still insane, but in a particular way. He asked me many silly questions. He was working in a school, but he couldn't teach. His job was to carry mortar for the school's masons. He asked me questions about whether I thought the plaster was poisoned, which of the masons was better, which of the masons was most likely to be putting poison in the mortar."

Having lost so much, facing persistent and continuing attacks, repeatedly brought to witness the public self-confessions of sundry associates and model confessors, and isolated from the familial and social support that otherwise might have helped to sustain them, some lost the capacity to distinguish truth from falsehood, lost their own sense of identity, and hovered at the edge of mental collapse. In the twilight between reality and breakdown, some may actually have come to believe the false accusations against them. While this led some, like Song Erli's friend, to false confessions and madness, it led others to suicide.

In a short story called "Who Am I?" Zong Pu writes about such a suicide, describing a female intellectual and her thoughts in the last few minutes before she drowns herself in a place many chose to commit suicide during the Cultural Revolution—the lake at Peking University.

Wei Mi, the heroine of the story, returns home late one afternoon to find her husband's body swinging from the kitchen ceiling. Having had all the research materials they had gathered over the years confiscated and destroyed, and knowing that shortly they will be confined to cattle pens, husband and wife have agreed that death is preferable to a life that has lost all meaning. Wei Mi, upon seeing the body of her husband, jumps from the window of their apartment, injuring herself without dying. A passerby, seeing her crumpled body and its head half shaved in the *yinyang* haircut, kicks her, accusing her of being a *niugui sheshen,* a phrase that is officially translated as "freaks and monsters," but which means, more literally, "ox ghost and snake spirit." As the injured and disoriented heroine crawls toward the lake, the young man's accusation becomes the shouts of *niugui sheshen* yelled against her at a recent struggle session. Wei Mi becomes an "ox ghost," that mythical monster who wreaks destruction on humans, who has fangs and eats people, devouring them with his fangs. Her face becomes black and her body is covered with bloody mouths, mouths with fangs, bloody from having eaten children, her students, because the heroine is a teacher. Continuing to crawl, unable to walk upright, she becomes the snake spirit, and Chinese mythology and biblical imagery meld as Wei Mi thinks of the serpent condemned forever to crawl on the earth for having seduced Eve with the fruit of knowledge. Only as Wei Mi is gasping her last does she look toward the sky and, seeing a flock of geese form the wedge-shaped Chinese character for "man," realize too late that she is human.

Zong Pu's description is not mere artistic device. For most Chinese, the label *niugui sheshen* carries with it frighteningly vivid visual images. Ox ghosts and snake spirits are the monsters of which Chinese nightmares are made. In time, at least some of those labeled ox ghosts and snake spirits began to identify with those images. It was 1972, shortly after his wife's death, when writer Ba Jin first sat down, pen in hand, to put his grief into words. For several hours a day, day after day, he sat before a blank piece of paper. The words wouldn't come. Ba Jin wondered whether, after all those years in a cattle pen, he really had become an ox ghost. Many people, even today, continue to refer to themselves as ox ghosts and snake spirits. There are even cases of individuals who, for some time after they were rehabilitated, for some time after that label was removed, continued to insist that they really were *niugui sheshen,* ox ghosts and snake spirits.

The incidence of madness seems highest among the young. Professor Hong Wenhan describes the descent into madness of his young daughter, Xiao Tao.

"I think my wife never liked Xiao Tao that much," Professor Hong begins. "Not just because she was a girl but because after she was born my wife was very ill. She was depressed, and there was some sort of sickness in her womb. She took Chinese medicine for it, but it never seemed really to get better, so she was very weak. So my wife kept saying, 'If I hadn't had Xiao Tao, I wouldn't have this sickness. My health would be better.' And directly to Xiao Tao she would say, 'If I had just had your brothers, I would be happier than I am having you.' I think she thought when she said those things that the little girl was too young to understand. But maybe Xiao Tao did understand.

"When the Cultural Revolution began and Jiang Qing became so involved, already many people didn't like her. But most people would admit that only within their families or to their very closest friends, and even then they would never speak of Jiang Qing by name. And most people would never say anything about her in front of their young children. But my wife one day said to me, right in front of Xiao Tao, that Jiang Qing was a bad woman. Just like that.

"Not long after that, at school one day, Xiao Tao just blurted out, 'Jiang Qing is a bad woman.' Her teacher was some kind of revolutionary, and when she asked Xiao Tao where she had heard that, Xiao Tao told her. So they put a dunce cap on Xiao Tao's head and paraded her through the streets. She was so tiny at the time, just a little girl, and the dunce cap was taller than she was high. She was only nine years old.

"Then they came here. The Red Guards. They took my wife away. I never saw her again after she went to jail. They wouldn't let me visit. By the time I heard anything again, she was already in the hospital. She had cancer, and she had been refused medical treatment until it was too late, because she was a counterrevolutionary. By the time they put her in the hospital, there was nothing that could be done. So she died.

"It was right after that, right after she learned that her mother had died, that Xiao Tao became insane. It is the kind of disease we call *yi feng* or *jingshen fenlie* [schizophrenia]. Sometimes she would act very happy and laugh a lot and have lots of energy and always be running. At other times, she would just be so sad. When she walked, she would keep her arms straight at her sides, stiffly, without moving them at all. And her eyes, they always seemed just to be staring. You couldn't talk to her to carry on a conversation. There seemed to be no logic to what she was saying. It was all just nonsense.

"So I put her in the mental hospital. I thought it would help her, make her better. But I think it only made her worse. There were mostly older people in the hospital, and they taught her to smoke and to curse. She was just the same after the mental hospital, only worse because of the smoking and the cursing. I don't want my daughter to smoke.

"My sons say that because of Xiao Tao, they are having trouble finding wives. It is true, when my eldest son brings a girlfriend home, Xiao Tao curses his girlfriend with the language she learned in the mental hospital, and tells my son's girlfriend to get out. Maybe it is true that some girls are afraid of becoming friends with my sons. People say that girls are scared of my daughter and that girls are afraid that if they married one of my sons, maybe their children would be mad. And I know what the younger people in the neighborhood say, too. They call Xiao Tao a witch.

"My sons want me to send Xiao Tao away. They want me to send her back to the mental hospital forever or to marry her off to some illiterate peasant out in the countryside somewhere, just to get rid of her, just so their lives can be smooth, so they can find someone to marry. Xiao Tao is twenty-four years old now. But how can I send her away? She is my little girl. I don't blame her for what happened.

"Xiao Tao looks after me, takes care of me, like the mistress of the family. She has never had a job, but still she goes to the market to buy the vegetables and the meat. She cooks for the family, and she is quite a good cook, too. And she can sew.

"Xiao Tao is so pretty. She looks so much like her mother. And now that she is grown, she wears her mother's clothes. Her mother was very beautiful, and she dressed very well, and Xiao Tao knows how to take the best of her mother's clothes and put them together in such a way that they match and look pretty. Perhaps Xiao Tao isn't as beautiful as her mother, but still she is very pretty. How can I send her away?"

Psychiatrists would argue that the Cultural Revolution is not the cause of Xiao Tao's madness. Schizophrenia is an illness to which individuals are predisposed and is not precipitated by particular distressing events. But friends and neighbors who still remember seeing Xiao Tao paraded through the streets in a dunce cap as high as she stood tall and who view her today with a mixture of sorrow and horror, looking so uncannily like her mother and emphasizing that likeness by dressing in her mother's clothes, would not accept the judgment of the professionals.

BEYOND the false confessions and the madness and the suicide which so pervaded the Cultural Revolution, there were still those who refused to succumb to their fate, those who were able despite their circumstances to find meaning in their suffering. Viktor Frankl, drawing from his own experiences in Nazi concentration camps, argues that when man has been stripped of everything, when all vestiges of the external trappings of dignity and integrity have finally been removed, when humiliation and degradation have become the constant and inescapable facts of human existence, when there is little left to distinguish man as human being from man the animal and beast, we are left still with one final choice, the last and inalienable of human freedoms: we can choose how we will respond to our circumstances, no matter how miserable they are. We can choose to find meaning in suffering.

Few, in the worst of times, are capable of achieving this. But those who do stand as universal statements of the best to which man can aspire.

The ideals for which they lived during the Cultural Revolution, the values that gave life meaning, were rarely lofty. J. D. Salinger noted, "The mark of an immature man is that he is willing to die for noble ideals; the mark of a mature one that he will live for humble ones."

It was above all for their families that they lived; their families kept them alive. One unintended consequence of the Cultural Revolution, an unexpected result of the inclusion of entire families in the web of attack, was a strengthening of familial bonds. If the isolation that occurred when members of the family drew a clear line of demarcation is one theme of the Cultural Revolution, another is the solidarity of those who refused to betray each other. The primary target of attack within any given family bore, in how he responded to his plight, responsibility not only for himself as an individual but for his family as well. When individuals persisted in the face of extremity, they did so not only for themselves but for their families too. In these cases, familial bonds served as protection against a hostile state. Family loyalty, love, and devotion are universally offered as reasons for persistence in conditions of adversity, but loyalty to the family during the Cultural Revolution had a meaning that was distinctively Chinese.

Jiang Xinren, it will be remembered, was kept from suicide by thoughts of his family, by what his death would mean for them. You Xiaoli and Li Meirong lived for their children. "It was my wife and son that kept me from committing suicide," Huang Chaoqun says. "My wife had already suffered so much, and without me she would have suffered even more. And my son was only nine years old when the Cultural Revolution began. I didn't want him to grow up an orphan. If a person committed suicide, they would say that he was afraid of being punished for his crime, that he was separating himself eternally from the people. I always thought that the Cultural Revolution could not last indefinitely. The situation would eventually change and the truth would come out. But if I had died, everything would be ended."

PEOPLE still fell in love during the Cultural Revolution, and they found meaning in love. Young people continued to get married. Tao Zhu's daughter, Tao Siliang, fell in love and got married while her father was under house arrest, and the pleasure he drew from his daughter's romance made Tao Zhu's confinement a little easier to bear.

More than love, Chinese found, as they always have, meaning in their children. Not only did the birthrate go up during the Cultural Revolution, but the baby boom of that period was a contributing factor in the later decision to limit the number of children in China to one per family. It is the baby-boom children born in the aftermath of the three bad years and during the Cultural Revolution who are being asked to limit their own children to one, in the optimistic hope that the population of China will peak at 1.2 billion in the year 2000 and then begin a long-term downward trend.

People fell in love during the Cultural Revolution not only in the normal course of reaching young adulthood, but illicitly, too, in the loneliness of the ostracism which engulfed the lives of victims. Kindnesses went far with the ox ghosts and snake spirits, and when two societal outcasts, separated as they often were from their spouses, found that by helping each other and sharing some of their misery the pain was at least temporarily diminished, romance was a likely result. The May Seventh Cadre Schools were particularly fertile ground for the blossoming of romance. Indeed, for many under attack in the cities, the May Seventh Cadre Schools were havens. The struggle meetings stopped and so did the isolation. The ox ghosts and snake spirits were together with others of their kind. The air was fresh and clean, healthy and invigorating. But separated as they were from their spouses and families, and lonely so far away from home, often on desolate and barren land, with so little to do, so little to read, and nothing to occupy themselves at the end of a day of work in the fields, men and women often turned to each other for companionship, comfort, and love.

Qiu Yehuang had studied in the Soviet Union, and he knew how to play the guitar and sing a few Russian folk songs. His music sometimes provided the backdrop for burgeoning romance, and was instrumental in his own. "The May Seventh Cadre School where I lived was in a very remote area of the countryside, a very poor area," says Qiu Yehuang of the place where he spent two years. "It was so remote that it took eight hours by truck just to get to the nearest railway station.

"At night there was really nothing to do. There was no electricity, so it was impossible to read, even if you had been able to smuggle in a book or two. We were supposed to have political study sessions, to remold our ideological thinking, but no one took them very seriously. Often, at night, I would sit outside and play the guitar and sing Russian folk songs. They were sad and mournful songs, but they expressed what was in my heart, so it made me feel better to play and to sing. Often as I was sitting there singing other people would gather around me and sit there in a semicircle to listen. The women in the school in particular seemed to like those sad and melancholy songs. At that time there were only six or seven songs that were permitted in China—revolutionary songs like 'The East Is Red' or 'Sailing the Seas Depends on the Helmsman.' Once while I was singing the guy who was the candidate for membership in the party came up to me and said he didn't think I should play those songs. He said they weren't revolutionary. I told him I didn't know any other songs and continued to play. And everyone around me supported me in this.

"We were far away from our families at the cadre school, and except for people who had to return home because their relatives were sick or had died, we were allowed to visit home only once a year. People were lonely out there in that remote and desolate place. We were weak and hungry. And relations among some of the people in the cadre school became very close. Some people fell in love. Sometimes a man and a woman would disappear into the woods, alone, for three or four hours. At first maybe it wouldn't be noticed, but after a few times, someone would notice, and there would have to be a public criticism. It would never be a direct criticism. People would never be mentioned by name. But we would be reminded that we were there to serve the revolution, and there would be a speech, and everyone would know what the leaders were talking about. It was hard, with so many people in such close quarters, to keep a secret.

"I fell in love at the May Seventh Cadre School. But no one ever found out. We never went into the woods together, so we were able to keep it a secret from everyone. Maybe it wasn't love really, but it seemed like love. Because it was so lonely there and my wife and I had such trouble talking during the Cultural Revolution. This other woman and I could talk to each other and comfort and support each other. And she liked to hear me sing the Russian folk songs. She left the cadre school before I did. We exchanged letters once but after that I never heard from or saw her again. By now, I think I have almost gotten over her."

Love that was not sanctioned by the state was not always regarded so benignly as in Qiu Yehuang's May Seventh Cadre School. Yang Yiren and Lin Xiaohe were both teachers in the same middle school. They both came under attack during the Cultural Revolution and were assigned the job of uprooting the bourgeois plants that had earlier brought color and life to the grounds of their school. Kneeling on the ground all day and miserable with their lot, they began helping each other, confiding in each other, and in time they fell in love. Their respective spouses had already been sent away.

One night late, the couple were together in Yang Yiren's apartment when the Red Guards broke in for one of the inspections of household registration that served during the Cultural Revolution as a supplement to the house searches. Counterrevolutionaries often tried to flee the justice the revolutionaries were meting out, and the inspection of household registrations was a means of rounding up those who were being illegally protected by family and friends. It was also a way of discovering illicit love affairs. Yang Yiren and Lin Xiaohe were discovered having an affair.

The next day, to the fascination and merriment of the watching crowds, the couple were taken together on a street parade through the city. They were tied together at the neck by a rope, and each wore the usual placard around the neck. There was something different about this parade, though. The placards labeled the accused not as counterrevolutionaries or any of the other variety of political criminals but as adulterer and adulteress. And Yang Yiren and Lin Xiaohe were both completely naked. The crowd grew larger and larger as the street parade progressed, laughing, applauding, jeering, and spitting at the miserable, hapless, humiliated couple.

When the street parade was over, Lin Xiaohe spoke to no one but went immediately to her children's room. She hanged herself from the bunk bed in which her children slept. When the Red Guards were informed of her death, they moved the body, bunk bed and all, to the courtyard in front of the house, organizing other ox ghosts and snake spirits facing similar temptations to come take a look at what could happen to them if they should succumb to illicit affairs of the heart. It was four days before the body was removed. No one dared to cut it down.

THEY found meaning, too, in the work they were assigned, however menial, humiliating, and degrading that work was meant to be. Huang Chaoqun, for years, was officially charged with watering the fields on the farm to which he was assigned. All day every day during the growing season he spent in endless trips to fetch the water, carried then over his shoulder in buckets attached one to each end of a bamboo pole, to be applied ladleful by ladleful to each individual plant. And because the plants flourished and then produced food, it was a task in which the white-haired senior professor came to take considerable pride.

Li Meirong—born, bred, and to all appearances permanently rooted in the city—spent a good part of the Cultural Revolution in the countryside. She too ultimately found meaning in her work. One of the first tasks to which the former middle school teacher was assigned was fetching water, "an easy task, really," she says. "There was no running water in the village. Instead, there was a village well, and all the water came from there. My task was to draw the water from the well and then to take several pails of it back to the village. You lowered the bucket on a rope attached to a pulley down into the well and then you had to use both hands and your shoulders to turn the crank that brought the bucket back up. The first day I tried it, I could only manage to draw one bucket of water. It was very hard for me because I wasn't used to such heavy labor, and my arms and shoulders and back ached with all the effort. After drawing that one bucket of water, I put it on the wheelbarrow to wheel it back to the village, but I was so clumsy with the wheelbarrow that by the time I had arrived back in the village, all of the water had spilled over the sides of the pail.

"But I got better at it. After about two weeks, I was almost an expert. I could pull up nine buckets of water all in one trip and put them all in the wheelbarrow, four on each side and one at the tip, and wheel the barrow back to the village hardly spilling a drop."

Later, Li Meirong was assigned to a May Seventh Cadre School, where she was a member of a squad whose task it was to grow corn. "I had never known what it was like to plant corn," she says. "In China, the methods of farming are still so primitive. There are no machines. To plant corn, you take three or four kernels and put them into the soil with your hands. Then when the plants start to grow, you have to go back to each plant and pull away the leaves so there is only one plant left. It is backbreaking labor. Peasants squat when they do it, but it was often difficult for us city folk to squat, so we would kneel. Planting one row of corn, or thinning one row of corn, would take me three hours."

Li Meirong persisted in learning, and eventually she was winning red flags as the best cultivator of corn in her school. She returned finally from the countryside with a lifelong appreciation of the effort and skill, the backbreaking labor, involved in producing the basic necessities of life. "Living in the countryside for those several years has made me a better person," she says. "I am better for having been there. In that sense, the experience was a good one. Before, as a teacher, life had been very simple. I had very few friendships outside the school and my life revolved around the school and my students. It was a simple life, an easy life, and in some ways I was like a student or a young person myself. There was a certain lack of maturity on my part, since all my relations were with students.

"Above all, I have a much greater appreciation of the peasants now, of how food is produced. I had never known how much backbreaking labor goes into producing just one bowl of rice or just one portion of vegetable. I had never appreciated how much the peasants have to suffer and endure to produce the food for us in the cities to eat. I have tried to teach my children this, to teach them to appreciate what the peasants endure for us. If they leave even a small bit of rice in their bowls at the end of a meal, I remind them of how much the peasants suffered to produce even those few grains of rice. I tell them they should show their appreciation by leaving nothing in their bowls."

NEVER before and never since have the bathrooms at You Xiaoli's university been so clean and so fresh and sweet-smelling as they were when You Xiaoli was in charge.

Qiu Yehuang, whose good friend was assigned to clean the public toilets in Peking, is anxious to impress upon the foreigner just what it meant during the Cultural Revolution to be assigned the task of cleaning the public toilets. "Have you ever seen one of those public toilets?" he demands. "It's a big room. Holds maybe twenty people. There are no dividers, so people can see each other. There are two lines. You're squatting here and another one is squatting there just next to you with nothing in between. They're awful. I hate them. I always try to wash myself at home afterward. The places smell. There is water on the floor, urine. There is no water, no toilet paper. In Peking, there are thousands of toilets like that. To clean them, people from the suburbs, from the people's communes, come to collect the manure, to use it as fertilizer. They drive in in a horse cart. The horse is pulling a big wooden container, like a wooden cart. They take it away in that.

"During the Cultural Revolution, the ox ghosts and snake spirits would have to bring water in and wash the floor and the steps. Then they would bring in some wood ash and dust the ash on the stuff to reduce the smell. Then when it got full, they would call the people's commune to bring their cart to pick up the stuff.

"But since intellectuals worked mostly in office buildings, they had to clean flush toilets. Those places weren't so dirty."

You Xiaoli was an intellectual, so the toilets she was in charge of cleaning were not so unappealing as the public toilets of Peking. "I was proud to clean the toilets," says You Xiaoli of the four years when that was her job. "I cleaned them wonderfully. I thought, 'I can do nothing for my people now. This is all I can do, so I'll do it as well as I can.' Before, I hadn't known that this was useful work. Now I know it. Today, people still say that we have never had such clean bathrooms as when You Xiaoli was cleaning them. It was punishment, but I also thought it was the kind of work that should be done well. The person who did the work before me was considered the lowest of the low. But it is also important work, and the people doing this kind of work should be told that it is important work. I used to put flowers in the bathrooms, to add some color and so they would smell nice. I was criticized for that. They said, 'You can never be reeducated. Even when you are an ox ghost and snake spirit, you still put flowers in the bathroom.'

"One day I was forbidden to wash my hands after cleaning the toilets, before I ate. The Red Guards turned off the faucet and forbade me. They said, 'You can't wash your hands.' Of course, I thought my hands were dirty, and I felt bad, embarrassed. But then I thought that the peasants in the countryside don't have much water, that they have to spread manure with their bare hands, that they can't wash afterward and they still have to eat. Then I stopped feeling sad. The Red Guards watched me eat, and they laughed. They thought it was a joke, punishment. But it made me know the life of the peasants.

"They criticized me for using too much water, for wasting too much soap when I cleaned. I had never noticed before what difficult work it is to keep bathrooms cleaned. But now I know it is important, the kind of work that more attention should be paid to. I remember reading Gorky, *My University*. He learned from society, said that society was his university. For me, the four years I spent cleaning toilets—that was my university."

For all the criticism she received for the bourgeois manner in which she insisted on cleaning the bathrooms, You Xiaoli was also rewarded, ironically, for her efforts. Before the Cultural Revolution, You Xiaoli had been the head of a research institute, the sound for "institute" in Chinese being *suo* and her official title—head of the institute—being *suozhang*. The sound for "toilet" in Chinese is also *suo,* and so well did You Xiaoli perform her assigned duties that her title was restored during the Cultural Revolution. She became the head of the toilets—the *suozhang.* "Conscientious people are still conscientious, no matter what," says You Xiaoli.

Chen Quanhong found meaning during the Cultural Revolution from another man, an old army officer, whose fate was similar to Chen's. After having been released from confinement, Professor Chen was given a job as a beast of burden, pulling carts with loads that often weighed more than 2,500 pounds and for which he received remuneration first of twenty-five cents a day and then, when his skills improved, of fifty. But serving as a beast of burden was not an occupation that this devotee of Chinese history and classics initially found particularly meaningful. Then he met an old army cadre assigned to the same job.

"He seemed not at all discouraged and was so full of energy," Chen Quanhong explains. "I asked him where he found the strength, the energy, the courage. He said that the laboring people of China had been pulling loads like that for centuries, that that was their lot. 'What the laboring people can do, I can do, too,' he said. Generation after generation, if need be. 'There is nothing special about me,' he said. So this old Red Army cadre encouraged me to be a good worker, and I really did become a good worker. I continued in my transportation job, pulling heavy loads, but I became an advanced worker, a model worker."

Liu Zhiping had always wanted to be a teacher, and her goal today is a reality. She is a teacher, a young instructor, in the university from which she finally graduated. But never has teaching had quite the same meaning as when she was in the countryside and the mining town during the Great Proletarian Cultural Revolution. Not only did her students appreciate what Liu Zhiping was able to teach, but they taught her, too. From them she learned that her identity did not depend on her father, that she could always find ways to be of use to society, that the Chinese people, despite the movement that was pulling them apart, could again be united as one.

"I felt, after those experiences, that China was united, that China was one big family, one nation, that other forces, other people, were pulling it apart," says Liu Zhiping sadly. "I knew that the Chinese people could be united again, and this made me feel very patriotic.

"And I felt very independent after that, as though I could be separate from my family, as though my problems at school weren't that important. I knew that if things went badly when I returned to school, if I couldn't stand it again, there would still be a place for me, still be something I could do. And I still feel that if there were another Cultural Revolution, I could return again to the countryside. I could work in the fields, or the mines, or be a teacher. And I would be welcomed there, warmly welcomed. Because we are all Chinese. It made me stronger, better able to face my school, to know that there was an alternative that was not so bad."

Song Wuhao had arrived in the countryside in the depths of despair, despised by the society in which he had been raised and having sinned grievously against his father. But he too ultimately found meaning in his work. Song Wuhao could not really be a scientist in the poor and backward part of the countryside where he and his brother lived, but he could bring scientific principles to bear on some of the problems confronting the peasants. He and his brother were instrumental in introducing electricity into the village where they lived, and with their help the peasants were able to bring running water to the village—not into their homes, but to the village common. Song Wuhao, after several years, was elected the brigade's accountant.

In all those years, as he grew more useful to the peasants with whom he lived and as he came to earn their respect, Song Wuhao never gave up hope that even though he had never even graduated from middle school, someday he might be given the opportunity to go to the university, to be trained as the scientist he still so desperately wanted to become. From his confinement in the cattle pen, and despite what had happened between them, Song Wuhao's father continued to nurture his son's hope. "My father, mother, grandfather, all are intellectuals," explains Song Wuhao. "For generations, my family have been intellectuals. So my father was very unhappy, depressed that we seemed unable to enter the university. But he kept telling us that the country couldn't remain in that state of upheaval. He said that the country was backward and that eventually, when the turmoil was over, our country would need us young people. He said that if we had no education, no culture, we would really be no different from the peasants, that we must therefore continue to study in what spare time we could find."

At night, after a full day of backbreaking labor in the fields, Song Wuhao continued first by kerosene lantern and later by feeble electric light to study. Universities, closed since the onset of the Cultural Revolution in 1966, began to reopen in 1972 to a new kind of student—the workers, peasants, and soldiers. Technically, Song Wuhao was eligible to apply. Living in the countryside as he had for four years, his household registration moved from Peking to that remote and awesomely beautiful area, he was classified as a peasant. In the summer of 1972, the county in which he resided gave an exam, locally conceived and locally administered, to university aspirants. Song Wuhao ranked first in the county. But political criteria were more important for college entrance at that time than academic ones, and Wuhao was therefore not allowed to enter the university. His father, after all, was a counterrevolutionary and a spy.

For five years, Song Wuhao took the university entrance exams. For five years he and his younger brother alternated between first and second place. In 1977, with Deng Xiaoping back in power and anxious to retrieve the country from the abyss into which it had fallen, the sins of the father no longer precluded the education of the son. Song Wuhao left the countryside to become a student of biochemistry at the university where his father had once been a senior professor.

Song Wuhao is not unique in his determination and persistence. Some of the best English spoken in China today comes from the mouths of young adults who were sent to the countryside during the Cultural Revolution and who studied at night over kerosene lights and listened in the dark to the shortwave radios they had surreptitiously brought with them. The classes that entered Chinese universities in 1977 and 1978, the first two years after college entrance examinations were reintroduced, classes peopled by the sons and daughters of the victims of China's Cultural Revolution, the young people who had spent often ten years of their lives in the Chinese countryside, are among the finest students that post-Liberation China has produced.

AND they found meaning in their suffering through the small acts of rebellion their circumstances occasionally permitted. Rebellion was rare during the Cultural Revolution, understandably so. "We must remember that people are capable of greatness, of courage, but not in isolation," Archbishop Anthony Bloom reminds us. "They need the conditions of a solidly linked human unit in which everyone is prepared to bear the burden of others." For most, the courage required for small acts of rebellion came only in the May Seventh Cadre Schools, where the isolation and loneliness of the Cultural Revolution were replaced by the solidarity of "squads" organized along military lines but composed at least of individuals who became friends. It was easier in the May Seventh Cadre School to be brave.

Huang Xing in that regard was unique. His small acts of rebellion began early, even before he had been sent to the countryside. Huang Xing is a man with a very strong sense of identity, a man who knows who he is, a man who always knew—and knew that his colleagues knew, too—that he was innocent of the charges against him. Witnessing the spectacle into which the politics of the Cultural Revolution degenerated, Huang Xing concluded early that the movement was theater of the absurd, and he refused to play his part. He refused to perform his role as victim. At the struggle meetings against him, Huang Xing was in the habit of appearing to wander off into space, even, indeed, to catch a little snooze. His detractors were infuriated with the lack of seriousness with which he greeted the accusations against him, but they never touched a hair on his head.

At some of the accusations, Huang Xing could only laugh. Locked in a cattle pen and subjected to regular interrogations by the young Red Guards, Huang Xing was questioned at length about his connections, extending all the way back to the 1930s, with the notorious Fei Zhengqing. The Red Guards, it seemed, thought that the notorious Fei Zhengqing was the brother of the well-known and also notorious rightist Fei Xiaotong. "I let them go on making fools of themselves," laughs Huang Xing. "Then I pointed out that Fei Zhengqing was the Chinese name of the American China scholar John King Fairbank."

Huang Xing even seemed to enjoy the May Seventh Cadre School. "The May Seventh Cadre School wasn't so bad," he recounts. "First of all, I was excused from the political meetings. I was considered a counterrevolutionary, and counterrevolutionaries were excused. And then there was the fresh air, the stars at night, the blue of the sky during the day, the peace. It really wasn't bad."

At the May Seventh Cadre School, Huang Xing continued to engage in small acts of protest. "It was during my stay at the May Seventh Cadre School that my status changed from someone who had been a counterrevolutionary in the past to a counterrevolutionary in action, a present-day counterrevolutionary. I still remember it. One day a guy in uniform came to me to make the formal announcement that I had been accused of being a present-day counterrevolutionary. I laughed at him. He said, 'This is serious. The crimes you have committed are serious. The accusation against you is serious.' I laughed again. It was absurd. Ridiculous.

"I was still at the May Seventh Cadre School, in 1972, when word came that I had been rehabilitated. The news spread, and everyone came over to congratulate me. Everybody wanted to shake my hand. One of those people was that guy in uniform who had accused me of being a counterrevolutionary in action in the first place. He stuck out his hand, but I refused to take it. 'Why do you want to shake hands with me? Aren't I a counterrevolutionary in action?' I asked him. His face turned red."

AT Qiu Yehuang's May Seventh Cadre School, the intellectuals conspired to treat an aspirant for party membership the same way they, the intellectuals, had been treated in the cities—they moved to ostracize him.

"While we were living in the village, each day we would eat together in a different peasant's house, so by the time we had left the village, we had eaten in just about everybody's house except the landlord's," Qiu Yehuang begins by way of background. "Since we were guests, the peasants would always try to fix something special for us, and they would always try to urge us to eat more. But one of the people in my group was a candidate for membership in the party, and in order to be admitted into the party, he had to demonstrate how enthusiastic he was about everything, how ideologically correct he could be. We all disliked him, and we hated being a member of his group when we were eating in the village. Whenever the peasants would offer us more food, he would always say, 'Oh, no, I can't accept food from the poor peasants. It wouldn't be right.' So we had to say no too. There we were, weak and hungry and starving. There was lots of food sitting right in front of us. But we couldn't eat.

"So we ostracized him. We wouldn't speak to him. Not a word. If he was working in one part of the field, we would all move to another part of the field. Four of the people in my group were women, and they weren't afraid of him at all. They could be very frank and forthright with him. One day, he pretended to be very polite and sincere and contrite, and he came over and asked us very humbly why we refused to talk to him. The women started yelling and cursing at him, and they told him. They told him that it was because he wouldn't let us eat the food that was sitting right in front of us and that he was always so damned enthusiastic about that miserable place."

Li Meirong's rebellion was the most audacious of all. "One of the things they did at the May Seventh Cadre School," she explains, "was to keep shifting people from squad to squad, from the corn-growing squad to the rice-growing squad to the vegetable-growing squad, from one study class to another, from one dormitory to another. They didn't want people to get too close, too friendly. They didn't want us to get too comfortable. And every time you switched squads, you had to learn how to plant a different kind of crop, change your dormitory, change your bed, eat in a different dining hall, make another set of friends.

"I have the type of personality that can be nice and cooperative and malleable for long periods of time. People say 'do this' and I do it, 'Do that' and I do it. I cooperate. But slowly I get angry and gradually the anger builds. Finally, it reaches the point where I can take it no more, when I put my foot down, when I say no. That was what finally happened at the May Seventh Cadre School with all those changes of squads.

"One day, the cadres announced that there was going to be another reshuffling of the squads. Some people would be moving to different dormitories. Some would plant different crops. I had already been moved so many times and it had made me so angry that this time I just refused. I told them I would not move. Not my squad, not my bed, not my dormitory, not my dining hall.

"Suddenly, I wasn't afraid anymore. I thought that this May Seventh Cadre School was the end of my life, that there was nothing left for me to do except this school. It didn't matter to me if they wanted to criticize me. I told them they could criticize me. They could stand me up on a platform in front of the entire May Seventh Cadre School and criticize me and hope that I lost face. I took my cheek in my hand—I had gained weight at the cadre school—and told them that my face was very thick. It was several inches thick. I could afford to lose some face. I could lose lots of face being criticized on a platform and still there would be plenty left. So it didn't matter if they criticized me. It didn't even matter if they wanted to kill me, if I should die. What would it mean if I were to die? Hadn't I come to the May Seventh Cadre School for the rest of my life? To die? It only meant that I would die sooner. That's all. But I absolutely refused to move. I was going to stay in my own bed, in my own dormitory room. I was going to continue growing corn. I wasn't going to shift around again.

"So the cadres called a meeting. Each squad was supposed to have a meeting at noon where the cadres would announce the changes. But first the cadres had to have their own meeting. At noon, we all brought our stools to the field where the meeting was to be held. Then we waited. And waited. The cadres were still having their meeting. They couldn't decide what to do. I wasn't at all certain what they would do, either. But I was not frightened. At last, I was no longer afraid. When I went to the meeting, I just carried my stool and sat down and looked very nonchalant. Finally, the cadres arrived and the meeting began.

"They started calling names. 'So and so will now plant corn instead of rice. So and so will move her dormitory room. So and so will move from the rice squad to the vegetable squad.' On and on they read. Name after name. I still hadn't heard my name. My good friend was sitting right next to me, and she kept turning to look at me. But I wouldn't look at her. I just sat there, looking straight ahead, being very nonchalant, wondering whether they would call my name. Still, they kept reading on.

"And then it was over. They were finished. They hadn't read my name. Everyone in the school, everyone but me, had gotten a new assignment. But they hadn't read my name. So I could stay where I was. In my own bed. My own room. My same study group. Planting corn. There is an old Chinese saying for this. 'When you are weak, you will be oppressed. When you are strong, people will fear you.' That's what happened. I was strong, tough, hard. And they were afraid. What could they do to me? They weren't going to kill me. They couldn't send me to prison."

Li Meirong was also able to take mild but sweet revenge against one of her accusers. It was teacher Wu who had led the attacks against Li Meirong, teacher Wu who had taunted Li Meirong about her Western-shaped eyes, her stylish clothes, her connections overseas. As the Cultural Revolution spread, and all of the country's urban educated were deemed in need of reeducation, teacher Wu, too, was sent to the May Seventh Cadre School where Li Meirong had already been for a year.

"I hadn't forgiven her then, and I don't forgive her now. Her, in particular," she says. "I had heard that she had been sent to the school. Some friends had told me. But I hadn't seen her yet. Then one day, I met her in the bathroom. She couldn't take it. Couldn't take all the work. There she was in the bathroom getting sick with vomiting and diarrhea. The peasant food bothered her, so she developed stomach trouble. And her legs were all swollen, huge, so she could barely walk. Working in the fields, in the rice paddies, you have to stand in water, and there were all sorts of insects that would bite into your flesh and work their way in through the skin. That's why her legs were so swollen. She had had to work in the paddy fields.

"Not that teacher Wu had never been to the countryside before. She had been to the countryside. When the teachers at my school had been sent to the countryside in the past, to do our stints of manual labor or to help with the harvest, teacher Wu would always accompany us. But teacher Wu was a cadre. She never did manual labor in the countryside. She would just sit in an office all day, barking out orders, like a big official. She had never done physical labor before.

"By that time, I was getting red flags for my work at the school, for being best at physical labor, best at studying Chairman Mao. When they would give me the red flags, though, I would refuse them. I would say, 'Send them to my school. Give them to my school.' And I really did get fat at the May Seventh Cadre School. So when I saw teacher Wu, I said, 'Teacher Wu, I thought you could do everything. But look at you. Your legs are all swollen. You are sick. You are vomiting and having diarrhea. Are you having some trouble with physical labor, teacher Wu? I'm really doing well here, as you can see. I'm thriving on physical labor. I'm even winning red flags. It's really so good to be here.' "

EIGHT

HOU YI ZHENG:
THE LONG-TERM EFFECTS

IT was the fall of 1977 when a thin, weak, and bedraggled You Xiaoli was summoned to the office of a newly formed organization on her campus—the *pingfang weiyuanhui*. Set up shortly after the overthrow of the Gang of Four in October 1976, the announcement of the establishment of the *pingfang weiyuanhui* had been made with considerable public fanfare. The responsibilities of the new organization were weighty, and it was important that its members be entirely above suspicion. With the public announcement of its formation was the encouragement to anyone knowing of any reason any of its members were not worthy of the post to submit their concerns, unsigned, to a private post office box established especially for the purpose. The *pingfang weiyuanhui* was the "rehabilitation committee," the committee established to investigate the charges leveled against the victims of the Cultural Revolution, the committee sanctioned to rehabilitate those who had been falsely accused.

"The former verdict against you is wrong," said the leader of the rehabilitation committee to You Xiaoli. "You are not a capitalist roader. You are not a spy. You are a good professor. Your salary will be returned to you."

Three months later, You Xiaoli stood again before the leading members of the rehabilitation committee. She was given an envelope containing, in cash, some $1,800 worth of Chinese currency. You Xiaoli's salary, when the Cultural Revolution began, had been a little more than $60 a month. When she came under attack in the summer of 1966, it was reduced to $7.50 a month. When Deng Xiaoping returned to office in 1973, he had made an effort to see that the salaries of intellectuals under attack were restored. In 1975, his efforts trickled down to benefit You Xiaoli, and she began receiving her full salary again. Technically, though, she was still owed a total of nearly $6,000 for the nine years her salary had been reduced.

But certain expenses had been deducted from the total You Xiaoli was owed. Money had been deducted for twelve years of faculty union dues. Money had been deducted for big character poster paper and for ink and brushes. Early in the Cultural Revolution, shortly after she had come under attack, You Xiaoli had thought she might write her own big character poster explaining and defending her position. As an ox ghost and snake spirit, she was not entitled to write a big character poster, and with only $7.50 a month in income, she could not afford to buy the writing materials to post one on her own. She had bought the materials on loan. For the twelve years from 1966 to 1978, $13 a month had been deducted for rent—a rent several times the national average in China and the period coinciding not only with the duration of You Xiaoli's disgrace but also with the time her apartment had been occupied, rent-free, by the revolutionary rebels. The revolutionary rebels, in fact, were still living in You Xiaoli's apartment. Housing was in short supply, and the revolutionary rebels had yet to be assigned a suitable apartment.

The revolutionary rebels had saved the jewelry they had confiscated from You Xiaoli's apartment, jewelry that she had inherited from a distant and wealthy relative. She was persuaded to sell the jewelry—diamonds, rubies, emeralds, and gold worth tens of thousands of dollars—to the state, and for her patriotic sale she received additional compensation. You Xiaoli was paid 100 *yuan* for her inheritance, about $50.

But You Xiaoli was comparatively well compensated. The Communist Party members on her campus were additionally charged with twelve years of dues for their membership in the party. Out of patriotism for their country and gratitude that their names had been cleared, they were encouraged to donate the remainder of what was owed them for the good of the party and state. The campus was covered with posters lauding the generosity and selflessness of those loyal members of the party who had refused to accept even a penny of compensation.

You Xiaoli spent the three days following the return of her salary on a shopping spree. During the repeated house searches in the summer and fall of 1966, her apartment had been stripped bare. Between them, You Xiaoli and her husband shared a broken comb. Her husband still had a razor, but his $7.50 a month was not enough to afford the razor blades. "But we still had a pair of scissors," You Xiaoli explains, "so I cut his hair and he cut mine. And I cut his beard with the scissors, so there were some long hairs and some short. Many people were like that, the old professors. They had no money to buy a new razor or shaving cream or soap. You couldn't do anything about it. So once you are very, very poor, you can't be clean, civilized. You can't be anything."

Nothing that had been taken from You Xiaoli's apartment was ever returned. Everything had to be replaced—beds, tables, chairs, wardrobes, cooking stove, clothes. "I bought everything secondhand," You Xiaoli explains, "because otherwise it would be too expensive." She and her husband borrowed a two-wheeled cart—there was no other way for them to transport the furniture —and with You Xiaoli pulling (it was a skill her husband had never learned) and her husband pushing, the couple spent three days hauling their newly acquired merchandise home. In three days, nearly the entire $1,800 in back salary had been spent.

As they were out making their purchases, You Xiaoli and her husband had stopped in the locker room of the local sports stadium to weigh themselves for the first time since the Cultural Revolution began. You Xiaoli weighed eighty-two pounds, her husband ninety-seven.

On the third day, with all her purchases safely at home, You Xiaoli removed from its wrapping the small hand mirror she had bought on her shopping expedition, held it before her, and stared in horror and disbelief into the eyes of a stranger, a face she did not know. She had not seen her own reflection in more than a decade. "I didn't know myself at all," she says. "I saw an old, old woman there with a wrinkled face, and thin, the cheekbones sticking out so sharply, and ashen-pale, white-haired. Before the Cultural Revolution, I didn't have white hair. And I found myself even shorter than before. Of course in such a little mirror, I couldn't see tall or short, but I felt shorter. I had gone from forty-five to fifty-seven years old. Of course, it's a time to grow older. But old doesn't mean *so* thin, *so* wrinkled."

"My husband also couldn't recognize himself in the mirror. So I asked him how it was that I could recognize him and he could recognize me. It was because we had been looking at each other all the time."

With You Xiaoli and her husband both officially rehabilitated, the requests for forgiveness began. Both husband and wife received letters from their former students, the students who had attacked them during the Cultural Revolution, apologizing, asking for forgiveness, explaining that they had not known what they were doing, that they had fallen under the influence of the Gang of Four. Zhu Que, then in her early forties, a fellow teacher who had viciously attacked them both, came to visit them one night and cried. She had been forced to hurl those accusations, forced to lie, she sobbed. The revolutionary rebels who continued to occupy their apartment, waiting until they were assigned proper housing, became increasingly solicitous of You Xiaoli and her husband. "Professor You," they would say, "may I go shopping for you? You are so tired. Please let me help. Let me do something for you."

As You Xiaoli began eating again, her diet no longer confined to the sweet potato buns and the two pickles a day, as she began sleeping longer and resting better, she began gaining weight. And as she thought her health was improving, "you just couldn't believe it," she said. "My skin was just like fish scales falling off—the face, the fingers, the whole body. It was terrible. I went to the doctor. He said it was like that for many, many people after the Cultural Revolution. From lack of food. You know, for almost ten years, we didn't have any oil. No oil whatsoever. So you become dry from no fat, no oil."

It was later that You Xiaoli began to be troubled by visions.

In the autumn of 1979, two years after You Xiaoli had been formally rehabilitated and cleared of the numerous charges against her, she was standing in front of a small class of students, only a handful of people, delivering an informal lecture. It was not the first time since the Cultural Revolution You Xiaoli had lectured to students. Nor was the classroom unfamiliar to her. She had lectured in it many times before the Cultural Revolution. She had been in it many times during the Cultural Revolution. It was one of the rooms where she had often been brought for struggle sessions. It was one of the rooms where her students had beaten her. During the Cultural Revolution, the room had been covered with slogans, painted in huge red characters on the walls. The walls had only recently been whitewashed.

As You Xiaoli was talking, she glanced casually, without thinking, over the heads of her students, and her eye was caught by the red revolutionary characters that could still be seen beneath the whitewash. You Xiaoli stopped talking. "Suddenly there wasn't just a handful of students," she says. "Suddenly I saw there were more and more and more people in the room and very soon there were lots of students sitting there and they were all the old Red Guards and it wasn't I who was lecturing to the students. It was a struggle meeting against me. I had the feeling I used to have when I was beaten. I used to be beaten so badly my nose bled, and also I still had my period during the Cultural Revolution and sometimes I would stand in the struggle meetings for so long that the blood would come down my leg, and that day I could feel the blood running out of my nose and down my mouth. I could taste the blood in my mouth and then I could feel it go down my chin and down my neck and down my chest and suddenly I could feel the blood going down my leg.

"And then I heard a song as though coming from very, very, very far away and then suddenly it was only the handful of students again. I asked what had happened to me. I was so pale. One of the students gave me a cup of hot water, and I finished my talk. That's all. The wall had been whitewashed and the characters were just a little bit still there and they caused my vision."

The vision of the struggle session against her is not the only one You Xiaoli has had.

IN attempting to describe the long-term effects of the Cultural Revolution on themselves, their families, and their friends, Chinese sometimes say that it is a case of *hou yi zheng,* meaning that after the disease is cured, a sickness remains. More formally, *hou yi zheng* may be translated as "sequela," meaning "a morbid condition left as the result of a disease." It is a term employed with some frequency by those who study the long-term effects of immersion in extremity. For if a disaster "splinters the silence for one terrible moment and then goes away," the tragedy of a disaster is not merely in the terrible moment but in the long-term effects on those who survive it. Many of those who survived the extremity of the Nazi concentration camps were liberated only to succumb afterward to the sickness psychiatrists once labeled "concentration camp syndrome" or "barbed-wire syndrome." Veterans of the Vietnam War returned to the United States in a reasonably healthy mental state. Today, many are burdened with deep psychological wounds.

Not only do survivors of extreme situations remain victims of their survival, but there is a universality to the sequelae that transcends the particular extremity. Psychiatrists who have studied survivors of extreme situations would argue that any form of extreme stress is likely to produce a similar pattern of long-term response, a similar set of symptoms which together are now labeled "posttraumatic stress disorder" and under which may be subsumed such disorders as concentration camp syndrome and combat fatigue. Leo Etinger, studying survivors of concentration camps, Kai Erikson, studying survivors of the Buffalo Creek dam disaster, and many who have studied the survivors of Vietnam combat have noted an almost photographic identity in survivors' descriptions of their continuing distress—symptoms that include a sense of guilt and a fear that the disaster might recur, nightmares, failing memory and difficulty in concentration, nervousness and irritability, depression, fatigue, sleep disturbances, headaches, emotional instability, and alienation.

Moreover, the nature of the distress experienced by victims of extremity differs in fundamental respects from other mental disorders. Traditional Freudian psychoanalytic theory posits a relationship between early childhood experiences and later neuroses, but posttraumatic stress disorder is testimony to the fact that traumas that occur in adult life can have long-lasting psychological consequences.

The symptoms of distress are sometimes delayed for months, even years, after the experiences of extremity. Many concentration camp survivors who were studied in the first year after their liberation appeared, psychologically at least, to function remarkably well. Their psychological wounds did not appear until later. American soldiers serving in Vietnam showed a lower incidence of combat fatigue than combat soldiers in any other war. But some have argued that by 1978, five years after the end of American combat involvement, as many as half a million veterans of Southeast Asian combat were suffering from posttraumatic stress disorder. For many, the symptoms did not appear until years after their return, and psychiatrists and psychologists predict a steady increase in new outbreaks of this disorder until at least until the mid-1980s. You Xiaoli did not begin to have visions until two years after she had been rehabilitated and the charges against her were cleared.

The Cultural Revolution differs in important respects from other extreme situations. Each extreme situation has a particularity all its own. But despite those differences, the themes that emerge from listening to Chinese talk about the long-term effects on them, their families, and their friends of having been victims of the Cultural Revolution and the themes of the "literature of the wounded" about the Cultural Revolution are precisely the symptoms experienced by a wide range of people from a variety of cultures who are suffering the psychological consequences of immersion in extremity—the symptoms of posttraumatic stress disorder. For many of its victims, the Cultural Revolution is not yet the "thing of the past" the Chinese government sometimes insists. Given the delay between the experience itself and the manifestations of its wounds, the ghost of that episode may still return to haunt its victims.

It is the tragic but nearly universal fate of those who have survived extremity to be burdened in their survival by a strong sense of guilt. And the tragedy of survivors' guilt is only compounded by the fact that those responsible for the victims' suffering often face the world with a conscience unencumbered by guilt. To be sure, many of the pleas for forgiveness at the conclusion of the Cultural Revolution by students who had participated in it as rebels were based on genuine contrition. Yao Baoding, Li Meirong, Huang Chaoqun, and You Xiaoli all received letters and visits of genuine and heartfelt apology. And all of them have forgiven their students. Li Meirong speaks for them all. "I don't blame the students," she says. "Even when they were torturing me, I told the students that I did not blame them. I said that over and over. I blamed Mao Zedong, not them. He was the one who told the students to go out and smash the 'four olds,' to rebel against their teachers. They were young. They didn't know what they were doing. It was the atmosphere of the time. Young students in China were taught to believe in class struggle, to believe that some people were the class enemies. They were taught to hate the bourgeoisie, and they didn't know any better. How could they have known better? Who would have told them?"

Other pleas of forgiveness, such as that offered by Zhu Que to You Xiaoli, were more likely to have been based on simple expediency. With the victims of the Cultural Revolution cleared of the accusations against them and restored to their former positions of influence and power, a well-timed, if not entirely sincere, apology served to preempt the possibility of retribution by the persecuted on the persecutors. But contrition and repentance are not traits in which the persecutors seem to abound. Many victims of the Cultural Revolution wait in vain for apologies from former friends, colleagues, relatives, students, and subordinates.

One of the peculiarities of China's Cultural Revolution is that persecutors and persecuted continue after the fact to live and to work side by side. Huang Chaoqun, several times a week, still sees the man who directed the house searches of his apartment. Often that man is wearing Huang Chaoqun's favorite sweater, which was seized during one of the raids. "We in China have a different sense of private property," notes Huang Chaoqun wryly.

Three times a week at the same time and place, Yao Baoding is going up the stairs as the man who served as his principal interrogator for two of the six years he was incarcerated is going down. They nod and wish each other good day like barely acquainted colleagues. "I have often wondered what he really thought during those interrogations, whether he really believed that I was a spy," says Yao Baoding. "Surely he acted as though he did. There was a sense of self-righteousness about him. He was a rather mean interrogator, a little nasty. I have tried to put myself in his position then. I have tried to imagine how I would have behaved in that situation, whether I would have believed that I was a spy. Perhaps so. Perhaps not. I don't know. I have thought about inviting this man over for tea, to talk about the Cultural Revolution, to ask him what thoughts were running through his mind. Better yet, I have thought about asking him over for a few drinks together, to get drunk. I'd like to talk to him. But that isn't possible now. Not now. It's still too early."

It was Bruno Bettelheim, writing about the survivors of Nazi concentration camps, who first introduced the concept of survivor's guilt. Robert Jay Lifton, writing of the survivors of Hiroshima, also analyzes this phenomenon. In its purest form, survivor's guilt is absolutely elemental, best expressed by Elie Wiesel, the eloquent spokesman for the survivors of Nazi concentration camps, who writes, "I live and therefore I am guilty. I am still here because a friend, a comrade, an unknown died in my place."

At a secondary level, survivor's guilt is related to what people did in order to stay alive, to what they felt when others were chosen to die and they were not. Concentration camp survivors today express guilt that they were sometimes able to secure easier jobs for themselves, and thereby preserve the physical and psychological strength so necessary for survival, that they rejoiced when others were chosen to die. Elie Wiesel writes of the shame he will feel forever for the one fleeting moment when he wished himself relieved of the burden of caring for his father, the better to struggle for his own survival. Survivors of the Buffalo Creek dam disaster tell of watching friends and neighbors sweep by, arms outstretched, crying for help, drowning in the morass of flooding sludge, as they, too numb and too focused on their own survival, failed to proffer help. Today, they feel guilty. Among Vietnam veterans, the most painful manifestations of survivor's guilt are often among those who served as medics, who continue to blame their own incompetence for the deaths of comrades whose lives, in reality, were beyond saving.

At still another level, the feelings of guilt, expressed particularly by survivors of the concentration camps and the bombing of Hiroshima, relate to people's feelings that they were either complicitous with the political system that brought about the disaster or that their protests were not sufficiently strong.

The elemental guilt so starkly phrased by Elie Wiesel—"I am alive and therefore I am guilty"—is not one of the legacies of China's Cultural Revolution. But the secondary elements of survivor's guilt are pervasive. There are those who feel guilty today because they believe they were complicitous in the political system that produced the Cultural Revolution or, particularly among the young, because they took part in the persecutions of the Cultural Revolution itself. There are those who feel guilty for having betrayed their relatives and their friends. And there are those who feel guilty because they were unable to protect their family members from attack.

Zhao Wenhao, describing the feelings of guilt that burden him still, offers a complex statement of what he and many of his compatriots feel. He speaks of the guilt so many feel for having so often to express themselves in ways that they did not believe, for the lies people so often felt they had to tell. He regrets the unquestioning belief he once had in China's Communist Party, and he is additionally burdened by a sense of guilt over his mother's death during the Cultural Revolution.

"None of us are innocent," Zhao Wenhao says. "Not really. Not completely. Not even those of us who were victims. Perhaps somewhere in China is someone, are some people, who have always been honest, who have always told the truth, always spoken what was in their heart, who have never had to speak words that they did not feel. Who they are, where they are, I couldn't say. For all of us, at one time or another, have had to speak words that we did not really believe. Because the political line has changed so often, so dramatically. Only people who do not think at all, who have lost the capacity for thought, could follow all those changing lines, could believe all the shifts in line. There are people like that, people who blow with the wind, without ever questioning or thinking. But they have lost the capacity for thought and therefore, perhaps, the capacity to be human. They are torpid.

"When the Cultural Revolution began, and the attacks against me started,

I believed those attacks. Many of the attacks had to do with status and privilege, and I thought at the beginning that, yes, perhaps we intellectuals did have too much status, too many privileges. So I felt guilty.

"But later, I felt guilty for another reason. Because you see, as a young boy before Liberation, as a young man after Liberation, I believed in the party. Not just believed in the party. I believed that the party was China's savior, China's Messiah. And so, as the Cultural Revolution progressed, I felt guilty for having believed, for having been so unthinking, for having followed so blindly, for having accepted so unquestioningly, for having glossed over my doubts.

"And for what I had done. Like the antirightist campaign. I participated in the antirightist campaign. Criticizing people. Innocent people.

"And then, while I was cleaning the toilets, my mother came under attack. She was in another city, and there was very little communication between us. But I knew that she was suffering, suffering badly, that she needed me, that I should go to her, to try to help her. But I couldn't. They wouldn't let me go.

"And then I learned that she had developed cancer. I believe that it was my mother's emotional state, her fear, her anxiety, her worry, that led to her death. But even as she was dying, they wouldn't let me visit her, wouldn't let me help her. And I felt guilty for that. It was only when she was on her deathbed, actually dying, that I finally got permission to go to her.

"So, yes, many of us feel guilty about the Cultural Revolution. I don't mean to suggest that we *should* feel guilty, that we really did something wrong. But, still, I feel that this guilt is a good thing, not a bad thing. It shows that we still have a conscience, that our consciences are intact. And so long as we have our consciences, so long as they work, there is hope."

On the part of young people who began as active supporters of the Cultural Revolution and later became its victims, guilt is often based on remorse for actions deliberately committed and deliberately designed to bring injury. Jiang Xinren, who spent two months in a darkened cattle pen and later took up loaded guns and used them, who woke up one morning and asked himself what he had been doing and why, is one of those young adults who is wracked today not with guilt *(neijiu)*, he says, because "guilt" is not sufficiently strong to convey his feeling. He has yet to find a word that could properly express the depth of his shame.

The guilt that Jiang Xinren feels today is complex, twisted, tortured, contorted, overwhelming, and sometimes even debilitating. For Jiang Xinren, at odds with the Chinese Confucian tradition, has become convinced that his behavior during the Cultural Revolution was less due to the exigencies of the situation, to the madness into which his country was plunged, the mob psychology, the hysterical, contagious, violent bravado that afflicted him and his peers, than to the fact that he, Jiang Xinren, is evil. "Many Chinese," says Jiang Xinren, "feel, 'If it weren't for the Cultural Revolution, I would have been good. I did it because of the Cultural Revolution.' But my perception of man is that man is evil, including me. I think I am evil. For me, the Cultural Revolution was like a pressure cooker. Everything went so fast, explosion-fast. Usually you'd need five or ten years to have so much evil. But during the Cultural Revolution, it happened in five or ten days. But if there were no Cultural Revolution, it still would have happened. It would just have been slower. When I think that I did wrong, that I am wrong, it's not because of the Cultural Revolution or the system or because Mao used me. Yes, Mao used me, yes, society, the system, has something wrong with it. But it's not 'If not for Mao, the Cultural Revolution . . .'"

Jiang Xinren feels guilty for his nation, his people. He feels guilty for being Chinese. "After the Cultural Revolution," he says, "I felt, 'I am guilty, ashamed, for being Chinese.' I didn't want to be Chinese. I felt that if I had the choice to be born again, I wouldn't choose to be Chinese. I feel guilty because there is no Chinese intellectual who can speak the truth to the whole world, who can stand up like Solzhenitsyn. The Chinese nation doesn't have a Solzhenitsyn or a Sakharov. Even Poland has its Walesa. China as a nation is guilty. If China had a Sakharov or a Solzhenitsyn there would be a future."

Often, in his guilt, Jiang Xinren feels like punishing himself. "Sometimes I want to beat myself to make myself feel comfortable," he says. "My friend taught me that, and I feel that way, too. Sometimes when I'm sick I don't want to see a doctor. I prefer to be sick for a couple days. For me that's much better. Because when I'm sick, that will make me take a really good rest. I'll have a good sleep and will think of nothing, forget everything. Because my whole body focuses on being ill. So I can forget other things. That's why I want to beat myself. So it will hurt and I won't have to think.

"I want to forget. If there is a big shower, a rainstorm, I don't want an umbrella. I feel comfortable in the rain. Once in the countryside, there was a really big storm, with very strong thunder. Everyone else wanted to go home. But I went to the river to swim. I know what common sense says. But I felt comfortable. There were big waves coming over my head, covering my head, strong thunder. But I felt so comfortable. There was no government, no security system, no one following me, no one to hurt me. I could say everything. I said things. I used all my dirty words, everything that I could say. Except for Mao. The words against Mao I kept in my head. When I was there in the river, I thought I would die in the water, but I wasn't afraid of death. I just didn't want to go back to China."

Today, Jiang Xinren has many types of nightmares. Often he dreams he is being attacked—by rival Red Guards, by the Public Security Bureau. He can see their faces. He recognizes their faces. He knows their names. But the nightmare Jiang Xinren has most is simply the picture of his closest friend, his face drained of blood, lying beside him as he, Jiang Xinren, is powerless to save his friend's life. "My friends always tell me that my mind has problems," Jiang Xinren says.

SONG WUHAO, fifteen and fanatic when the Cultural Revolution began, who remained silent in his conviction that Cao Diqui and Chen Peixian were good revolutionaries after all, who was forced under torture to beat his own father, is also tormented by guilt. It is to expiate his guilt, not merely his own but the guilt of his generation, that he talks.

"I feel I must apologize to my country and my people," he says, crying. "I must fall on the ground on my knees and beg for their forgiveness. Because if we fanatic young Red Guards had not done what we did, the country would not have been paralyzed. If we had not done what we did, what happened to my father—what happened between me and my father—would never have happened. On the one hand, it is true that we were used by the Gang of Four. But on the other hand, in terms of the entire history of what happened, we, I, my generation, still have a share of the responsibility. We doubted. We recognized they were evil. We opposed them in our hearts. But we did not oppose them openly."

THERE are also young people who emphatically, insistently, stridently refuse to feel guilty today for their actions during the Cultural Revolution. Song Erli is one. Song Erli never beat anyone during the Cultural Revolution. He never took up guns. But he did turn against his father. He did publicly and forcefully draw a clear line of demarcation from his father. "Perhaps you think this is something shameful," Song Erli says. "But I didn't feel ashamed at the time. I thought it was revolutionary.

"One of the Confucian credos is that a son shouldn't inform on his father, even if the father is a bandit. That meant that the family bond was more important than the social bond. But the Communists encouraged you to inform against your father if your father was a counterrevolutionary. That was our education, my education, from the very beginning. In the 1950s, when I was in primary school, I would tell the teachers what my parents had said that was bourgeois. So when I read accusations that the Communists were ruining China's moral principles, I thought that was ridiculous. Because I thought revolutionary principles should come above all. I also thought that was modern, because in modern society family bonds were not so important. So I could hardly tell whether informing on my father, if my father was a counterrevolutionary, was wrong or not. And during the Cultural Revolution, there was nothing like personal integrity, a sense of truth. People discovered that the Cultural Revolution was chaos, so anyone could attack anyone, there was no revolutionary integrity. So if you wanted to save your own neck, get out of a beating, you could just tell a lie. There was no shame in telling a lie. Because everything was so chaotic. I was a revolutionary rebel, and I thought that my behavior was revolutionary. But perhaps I did it for personal reasons, too. I thought that my mother, even though she bore the label of rightist, wasn't really counterrevolutionary. And, secretly, I sympathized with her. But my father truly was counterrevolutionary, and I hated that. I hated my father. So the reasons are both personal and ideological. So I took the chance for personal revenge against my father. But I didn't know that at the time. I thought I was being revolutionary.

"I did something wrong, and what I did was disastrous to my family. They had to move out of their apartment into one small room. I shouldn't have joined the Red Guards to oppose my father. I regret that. But so much happened so quickly during the Cultural Revolution, you hardly had time to feel that you had done something terribly wrong. You must understand that these things were so common. Everyone did something wrong to others. But I never beat other people. Friends, people I know, people who took part in the atrocities, today have no memory of what they did. When I told one person that this professor had died of cancer, I remembered vividly the scene where he and others had beaten that professor to the ground during the movement to purify the class ranks. But I saw no sign of a guilty conscience when I told him that.

"Do you really think the Chinese suffer so much from a guilty conscience? The Westerners have guilty consciences because of Christianity, because of the idea of sin. But in China, where material considerations are primary, questions of guilt, questions of conscience, are a luxury. Westerners have too much time, too much money, so they feel guilty. American plays are obsessed with psychoanalysis, psychiatry. This endless introspection, the analysis of the inner mind, appears artificial to the Chinese eye. I can cite many concrete examples to show how people involved in events during the Great Cultural Revolution are not yet ready to repent. In fact, everybody finds excuses. Many of those who had been responsible for knocking down others as rightists were reluctant to rehabilitate their victims. I have seldom met people who bear a guilty conscience for what they did in the Cultural Revolution. I, of course, also did something wrong which I regret. But I seldom suffer from a guilty conscience."

MANY adults were confronted during the Cultural Revolution with extremely difficult, "no-win" choices, choices that sometimes involved the apparent necessity of sacrificing one member of the family in order to save other members. Such choices were faced most frequently by women who sometimes believed that by attacking their husbands—"drawing a clear line of demarcation"—

they might be able to save their children. Such was the case with Maomei's mother in the story "Anecdote from the Western Front." In a scene central to the story, Maomei writes a letter to his mother, exonerating her from guilt in the death of his father. In it, Maomei adds to the official grounds for exoneration—having fallen under the influence of the Gang of Four and of feudalist thought—his more personal recognition that his mother had attacked her husband in order to save the children.

Today, many adults in China feel guilty for having betrayed their relatives and their friends. The mother of Zong Fuxian's best friend, the woman who had stood up at the meeting where her husband read his false confession declaring himself a spy for Japan, the woman who had led the shouting of slogans denouncing her husband has been wracked ever since by guilt. "The mother has carried a heavy burden," recounts Zong Fuxian. "After the downfall of the Gang of Four, the father was proved innocent of the charges and was rehabilitated and allowed to resume his former position at the institute. But the family that had been shattered by the Cultural Revolution could never be rebuilt. The husband could never be rebuilt. He said that given the circumstances in which he found himself during the Cultural Revolution, hearing his wife stand up and lead the slogan shouting against him was worse than any torture, any pressure, any slogan that had ever been used against him. He could not forgive her. He would not forgive her.

"After that, the mother became mentally ill. She herself felt she was guilty for what she had done, and that guilt was only compounded and reinforced by the fact that her husband would not forgive her.

"Their son, my best friend, has another view. He says that not all the blame should be placed on his mother, that she should not be made to assume full responsibility for having stood up and shouted those slogans. He points out that she had been under heavy pressure to denounce her husband, to draw a clear line of demarcation. And he points to the fact that his father could not stand the pressure, could not bear the torture, that it was *he* who had confessed to being a spy for Japan. How then could his mother be blamed?

"But the husband still refused to forgive. Even when he was lying on his deathbed with his wife there beside him, he still refused to forgive."

THERE is still another kind of guilt in China today, a guilt all the more tragic because the people who feel it are blameless and were largely powerless to prevent the attacks against those about whom they now feel guilty. They are people who were, within their own families, the primary focus of attack. They did not betray other members of their family, but they were helpless to protect them from similar attack. The case of China's great twentieth-century novelist Ba Jin is a good example.

Ba Jin's wife, Xiao Shan, died of cancer during the Cultural Revolution, a death that Ba Jin, like so many Chinese who share his view of cancer, attributes to the depression and anxiety that overcame her during this period. But it is not the Cultural Revolution that Ba Jin blames for the death of his wife. One small part of his reminiscences of Xiao Shan is an accusation, an outcry, against the Great Proletarian Cultural Revolution. But the thrust of his message is an accusation against himself. It was because of him, Ba Jin argues, because she was his wife, that Xiao Shan came under attack. This man who had to kneel on broken glass before ten thousand people claims that he was never beaten during that time, that it was his wife who suffered and died because of him. He says that he regrets ever having written literature, because what he wrote was the precipitating factor in the accusations against his wife and his children. He says he would willingly have suffered a thousand, even ten thousand, slashes of a knife against his flesh in order to have saved his wife. He proclaims himself guilty for her death. He wishes he could have died for her. When he dies, he wants his ashes mixed together into eternity with hers.

Some of Ba Jin's compatriots, Zhao Wenhao and Jiang Xinren included, believe that the profundity of the guilt Ba Jin expresses goes deeper than the death of his wife. During the antirightist campaign of 1957, a campaign which left many of Ba Jin's fellow writers labeled as rightists and unable to practice their craft, Ba Jin had participated in the attacks against his friends and colleagues, people he knew to be innocent. And then during the Cultural Revolution, Ba Jin himself was attacked, and Ba Jin too was innocent. The guilt that Ba Jin can only express in terms of his wife, say some of his compatriots, is also the guilt he feels for the attacks in which he participated in 1957. Of course, argue Zhao Wenhao and Jiang Xinren, Ba Jin feels guilty.

Ba Jin's reminiscences of Xiao Shan have been read as a modern-day literary equivalent of Emile Zola's manifesto "J'accuse." But this is a misreading both of Zola and his relationship to the Dreyfus case and of Ba Jin and his relationship to China and the Cultural Revolution. The thrust of Ba Jin's message is not "j'accuse" but "je m'accuse." What is more, Ba Jin wrote his reminiscences not amid the morass of mass hysteria that was the Cultural Revolution but at its conclusion, when the words he wrote, the sentiments he expressed, were not only permissible but encouraged. Emile Zola defied the mob. That is not what Ba Jin ever did. "When the situation is good," says Jiang Xinren, "Ba Jin speaks the truth. When the situation becomes bad, he closes his mouth. He never says anything. He never stands up. Of course he feels guilty, yes. But he doesn't have the courage to tell the truth." In this regard, Ba Jin is not alone among Chinese intellectuals. Few found the courage to defy the mob during the Cultural Revolution. Few had the courage to defy the state.

THERE is an analogue to the guilt felt by Ba Jin for the death of his wife in the guilt felt by the many mothers who came under attack during the Cultural

Revolution who were powerless to protect their children. There are those who say that there was almost an entire generation of children who grew up in China with living parents but were raised nearly as orphans. For parents did not have to be incarcerated for their children to have to go for long periods of time without adult supervision. In many work units, the political meetings and the struggle sessions lasted so far into the night that neither parent could return home in the evenings. They could return home only on Sundays. But when one or both of the parents were under attack, the problems were different. The children often also came under attack and the parents were often unable to protect them.

Shortly after the attacks against her had begun, after she had been accused of being a landlord and a spy, Li Meirong bicycled home from a struggle session late one evening to hear, before she entered, the sounds of crashing furniture and the accusatory shouts of young Red Guards. It was the first in the series of house searches that would ultimately leave her home stripped of all possessions and her family confined to the kitchen. Li Meirong hesitated, waiting. She knew both that her husband and her seven-year-old son were inside and that should she enter she would most likely be beaten. She feared for the safety of her son. She was torn. But she decided to bicycle to the apartment of an old family friend and returned to her own home only several hours later.

Li Meirong's son was in primary school then, and while classes in the school were suspended, the children still had to go to school to participate in political meetings and struggle sessions. Some of these struggle sessions were directed against Li Meirong's son, who was accused of being a *gouzaizi*, a "son of a bitch," and the "offspring of a counterrevolutionary." On the way home from school, he was similarly taunted. He did not understand what was happening to him, why he had been singled out for such hostility, and his mother had difficulty in explaining. And Li Meirong was powerless to protect him.

Today, Li Meirong dreams for many who were mothers during the Cultural Revolution and who were unable to protect their children. Sometimes she dreams that her children are being attacked and that she is trying to defend them. Li Meirong is down on her knees pleading, as they are hitting her children. Sometimes she wakes up at night with her arms flailing against invisible attackers, and she is crying. She is pleading, *"Tamen jiushi xiao haizi, tamen jiushi xiao haizi"*—"They're just little children, they're just little children." Chinese women unable to protect their children during the Cultural Revolution continue today to try to protect them in their dreams.

Individuals who have survived extremity are further burdened in their survival by a fear that similar disaster might strike again. Often that fear can be triggered by apparently commonplace situations and events—a change in the weather, a certain smell, the sight of a uniform. Survivors of concentration camps, long after they had been freed, continued to experience enduring distress at the sight of an armed policeman or the sound of the late-night ring of a telephone. Survivors of the Buffalo Creek dam disaster, two years after the event, continued to form flood watches and to prepare their families for flight whenever it rained. Some Vietnam veterans still will not sit with their back to a door, and some still duck for cover at the sound of a truck's backfire.

In China, some are still startled and suffer heart palpitations at a knock on the door. The house searches were always preceded by a knock. Huang Chaoqun is still startled whenever there is a knock. Jiang Xinren's father was, too, until he died. "During the Cultural Revolution," explains Jiang Xinren, "there were so many house searches and inspections of household registrations. There would always first be a knock on the door, and then they would just come in."

Early in the Cultural Revolution, while Jiang Xinren was in other cities engaging in revolution, his family's large apartment had been searched and the family relegated to a single room. "Before, they had the whole big apartment to live in," says Jiang Xinren, "but now they had only one room. At night, my brother, sister, and I gave the room to my parents so they could sleep, and we slept outside. Not really outside, but in the corridor outside the apartment. After we began sleeping in the corridor, we couldn't knock on the door anymore, because that upset my father. Instead, we would have to call out, 'Can I come in?' And at night, if my father was in bed and there was a loud noise, he would think it was a gunshot and that I was being killed, and he would jump out of bed and start yelling that they were killing his son."

Once Huang Chaoqun was wakened late at night out of a deep sleep, his wife shaking him and demanding over and over and over, "Get up, get up, get up. The Red Guards are coming."

"Don't speak nonsense," Huang Chaoqun retorted.

"Yes, they are coming. The Red Guards are coming. I'm a hundred percent sure the Red Guards are coming."

Mrs. Huang had heard a fire alarm go off. It was some time before her husband could calm her.

Chen Da'an still gets up five or six times during the night to see if the door and windows to her apartment are locked. Chen Da'an was a young and pretty teacher during the Cultural Revolution, and she was locked in her own private cattle pen. While in captivity, during the middle of the night, she was on repeated occasions raped by one of the members of the workers' propaganda team.

The strains of "The East Is Red," the theme song of the Cultural Revolution, precipitate images of bloody street battles in others. One of Yang Qing's first memories of being alive is a bloody Red Guard battle. The majestic, inspiring, defiant strains of "The East Is Red," the regal ode to Mao, were blaring relentlessly in the background. Today, whenever she hears the song, the scene of battle reappears in her mind's eye. "It was a clear, sunny day," she recalls, "crisp and cool. On the street and sidewalk in front of my house were lots of people, crowds of people, all lively, hustling and bustling. Then suddenly there was a lot of noise, and people were running, scattering in all directions. Except that some people were just lying in the street, bleeding. The noise had been gunshots. Those were the Red Guards and that was the Cultural Revolution. This is the first thing I remember about being alive. Now, whenever I hear 'The East Is Red,' I see that day."

Li Meirong spent a year as a visiting scholar in the United States. Walking down the street one day, she passed a poster shop that had in its window a caricature mocking former President Richard Nixon. Li Meirong was rooted in terror and then had to stop herself from running away. She thought of Chairman Mao, imagined she saw him in the caricature, and knew what would have happened in China had anyone dared display a parody of him. "They would have been killed," she asserts. She remembers feeling similar fear watching a television program in honor of Ronald Reagan shortly before his first inaugural. A comedian did a series of satirical imitations of American presidents—Kennedy, Johnson, Nixon, and Reagan—with the soon-to-be-inaugurated president sitting in the audience. Li Meirong was terrified, knowing that Reagan was watching the performance, and she was confused and uncomprehending when he actually laughed and applauded what he saw. She was thinking again of what would have happened in China had anyone dared to satirize Mao.

You Xiaoli's visions are always involuntarily triggered by a fleeting, almost commonplace event that nonetheless can be directly traced to what she experienced as an ox ghost and snake spirit of the Cultural Revolution. "Once, walking down the street," she recalls, "I saw a bicycle accident. Not a bad one. Two bicycles had an accident, just in front of me, on the street. The two riders started fighting, each saying the other was to blame. It had nothing to do with me. It was just two guys quarreling. But suddenly I had a vision of two people beating each other. I was walking on the sidewalk and by then the two men quarreling were alongside me but I saw something in front of me. It was the Red Guards fighting with each other terribly. With stones, throwing stones at each other. Other people could hide in their rooms when the Red Guards had their battles on our campus, but we ox ghosts and snake spirits still had to sweep the grounds, so a stone could hit us. And that's what I saw inside me, with my mental eyes, two groups of people fighting there. I couldn't go forward. I just couldn't move at all. And suddenly I felt as though my nose were bleeding, and my blood was so hot and down to my mouth, my neck, my chest. And I couldn't move at all, so I sat down on the sidewalk.

"Then a student of mine came across and asked me what was wrong. She took me to the clinic. The doctor said I was so pale."

The doctor did a thorough examination of You Xiaoli. They were afraid it was a problem with her heart. But nothing was wrong. All the tests, her blood pressure, the X-rays, were normal. The doctor gave her some tranquilizers. She never told him about her visions. She was too embarrassed.

"I never saw ghosts before the Cultural Revolution," continues You Xiaoli. "Now, after the Cultural Revolution, I always see ghosts. Like when I take the bus to go into town and somebody sits in front of me or stands there, and suddenly I feel they aren't real people. They're ghosts. I see their faces change into ghost faces—*niutou mamian*—ox heads and horse faces. I don't know what triggers that."

If the fear that the Cultural Revolution could happen again is often expressed involuntarily, triggered by random and often apparently trifling events, that fear is also expressed more consciously. For once extreme events, however unique, occur, their particular horrors enter into the realm of future possibility, permanently altering the way human beings perceive their world, welding fear to the mind like mortar to brick. Thus survivors of the Nazi Holocaust have taken as their clarion call the slogan "Never Again," and survivors of Hiroshima have devoted themselves to the cause of peace.

Indeed, some Chinese draw a distinction between their subjective and their objective view on this question. Objectively, they argue, conditions have changed sufficiently, sufficient reforms have been introduced, to prevent another Cultural Revolution. Subjectively, though, they are still afraid. Many have mapped out strategies for how they will survive the next Cultural Revolution. Song Erli will be less of an idealist, more realistic about the use and abuse of power. Liu Zhiping would flee again to the countryside. But still, she says, "I couldn't take it again. I would not survive."

Other people, however, do not make such distinctions between their objective and their subjective views. "No one would ever say that the Cultural Revolution will never happen again," says Bai Meihua. "We are all afraid it will. We don't say this out loud, publicly. People, for instance, want to curse Jiang Qing. But everyone is afraid of saying anything against her in public. They are afraid she might come back into power again. So people never say what they really think.

"At present, there is no indication that there will be another Cultural Revolution. But we dare not say that we can never have another Cultural Revolution. Because in China, after Liberation, there have been so many movements, so many changes. What happens, what will happen, depends on the leaders. Now, Deng Xiaoping controls everything. But what will happen after he dies? Deng has experience, particularly with the military. Younger people in the government couldn't control China, couldn't control the army. If there were to be another Cultural Revolution, it would come from the army. There are still many revolutionary rebels in the army, and it is impossible to take power away from them, to take all the power out of their hands. Maybe some of these revolutionary rebels are even high-ranking military leaders.

"Hu Yaobang isn't any good, either. All he does is talk political theory, nothing but empty talk. People want peace, quiet, security. They are worried about practical problems, about their own families, their food, where they are going to live, the problem of crowding. They're not interested in politics. The last thing they want to hear about is politics. They want to find practical solutions to their problems. In my office, when the leader has to give a political report, we all have to go. But during the meeting, when you look around the room at the audience, you see that some people are reading, some people are sleeping, some people are talking, but no one is paying any attention. Even the leader gives these reports only because he has to. He doesn't enjoy doing it, and sometimes we tease and joke about how he has to do it.

"I hope there are no movements again in China. Everyone in China is afraid of any kind of movement. We want to lead a safe life, a secure life. One reason China is still so poor today is all the movements we have had. They never stopped. If there were to be other movements, some families would have a very bad experience, a very sad experience, especially we cadre families. Our parents would be pulled down again, be put into prison again.

"My father, though, wouldn't agree with my point of view," Bai Meihua adds, "although I can be very frank with him and tell him how I feel. We call him *hongqi,* the red flag."

SOME people, women in particular, are afraid less that the Cultural Revolution will happen again today or tomorrow, to them and their generation, than that it will happen to the generation of their children. You Xiaoli is such a woman. "I think there will be another Cultural Revolution just as I think there will be other wars," says You Xiaoli. "So I tell my son to prepare to live during another war, another Cultural Revolution. But he says that every revolution is different from those of the past, that there will be another Cultural Revolution but that it won't be the same as the one I had.

"It isn't fear that makes me feel this way, feel that there will be other Cultural Revolutions and that I want to warn my son. I am old enough. Maybe I won't experience another one. I will pass away when the next one comes. My son is the one who will meet another Cultural Revolution. That is why I don't like him to be that way. I want him to be honest, to always speak the truth. I want him to think, to see that things are more complicated, not so simple as he makes them out to be, so that when the next Cultural Revolution comes, he will know how to deal with it. But he refuses to learn from my experience. He thinks there can't be two movements alike, two movements of the same kind. He says, 'Don't worry. We have to experience our own Cultural Revolution.'

"Maybe we can prevent it. But now I think there is still a danger. If our central government and provincial government can lead successfully . . . I am not so sure. If the country becomes rich enough, if the living standard becomes good enough, if we are progressive enough, maybe when the leftists launch another Cultural Revolution, people—most of them—won't believe. But if the country is not that rich, if we don't make progress, if we are still backward, maybe most people would believe that the intellectuals, the professors, are the spiritual aristocratic class and that cadres are capitalist roaders. It is quite possible. That is why I think we should have real equality. The sooner we abolish privilege, the sooner we abolish the back door, the better.

"That is why sometimes, even today, I still go back and clean the toilets on campus. When people see me cleaning the toilets, they think I have gone mad. They can't understand it. But I do it to make me remember. Because I think if I ever forget, if I ever completely forget how I was treated during the Cultural Revolution, maybe I would do something wrong. Maybe I would come to see myself as a leading member, maybe I would come to consider manual labor as a form of punishment. Because when the ultraleftists rise again, they will use the faults, take advantage of the faults of the cadres and the intellectuals, including me. That is why I like to lead a more simple life, to do manual labor. That is why I want my son to continue to lead a simple life, to do manual labor, not to become a part of a spiritual aristocratic class but to lead a certain kind of simple life."

THE most poignant expressions of the fear that the Cultural Revolution could happen again are to be found in the nightmares from which so many in China continue to suffer. If, during their waking hours, most are able to forget the Cultural Revolution, it often comes back to haunt them asleep, as scenes from that period are repeatedly replayed in their dreams. Bai Meihua used to see scenes from her own experiences replayed as though on film, and Qiu Yehuang still dreams of the things he saw—the murders, the killings, the blood. "I think it's because I saw a lot of murdering," he says. "In my mind asleep appear some frightening scenes of murders, of the Red Guards killing people. It's not always killing people, though. I see them shaving women's heads, putting on tall paper hats, the street parades, the awful scenes in Peking. When you are a child and you hear frightening stories and you dream, when you dream, you're frightened. But you don't feel you're one of them. Your mind isn't as frightened. But when I have these dreams, I am frightened, and when I wake up I am almost crying."

Li Meirong still dreams that they are beating her. She is down on her knees, and they are beating her, and she tries to strike back. Huang Chaoqun still sees his old friend and former student Lao Qian. Lao Qian was accused during the Cultural Revolution of being a capitalist and a spy, and while Huang Chaoqun was confined to his cattle pen, Lao Qian committed suicide. But Huang Chaoqun has never quite believed that Lao Qian committed suicide. He never seemed the type. He had been such an ebullient, happy-go-lucky man, so stable, so durable. And Huang Chaoqun never saw the body. Sometimes Lao Qian comes to Huang Chaoqun in his dreams. "They beat me to death and then burned me and said I drank insecticide," Lao Qian says to Huang Chaoqun. But Huang Chaoqun's other friend, Zhang Shimei, insists that Lao Qian really did take his own life. "Zhang Shimei told me that Lao Qian really *did* commit suicide," says Huang Chaoqun. "Because he couldn't stand the torture." But Huang Chaoqun is not yet convinced. His dream keeps telling him otherwise.

You Xiaoli, too, dreams of those who died. "Sometimes I see colleagues who committed suicide or who died during the Cultural Revolution," she says. "Actually, they weren't good friends when they were alive, just fellow ox ghosts and snake spirits. And in my dream I see them and they look so sad. Once there was a lady, she was much older than I, and she said, 'Oh, You Xiaoli, I should have waited longer. If I had waited, I could still be here.' And then I woke up.

"Sometimes in my nightmare I feel that someone hanged me from the ceiling, and then they put up a big character poster saying that the spy You Xiaoli committed suicide. And I want to say that no, I didn't commit suicide, that they did it, but since my neck is so tightly strangled by the rope I can't scream. But I wake up screaming and my husband says it's like I was choking and trying to scream.

"And sometimes I wake up from a backache, and when my back hurts I have the same nightmare. I dream they are jumping on my back again. But really it's just my back that hurts. Whenever I have a nightmare, I wake up and I am all sweaty. It's horrible. I feel exhausted and tired as if I had been doing heavy labor."

THE dreams of mothers like Li Meirong who were unable to protect their children during the Cultural Revolution have been passed down to the next generation of women, to Liu Zhiping's generation, the generation that was young and unmarried at the time of the Cultural Revolution, who now have children of their own, and who fear that what happened to them may someday happen to their children. When Liu Zhiping was asked if she ever dreamed about the Cultural Revolution, she said, "Yes, I have dreams, nightmares. I can tell you the one I had this morning.

"It was about my daughter. They were trying to snatch her away from me. You will meet my daughter, and then you will know that she is pretty, so very pretty. I love her. In the dream, they try to snatch her away, and as I try to grab her back, somebody else comes and grabs her away. But as they are trying to take her away, as I am fighting for her, trying to protect her, she becomes very small, and fat, and black, like an ugly black ball. Even her grandmother comes and tries to snatch her away, but her grandmother looks old and shriveled and ugly, like the wolf grandmother. I keep trying to fight for my daughter, to protect her, but at the end, she is nothing but a little ugly black ball.

"During the Cultural Revolution, I thought I would never get married and have children," Liu Zhiping continues. "I even vowed not to get married and have children. I knew I could only bring trouble to a husband, and I don't want my daughter to go through the same experiences I had. I am afraid for my daughter and my husband still."

Liu Zhiping's dream about her daughter is also a dream about herself during the Cultural Revolution, about her running away from school, the school's snatching her back, and her running away yet again.

THE nightmares, the guilt, the fear, the involuntary intrusion of incandescent memories of the past, the visions in which You Xiaoli actually relives the past, are among the symptoms of posttraumatic stress disorder. Liu Zhiping describes many of the remaining symptoms in herself.

It is true that Liu Zhiping found meaning living among the peasants and the miners during the Cultural Revolution, true that their acceptance of her generated renewed confidence in herself, true that she believes she could always go back. But the price of the meaning she found has been high. "I think that there is a sickness in my brain," she says, "a sickness from the Cultural Revolution. I can't sleep at night. Usually I go to bed at one or two o'clock in the morning, but even then I can't sleep. I have some medicine, some pills to take, but they don't seem to help. I feel as though I forget things, that my brain just can't remember, isn't as quick as it used to be. I forget things. Sometimes I get impatient and lose my temper. With my husband. I yell at him sometimes.

"I think those years were very hard on me. That walk—our Long March —was difficult, especially the days when it was so cold. The months in the mine were even harder, though. I am not really very strong, and pushing those carts required enormous strength. I did it, yes, but it was very hard, and I don't know that I could do it again.

"My friends see me now, friends from my university, and they don't recognize me. They all say how much I have changed. I look so old.

"My face. It's all puffy, and my husband, even my husband notices. He says I look yellow. He is right. My skin has become yellow. My face.

"I can't talk to my husband about these things. When he asks me what is wrong, I just say that I have been working too hard, that I am very tense about all the work there is to be done.

"And I have other dreams, too. Sometimes I dream I am being attacked by tigers. They attack me and claw at me. When I wake up after these dreams,

I have to sit on the bed, like this, with my hands over my eyes. Sometimes I sit for ten minutes. I have to keep telling myself that it wasn't real, that it was only a dream. Whenever I get so upset, I just have to keep telling myself that they are only dreams. They *are* only dreams."

JIANG XINREN describes similar symptoms in his father. "The change in my father was so sad," he says. "He had always been a very kind and gentle man before. But something had happened to change him. For instance, if he had put a newspaper on the table and my mother had moved it just the slightest bit, he would get angry and yell at her. He was always angry at us for just the smallest thing. And he would forget things. He would put a glass down on the table one minute and then forget where it was immediately and get angry. For weeks he would be unable to sleep at all. Not at all. Sometimes he would just sit up the whole night, smoking, and not saying anything, staring straight ahead. He didn't talk much anymore.

"We all understood why he was like that. It was because when he went to work, he wouldn't say anything all day. He couldn't say anything. Not a word. Because he was afraid that if he said anything, he would be attacked. So his anger would gradually build up during the day, and at night he would take that anger out on us. It was *shenjing shuairuo*"—neurasthenia.

YOU XIAOLI describes the symptoms of depression from which so many suffer, symptoms Liu Zhiping shares. "Every morning I wake up very, very early, and when I wake up I feel so sad, so hopeless, for no reason, so depressed. I just want to cry. I immediately turn on both lights, and I feel better then because I'm not in the dark, because in the dark I feel cold and see shadows moving back and forth. But still I feel like crying. So as soon as possible I pick up a book and read and focus my attention on reading, and then everything is all right. If I read a book that is glad and happy, I feel good. If I read a sad book, I also feel better, as though it's not just my sorrow but that I share my sorrow. If the weather is dark and cloudy, I feel worse. Two days ago, the whole day it rained, and it was so dark outside and I had to listen to the rain, and I felt so bad, as though someone were crying outside. And then I went to the window to look out to see if someone was crying, even though I knew it was just the rain. If it's raining when I wake up, then I always have to get up and see if someone is crying outside.

"Before the Cultural Revolution, the weather didn't mean anything. If it rained, I thought it was good because it meant the peasants had rain, that it was good for a plentiful harvest. But after the Cultural Revolution, it wasn't like that. I used to like snow, but after the Cultural Revolution, even snow frightened me. Once after it snowed, I had a dream about a huge white monster with a bloody mouth and fangs, and I fell into the monster's mouth and went falling down, down, down, down."

A numbing of responsiveness to the external world is yet another manifestation of posttraumatic stress disorder, and many victims of the Cultural Revolution suffer, too, from such psychic numbing. The younger brother in Liu Xinwu's "Awake, My Brother" is described as cold, detached, dispirited, unresponsive, withdrawn from the mundane world, without interest or hope. His eyes are without luster or gleam. He has lost trust, faith, ideals. His elder brother asks, "Don't you have any heart at all? Don't you feel?"

"My heart has turned to stone," says You Xiaoli. "When you have cried and cried and cried, finally you have cried all your tears. When your heart has bled and bled and bled, finally there is no more blood. Then you turn to stone."

BEYOND the psychic scars of the Cultural Revolution are the physical wounds that persist, the recurrent aches and pains that all attribute to their suffering during the Cultural Revolution. The knee that Liu Zhiping injured during her Long March, the arthritis of Song Wuhao, Jiang Xinren, and Li Meirong, Huang Chaoqun's stomach problems and Professor Song's shortness of breath, the pain in You Xiaoli's back and leg—all are the constant, nagging, quiet reminders of a past that continues to exact its toll.

Many of the wounds that continue to grate are lumped by those who suffer from them under the category of *shenjing shuairuo*, "weak nerves" or neurasthenia, a classification that has long since disappeared from the medical terminology of the West. The insomnia and nightmares, the sudden outbursts of anger, the exaggerated startle response to a knock on the door or an alarm going off, the forgetfulness and inability to concentrate, the difficulty some have in making decisions, the wakening early in the morning feeling sad and lonely and depressed, even the visions of You Xiaoli, all are seen by those who suffer from such symptoms as manifestations of neurasthenia. "The Chinese just call everything *shenjing shuairuo,*" says You Xiaoli. The psychic numbing and the heart that has turned to stone, the alienation, are more difficult for them to categorize. What they do know is that those symptoms, those feelings, were not there before the Cultural Revolution. The nagging persistence of the small aches and pains are easily explained as physical wounds that never had a chance or the treatment to heal. But by whatever name the Chinese may choose to label their wounds, the configuration of symptoms of their enduring distress bears uncanny resemblance to the universal sequelae of immersion in extremity that psychiatrists in the United States now label posttraumatic stress disorder.

Indeed, there is a tendency for some Chinese to express their psychic distress more in physical than in mental terms. A survivor of a Nazi concentration camp might exaggerate the long-term effects of that experience by expressing a fear of going crazy. Liu Zhiping, though, says she thinks she has a sickness in her brain, and Jiang Xinren's friends tell him there is something wrong with his mind.

Most would recognize their continuing distress as in some sense psychological, or at least as psychologically induced, but the cures they seek, their quest for a respite from the pain, are medicinal. It is the quest for sleep that most preoccupies them, and for many whose stories are included here, sleep can be induced only by *anding*—a drug like Valium—sold in some parts of China without prescription and one that in any case is freely and liberally prescribed. Once the discovery is made that *anding* is capable of inducing sleep, sleep for some becomes possible only with its use. When You Xiaoli's husband once hid her *anding* in a vain attempt to break her habit, You Xiaoli tore their apartment apart in an attempt to find her pills. Without *anding*, sleep simply would not come.

Neither You Xiaoli, Liu Zhiping, Song Wuhao, Jiang Xinren's father, nor Jiang Xinren himself has ever consulted a psychologist or a psychiatrist. The thought would never occur to them. Psychiatrists in China are directly attached to mental hospitals, and mental hospitals are the exclusive preserve of the mad. Indeed, psychiatrists in China are finding that their schizophrenic patients are exhibiting new and hitherto unseen symptoms that bear no small relation to the political upheavals to which their country has been subjected —patients who deny being the children of their parents, who suffer from the delusion of imminent catastrophe, the delusion of being despised, the delusion of imminent arrest, the delusion of being slandered. There are even those suffering from metamorphopsia—people drawn repeatedly to look at their image in the mirror, in the conviction that the image they see is markedly different from the image they saw in the past.

Those who suffer still from the symptoms of posttraumatic stress disorder are hardly mad. They are functioning members of Chinese society. The wounds from which they suffer are invisible to all but their closest, most trusted relatives and friends. Their screams really are silent—so silent that many were able to share their pain only after tens of hours of discussions, only after an arduous decision to trust, only after having been assured that they were not alone in the manifestations of their pain. So silent are their screams that behind those who were able to share their pain must be many more who could not.

THE symptoms of other victims of the Cultural Revolution are more obvious. Others are and remain debilitated. Bai Meihua's friend who went mad after her parents had been incarcerated and her boyfriend had left her is still, Bai Meihua says, mad today. Song Erli's friend who was forced to confess to being a member of the nonexistent May Sixteenth elements is still afraid that the masons with whom he works are putting poison in the mortar. Jiang Xinren's friend still smiles without speaking.

For some, the breakdown occurred not during the Cultural Revolution but after. Many who waited until the end to collapse are women. Such women were usually in their forties or fifties when the Cultural Revolution began, were married to men who became victims of the Cultural Revolution, had as their primary function that of housewife, and had as their primary tasks during the Cultural Revolution, in the face of overwhelming difficulties, the responsibility for holding together their families and their households. For the full ten years of the Cultural Revolution, these women, despite the enormous difficulties with which they were burdened, performed those tasks admirably. But when their husbands were rehabilitated, the strength they had maintained intact during their period of tribulation suddenly melted away. Sometimes the behavior of these women was not only disoriented, but bizarre. Chang Rujuan describes the insanity of her mother.

"My mother was in her late forties when the Cultural Revolution began," says Chang Rujuan. "Earlier, she had worked in a factory for many years, but she had retired some time before. She was a party member, an old revolutionary cadre from the days of the War of Resistance against Japan. Her family had been very poor before Liberation. Very poor. And she had never received an education. She could read a few characters, write a little, but really she was nearly illiterate. But she had such faith in the party, such trust. She always had. She had so much faith that only under the party could China make progress. She was so proud to be a member.

"And she was a good wife, too. Too good, maybe. Some people think that what happened to her after my father was rehabilitated was really to spite him—for all those years when she had been such a good wife. I don't think my father ever even had to pour himself a cup of tea. She always did it for him. She took hours preparing his meals. Such a good wife. And his clothes were always clean, perfectly mended. And of course she did all the housework. They were of the older generation in which women did all the housework.

"My father was accused of being a counterrevolutionary after the Cultural Revolution began. He was an intellectual, at the academy, a scientist. Every day for weeks on end he had to leave the house early in the morning to go to meetings, criticism meetings, where he would be attacked. Some days he would go on the street parades with an accusatory placard around his neck, and people would yell at him and spit at him, and accuse him of being a counter-revolutionary.

"Nothing really happened to my mother, though. She just stayed at home. But she seemed to take it harder than others. I don't know why. Maybe because she had so much faith in the party and couldn't understand why it was turning against my father. Maybe because she had so little education and couldn't understand as well as the intellectuals what was happening.

"It seemed that all my mother did during that time was cook. My father would be gone all day, and my mother would spend all that time cooking meals for him to eat when he returned. It was difficult, difficult for her even to buy food then. My father's salary had been cut back to seven dollars and fifty cents a month. The average worker's salary then was twenty dollars a month, so all my father's income had to be used on food, and still it was only barely enough money. But somehow, my mother always had a hot meal waiting.

"My father wasn't really a counterrevolutionary. He had been falsely accused. He was lucky. His rehabilitation came early, several years earlier than for his colleagues. When he was rehabilitated, my mother threw a big party, inviting lots of guests—not people who were still accused but others who had already been rehabilitated and people who hadn't been attacked. She even invited some of the Red Guards who had attacked my father in the first place.

"She drank a lot at the party and began laughing loudly, almost hysterically. The next morning, when she woke up, she didn't recognize anyone. Not me. Not my father. Not my brother. No one. At first, we thought she was just kidding, pretending, that it was just some kind of joke. But gradually we realized she wasn't pretending. Eventually, she was able to recognize my father, but to the very end of her life, he was the only person she ever recognized again. I was already married then, but I lived nearby, and I had to go every day to do the cooking and help with the laundry and the housework. She couldn't do anything anymore.

"We kept thinking she would get better, but she didn't, so my father and I decided we had better send her to a mental hospital. But mental hospitals are horrible places. The so-called nurses are cruel to the patients. Mainly, they just don't want the patients to cause any disturbances. So they give the patients a powerful drug to make them quiet.

"When my mother came back, she was very quiet at first, and we thought maybe she would be okay again. But then something started happening. Whenever I went to the house, as soon as she saw me, she would kneel down on her knees, the palms of her hands pressed together, and start pleading. She would beg me not to take my father away, saying that he was innocent, that he had done nothing wrong. If she got outside, she would run up to people saying that she knew they were after her husband, coming to take him away. Then she would start hitting at them and beating them. She was always like that.

"One day, she was leaving the apartment. I don't even know where she was going. My father doesn't either. But when she got to the corridor, she just fell down and died. As quickly as that.

"My father retired after that. For a long time, he hardly went out at all, and he didn't like anyone to go visit him. He wouldn't read or anything. He just sat in his chair all day, staring straight ahead. He has gotten better lately, though. He even does a little work now."

IN other cases, the reaction of women who collapsed after the Cultural Revolution was one of apparently severe clinical depression.

In 1980, Arthur Kleinman, a psychiatrist, anthropologist, and China specialist, conducted a study of neurasthenia at the Hunan Medical College. Neurasthenia, as Kleinman interprets it, is often (although not always) a form of clinical depression—not the type of depressed mood from which most people suffer from time to time but a serious form of depression, a potentially deadly disease. Clinical depression can be accompanied by a general, profound, and implacable sense of hopelessness, and in that state of utter and unremitting despair, a small but significant portion of the clinically depressed attempt suicide. Some succeed.

One of Kleinman's patients in Hunan was a woman whose depression had begun only at the conclusion of the Cultural Revolution. The woman was the wife of a "rightist." In 1958, her husband had been sent to live in the countryside, able to visit his family only once a year. They had four children, and the woman—because of her husband's background—was unable to find work. She had only a very limited income on which to support her family. During the Cultural Revolution, the situation for her husband, the woman herself, and the family worsened considerably. Her depression began in 1978, just after her husband was rehabilitated, promoted to an extremely responsible position, and returned home to live with his family after having been absent for nearly twenty years. In her interview with Kleinman, the woman began by denying that the onset of her depression was related to difficulties of readjustment in living with her husband. She tried to explain why she was depressed. Kleinman paraphrases her explanation:

> Suppose, she said, looking at the ground, you were climbing a mountain and this mountain was very steep and terribly difficult to climb. To the right and the left, you could see people falling off the mountainside. Holding on to your neck and back were several family members so that if you fell so would they. For twenty years you climbed this mountain with your eyes fixed on the handholds and footholds. You neither looked back nor ahead. Finally, you have reached the top of the mountain. Perhaps this is the first time you have looked backward and seen how much you had endured, how difficult your life and your family's situation had been, how blighted your hopes. . . . She ended by asking me if this was not a good enough reason to become depressed.

Yet for all the invisible wounds that have yet fully to heal, Studs Terkel is right when he points out, "That there were some who were untouched or indeed did rather well isn't exactly news. This has been true of all disasters." Those who did rather well during the Cultural Revolution, or so its victims would argue, were the careerists, the opportunists, the *fengpai*—those who blow with the wind, those willing to scramble up the ladder of success over the backs of their fallen, disgraced, and unfairly discredited colleagues. The majority of urban folk were doubtless, like Qiu Yehuang, *xiaoyaopai*, nonparticipant observers of their society in disintegration. Yet few, in the cities at least, were genuinely untouched. Even workers in factories were required to participate, at least as observers, in the struggle sessions, and many spent idle and boring weeks when the intensity of the struggles had brought work in their factories to a halt.

It is also true that some who survived the Cultural Revolution as victims have also done rather well, that some seem to have emerged from their tribulations unscathed. Indeed, a psychologist confronted with people who appear initially to be little changed following immersion in severe and prolonged stress might be led to suspect that such individuals are deluding themselves through denial. Most psychiatrists recognize that during immersion in extremity, denial in the form of "psychic numbing" or "emotional anesthesia" serves a positive function, as a coping mechanism essential to survival. Several whose stories are included here remember that they felt nothing, that they were incapable of feeling, in the midst of the Cultural Revolution. It was after it was over that the pain became unbearable. The woman who spent twenty years climbing a mountain, her children clinging to her back, was practicing denial or "psychic numbing." And while she may be suffering today from depression, what is just as important is that she did reach the top of her mountain, carrying her children with her.

MANY psychiatrists would also argue that however natural and frequent denial as a response might be, once the stressful event has passed, denial becomes maladaptive. Denial does not allow an individual to integrate significant events of his life into his overall view of the world. What appears initially as continuity might be regarded instead as an inability to adapt. But specialists and laymen might well differ in the interpretation of the function of denial in the wake of the Cultural Revolution. No Chinese whose story is included here has ever pretended to be able to explain the Cultural Revolution—or in any case not fully, not completely. No one has yet been able fully to integrate that experience into his or her life. For most, it is not a question of picking up the pieces, sorting them out, and moving on. Rather it is a question of leaving the pieces scattered around like so much rubble and still standing up and going on. The remarkable resilience of so many Chinese who have gone through so much may be to a large extent a function of denial. And the failure fully to confront the implications of the Cultural Revolution is also a way of continuing to find meaning in the past.

One of the apparently universal features of old age is a retrospective stock-taking of one's life, an effort not uncommonly accompanied by depression. Literature provides us with examples. In one of the final scenes of di Lampedusa's *The Leopard*, the protagonist of the novel, Don Fabrizio, knows that he is dying and begins drawing up a balance sheet of his life, "trying to sort out of the immense ash-heap of liabilities the golden flecks of happy moments." "I'm seventy-three years old," Fabrizio thinks, "and all in all I may have lived, really lived, a total of two—three at the most." Some Chinese, now Don Fabrizio's age, refuse to engage in the retrospection that is ordinarily a part of growing old. "It is sad to be old," one man now in his mid-seventies who was a victim of the Cultural Revolution said, "so I do not want to look back and dare not look forward. I can only enjoy my present." Other Chinese now in middle age, Chinese like Li Meirong, wonder after all they suffered during the Cultural Revolution where they will find the pleasant memories to comfort them in their old age, wonder whether they still have enough time left to build a reservoir of happy moments upon which to draw when they get old.

When her name was finally cleared and the time had come for Li Meirong to leave the May Seventh Cadre School and return to teach at the school where she had been so bitterly and viciously attacked, she made one final act of protest. She refused to return. The school sent a delegation to the cadre school to implore her to return. But still she refused. "I told them I didn't want to go back," she says. "I would never go back to that school. I said that I was perfectly happy at the May Seventh Cadre School, that if they couldn't find another school for me, I would stay at the cadre school the rest of my life. Or I would go live with the peasants in the countryside. That would be just fine."

So they found another school for Li Meirong—a university, which is where she had always wanted to teach anyway.

When Li Meirong's back salary was returned to her, she refused to use it to replace the furniture that the Red Guards had taken away and never returned. "I never want beautiful things again," she says. "Nothing can ever be the same after the Cultural Revolution. Chairman Mao said that China needed not one Cultural Revolution but many Cultural Revolutions. So the Cultural Revolution could happen again. And when it happens again, I will not survive. I will be killed in the next Cultural Revolution. Things are better now, but you can never be certain that it will never happen again.

"I am getting older now," continues Li Meirong. "And I wonder now, as I look back on my life, where the pleasant memories will be to comfort me when I really do get old. If I look back far enough into my childhood, when I was just a little girl, yes, there are pleasant memories. Memories of my grandparents, who treated me well. Memories of growing up in the big house. Those are good memories, memories that can make me smile. But after that, the memories aren't so good. Even of the early days after Liberation. Yes, they were days of hope, days of expectation, but it changed so quickly, and now, looking back, they don't seem so good anymore. So I wonder what will comfort me in my old age. I want, between now and the time I die, to build memories that I can look back on with fondness." Perhaps the Chinese know earlier than we, younger than we, that the meaning of old age is often in the memories that it provides.

Perhaps there also comes a time, past middle age, when life is beyond reinterpreting, when it is too late to reinterpret one's life and still be able to find among the "immense ash-heap of liabilities" those "golden flecks of happy moments." Perhaps the persistence of denial permits those who are approaching the end of their lives to look back and still find meaning.

At least that is one way of interpreting You Xiaoli as she tried to explain why, after all she has suffered and endured in his name, recognizing all his faults, she still loves Chairman Mao. In terms of sheer physical abuse, You Xiaoli was tortured during the Cultural Revolution beyond the limits of human endurance. Her physical wounds today are not invisible. And yet she has survived. She was accused of a multitude of sins during the Cultural Revolution, from opposing Chairman Mao, to being a counterrevolutionary, to being a spy. You Xiaoli is the illegitimate offspring of a rape by a landlord of his servant. She never knew her father. Her mother died of starvation on the streets of Shanghai, and You Xiaoli joined the Communist movement at the age of sixteen. Until the Cultural Revolution, the "Liberation" of China had treated her very well. You Xiaoli is now in her mid-sixties, and she thinks of herself as an old woman.

"Ever since I was a young girl of only sixteen," explains You Xiaoli, "I have believed in Chairman Mao. I have believed that without Chairman Mao I would have no future, no happiness. I suffered in the old society, and then suddenly, in 1949, I was liberated. The party sent me to the university to study and then on for postgraduate work as well. I read Marxism-Leninism/ Mao Zedong Thought. My situation got better. I got a good position. It was Chairman Mao who rescued me from being such a poor girl before Liberation.

"I know that Chairman Mao believed in violence. He said that revolution is not a dinner party, that revolution is violent. During the movement against counterrevolutionaries in 1955, Chairman Mao said that we had killed a number of people but that still the number of people we killed was not so great. We did kill many people. We killed many more people than Qin Shi Huang.

I know that. And Chairman Mao abused his power. Like firing Peng Dehuai. Peng Dehuai was a good man. Chairman Mao shouldn't have fired him. I know that, too.

"During the Cultural Revolution, I kept thinking Chairman Mao doesn't know how much we are suffering; he doesn't know what is going on here. Actually, I think I didn't really believe that, but it was easier for me to think that. It was more comfortable that way. And then another quotation from Chairman Mao would come out, and we ox ghosts and snake spirits would all have to recite it and then we would suffer even more. People destroyed themselves because they loved Chairman Mao so much, because they just couldn't admit that he was wrong.

"But I still love Chairman Mao. His motives were good. He wanted to prevent China from becoming like the Soviet Union, from becoming revisionist. If I ever thought that Chairman Mao had done something wrong to harm the Chinese people, something about me would change. I would lose my own sense of self-confidence. All my beliefs would have to change. And my past. All my past experiences. What would happen to them? If I didn't love Chairman Mao, how could I look back over my life?"

DESPITE the difficulties of integrating a stress-filled past with the realities of the present and despite the natural human tendency toward denial and repression, the possibility nonetheless exists that some will survive extremity relatively unchanged and that others may even experience psychosocial growth. The most inclusive and sophisticated models of human response to stress incorporate those possibilities. Individuals capable against all odds of refusing to succumb to their circumstances are the stuff of which great literature, reportage, and myth are made. John Hersey, writing about the aftermath of Hiroshima, describes the physician who, in what was as close to living hell as man has ever experienced, continued somehow to treat the wounded and the dying. Arthur Miller portrays the unexpected courage of the morally flawed and otherwise ordinary John Proctor, who goes to his death for refusing to confess to a crime of which he is innocent. There were those in the Nazi concentration camps who, facing their own imminent deaths, continued to minister to the needs of their suffering brethren. Few treatments of the Holocaust have failed to pay homage to the dancer who, as she was being led to her death, was called upon by her captors to dance just one more time. Naked and emaciated, her spirit summoning its final measure of beauty, grace, and strength, she danced her final dance. And when it was over, she seized the gun of her guard and shot him dead.

The Cultural Revolution, like most great disasters, has few who were heroes or martyrs, but a few do seem to have come through their experiences relatively unchanged. And if none who were victims "indeed did rather well," some, however painfully, experienced psychosocial growth.

Yao Baoding and Huang Xing seem to have survived the Cultural Revolution relatively unchanged. Yao and Huang stand at opposite ends of the Chinese political spectrum. Yao Baoding was an ultraleftist who spent six years in solitary confinement. He supported the Cultural Revolution then, and he supports it now. Yao was able to find meaning in his imprisonment because he believed he was suffering for a revolutionary cause. Huang was, and still is, a member of the Democratic League, the organization formed in the 1940s as an alternative to both the Nationalists and the Communists and revived again at the conclusion of the Cultural Revolution. He survived the Cultural Revolution by concluding early in the movement that it was theater of the absurd and refusing to play his role. Both are older men, now in their mid-seventies.

But Yao Baoding and Huang Xing, despite their vast political differences, do have a number of things in common. Both have very strong personalities and a very strong sense of their own identities. Each has a mission in life, missions in which they believe, even now, with a passion. Yao Baoding is an ardent and excellent teacher, beloved by his students, and Huang Xing is in the arts. Work toward their goals had been interrupted during the Cultural Revolution, but their missions had been resumed at its end, and both were in a position in Chinese society to fulfill their goals. It was these two men who, when asked what was worst about the Cultural Revolution, both said it was the wasted years. "I kept thinking during all that time that I was in jail," says Yao Baoding, "that when it was over, when I was out, I would make up for those wasted years. I kept thinking, 'I have to make up for these years.' I still don't know whether I have."

Both Yao Baoding and Huang Xing expressed strong resentment against new party retirement policies, because they think they have little time left to accomplish their goals. Neither of them wanted Communist Party bureaucrats telling them they had to retire before they had made up for the time they had lost, before they had accomplished the goals that had given their lives meaning. "Usually when people talk about the wasted years," says Huang Xing, "they're talking about the younger generation, the 'lost generation.' But the older generation also lost ten years, ten years of service to the country. For some people ten years, for others—the rightists—twenty. We also want to make up for those wasted years before we die. For my generation, our time is short. You see lots of resistance to retirement by older people now, and they're being criticized for resisting. Everyone thinks they want to hold on to their privileges, their apartments, their cars, the things that come with being a big cadre. But that's not true. We're resisting because we feel we still have something to contribute to our country. We have to make up for those wasted years when we couldn't make our contributions."

It is difficult to be certain, of course, but Yao Baoding and Huang Xing were probably little different at the end of the Cultural Revolution from what they were before.

DEEP in the psyche of Western culture, tracing no doubt to the biblical story of Job, is a belief that suffering has a salutary and purifying effect, that we are stronger, wiser, and in some sense better for having suffered and endured. But fate does not often choose to test the integrity and the character of those of us who are best, those most likely to suffer and endure. The import of Job is not that he is typical but that he is extraordinary, a rare example of the best to which man can aspire. It is for inspiration that we turn to the Book of Job, not for confirmation of what we are. Of all the possible responses to extremity, psychosocial growth is the least likely, the least frequent, and therefore all the more admirable when it does occur.

The dominant legacy of the Cultural Revolution is the invisible wounds, the slow, silent screams. But a process of growth, for a few, has also taken place. That process, when it has occurred, has been exceptionally painful, for it has involved individuals redefining themselves, their roles in Chinese society, their own political positions, and their place in the Chinese polity.

Outsiders might differ on what types of new Chinese political views represent "psychosocial growth," but the most frequent type of growth is political. Most would agree that the new skepticism of China's young, the refusal to accept party pronouncements on faith, is a healthy trend. Whether such young Chinese as the Democracy Wall dissidents, who knowingly courted arrests in order to express their views, should be similarly judged is a matter of controversy. Viewed from the perspective of the Western democratic tradition, their heroic challenge to orthodox authority might be viewed as psychosocial growth. Viewed within the realities of the current Chinese political system, where dissidence is bound to be crushed and where the system of justice is remarkably adept at eliciting unwarranted false confessions, such challenges might be viewed as politically and socially maladaptive. How does one judge nearly certain martyrdom in the face of political repression?

But there are different examples of political growth as a result of the Cultural Revolution. Zhao Wenhao has used the Cultural Revolution as an occasion to analyze anew the history of the Communist Party in China and the implications of Mao's thought. He recognizes both the realities and the inevitabilities of Chinese politics. He sympathizes with the dissidents but recognizes the limitations of dissidence in the current Chinese polity. It was Zhao Wenhao who, in discussing the question of the sense of guilt that burdens so many victims of the Cultural Revolution, began by saying that "none of us are innocent, not even those of us who were victims."

"To a certain degree," says Zhao Wenhao, "I think that the Cultural

Revolution was not an aberration but rather an extension of policies that began in the 1930s and 1940s, maybe even earlier. The rectification movement in Yenan was itself a miniature Cultural Revolution. Many innocent people were persecuted. On a smaller scale, what happened during the Cultural Revolution had happened before. Before the Cultural Revolution, there were many political campaigns, and these were all Cultural Revolutions on a smaller scale. It had happened again and again.

"So the disaster of the Cultural Revolution was inevitable. The seeds of the Cultural Revolution were inherent in the whole nature of politics. The nature of all these movements was the same—the campaign against Hu Feng, antirightist campaigns, antirevisionist campaigns, the anti-right-deviationist campaign after the purge of Peng Dehuai—all these campaigns took place in the 1950s. Then at the tenth plenum in 1962, Mao put forward the slogan of class struggle.

"But it goes as far back as Mao's investigation into the peasant movement in Hunan in the 1920s. Mao praised this kind of movement then. During the Cultural Revolution they put dunce caps on people. Mao praised putting dunce caps on people in that article. And during the Cultural Revolution, everyone repeated the phrase 'revolution is not a dinner party' from that article.

"There is an identity crisis in China now, similar to what Emile Durkheim describes when he writes about anomie. Norms are the final ground for any human behavior, but now the norms are being shattered, and there are no substitutes, so we are facing a period of anomie, especially the younger generation. People are not sure what they want. They want change, but as to what kind of change is adequate, they are not so sure. I have some sympathy with some of the Democracy Wall dissidents like Wei Jingsheng, but I don't quite agree with them. The changes they were calling for were too radical, and to pursue such radical changes could only bring another disaster to China. I agree with some of Deng's policies. I think perhaps he is the right man for the job right now, even though I have some doubts about some of his policies. But in the future, perhaps Deng will not be the right man for the job.

"So it is hard for me to say what my own attitude is. People say this is a period of exploration. We are reassessing our previous conceptions. Some people are skeptical. They doubt everything. Skepticism always works at times of crisis; skepticism shakes old beliefs. But unless we find something positive, some really positive alternatives, we cannot really change society. The rule of the party is an established fact. We cannot bring about reform, we cannot change China, without taking account of this fact. The party is the only organized power in the country. So I don't know what will happen. I believe China will change eventually. Of that I am sure. Today, I don't know what kind of changes there will be, and sometimes I find myself furious with the patience of my own people. Many people are very sad, very pessimistic about the future. In the long run, though, I think the changes will be for the better. But before that, there will be some setbacks, some serious ones."

THERE is also a different type of psychosocial growth, growth that is not political but personal. Martyrs like Yu Luoke were rare during the Cultural Revolution, but a few at least were saints.

You Xiaoli was a saint.

Despite the torture that You Xiaoli was forced to endure, she never confessed to crimes of which she was not guilty. She never betrayed her family, her friends, her colleagues, or her comrades. She refused to lie. Given the circumstances in which people found themselves during the Cultural Revolution, You Xiaoli's is a most remarkable achievement indeed. Of the people whose stories are included here, You Xiaoli is the only one for whom that can be said, the only person who emerged from the Cultural Revolution as innocent as when it began.

"Why didn't I confess?" she responded when first asked about her refusal to succumb. "Because I wasn't guilty. It would have been ridiculous for me to confess."

The roots of You Xiaoli's tenacity, the strength of her integrity, the source of her resistance, are to be found, as character usually is, in her childhood, in the early admonitions of her mother. You Xiaoli's mother was a fanatically, even perversely, religious Christian, a believer in the second coming of the Messiah. The lessons of God's love and kindness in You Xiaoli's religious training were buttressed by the threats and intimidations of the demons and monsters of Chinese myth, dressed in biblical guise. You Xiaoli was brought up to believe in heaven and hell. "My mother told me," she recalls, "that if you do something bad, then at the end of time, or the end of the world, or sometime, you will be punished, even if you are not punished in this world. And if you do good, anyway you won't go to hell. She believed that if you do good, at the very end you will receive good; if you do bad, you will be punished."

You Xiaoli was taught not to lie, taught never, ever to lie. As the offspring of a rape by a landlord of his maidservant, You Xiaoli as a young child lived in the home of her father without benefiting from his riches. Her mother cooked for her master, You Xiaoli's father, but neither she nor You Xiaoli nor You Xiaoli's brother was allowed to sample the master's fare. You Xiaoli, surrounded by opulence, often went hungry. It was under such circumstances that the prohibition against lying was scratched ineradicably on her young and malleable mind. "I remember when I was very, very small," You Xiaoli says, "my mother was preparing some food for my father. I even forget what food. But I wanted very, very much to have a piece, just a small piece. My brother said we could each take a piece from the pot, and no one would ever know.

But actually, we didn't do it. So when my mother came back, I told her that we had discussed it and thought about it and thought that it was okay, but that we didn't do it. She asked whether if we had taken some, would we tell. She told me a story about a neighbor's daughter who took a piece of pork or fish or something from the pot and when her mother came back, the girl lied and said it was a rat who ate the morsel. Then at night, the girl felt a pain in her heart, and then she felt a snake biting her heart, and she wasted away and died. And then after her death, again she was punished because she had told a lie in her lifetime, and my mother told us about the fire in hell and all sorts of horrible stories. She said that Cain killed his brother and cheated—whom?— God or somebody, and then he was wandering all his life. They weren't really Bible stories, just invented stories. She said that nobody will punish you on this earth as much as you will punish yourself.

"That girl whose heart was eaten by the snake was a real person in my neighborhood, a real thing. I believed, not that it was a snake but like a snake biting you there. Even now, to this day, I think if you tell a lie you will feel like a snake on your heart. I really believe that. Why should people tell a lie? Because they are tortured? You can't possibly be tortured worse than being crucified. That makes you die a very slow death. That's all. I expected during the Cultural Revolution to be tortured to death. But I would never lie."

Today, You Xiaoli believes that the most remarkable achievement of her entire life is that she retained her integrity throughout the Cultural Revolution, that she never lied and never betrayed her colleagues or her friends. Survivor's guilt may be the dominant legacy of the Cultural Revolution, but it is not a legacy of which You Xiaoli is a part. It is her achievement during the Cultural Revolution that remains You Xiaoli's greatest source of happiness.

"Before the Cultural Revolution," says You Xiaoli, "I didn't know what kind of person I was. I didn't know that I could be the type of person who would not confess under torture, who would not betray other people. And I never knew how good it would make me feel to realize that I am that type of person. Today, when some other people walk into a room and meet other people, they feel embarrassed, uncomfortable, because they betrayed their friends during the Cultural Revolution. But now, everyone thanks me for not betraying them. They like me more. They thank me for not having done anything to harm them. They say that I am *laoshi*—that means that I am honest but not that smart. It means that I could never hurt anyone, never cause anyone to suffer. It also means that I could never become wealthy or famous or get a ranking position. Maybe it is better to be honest and smart. But I feel comfortable. It is because of my conscience. My conscience is clear, and that makes me much happier than other people. The thing that makes me happiest today is that I feel no guilt. In all my life, to this very day, that is what makes me happiest. That I feel no guilt."

NINE

HOW COULD THEY HAVE BEEN SO CRUEL? "FOR THE BANE AND THE ENLIGHTENING OF MEN"

IT is Aldous Huxley who reminds us how thin the veneer of civilization really is. Civilization in one of its aspects, he says, "may be defined as a systematic withholding from individuals of certain occasions for barbarous behavior. In recent years we have discovered that when, after a period of withholding, those occasions are once more offered, men and women, seemingly no worse than we are, have shown themselves ready and even eager to take them." China's Great Proletarian Cultural Revolution was one such recent occasion.

Some in China even believe they can identify precisely the incident when, after a period of withholding, the occasion for barbarous behavior was once more symbolically offered. It was on August 18, 1966, at the Red Guard rally, a million Red Guards strong, when Chairman Mao descended from the podium and into the crowd, admonishing middle school student Song Binbin—"Polite Song"—for the gentility of her name. Afterward, Song Binbin changed her name to Song Yaowu—"Song wants violence," "Song wants the opposite of civil order"—and Song Yaowu engaged herself in violence. Some say Song Yaowu even went so far as to kill.

How could they have been so cruel? How could they have done such things to each other?

"It's in the genes," Yang De asserts, "inherent in the Chinese race, transmitted from generation to generation." But Qiu Yehuang is slower to respond. "This is a good question," he says. "I have been considering it myself."

Many Chinese have been considering this question. There is no simple or easy answer. No single explanation will do.

"First of all," cautions Qiu Yehuang, "you can't say that all Chinese are cruel. Ninety-nine percent of the Chinese people are good. Less than one percent showed cruelty. But if one percent were cruel, there were ten million who were cruel, and ten million cruel people can do a lot of bad."

Why then were the ten million so cruel? Qiu Yehuang sees the question in historical perspective, in terms of the rise and decline of Chinese civilization. He touches thereby on the profoundly unnerving and ultimately humbling question of whence our moral values come, what Hannah Arendt calls "one of the central moral questions of all time, namely . . . the nature and function of human judgment."

It is both to China's ancient and modern past that Qiu Yehuang turns for an explanation, to the whittling away of moral values that accompanied the decline and fall of the last of China's dynasties, the Qing, to the value of revolution and struggle that replaced the Confucian ideals of harmony, righteousness, and respect for one's fellow man, and to the absence of any objective and absolute moral standard outside that decreed by the Communist Party and against which one's behavior could be measured.

"How could we be so cruel? Maybe you don't know all of Chinese history for the past four thousand years," he begins. "Generally speaking, since civilization began developing, the cruelty of human beings has been getting less and less. We have become more civilized. China has such a long history. Our ancestors five thousand years ago were cruel; they killed other people for little reason or no reason. If you read ancient Chinese history, you'll find that the Chinese were much, much more cruel than Hitler. In the Xia dynasty, four thousand years ago, they were killing people as we kill fleas, with no consideration. The interesting thing is that four thousand years ago Xia Jie called himself a sun and later Mao did the same. Then later there was Confucius and other philosophers like Lao Tzu. People became more decent, milder. They didn't kill, they had respect for other people, they loved other people. The influence of Confucius and Lao Tzu lasted for thousands of years.

"But at the end of the Qing dynasty, especially before and after 1911, lots of foreign theories came into China. Those theories and conceptions I agree with. I like them. I think they're correct. But everything has its negative side.

The Chinese started to criticize Confucius—'old number-two Confucius' they called him, *Kong Lao Er.* This was a way of vulgarizing Confucius. It was during the high tide of the May Fourth Movement. Of course, I don't think Confucius's theory was totally correct. Some of it was wrong—such as the part that says a lady should always obey her husband, the 'three obeys and four modests.' I think that's wrong. Confucius was discriminating against women. A lot of things like *xiao*—filial piety, offering sacrifices to the ancestors and parents—are also wrong. We want children to respect us, but if we're wrong we should let children oppose us. So Confucius wasn't totally correct. But I also don't like the way they criticized him and threw everything out. Because lots of what he said was correct—loyalty, honesty, respect for other people. Confucius was like the Bible.

"What I'm saying is that revolution is sometimes good. But when people start a revolution, sometimes they overdo it. That's almost unavoidable some-times. So they criticized the Qing dynasty, but they criticized things that were correct, too. It was the same with the Russian revolution and the French revolution. Those revolutions degenerated into vandalism. Revolution some-times has negative effects.

"So I think that starting in 1911 and going on to the Cultural Revolution, a lot of correct things were destroyed. People didn't know what was right and what was wrong. People just believed. People just believed Chairman Mao. What he said was correct. People weren't thinking. They were just following. Especially since 1948, when the power of the Communist troops became obvious and they occupied lots of territory.

"Yet some principles should occupy people's thinking. Communism be-came the only correct idea in China. People forgot loyalty, honesty, respect for other people. People forgot what was good, they forgot about teaching the good, they didn't tell people how to love other people. No one taught children to love their parents.

"And then communist theory maintained that our society develops through fighting. It also said that the only good class was the proletariat. The bourgeoi-sie and the landlords and the rich peasants and the rightists and the bad elements had to be destroyed. And the Communist government did destroy them. They shot lots of people to death. Young people were taught to believe that if you want to keep China the number-one revolutionary country, you have to kill all those people, just the way that if you want to keep your room clean you have to kill all the flies and fleas. We have taught that this is the correct thing, and so of course young people behave that way.

"If there are one or two small insects on the ground, and you kill them with your shoe, you feel cruel. If you kill a thousand, then you lose that feeling. You lose your humanity. It was the same with the Japanese and the Germans. First the Japanese killed one Chinese, the Germans killed one Jew. Then they killed ten and then a hundred. You lose your conscience. The Chinese say 'fight with red eyes.' If you have red eyes you are angry, upset, you kill everything. It didn't all happen at the beginning of the Cultural Revolution. At first they just hit a few people. Then they killed a few people. It was gradual. Then gradually —how many did they kill? Millions."

Qiu Yehuang is right. The history of China from the final years of the Qing to the country's "liberation" by the Communists, from 1949 to the Great Proletarian Cultural Revolution, is also the history of an erosion of moral values, a decline in the capacity of the Chinese people to make reasoned moral choices or even to recognize choices as moral. As the first generation born after Liberation comes to maturity, the generation gap that preoccupies so many in China today is, in one of its manifestations, a gap in the perception and recognition of morality.

When Wu Gengsheng and Gao Cuixia, Li Weiguo and Qiu Yehuang attacked innocent people during the antirightist campaign of 1957, they knew both that the people they were attacking were innocent and that by a moral standard in which they still believed what they were doing was wrong. They knew at least that they were acting not out of morality but out of expediency. Wu Gengsheng and Gao Cuixia had attacked in order to get ahead, to climb higher on the ladder of political success. Qiu Yehuang and Li Weiguo had attacked in order to avoid being attacked themselves. When Bai Meihua participated at the age of thirteen, early in the Cultural Revolution, in the house search and beating of a high party official, she seemed unaware that there was a moral standard against which her actions might be judged wrong. Minister Chen had been deemed by Mao a counterrevolutionary. Of course he deserved to be attacked. To this day, Bai Meihua feels no guilt for her attack on Minister Chen. She exhibits no remorse.

In 1980, when the Cultural Revolution was over and an American scholar in China had occasion to teach her class the Ten Commandments, there was one commandment her students simply did not understand: "Thou shall not bear false witness against thy neighbor." Products of China's Great Proletarian Cultural Revolution, her students had grown up steeped in false witness. The Cultural Revolution was the bearing of false witness run rampant. That the bearing of false witness was wrong was a concept never taught to the Cultural Revolution generation.

You XIAOLI, born only a decade after the collapse of the Qing dynasty and educated by the last generation to be educated under the Qing, touches on these generational differences in her effort to explain. "The people who were cruel weren't all of the same kind," she begins.

"The middle-aged were one kind of cruel. They knew that if you followed the party policy and followed the leaders' commands, you would please the leadership and you would be promoted and you would climb up the ladder.

There were lots of people like this. They wanted to have a future in China, and to have a future meant to be a high-ranking cadre, to have a good salary, a nice house. So among them cruelty was the result of egotism and selfishness.

"And then there was another kind of cruel. There were people who hated you even before the Cultural Revolution. Sometimes they had reason, sometimes not. For instance, there were people who hated me because I always told the truth. If I thought that something was wrong or that someone had done wrong, I always said so. I always said what I thought directly to the person. During the Cultural Revolution, those people beat me, or influenced people who beat me.

"We old intellectuals, when we were small, studied the old traditional beliefs—that an intellectual may be killed but he can't be insulted, that an intellectual won't bow before people just for a bowl of rice. That means that an intellectual would rather be poor. And then when my generation was older, we were educated in a Western-style education, to care more about knowledge, to know the world, to know people, to enjoy art, literature, music. We learned all kinds of self-enjoyment, but not vulgar things. We had our own spiritual world.

"But the middle-aged intellectuals were given a Soviet-style education. They think that everyone belongs to some category of class, that you carry with you the nature of that class. They believe in class struggle. They think that it is the most heroic activity. 'The happiest thing is to fight with the people, to struggle with the people, to struggle against the class enemy.' This is Chairman Mao's saying. He especially emphasizes the endless happiness that is supposed to come from struggle against other people. No wonder we had so many political movements. No wonder we were always struggling with people. Middle-aged people believe in Marxism-Leninism Mao Zedong thought. The little red book is their Bible, and they worship political idols. My generation, the older generation, doesn't do that. We aren't that stupid. The middle-aged generation could be cheated. They couldn't cheat us.

"And then there were the young people, the Red Guards. Some of them were innocent. They were educated to fight against everything reactionary. It was considered heroic to do so. For instance, I, or an old cadre, or an old reactionary, we were the enemy. So they could kill you, and that made them heroic. They were innocent."

You Xiaoli is not alone in thinking this of the young Red Guards. Among those in China who refuse to accept the premise that the distinction between good and evil is primarily a function of class, there is a widespread belief that elemental morality is not instinctual but learned, that the difference between right and wrong must be taught, that morality is a product not of the nature of man or of class but of education. In this view, the young of China of course behaved badly, because they were educated badly. And if the fault lies not with the young but with their education, then they must be forgiven, for they knew not what they did.

THE young, too, recognize the effect of their education on their behavior during the Cultural Revolution. "In terms of explaining the violence," says Jiang Xinren, "you must remember that I grew up in 'New China.' Chairman Mao always said that political power grows out of the barrel of a gun. During the Cultural Revolution, we were struggling for power. It was a movement to seize power. So it was only natural that we should have used guns. Chairman Mao said that violence was right in a revolution. He said that a revolution was not a dinner party or doing embroidery. So of course there was violence."

APART from the shape of the violence, which he lays to Mao's theory of revolution and power, Jiang Xinren finds the roots of the Cultural Revolution itself in the darker side of traditional Chinese culture. You Xiaoli and Qiu Yehuang extol the traditional Confucian values of benevolence, righteousness, and harmony, but he sees the older ways as a hotbed of jealousy, antagonism, and gossip.

In explaining the failure of capitalism to develop in China, John King Fairbank has pointed to the fact that in contrast to economic man of the West, who prospers most by producing more, the goal of economic man of China was to grow rich not by increasing production but by increasing his own share of what had already been produced. The size of the pie, in Chinese eyes, remains the same. The trick is to seize a larger share of the pie.

Jiang Xinren uses Fairbank's argument to explain how in a society where the pie is static and does not grow, jealousy and competition—ruthless, unbridled competition—is the result. For Jiang Xinren, jealousy Chinese-style was one of the underlying reasons for the cruelty of the Cultural Revolution. "In China," he says, "everyone is jealous. If you have rice to eat, they want you to eat gruel. If you have gruel, they want you to put your spoon down and not have anything to eat. During the Taiping Rebellion, the Taipings were trying to overthrow the Qing dynasty. And at the same time several Western countries were attacking China. The leaders of the dynasty preferred to give control of the country over to foreign armies rather than to give power to the Taipings. The Chinese always separate into different groups that are opposed to each other. They never can get along.

"So Mao could always use one group of people to attack another group of people. In China, you could never change the classes smoothly as in the United States. In China, you always have to have revolution. You can't change anything smoothly or slowly. It's still true. That's why China has never had a really democratic movement. You just get a new emperor coming in after a change in dynasty. So that's why the Cultural Revolution happened in China, not another country. It was jealousy gone wild."

With his boxerlike mind, agile and quick, Song Erli attacks the question of cruelty during the Cultural Revolution like a punching bag, from every angle, —ignorance and fear, cowardice, blind faith, the psychology of the mob. "For one thing," Song Erli begins, "people were cruel out of fear. If you weren't cruel toward the class enemies, that meant you'd lost your class stand and were no longer revolutionary. That isn't so dangerous to idlers, but it is dangerous to those who aspire to power, and at any given time there will be people who aspire to power. Otherwise there would be a vacuum. So it was a combination of ambition and fear that made people so cruel.

"I saw with my own eyes a classmate of mine who had never been an activist before the Cultural Revolution. He was something of a coward. He was of pure red class origin, a peasant, and I saw with my own eyes how he beat some professors. He assembled the professors under the scorching sun in the summertime, and he abused them. And then for some reason I don't know he grabbed a professor by the collar and boxed him in the ears and threw him on the ground. It was a terrible scene. Then I knew he was a coward. If you beat an old professor, what kind of person are you? What kind of person beats an old professor?

"I had read so many novels about how bravely the People's Liberation Army soldiers had faced death by charging the pillboxes of the Guomindang, and I had said, 'How courageous! What spirit!' But then after the Cultural Revolution, I understood that it was very easy. It requires no courage to go to death when you're in a mob. In fact, the more ignorant you are, the braver you are.

"Even those who went to the execution ground and had faith—that wasn't so difficult. During the Cultural Revolution I found many people who went to their deaths out of blind faith. Yes, really to their death. It wasn't hard to be brave. Not with blind faith. And not just blind faith in Mao or the revolution or the revolutionary cause—belief in your faction. It was very stupid. I myself did some very dangerous things just because my comrades discussed the matter and decided to do it. It was ridiculous, really. So the factions produced mob psychology. It wasn't personal psychology. It was the mob. It brought out the animal in you.

"It was ignorance, too. Once I was traveling by foot into the countryside and I went to a village. I couldn't find anyone. But I heard a noise and went to a house and found some young people torturing some bad elements—the landlord's wife and sons. One of the landlord's sons was made to kneel on two bricks.

"So I went in and I was welcomed as a Red Guard from the city. I asked, 'What are you doing? What's wrong with these people? What have they done?' A young boy, very young, said that it was the duty of every revolutionary youth to keep an eye out, that a counterrevolutionary comeback was possible —or something like that, some revolutionary teaching they got in school. We all had this kind of revolutionary teaching session every few days in school. I had been in the countryside conducting the Socialist Education Movement, and we had struggle meetings against the landlords and rich peasants. These were presided over by me but attended by the peasants themselves. In those sessions peasants were lenient—or at least not so cruel as the young kids I found torturing the landlord's wife and sons. I think it was not entirely ignorance that made those young kids so cruel. Their fathers had lived and worked in the village with the landlords. They hadn't been treated cruelly when they were tenants of the landlord; the kids knew that. I think they were so cruel in their own practical interest. Those peasant children had to try to build up their sense of superiority. They were poor peasants, of poor peasant family origins, like everyone else in the village. There were so many peasant boys and girls. They all wanted to think they were superior to the others. In an egalitarian society, what can you do? You have to become politically superior. It's human nature to climb over others. It was very practical, their behavior."

After letting his mind ramble, looking at the question of cruelty from all sides, Song Erli settles finally on a fundamental flaw in China's egalitarian socialist system. It is not just that the size of the pie remains the same and that people inevitably fight to increase their share. It is also that there is only a single flavor of pie—the pie of political power. Other societies confer status and reward on a myriad of occupations, contributions, accomplishments. In other societies, there are many routes to success. In China there is only one, the path of political power.

"In other societies, the smarter people have choices—they can try to become lawyers or millionaires. In China, too, there are some people who are smarter than others. But in China, everyone has to crowd into a very narrow riverbed. This society intentionally encourages a desire for power and superiority. So in the case of the peasant lads, it wasn't simply a desire for power that led them to behave that way. It was a desire to be superior. But the only way was through power. So everyone struggles for power and the riverbed overflows and there is a flood."

AND finally, of course, the people who suffered through it put the blame for the Cultural Revolution and the cruelty it engendered on the man who conceived and led it, on the man in whose name the struggles were waged, on Chairman Mao himself. "In the case of the Cultural Revolution," said Liu Zhiping, "if you really look at it closely and if you are really honest, there were lots of people involved, yes, lots of authorities giving instructions. But there wasn't really a Gang of Four giving instructions. In the end, it was one man, the authority of just one man. It was Mao Zedong. That is why I sat on my bed and read his four volumes over and over and tried to figure out what principles of Chairman Mao applied to the reality of the Cultural Revolution. I couldn't find those principles. Chairman Mao said that China should be united, but that wasn't happening in the Cultural Revolution. There were always two groups opposing each other, and there seemed to be no way to unite those groups. Chairman Mao said that ninety-five percent of the people had to be united and that only five percent were bad. But there had been so many movements, and every time it was a different five percent that were bad, so really the 'bad' people were much more than five percent. But it was still Mao who led the Cultural Revolution. He was the one man behind it, the one authority. That is why China needs a rule of law. So it can never again be just one man. And that is why so many people feel cheated. Because they believed in that man."

Bai Meihua concurs. "Am I angry?" she asks. "No, I'm not angry. But I hate. I hate Mao. It isn't true about the Gang of Four. The Gang of Four didn't have much power at the beginning of the Cultural Revolution. It was only later that they began to get power, and even then they couldn't have done it without Mao. Some people talk about the Gang of Five, meaning the Gang of Four plus Mao. But even that is inaccurate. It was Mao. Mao began the Cultural Revolution. It was his Cultural Revolution, and for that I hate him.

"And there is a particular person, a particular revolutionary rebel, whom I also hate. After the two revolutionary rebel families moved out of our house, another revolutionary rebel moved in, a revolutionary rebel from Sichuan. He said he was there to make revolution. He never wore shoes. He went barefoot all the time. He said that during the Long March, the Communist Party members didn't have shoes to wear, so it was revolutionary to go barefoot. In the room that he occupied was a picture of my family, my parents and the three children. It was a big picture, framed, with glass. He took a brush and painted on the picture in black. Under my father, he wrote 'counterrevolutionary.' Across my mother's picture, he wrote 'wife of a counterrevolutionary.' And across the photographs of me and my sister and brother he wrote *gouzaizi*— 'sons of bitches.' We had a big fight with him about that. I don't know what he finally did with the picture. I think he must have ripped it up."

IT is difficult to add to the musings of those whose lives were so profoundly affected by the Cultural Revolution, those whose lives the movement so decisively changed. But from their own explanations it is possible to highlight five reasons for the tragedy—prosaic, commonplace, but true—that stand out as primary.

First, and most obvious, the people of China took their leader and elevated him beyond emperor to a god, exhibiting before Mao Zedong near-slavish subservience, blind obedience, unquestioning faith, offering to him the willing, even eager, sacrifice of their own freedom and independence of judgment. Many Chinese—all whose stories are included here, people who were intelligent, well educated, and good—seem genuinely to have loved Chairman Mao, to have loved the Chinese Communist Party. And even, particularly after 1957, as the ideals they had thought that Mao and the party embodied were relentlessly, inexorably undermined, they continued to cling to the hopes, the dreams, the expectations, the promises that the Communist Party and its chairman had inspired with the liberation of the country in 1949. So much did they love Chairman Mao, so greatly did they admire the party, so timorous were they before authority, that faced with conflicts between their own individual perceptions and what the party and Chairman Mao said was happening, many of them doubted not the party or Mao but themselves. The capacity for independent human judgment, in these circumstances, was grotesquely, pathetically, tragically, maimed.

China had never been a society where individual judgment was particularly encouraged. The role of the leader has always been important. Confucian doctrine counseled that when rulers behaved morally, their subjects would behave morally, too, that it was therefore the rulers and not the miscreants themselves who were responsible for the misbehavior of their subjects. That aspect of tradition had not notably changed with the coming to power of the Communists. It is to the leaders rather than to the system itself that Chinese look for an explanation of what has happened and for predictions of what will come. It is in leaders rather than individual citizens that responsibility is vested. Intellectuals, to be sure, have been recognized as capable of possessing the capacity for human judgment apart from the dictates of the ruler, and traditional folklore glorified those rare and exemplary martyrs—men like the Ming dynasty's Hai Rui, whose example had begun the Cultural Revolution—who stood up to challenge corrupt and evil authority. But in general, loyalty was lauded over independence of thought.

The ascension to power of the Communists served only to enhance traditional subservience before authority. On the one hand, by assigning all Chinese to a work unit, the Communist Party guaranteed jobs to everyone, thus eliminating the earlier tragedies of the impoverished and often starving unemployed. By introducing a ration system administered through the work unit, urban dwellers were guaranteed at least a minimum of nourishment, ending the spectacle of widespread starvation on city streets, the trucks that came through daily to gather the urban dead. The work unit even provided housing for its members, however crowded, shabby, and dilapidated that housing may have been. When luxuries were available, access to them was also often through the work unit—rations for certain types of fish and meat, extra watermelons and peaches in the summer, cabbages for the winter. Bicycles were allotted through the work unit, and movie theaters played to audiences composed of members of the several work units whose leaders had managed to purchase tickets in bulk.

The organization of China after 1949 fostered gratitude on the part of Chinese for the security the guarantee of livelihood assured them. But the security fostered dependence as well, dependence on the party and the state, and dependence on one's own work unit and the leaders within it. That dependence in turn fostered subservience born of both gratitude and necessity. When the basic goods of life are supplied by the state—can only be supplied by the state—the price of defiance, of independent human judgment, is high. What develops, or so it seems, is a tacit agreement—a certain sacrifice of critical judgment in return for security and the dependence that entails, the classic sacrifice of freedom in return for the guarantee of bread.

Second, by 1966, when the Great Proletarian Cultural Revolution began, there was in China no higher or separate moral code outside and beyond that of Party Chairman Mao Zedong, no agreed-upon principles of human behavior to which individuals or groups might appeal as legitimate. The Confucian code of ethics, having suffered its gravest attacks during the May Fourth Movement of 1919, had long since been discredited, and lest the people of China harbored any residual beliefs in the Confucian ethic, Confucius himself came under attack late in the Cultural Revolution, after the death of Lin Biao. The Ten Commandments of the Judeo-Christian tradition had never taken root in China, and the notion of an impartial rule of law was almost entirely absent. It is important even that it was Liu Shaoqi who was chosen as the "number-one party person in authority taking the capitalist road," for Liu Shaoqi was the Communist Party embodiment of bureaucratic procedure, due process by the Party's rules. It was Liu Shaoqi who had taken out the party constitution and shown it to his children in an effort to prevent them from engaging in violence against others. With the overthrow of Liu Shaoqi and those most closely associated with him, even the appeal to the party constitution became meaningless.

True, there were those who attempted to end the violence by appeals to Mao or those most closely associated with him. Some tried in desperation to stop the savagery of beatings by quoting Mao's strictures on discipline, or the slogan attributed to Jiang Qing: "Attack with words, defend by force." Sometimes they succeeded. But revolutionaries committed to Chairman Mao, revolutionaries like Jiang Xinren, could quote Mao to the opposite effect. In the end, there was no moral court of last resort beyond Mao to which individuals could turn, no basis for serving as the Emile Zola—or even the Lech Walesa —of the Cultural Revolution. On the basis of what moral code could individuals have defied either Mao or the mob and said no?

Third, the authoritative ethical code that did govern China—so-called Marxism-Leninism/Mao Zedong thought—declared that good and evil were a function not of the nature of man nor of the deeds he performed but of class. There is no human nature, Mao had said, only class nature. There were good classes and bad classes, and individuals within those classes were *ipso facto* good or bad themselves. Sin inhered not in individuals or deeds but in classes. Class, moreover, was a necessarily inheritable quality, good and evil thus being transmitted through the genes. True, through hard work and ostentatious manifestations of revolutionary zeal, the sons and daughters of "bad-class" parents stood at least a chance of being admitted to the circle. But they were the exception rather than the rule.

What is more, violence, according to the theory, was, in certain circumstances, at least, a permissible form of behavior toward individuals of bad class backgrounds.

Thus the theory left open the possibility of wholesale persecution of individuals not for what they had done or actions they had performed but for the class they were. It was members of the "bad" classes whose very lives were at risk during the Cultural Revolution—members of the capitalist class who were beaten to death on buses and trains, landlords who were beaten to death on campuses, not for deeds they had done but simply for who they were.

The theory further stipulated that at any given time, 5 percent of the population fell into the ranks of the enemy. As the revolution continued, the enemy classes seemed not sufficiently large to constitute the requisite 5 percent, and enemies had to be invented—enemies like Li Meirong, You Xiaoli, and Professor Song. And because the new enemies had to be guilty not merely because of their class but because of the deeds they had allegedly done, their crimes also had to be invented. The individuals whose stories are included here were flawed, as all human beings are flawed. With their backgrounds, their pasts, and their political views, it was not by chance that revolutionary China chose them for attack. But none were guilty of the crimes of which they were accused.

Fourth—and this is of key importance—Mao insisted that class and other enemies of the state be punished not by institutional means, not even through resort to secret police, but by means of mass participation in publicly administered social justice. The social environment, moreover, was so structured that not to participate in the process whereby pariahs were excluded from the circle was to risk being branded a pariah and being excluded oneself. Justice was in the hands of the mob. For if it is true that the courage to resist is nearly impossible in a state of isolation, it is no less true, as Song Erli points out, that the courage to do harm is often a product of the bravado of the mob. The Cultural Revolution was a spectacle, a public event. The attacks against the victims were staged in public struggle sessions. The capitalists and landlords were not killed privately, quietly, silently, behind locked doors, but in public, for everyone to see, by bands of youths who believed themselves brave, their deeds heroic.

And one must add finally, with Song Erli, that the riverbed of success in China was very narrow, that the avenues to recognition were few, the means by which human aspirations might be fulfilled small, the opportunities for the realization of one's human potential restricted. Revolution was good and revolutionaries were good people, as Song Wuhao points out, and the only way to be recognized as a revolutionary and therefore good was to join the ranks of the officials, to be vested with political power. But positions of power were scarce, and struggles for them inevitable. That the military was a major actor in the struggle for power and held in its hands the preponderance of force enabled it ultimately to enforce its will with a particularly efficient and orderly brutality.

BEYOND the crisis in confidence that China's leaders fear because of the challenge to their legitimacy it brings, and deeper and more serious by far, is the crisis of morality in China. Somewhere along the way, the elemental rules of human living together have been lost. China, as Zhao Wenhao has pointed out, is in a state of anomie.

There are those, like Song Erli and Wang Hongbao, who believe that modernization and morality are linked, that a new moral code can emerge only when China has solved its economic problems, when China achieves its goal of transforming itself into a powerful, modern nation-state. Wang Hongbao can still remember when and where he was when he reached the conclusion that Chinese morals can improve only with a rise in the standard of living. It was at a wedding in the countryside where he, like the other young people whose stories are included here, had been sent, he believed, to live the rest of his life.

The village was impoverished. "There was never enough to eat," he says. "People made gruel out of corn flour and sorghum. There were no vegetables and no meat. Everyone was very thin and had very little energy. Even the draft animals were so thin and so weak that they couldn't be used to plow the fields. People aged very quickly in the village, By the time a woman was forty, she was already old. Her teeth had fallen out, and her hair had turned thin and gray. The same was true of the men. Children were thin. Their arms and legs were thin, and their bellies were swollen. That was because they had worms. The children all had snotty noses, and their faces were dirty, black, and the black all mixed with the snot. The female students used to love to play with children in Peking. But here, they were afraid even to touch them. The children all had lice on their heads. They used to sit in front of their mothers, and the mother would go through the child's head picking out the lice and crushing them between her fingers. After a while, the mothers' fingers would get all black and bloody. This was very natural to the peasants. The mothers would sit there and talk to you while picking lice.

"Because there was so little food, people's manners when they ate were also very bad. I remember one time there was a wedding in the village, the first wedding I attended. At a wedding, the parents of the bride and groom invite many guests and have many tables, and serve special food. People, relatives from neighboring villages, come from all around. Their table manners were just awful. It is special food and everyone wants to eat as much as he can. So people just grab with their chopsticks and shovel things in their mouths as fast as they can, until everything is gone. Nobody puts anything on a plate. To put something on your plate would slow you down, and somebody else might get more to eat. Nobody talks to anyone else. They just eat and then wait for the next dish to come. That is why I think that the present movement for good manners can't really have much effect until the material conditions of people are improved. When people are hungry, they can't afford to be polite."

But You Xiaoli, who grew up in bitter, grinding, awesome poverty, would not agree with Wang Hongbao. "I was poor," she says. "But I knew the right way to conduct my life, how to behave properly. Knowing how to behave properly isn't because you are rich or poor. It has to do with whether you are educated." You Xiaoli had been educated.

But the education You Xiaoli received is no longer available in China, and soon You Xiaoli herself and the model she serves as will be gone. From where is the new moral code to come? It is a question for which there is as yet no answer.

Could the Cultural Revolution happen again? Of course it could. It happens every day.

Reduced in scale and stripped of the colors and flavor that render it unique, devoid of its cultural peculiarities, the Cultural Revolution is only one more variant in a universal repertoire of human tragedy that man seems doomed to repeat.

In the early 1960s, when Yale psychologist Stanley Milgram performed his famous experiments designed to test the limits of the average American's subservience to authority, he found that the vast majority of his subjects were willing upon instruction from authority and with only minimal persuasion to administer electric shocks to their fellow experimental subjects which they believed to be harmful, dangerous, and even potentially lethal. With the subjects writhing in pain before their eyes, begging and pleading for mercy, most of these ordinary Americans, uncomfortable but complying in the name of science and out of deference to authority, went right on increasing the voltage.

Albert Camus concludes his classic human statement of how man in extremity behaves by pointing out "that the plague bacillus never dies or disappears for good; that it can lie dormant for years and years in furniture and linen-chests; that it bides its time in bedrooms, cellars, trunks, and bookshelves; and that perhaps the day [will] come when, for the bane and the enlightening of men, it [will] rouse up its rats again and send them forth to die. . . ."

The lesson the Cultural Revolution teaches is nothing if not humility. For how can any of us be certain, without having been there ourselves, how we would behave in similar circumstances? Even You Xiaoli, the best to which we can aspire, had not known before the Cultural Revolution that she could be the type of person who would not confess under torture, who would refuse under pain of death to betray her relatives and her friends.

The germs of the Cultural Revolution are in us all.

EPILOGUE

ON BEING CHINESE

NEITHER education nor personal proclivity had prepared Jiang Xinren for life as an ordinary peasant in the countryside of China. But upon officially graduating from college, this young man who had grown up in his country's largest city was sent to his father's ancestral village to begin a new life. The existence he was able to eke out—$4.50 a month at the start, $6 when he gained some experience —was never enough in itself to keep him alive, and Jiang Xinren came to rely for his livelihood on the supplemental income sent by his father from Shanghai.

Life in the countryside only compounded the disillusionment that had already crumbled Jiang Xinren's view of the world. "People were very poor in that part of Guangdong," he remembers, "poorer than I ever imagined. And they all blamed it on socialism. They didn't like socialism. They all said that before the Communists came, it had been better. Actually, the area was very rich, and in terms of crops, each year produced enough for three years' worth of food. It was the taxes that made people so poor. So much was taken away and given to the state. Most people in the villages and in the surrounding area had relatives abroad, and they survived by receiving money from them. People were poor, but they weren't starving then. But I heard that during the three bad years, many people died."

But the eight years that Jiang Xinren spent in the Guangdong village were important to him. From his disillusionment and despair, from a world that had lost all meaning and value, he began slowly, painfully, to reconstruct a new and different view of the world, a world that started once more to make sense. "The control of the party was not so strong in the village, so it was possible to do things that weren't possible in the city," says Jiang Xinren. "For instance, I listened to the radio—to broadcasts from outside China, to the BBC and the Voice of America. I listened particularly to the news reports about what was going on in China. That was the way I learned about the downfall of Lin Biao two or three months before we received word about it in the village. The villagers didn't know anything about those things. They didn't read a newspaper and they didn't really care. I also listened to gospel programs, and that way I learned about the Bible. There is no Bible in China, no church, so that was the first time I heard.

"I also read books I had never read before." Jiang Xinren had found his family's ancestral home still standing, being lived in and tended by a poor relative. Jiang Xinren had moved in. "There were lots of books there from before the Liberation, and I read many of those old books," he explains. "Some of them, three or four, were attacks against communism, and I read those. I also read books about sex, and that was very important, too. Before then, I had always thought that sex was something dirty, even between husband and wife. It was something we never talked about, never. In our textbook, there was one very simple chapter on sex, but the teacher always skipped over it, so we never read it. Some of the books I read were love stories, romances, but there was one other book, not a romance, that was most important. It said that human beings need certain things to live, things like food and shelter, and that sex was one of those things and that sex was also necessary for procreation. The book didn't treat sex as dirty, and that was important to me, like a revelation."

Other books that Jiang Xinren read were ones he had brought with him and ones that he exchanged with other educated young people similarly exiled to the countryside. For when Jiang Xinren and his comrades had sacked the library and burned the books, they had been selective about what they had thrown to the flames and kept some of the best books for themselves. One of the books Jiang Xinren had saved was Khrushchev's autobiography. "It surprised me," said Jiang Xinren. "It said that North Korea attacked South Korea. I had thought that was a lie until Khrushchev said that. China has never said that." He read John F. Kennedy's *Profiles in Courage* and Orwell's *1984,* and a book on the Cuban missile crisis.

After he had been in the countryside for several years, the peasants discovered that a young man with Jiang Xinren's education and background had skills which they could use. "Since I had some technical expertise that the peasants didn't, they began calling on me for advice, about things like building bridges, as though I were a civil engineer," he explains. "In that job I got a lot more money—seventeen and a half dollars a month instead of six. And I got to travel a lot in a truck."

It was when he began to travel that Jiang Xinren's thoughts of leaving China began.

"In my last two years or so, the only thing that kept me going, that gave me hope, was my plans to leave China," he recounts. "Since my village had lots of relations with Hong Kong, someone brought me a very detailed map of Hong Kong so I would know what to do, where to go, when I got there. But it was impossible to find such a detailed map of China. So I used my truck to learn all about the countryside, to plan the escape route. And every day, knowing I would have to swim out, I practiced swimming for about three hours, gradually building my strength.

"When I finally decided to leave, I had to pay a peasant farmer a lot of money in order to stay at his house and wait for the right time to leave. In the end, though, the price of his help was that I had to take his brother-in-law along.

"The first night out, we had to stop on an island, because there were military patrols on the water, and we were afraid we would get caught. The next day, though, we made it. It was a twenty-hour swim, and for most of the time I had to carry the farmer's brother-in-law. He couldn't swim very well, and after about three hours out, he couldn't swim at all. So I had to carry him almost the whole way. Sometimes I could float, but even floating, I still had to carry him, and it was a lot of work. We didn't have any food during those two days. In the daytime, we couldn't swim at all. We had to stay on little islands to rest. We swam at night.

"We knew when we got to Hong Kong by the lights. Behind us it was dark, before us, ahead, it was light. There was no real dividing line between China and Hong Kong, just the lights to let me know I was there.

"When we got on shore, we went to a farmer's house and knocked on the door. I fell on his bed and went to sleep, unconscious, as though in a coma, and didn't wake up for two days. I was so exhausted from the swim, no sleep, no food.

"After I woke up, I called my aunt and uncle and they came to pick me up in their car. It was less than a week after that that I first went to church. My aunt was a very devout Christian, so I went to church with her. I feel that people need religion, especially young people, for the spiritual part of their lives.

"As for the young man I carried down the river with me, I know I saved his life. But he didn't really seem to think so, or at least didn't show me any particular thanks. We rarely saw each other in Hong Kong."

After several years in Hong Kong, Jiang Xinren was able to emigrate to the United States.

But it cannot be said that Jiang Xinren has found happiness or peace of mind. There is no escape from his guilt. The God Jiang Xinren has chosen, the God that gives his life meaning, is a mean and vengeful God, a God who defines man not in His own image and likeness but as a sinner—inevitably, incorrigibly, inescapably a sinner. It is the Christian notion of mercy that Jiang Xinren has found most difficult to accept, and hence he refuses to forgive either himself or the system from which he has escaped but still cannot leave behind. Often Jiang Xinren dreams that he is being snatched back to China, and just as often he wants to kill. For Jiang Xinren has come to hate not only himself but communism, too, and he believes that the only way to overthrow the Communist government is by force. "At first, after I left China," he says, "I always felt I was being followed, always had to look back over my shoulder to make certain that they weren't coming to snatch me away. And sometimes even now I dream that they snatch me back to China—the Communist government. It's always people I know. I recognize their faces. They are my old friends, people who work now with the Security Bureau. Sometimes when I wake up I think I am back in China. And sometimes I dream I am being attacked by the old Red Guards, the conservatives, and by the Public Security people.

"With the first type of dream, when I feel they are coming to take me back to China, I feel very frightened. With the second type of dream, when I feel I am being attacked, I wake up very angry. I feel I want to kill. When I am fully awake, though, I have to think of the Christian notion of mercy, that I should be merciful to my enemies. But that is the hardest of the Christian notions for me to accept. I can't feel mercy for my enemies. I still can't accept that part of Christianity, the pacificist concepts of Christianity, of loving the enemy, of turning the other cheek.

"I still want to kill. I want China to get rid of communism, and I still believe that the only way to do that is by force. There is no other way to get rid of communism than to overthrow it by force. And I want to overthrow it.

"Power still grows out of the barrel of a gun."

JIANG XINREN is unusual but not unique. Many former Red Guards exiled to the countryside of Guangdong escaped to Hong Kong during the decade of the 1970s, and many remain tortured, haunted, obsessed by the Cultural Revolution, consumed by fear and weighed down by hate.

Others less dissident but still disenchanted have found their way to the

United States, too, and the new era of normalized relations between China and the United States has made such emigration easier. In 1982, Wang Bingzhang, a revolutionary rebel at Peking Medical College during the period of the Cultural Revolution and the first Chinese since 1949 to receive a Ph.D. abroad, defected in Canada. Echoing Lu Xun from half a century earlier explaining why he left medicine to become a writer, Wang Bingzhang explained why he was leaving medicine to lead a movement for democracy in exile. "Medicine can only cure a few patients," said Wang, "but cannot cure the disease of a nation. In China, the people have suffered greatly, not because of lack of advanced science and technology but because of lack of democracy and freedom. The current political system is totalitarianism with a huge bureaucracy which suppresses the people, killing incentives and hindering production and development."

With Wei Jingsheng and other imprisoned dissidents listed among the editors, Wang Bingzhang began a new magazine, *China Spring*, dedicated to giving voice to the ideals of China's democracy movement. One of the democrats who has lent Wang Bingzhang her support is Lin Xiling, the fiery female student leader of the Hundred Flowers movement at People's University in 1957, imprisoned during the antirightist campaign that followed and released only after eleven years in prison and four in a labor reform camp. Lin Xiling, toughened by prison, unrepentant and outspoken, left China in 1982.

Liang Heng, in 1979–80 a student leader of the democracy movement at Hunan Teachers College in Changsha, married now to American Judith Shapiro and living in the United States, serves similarly as a less dissident but articulate young spokesman for the need for democracy and human rights in China. Together with other like-minded young Chinese intellectuals, committed to the reform of their country but living abroad, he now publishes a Chinese-language journal, *The Chinese Intellectual*, in New York. Liang Heng's book *Son of the Revolution,* describing his experiences as a young middle school student during the Cultural Revolution and unquestionably the best of its genre, is reminiscent of the stories told here by Bai Meihua, Song Wuhao, Liu Zhiping, Jiang Xinren, and Song Erli—yet another perspective to the *Rashomon* that is the Great Proletarian Cultural Revolution.

But most Chinese of the Cultural Revolution generation who have been afforded the opportunity of studying abroad—the overwhelming majority of them, in fact—return to their native land. The differences between Jiang Xinren, Wang Bingzhang, and Liang Heng—those who have left their own country to take up residence abroad—and their compatriots who remain in China are profound. Late in the last century and early in this, Sun Yat-sen absented himself from China in order to foment revolution from abroad, and his efforts are credited by his countrymen (mistakenly, new studies indicate) with the final toppling of the Qing dynasty that had ruled China since 1644.

By both the Communists and the Nationalists alike Sun Yat-sen is revered as the father of the new Chinese republic. Both parties trace their roots to this founding father of modern China.

But many Chinese are suspicious today of those who leave their homeland and seek to reform—no, to revolutionize—it from abroad. Among young adults of the Cultural Revolution generation, people now in their thirties and early forties, there is a sense both that attempts to reform the system from overseas are doomed to fail and that the more successful expatriate political movements become the more likely the current reforms in China will be brought to an unfortunate and precipitate halt.

SONG ERLI is one of those who worries about expatriates like Liang Heng and what he adamantly insists on referring to as Wang Bingzhang's "most stupid *China Spring.*" When Song Erli was released from incarceration after refusing to confess during the movement to ferret out the May Sixteenth elements and was sent to work as a laborer in the cold dark pit of a mine, it took him eight long years, one step at a time, to struggle toward the light of day. In 1979, he was permitted at last to take the entrance exams for graduate study at the Chinese Academy of Sciences. He passed with all flags flying.

Song Erli is exceptional, after all he has suffered, in continuing to express nostalgia for the Great Proletarian Cultural Revolution. "Today," he says, "some people regard the entire Cultural Revolution as suffering. But at a certain stage, the Cultural Revolution was a festival, a great event. It was the only time in thirty years that the common people, the workers, the students, had a say on important matters. It was a great democracy. The main spearhead of the Cultural Revolution wasn't against the intellectuals. The spearhead was directed against the high-ranking bureaucrats. Many of those cadres were hypocrites. I was just a small potato, a nobody, but I criticized those top-ranking hypocrites and got to know a lot about what they had so successfully hidden behind their moralizing, their pomp, inside their grand mansions. They had dark sides to their lives, and this was revealed. The Cultural Revolution let people see the hypocritical side of many bureaucrats, even the top-ranking ones. Like Ye Jianying's morally degenerate sex life.

"You may say that it was all an illusion, a false democracy. But it was a democracy. Can you find any other year, any month, any day in the thirty years since Liberation when the common people had a say? It was a revolution by the people, a revolution crushed by the combined efforts of the army, Mao, Lin Biao, and the Gang of Four.

"That is why Tiananmen was such a great event. Some of the poems were directed against Mao. The most famous poem of all, more famous than any of the poems praising Zhou Enlai, was directed against Mao. It said that we are not the fools, the stupid common people, of the days of Emperor Qin Shi

Huang. It said that the days of Qin Shi Huang have passed and that feudalism is gone for good. This was the message of the Cultural Revolution. I think Tiananmen was great, because it was the reappearance of 1966 without the mistakes, without people being misled.

"There wouldn't have been such an outpouring during the Cultural Revolution if there were not such a great cry for democracy. That cry is still there. It will never be quenched. In the years to come, those of us who put up the big character posters will always look back and remember the freedom of those days and our political zeal. Even me. Even though I was looked down upon as a son of a bitch, even though I suffered from my involvement with democracy and from my blind zeal. That was the tragedy of the Cultural Revolution. But from the bottom of my heart, I loved those days."

SONG ERLI is sober, though, about the possibilities for the introduction of genuine democracy into China, more willing to accept less than his ideal than some of his compatriots who have chosen to remain abroad. So Song Erli supports the reforms of Deng Xiaoping. The lesson the Cultural Revolution taught him best was the folly of his youthful idealism. "History has shown," he says, "that in a communist country, no reform is possible unless it is led by reformists within the Communist Party itself. Yugoslavia is a successful example. The Czechoslovaks and Hungarians would have succeeded if not for foreign military interference. Poland's Solidarity was doomed to fail. It was bound to trigger a military coup d'état, just like the action of the Chinese revolutionary rebels from the fall of 1966 to the summer of 1967, which ended in military takeover."

Song Erli believes that Deng Xiaoping's reforms are still being opposed by conservative forces in the government, particularly the military. "The army remains the last bastion of Chinese feudalism," he says. "They can't forget the days when they held all the power and were actually the masters of our country. Today, just as fifteen years ago, I still consider Xu Shiyou* and other military commanders like him the main danger of a coup d'état and the end to successful reform. The only condition for a military coup d'état is an economic disaster. The army is waiting for that. On the other hand, today the former revolutionary rebels, the intellectuals, and the reformists within the party headed by Deng all share the same goals. The revolutionary rebels during the Cultural Revolution were part of a democratic movement. The movement failed. But today, Deng is carrying out its will."

What worries Song Erli, the reason he so adamantly opposes Wang Bingzhang and *China Spring*, is the possibility that vociferous public attacks launched by defectors against the Dengist regime could serve as a pretext for

*Xu Shiyou died in 1985, after the interviews recorded here.

the conservative military to marshal its forces against the reformist leader. Song worries, moreover, that defections to the United States could provoke the Chinese government into stopping, or at least slowing, the flow of students and scholars abroad. Long-term reform in China, he believes, is fundamentally dependent on the introduction and acceptance of Western ideas. The more students and scholars who study abroad, the more of them who return to China, the better off in the long run China will be.

Song Erli is one of those scholars who has had a chance to study abroad. He is one of those who has returned to China. He returned in the summer of 1983.

And shortly after he returned, Song's greatest fear appeared to be becoming reality. It was a contagious fear, infecting many other of China's intellectuals, a fear born of the Cultural Revolution and all the other political movements that preceded it, a fear more real and more profound and certainly longer-lasting than the involuntary fears so many still feel from a knock on the door or the music of "The East Is Red." Just after he arrived back in China, the conservative forces launched what seemed at first to be yet another political movement, a campaign against "spiritual pollution" from the West—an attack against "bourgeois liberalism," humanism, individualism, values that Song Erli and his colleagues had come to appreciate during their studies abroad, values they associated with the democracy they had hoped might one day come to their country.

In the midst of the campaign against spiritual pollution, a letter from Song Erli was delivered to me, hand-carried out of China.

"China, my dear motherland, my lovely country," he wrote. "I can never tell you how bitterly I love it." But Song Erli was unhappy, miserably, profoundly unhappy.

"Perhaps you remember the final lines of T. S. Eliot's poem 'Journey of the Magi'?" he continued. "I love that poem."

I did not remember, and it was several weeks before I checked:

> We returned to our places, these Kingdoms,
> But no longer at ease here, in the old dispensation,
> With an alien people clutching their gods.
> I should be glad of another death.

China has wounded its young, grievously, repeatedly, and callously wounded them. Many feel alienated and betrayed. "Why is my country doing this to me?" Song Wuhao had demanded to know after his parents had been incarcerated and he was forced to flee to the countryside, stealing sweet potatoes from peasants and drinking water from streams. "This was a revolution and this is what the revolution was giving me."

What is most remarkable about China's young is not that their patriotic ties are tenuous but that they exist at all. For many of China's young remain deeply patriotic, committed to the service of their country. Patriotism still serves as a motive force propelling the country forward. Song Wuhao believed that he was speaking for all of China's youth when, after deploring what the revolution was giving him, he added, "But even in those darkest moments, I still loved my country. I was still patriotic. I still loved the Chinese people, the peasants and the workers."

Today, the dream that Song Wuhao has dreamed since he was only a little boy, the dream that led him initially into fanaticism, has finally come true. Song Wuhao has become a part of the circle. In 1982, his application for membership in the Chinese Communist Party was approved.

The other part of his dream has become a reality as well. Upon graduating from Qinghua University, Song Wuhao went on to graduate school at the Chinese Academy of Sciences, of which he became a member. Song Wuhao is a scientist now, a scientist at last. His patriotism has not diminished. "My responsibilities to my country are great," he says, "and the road ahead is difficult. The future of China belongs to us, the younger generation. The older generation will die off soon. I want to use my strength, my talents, my abilities, in the service of my country. Each person's talents and abilities are limited, so each of us has to give everything we have. It can't just be me and a few others. My entire generation must give. This includes the generation of peasant youth as well. They aren't stupid. They just haven't been educated. If they had the chance, they probably could study better than I. So now I feel I can contribute to the progress of my country and help my people. Now I have hope again."

Li Weiguo, too, prohibited earlier from joining the party because his unemployed father who had died on the streets from starvation had nonetheless once worked for the Guomindang, is also part of the circle now. He, too, has been granted membership in the party. "China needs me," Li Weiguo says.

But surprisingly patriotic though many of the Cultural Revolution generation remain, their patriotism is different in essence from that of the older generation, the generation of Huang Chaoqun, You Xiaoli, and Hu Guangzhi. One of the many unintended consequences of the Cultural Revolution is a widening gap between the generations, and one of the distinctions between young and old is a different sense of what it means to be Chinese, a fundamental difference in how the generations conceive of themselves.

Nurtured on the milk of socialism and revolution, educated in the love of socialist and revolutionary China, not love of China itself, the patriotism of China's young is tentative, provisional, judgmental. It is a patriotism that demands reciprocity, expecting something in return. It is the generation of Liang Heng and Song Erli who hurl to their elders the question posed by Bai

Hua in the movie *Unrequited Love,* the question for which the movie was banned: "Dad, you love our country. Through bitter frustration you go on loving her. But, Dad, does this country love you?"

The younger generation looks to the future, to reform and change. Its links to the past are tenuous. The China of culture and tradition and history is a China the young were educated to attack. The campaign against the "four olds" was a campaign against a fundamental part of China itself.

Among the older generation, horrified by the destruction caused by the campaign against the four olds, is a sense of the link between present and past that is possible only in a country as old and as laden with tradition as China and only on the part of individuals with a profound respect for their past. "When I was first beaten so brutally by the young Red Guards," Hu Guangzhi reports, "I had to ask myself what I was here for, whether there was any meaning to my life, whether it was worth living. My family originally had been very poor, from the poorest area of Gansu. Then in the Song dynasty, sometime in the tenth or eleventh century, they migrated to Shanxi. There things were better but still not that good. I thought of my father and his father and his father's father. All of them had suffered. So I thought that this was my fate. This was what I had to suffer, just as they had suffered, for the modernization of my country."

For some of the elder generation, it is not just that suffering is part of fate and therefore to be expected but that suffering is part of the definition of what it means to be Chinese. To be Chinese is to have suffered in China. To members of the older generation like Huang Chaoqun and You Xiaoli, those who through absence escaped suffering cannot be considered fully Chinese. However devoted some Chinese-Americans may be to serving the land of their ancestors, Huang Chaoqun can no longer accept them as Chinese. "They didn't suffer," he says. "They didn't go through the antirightist campaign or the Cultural Revolution."

"I don't like Liang Heng, either," he continues. "Liang Heng is someone who ran away from China. I look down on people who go to the United States and don't come back. The younger generation, like Liang Heng, they don't have the same ties of suffering and happiness with our people."

You Xiaoli concurs. "I would rather suffer together with my countrymen, starve with my countrymen, eat bad food, than be separated from my fellow compatriots. That's a Chinese attitude. You have to be proud of your country, your people. You have to do your part. My ancestors were traitors. They sold their country to foreigners. The warlords had the Japanese, the Guomindang had the Americans, the Communist Party had the Russians. Many sectors of the Chinese people had foreign people who supported them, making us more backward, backward, backward. This is what our ancestors did, so we suffered. So I have to work for the better future of my people, and maybe after ten or twenty generations, maybe my descendants can enjoy their lives like the Americans, maybe even better.

"We have a saying," she continues, "that 'a golden house, a silver house, still isn't as good as my own straw house.' Even dogs, no matter how poor the family, will never run away to a rich family. A dog would rather starve together with his poor family. I don't think we should be worse than dogs. We should at least be the same as dogs. That's why I don't like the Soviet writers like Solzhenitsyn. I don't like the Soviet writers who desert their homeland. A person should suffer everything with his own people.

"Maybe it's because of all the blood and tears that I have shed for this land. My mother's tears flowed on this land, and her blood, too. My mother's corpse is buried somewhere on this land. I haven't suffered as much as my mother did, but this is still where my blood was shed, too. This is where I have suffered for more than half a century. My tears have watered this land. My blood has watered this land. So I want to wait and see the flowers growing from it. If I don't work for my people, I would feel as though I had betrayed my mother."

For the elder generation of Chinese, the circle into which they would step is linked not by politics but by nationhood, by a devotion to their country and its people regardless of rulers.

To the older generation, to be Chinese is to live, even in suffering, and to die in China.

Liang Aihua is a returned overseas Chinese and heir to a family fortune waiting for her outside China. She and her husband, both scientists with advanced degrees, went back to China with their children in 1965, a year before the Cultural Revolution began. Liang Aihua's story has not been told here. For Liang Aihua, as for the Chinese government itself, the Cultural Revolution is a thing of the past. It is a past whose memories are too painful to recount, one she is not willing to resurrect. Liang Aihua lost both her husband and a son to China's Great Proletarian Cultural Revolution. At the conclusion of that decade, as restitutions were being made, Liang Aihua was approached by high Chinese officials and assured, in light of what she had suffered, that they would surely understand should she choose to leave. She chose to stay.

"Why do I choose to stay and work in my fatherland?" she asked. "China is a large country, and its population is huge. But its science and technology, its education and culture, are backward. The standard of living of its people is low. Every Chinese is going to have to work hard for the development of the country. If China could become richer and stronger more quickly, that would be good for the rest of the world, too. I am happy with my work right now. I have had the opportunity to study abroad, and I believe that what I am doing now is still of use to my country. That is the reason I stay. I am Chinese."

METHODOLOGICAL NOTE

THE technique I used in the interviews
upon which most of this book is based
was a psychological one, and more specifically, the type of interview technique that
such psychologists as Carl Rogers would
describe as "nondirected, empathetic,
and client-oriented." It is a technique I
learned through private consultations
with a psychiatrist for three hours a week
during the three months before I left for
China. While there were some basic bio-
graphical questions I tried to pursue with
everyone, I used no questionnaire, or
even an implied questionnaire. Rather, I
attempted to allow these people to relate
their own stories, and the stories of their
families and friends, in the manner that
had most meaning for them. The themes,
patterns, and threads that provide the
texture of this book thus emerge from the
interviews themselves rather than from
any preconceived sense of what those patterns would or should be.

My interviews in China were of two
types. Eight took place under the official
auspices of the Chinese Academy of

Social Sciences. These tended to be relatively short, lasting usually from three to four hours. With rare exceptions, these interviews tended to be more stilted, less revelatory, and less spontaneous than those conducted on my own. My research assistant was present at each of them, and usually one or more representatives of the Institute of Literature also attended.

The remaining forty-one interviews, including those conducted in the United States, were private, arranged through personal contacts. These meetings were much more lengthy, with many extending over a period of several months and some over a period of years. I have been able to interview one person for several hundred hours, two people for well over two hundred hours, and several others for over a hundred. Most lasted a total of between fifteen and sixty hours.

The people whose stories are presented here proved to be very uncomfortable with any attempt to tape-record our conversations. Quotations therefore are as accurate a representation of the actual words spoken as my note-taking and translation skills permit. Many of the quotations have actually been verified by the people who spoke them. The stories of such public personages as Liu Shaoqi, Tao Zhu, Wu Han, and Lao She which are included here are based primarily on published documents and no effort has therefore been necessary to protect their anonymity. The names of people I interviewed, however, have been changed to protect their anonymity, as have certain revelatory details. Occasionally, when the person speaking makes reference to particular people or events that would not be immediately clear to the nonspecialist reader, I have added brief identifying phrases, and the sentences as quoted in the text are not always presented in the precise sequence in which they were spoken.

Since so much of the material contained in the text is based on spoken interviews rather than written sources, I have rejected the conventional footnote format. Important references are to be found at the end of the book, identified by the chapter and page on which the reference was used. Finally, for the convenience of the nonspecialist reader, Chinese weights and measures in the text have been converted into equivalents familiar to the American reader. For interested specialists, it should be noted that American dollar equivalents for the Chinese yuan were arrived at by valuing the yuan at fifty cents. With the exception of China's capital city ("Peking" to most Westerners, "Beijing" in *pinyin*), most place names appear in *pinyin* spelling.

REFERENCES

PREFACE

p. iii For the description of the death of popular
novelist Zhao Shuli, see Chen Dengke, "Yinian Zhao
Shuli Tongzhi" ("In Commemoration of Comrade
Zhao Shuli"), in *Huiyi yu Daonian (Reminiscences
and Memorials)* (Hong Kong: Chunhui Publishers,
1979), pp. 118–119.

p. xi For a useful anthology of different perspectives
on the Cultural Revolution, see Richard Baum with
Louise B. Bennett, eds., *China in Ferment* (Engle-
wood Cliffs, N.J.: Prentice-Hall, 1971). For what is
still the best general overview of the early years of the
Cultural Revolution, see Stanley Karnow, *Mao and
China: From Revolution to Revolution* (New York:
Viking, 1972). Edward E. Rice, *Mao's Way* (Berkeley
and Los Angeles: University of California Press, 1972),
also covers the Cultural Revolution well. For a variety
of perspectives about the Cultural Revolution, see
Philip Bridgham, "Mao's 'Cultural Revolution': Ori-
gin and Development," *China Quarterly*, no. 29
(January–March 1967) and no. 34 (April–June 1968);
Lowell Dittmer, *Liu Shao-ch'i and the Chinese Cultu-
ral Revolution: The Politics of Mass Criticism* (Berkeley and Los Angeles: University of California Press,
1978); Robert Jay Lifton, *Revolutionary Immortality:
Mao Tse-tung and the Chinese Cultural Revolution*
(New York: Vintage, 1968); Hong Yung Lee, *The
Politics of the Chinese Cultural Revolution: A Case
Study* (Berkeley and Los Angeles: University of Cali-
fornia Press, 1978); Stanley Rosen, *Red Guard Fac-
tionalism and the Cultural Revolution in Guangzhou
(Canton)* (Boulder, Colo.: Westview Press, 1982);

Parris H. Chang, "Regional Military Power: The Aftermath of the Cultural Revolution," *Asian Survey*, vol. XII, no. 12 (December 1972); Jurgen Domes, *China After the Cultural Revolution: Politics Between Two Party Congresses* (Berkeley and Los Angeles: University of California Press, 1975 and 1977); Michael Ying-mao Kao, *The Lin Piao Affair: Power Politics and Military Coup* (White Plains, N.Y.: International Arts and Sciences Press, 1975); Jack Gray, "The Economics of Maoism," in *China after the Cultural Revolution* (New York: Random House, 1969); Jean Daubier, *A History of the Chinese Cultural Revolution* (New York: Vintage, 1971).

p. xii   For the origins of the Cultural Revolution, the continuing study of Roderick MacFarquhar is the most definitive. See Roderick MacFarquhar, *Origins of the Cultural Revolution*, Vol. I, *Contradictions Among the People* (New York: Columbia University Press, 1974), and Vol. II, *The Great Leap Forward* (New York: Columbia University Press, 1983). See also Theodore White, *Roots of Madness* (New York: Norton, 1968); Richard Baum, *Prelude to Revolution: Mao, the Party, and the Peasant Question, 1962–1966* (New York: Columbia University Press, 1975); and Richard Baum and Frederick C. Teiwes, *Ssu-Ch'ing: The Socialist Education Movement of 1962–1966* (Berkeley: Center for Chinese Studies, 1968).

For perspectives on China from people who have lived there recently, see especially Richard Bernstein, *From the Center of the Earth: The Search for the Truth about China* (Boston: Little, Brown, 1982); David Bonavia, *The Chinese* (New York: Lippincott & Crowell, 1980); Fox Butterfield, *China: Alive in the Bitter Sea* (New York: Times Books, 1982); John Fraser, *The Chinese: Portrait of a People* (New York: Summit, 1980), Jay and Linda Mathews, *One Billion: A China Chronicle* (New York: Random House, 1983); Steven W. Mosher, *Broken Earth: The Rural Chinese* (New York: Free Press, 1983).

For firsthand accounts from those who participated in or witnessed the Cultural Revolution, see Gordon Bennett and Ronald N. Montaperto, *Red Guard: The Political Biography of Dai Hsiao-ai* (Garden City, N.Y.: Doubleday, 1971); B. Michael Frolic, *Mao's People: Sixteen Portraits of Life in Revolutionary China* (Cambridge, Mass.: Harvard University Press, 1980); Neale Hunter, *Shanghai Journal: An Eyewitness Account of the Cultural Revolution* (New York: Praeger, 1969); Liang Heng and Judith Shapiro, *Son of the Revolution* (New York: Knopf, 1983); Ken Ling, *Revenge of Heaven* (New York: Putnam, 1972); Ruth Earnshaw Lo, *In the Eye of the Typhoon* (New York: Harcourt Brace Jovanovich, 1980); David Milton and Nancy Dall Milton, *The Wind Will Not Subside: Years in Revolutionary China—1964–1969* (New York: Pantheon, 1976); Sidney Shapiro, *An American in China: Thirty Years in the People's Republic* (New York: New American Library, 1979); and Yue Daiyun with Carolyn Wakeman, *To the Storm* (Berkeley: University of California Press, 1985).

For studies without an exclusive focus on the developments of the Cultural Revolution but which focus on particular groups or sectors of Chinese society that suffered during that period, see Thomas P. Bernstein, *Up to the Mountains and Down to the Villages: The Transfer of Youth from Urban to Rural China* (New Haven: Yale University Press, 1977); Deborah Davis-Friedman, *Long Lives: Chinese Elderly and the Communist Revolution* (Cambridge, Mass.: Harvard University Press, 1983); Merle Goldman, *China's Intellectuals: Advise and Dissent* (Cambridge, Mass.: Harvard University Press, 1981); and Susan Shirk, *Competitive Comrades: Career Incentives and Student Strategies in China* (Berkeley and Los Angeles: University of California Press, 1982).

p. xix   The description of the Cultural Revolution as a "human tragedy on the grand scale" is from Roderick MacFarquhar, *Origins of the Cultural Revolution*, Vol. I, p. 3.

p. xix   "Revolutions are ruptures of conscience" is from Harold Lasswell, *Politics: Who Gets What, When, How* (New York and Cleveland: Meridian, 1971), p. 42.

CHAPTER ONE

This chapter is based both on interviews with people who participated in the Tiananmen demonstrations and on published sources. The 1976 chronology of events in China can easily be followed in the *Peking Review* for that year.

By far the most useful source for a chronology of what happened at Tiananmen Square during Qing Ming festival 1976 is a picture book, *Renmin de Daonian (The People's Memorial)* (Peking: Peking Publishing House, January 1979). Also very useful is a lengthy article, "Mingyun" ("Fate"), *Dangdai,*

April 1979, pp. 4–65. Many of the Tiananmen poems are translated in *Chinese Literature*, no. 3 (1979).
p. 6 The story of the peasant belief that Zhou Enlai was both descended from and returned to the stars is told by the young man who appears in this book as Song Wuhao and his brother, both of whom were in the countryside at the time of Zhou's death. The belief is clearly based on Zhuge Liang in *The Romance of the Three Kingdoms* and is widely known to many Chinese.
pp. 9–10 There are a number of analyses of those who were China's leaders in 1976. For Mao, see the autobiographical account in Edgar Snow, *Red Star over China* (New York: Grove, 1961); Stuart Schram, *Mao Tse-tung* (Baltimore: Penguin, 1974); Stuart R. Schram, ed. and intro., *Chairman Mao Talks to the People: Talks and Letters, 1956–1971* (New York: Pantheon, 1974); and Dick Wilson, ed., *Mao Tse-tung in the Scales of History: A Preliminary Assessment Organized by the China Quarterly* (New York and London: Cambridge University Press, 1977).

On Mao's wife, Jiang Qing, see Roxane Witke, *Comrade Chiang Ch'ing* (Boston: Little, Brown, 1977) based on interviews with Jiang Qing; and Ross Terrill, *The White Boned Demon: A Biography of Madame Mao Zedong* (New York: Morrow, 1984). Many of the rumors that circulated about Jiang Qing in Tiananmen Square in April 1976 are almost certainly false, and neither Roxane Witke nor Ross Terrill even mention, for instance, her alleged affair with Zhang Chunqiao. Mao's peccadilloes (but not allegations of his fathering a child) are widely credited.

For the most recent biography of Zhou Enlai, see Dick Wilson, *Zhou Enlai: A Biography* (New York: Viking, 1984).

For a lengthy analysis of Hua Guofeng, see Michel Oksenberg and Sai-cheung Yeung, "Hua Kuo-feng's Pre-Cultural Revolution Hunan Years, 1946–1966: The Making of a Political Generalist," *China Quarterly*, no. 69 (March 1977), pp. 3–54. See also Andres D. Onate, "Hua Guofeng and the Arrest of the 'Gang of Four,'" *China Quarterly*, no. 75 (September 1978), pp. 540–565.
p. 15 The account by a Westerner who was in Tiananmen Square on Saturday, April 3, is David S. Zweig, "The Peita Debate on Education and the Fall of Teng Hsiao-p'ing," *China Quarterly*, no. 73 (March 1978), pp. 140–159.
p. 17 For support for the argument that scatology had long been employed in China as the finishing touch in accusations against foes, see Paul A. Cohen, *China and Christianity: The Missionary Movement and the Growth of Chinese Antiforeignism, 1860–1870* (Cambridge, Mass.: Harvard University Press, 1963), pp. 49–58. Late in the nineteenth century, Christians in China were particularly subject to accusations of lascivious behavior and obscene and barbaric customs. Priests, it was said, were castrated in their youth, and converts to the faith were forced to commit sodomy with them. On Sundays, following the Christian service, whole congregations were said to copulate together in great mass orgies of joy. Christians were said to delight in drinking women's menses, an allegation that provided the additional explanation of why the Christian barbarians smelled so terrible.
pp. 21–2 Derk Bodde's *China's First Unifier: A Study of the Ch'in Dynasty as Seen in the Life of Li Ssu* (Leiden: E. J. Brill, 1938) is still an excellent source on Qin Shi Huangdi and is the source (p. 11) of the quote about the burning of the books and the undying odium of Chinese scholars.
pp. 24–5 The story of Tangshan in the aftermath of the earthquake is told by a former PLA soldier who was there. See also *After the Tangshan Earthquake: How the Chinese People Overcame a Major Natural Disaster* (Peking: Foreign Languages Press, 1976).
p. 27 Arthur Miller's metaphor is from Inge Morath and Arthur Miller, *Chinese Encounters* (New York: Farrar, Straus & Giroux, 1979), p. 52. Miller's book is a superb account of the persecution and recovery of many Cultural Revolution victims in the arts. Miller's *The Crucible*, a play about the Salem witch trials, is widely read by intellectuals in China and is viewed by them metaphorically as about the Cultural Revolution.

CHAPTER TWO

pp. 30–1 A description of the visit to the United States of the first delegation of social scientists and humanists can be found in Anne F. Thurston, "New Opportunities for Research in China," *Items*, vol. 33, no. 2 (June 1979), pp. 13–25.
p. 31 It was to Harvard graduate student David Arkush that Wilma Fairbank gave her files on Fei Xiaotong. Arkush has since published a book on Fei. See R. David Arkush, *Fei Xiaotong and Sociology*

in Revolutionary China (Cambridge, Mass.: Harvard University Council on East Asian Studies, 1981). A number of Fei's own writings from the 1930s are available in English. Qian Zhongshu's wife, Yang Jiang, has written about their experience in the May Seventh Cadre School. See *Ganxiao Liu Ji (Six Sketches from a Cadre School)* (Peking: Xinzhi San Lian Publishers, 1981).

p. 31   A report on the fact-finding delegation to China can be found in Anne F. Thurston and Jason H. Parker, *Humanistic and Social Science Research in China: Recent History and Future Prospects* (New York: Social Science Research Council, 1980).

p. 33   For Camus's argument that human evidence must be preserved, see Albert Camus, *Resistance, Rebellion and Death* (New York: Modern Library, 1963).

p. 42   The story of the errant schoolboy may be found in Alphonse Daudet, "The Last Lesson," in *Monday Tales* (Boston: Little, Brown, 1901), pp. 1–9, or, in the original French, in Alphonse Daudet, *Contes du Lundi* (Paris: G. Charpentier, 1881), pp. 1–12.

pp. 45–6   The quotation about dancing in the ring is from Milan Kundera, *The Book of Laughter and Forgetting* (New York: Penguin Books, 1980), pp. 65–66.

p. 47   Liu Shaoqi's *How to Be a Good Communist* is available in English. See *Collected Works of Liu Shao-ch'i Before 1944* (Kowloon, Hong Kong, 1969), pp. 151–283.

p. 53   "This is a memory book" is from Studs Terkel, *Hard Times: An Oral History of the Great Depression* (New York: Washington Square Press, 1970), p. 17.

CHAPTER THREE

p. 55   Nie Yuanzi's big character poster can be read in *Survey of the China Mainland Press*, no. 3719.

An excellent source on the May Fourth Movement and on the role of Peking University during that time is Chow Tse-tsung, *The May Fourth Movement* (Cambridge, Mass.: Harvard University Press, 1960).

p. 56   Mao's statement that to the intellectual elite of Beida he didn't exist as a human being is to be found in Edgar Snow, *Red Star over China*, p. 151.

On the founding of the Chinese Communist Party and its rise to power, see Benjamin I. Schwartz, *Chinese Communism and the Rise of Mao* (Cambridge, Mass.: Harvard University Press, 1951).

pp. 57–8   For Zhou Peiyuan's confession, see Theodore H. E. Chen, *Thought Reform of the Chinese Intellectuals* (Hong Kong: Hong Kong University Press, 1960), p. 63.

p. 58   For Lu Zhiwei's statement, see Lu Chih-wei, "U.S. Imperialist Cultural Aggression as Seen in Yenching University," in Stewart Fraser, ed., *Chinese Communist Education: Records of the First Decade* (Nashville: Vanderbilt University Press, 1965), pp. 104–111. For his daughter's attack, see Lu Yaohua, "I Denounce My Father, Lu Chih-wei," in the same volume, pp. 136–141.

p. 60   For the statement that the peasantry provided the Communist Party with some 70 percent of its membership, see Suzanne Pepper, "Educational Development 1949–1957," in *The Cambridge History of China*, Volume 14: *The Emergence of Revolutionary China* (forthcoming).

Lucian W. Pye has written about the problem of modernizing China without modern men. See *The Spirit of Chinese Politics* (Cambridge, Mass.: M.I.T. Press, 1968), pp. 36–50.

p. 60   Lu Xun has written about drinking the blood of executed criminals for health and strength. See "Medicine," in *Selected Stories of Lu Hsun* (Peking: Foreign Languages Press, 1972), pp. 25–34.

For the statement that 70 percent of the men and 99 percent of the women in China were illiterate, see again Suzanne Pepper, "Educational Development 1949–1957."

p. 61   The story of Bishop Ignatius Gong Pinmei is told in *China: Violations of Human Rights* (London: Amnesty International Publications, 1984), pp. 19–21. His release was reported in the *New York Times*, July 4, 1985.

p. 62   The figure of 800,000 liquidations between 1949 and 1954 was reported by the *New York Times*, June 13, 1957, based on a report from Warsaw, before the final, revised version of Mao's speech was made public. The figure has not been repeated.

For Lin Xiling's statements during the Hundred Flowers movement, see Dennis J. Doolin, *Communist China: The Politics of Student Opposition* (Stanford: Hoover Institution of War, Revolution, and Peace, Stanford University, 1964), pp. 23–43; and Roderick MacFarquhar, ed., with an epilogue by G. F. Hudson, *The Hundred Flowers* (London: Stevens & Sons Limited Atlantic Books, 1960), pp.

140–141. Lin Xiling left China in 1982 and took up residence in France. She visited the United States in the winter of 1984–85. See Jean Leclerc du Sabon and Ba San, "Chine: souvenirs d'une idéaliste incorrigible" ("China: Memoirs of an Incorrigible Idealist"), *L'Express*, November 4–10, 1983, pp. 143–158.

p. 62   Zhou Enlai's estimate of support from China's intellectuals can be found in Theodore H. E. Chen, *Thought Reform of the Chinese Intellectuals*, p. 101.

pp. 63–5   The quotations from intellectuals during the Hundred Flowers movement are from Roderick MacFarquhar, *The Hundred Flowers*, and Theodore H. E. Chen, *Thought Reform of the Chinese Intellectuals*. The names of those who engaged in the criticisms are real.

p. 74   For an examination of Mao in Moscow in 1957, see Roderick MacFarquhar, *Origins of the Cultural Revolution*, Vol. II, pp. 8–19.

For one example of some of the fantastic claims that were being made for increases in agriculture, see Tao Zhu, "Refutation of the 'Theory of Limited Increase' in Food Production," *Red Flag*, no. 5 (August 1, 1958), translated in *Joint Publications Research Service*, #7837, pp. 39–51.

p. 75   For the Kwangtung figures, see "Kwangtung Party Conference Reviews Crop Conditions," *People's Daily*, May 31, 1959, translated in *Survey of the China Mainland Press*, #2032. For the national figures, see Basil Ashton, Kenneth Hill, Alan Piazza, and Robin Zeitz, "Famine in China, 1958–61," *Population and Development Review*, Vol. 10, no. 4 (December 1984), pp. 613–644.

p. 77   See Anna Louise Strong, *China's Fight for Grain* (Peking: New World Press, 1963), pp. 7, 39.

pp. 77–8   See Tao Zhu, "Literature and Arts for the Countryside," *Survey of the China Mainland Press*, #2992.

p. 79   For Minister of Defense Peng Dehuai's reservations during the Great Leap Forward, see *The Case of Peng Teh-huai, 1959–1968* (Kowloon, Hong Kong: Union Research Institute, 1968); and Roderick MacFarquhar, *Origins of the Cultural Revolution*, Vol. II, pp. 187–255.

pp. 79–80   For recent demographic studies of the "three bad years," see Basil Ashton et al., "Famine in China, 1958–61"; and Ansley J. Coale, *Rapid Population Change in China, 1952–1982*, Committee on Population and Demography, Report #27, National Research Council (Washington, D.C.: National Academy Press, 1984).

p. 80   For figures on the increase in life expectancy and decrease in infant mortality, see William C. Hsiao, "Transformation of Health Care in China," *New England Journal of Medicine*, vol. 310, no. 14 (April 5, 1984), pp. 932–936. For somewhat different figures on life expectancy, see Judith Bannister, "An Analysis of Recent Data on the Population of China," *Population and Development Review*, vol. 10, no. 2 (June 1984), pp. 241–271. For a comparative analysis of the crisis of the three bad years and a conservative approach to the number of possible deaths, see Thomas P. Bernstein, "Stalinism, Famine, and Chinese Peasants: Grain Procurement During the Great Leap Forward," *Theory and Society*, vol. 13, no. 3 (May 1984), pp. 339–377.

p. 81   For numerous instances of corruption during the recent Cambodian famine, see William Shawcross, *The Quality of Mercy* (New York: Simon and Schuster, 1984).

p. 83   See Milovan Djilas, *The New Class: An Analysis of the Communist System* (New York: Praeger, 1957).

p. 84   With respect to the question of whether Mao had a college education, Mao's biographer says, "The First Normal School [from which Mao graduated] was officially considered an institution of secondary education, and not of higher education. In a sense, therefore, Mao never acquired a university education. But the standards at the school were high, and in fact he learned as much as he might have done at a provincial university." See Stuart Schram, *Mao Tse-tung*, p. 37.

p. 85   The discussion on Lu Xun, *zawen*, and Wu Han is taken almost entirely from James R. Pusey, *Wu Han: Attacking the Present Through the Past* (Cambridge, Mass.: Harvard University East Asian Research Center, 1969).

p. 88   For a thorough analysis of Mao's changing conception of class and its implications for Chinese society, see Richard Curt Kraus, *Class Conflict in Chinese Socialism* (New York: Columbia University Press, 1981).

CHAPTER FOUR

p. 95 The text of the "Sixteen Points" can be found in Richard Baum, *China in Ferment*, pp. 99–107.

Chairman Mao's letter to the Red Guards of Qinghua Middle School can be found in Stuart Schram, ed., *Chairman Mao Talks to the People*, pp. 260–262.

pp. 96–7 For the classic description of the Long March, see Edgar Snow, *Red Star over China*, p. 190.

p. 103 For the case of Lü Liuliang, whose body was disinterred and decapitated decades after his death, see Thomas Stephen Fisher, "Lu Liu-liang (1629–83) and the Tseng Ching Case (1728–33)" (unpublished Ph. D. dissertation, Princeton University, 1964).

p. 104 See John Avedon, *In Exile from the Land of Snow* (New York: Knopf, 1985).

p. 105 This passage is from *ibid.*

p. 107 Lowell Dittmer, *Liu Shao-ch'i and the Chinese Cultural Revolution*. The quotation is on p. 3.

Liu Shaoqi's statements to his children are told by his children, Liu Pingping, Liu Yuan, and Liu Tingting, in "Shengli di Shenghua Xian gei Nin: Huainian women de Baba Liu Shaoqi" ("Presenting You the Flowers of Victory: Remembering Our Father, Liu Shaoqi"), *Gongren Ribao (Workers' Daily)*, December 5, 8, and 12, 1980. I am grateful to Madame Liu Shaoqi (Wang Guangmei) for giving me these articles. A daughter by an earlier marriage, Liu Aiqin, has also written about her father. See *Nuer de Huainian: Huiyi Fuqin Liu Shaoqi (Reminiscences of a Daughter: Remembering My Father, Liu Shaoqi)* (Hebei: Hebei People's Publishers, 1980).

p. 108 The accounting of the extent of purges during the Cultural Revolution can be found in Jurgen Domes, *China After the Cultural Revolution: Politics Between Two Party Congresses* (Berkeley and Los Angeles: University of California Press, 1975).

p. 109 For traditional rules holding a whole family accountable and liable to execution for the crimes of one member, see Wallace Johnson, trans., *The T'ang Code: Volume I, General Principles* (Princeton, N.J.: Princeton University Press, 1979), pp. 18–21.

p. 111 For an unattributed translation of Yu Luoke's "origin theory," see Gordon White, *The Politics of Class and Class Origin: The Case of the Cultural Revolution* (Canberra: Australian National University Contemporary China Center, 1976). For an article eulogizing Yu Luoke and describing his death, see "Huapo yemu de yunxing: ji sixiang jiefang de xianqu Yu Luoke") ("A Meteorite Breaks the Curtain of Night: Remembering the Pioneer in Liberating Thought Yu Luoke"), *Guangming Ribao*, July 21 and 22, 1980. Yu Luoke's sister, Yu Luojin, has also written about her brother in "Yige Dongtian de Tonghua" ("A Winter's Fairy Tale").

pp. 111–12 The story of Maomei's mother is told in Xu Huaizhong, "Xixian Yishi" ("Anecdote from the Western Front"), in *1980 Duanpian Xiaoshuo (Short Stories of 1980)* (Peking: People's Literature Publishing House, 1981), pp. 30–80. Tang Lin's story can be found in Lu Wenfu, "Dedication," in Lu Xinhua et al., *The Wounded: New Stories of the Cultural Revolution, 1977–78*, trans. by Geremie Barme and Bennett Lee (Hong Kong: Joint Publishing, 1979). Many short stories and short novels from China about the Cultural Revolution have now been translated. For some of the best, see Chen Jo-hsi, *The Execution of Mayor Yin and Other Stories from the Great Proletarian Cultural Revolution* (Bloomington: Indiana University Press, 1978); Helen Siu and Zelda Stern, eds., *Mao's Harvest: Voices from China's New Generation* (New York: Oxford University Press, 1983); Liu Binyan, *People or Monsters? And Other Stories and Reportage from China After Mao*, ed. by Perry Link (Bloomington: Indiana University Press, 1983); Perry Link, ed., *Stubborn Weeds: Chinese Literature After the Cultural Revolution* (Bloomington: Indiana University Press, 1983); Gu Hua, *A Small Town Called Hibiscus* (Peking: Panda Books, 1983); Yang Jiang, "Six Chapters from My Life 'Downunder,'" trans. by Howard Goldblatt, *Renditions*, no. 16 (Autumn 1981).

pp. 116–17 For the house search in China's most famous novel, see *The Dream of the Red Chamber: A Chinese Novel of the Early Ching Period* (New York: Grosset & Dunlap, 1958), pp. 529–541. For the contemporary literary description of a house search, see Zong Pu, *San Sheng Shi (Stone of the Three Reincarnations)* (Tianjin: Hundred Flowers Arts and Literature Publishers, 1981), pp. 129–133.

p. 118 For Lu Xun's explanation of why he gave up medicine, see *Selected Stories*, pp. 2–3. "The True Story of Ah Q" is included in the same volume, pp. 65–113.

For Mao's "Report on an Investigation of the Peasant Movement in Hunan," see *Selected Works of Mao Tse-tung* (Peking: Foreign Languages Press, 1967), pp. 23–59.

p. 121 The story of Liu Shaoqi's youngest daughter crying out at the struggle session against her parents is told in the previously cited series of articles by his children.

p. 122 The struggle session against Wang Guangmei at Qinghua University is described in several sources. See Ken Ling, *Revenge of Heaven*, pp. 198–214; Stanley Karnow, *Mao and China*, pp. 326–331; Edward Rice, *Mao's Way*, pp. 344–347; Lowell Dittmer, *Liu Shao-ch'i and the Chinese Cultural Revolution*, pp. 103–104. For an entire book on the Cultural Revolution at Qinghua University, see William Hinton, *Hundred Day War: The Cultural Revolution at Tsinghua University* (New York: Monthly Review Press, 1972).

p. 123 The scene outside Zhongnanhai in July is described in Lowell Dittmer, *Liu Shao-ch'i and the Chinese Cultural Revolution*, pp. 105–106. Both the struggle session of July 18 and the one of August 5 are described in the previously cited article in *Gongren Ribao* by his children.

p. 126 The description of Qincheng prison outside Peking where Wang Guangmei was incarcerated is from Wei Jingsheng, "A Twentieth Century Bastille," in James D. Seymour, ed., *The Fifth Modernization: China's Human Rights Movement, 1978–1979* (Stanfordville, N. Y.: Human Rights Publishing Group, 1980), pp. 214–219.

pp. 129–30 The description of what happened to Wu Han's children is in Liao Liao, "Xiangqi Wu Xiaoyan—Wu Han de Nuerl" ("Thinking About Wu Xiaoyan—Wu Han's Daughter"), in *Huiyi yu Daonian (Reminiscences and Memorials)*, pp. 38–42.

The visit by her children to Wang Guangmei in prison is told by her children in the previously cited *Gongren Ribao* article.

p. 131 Information about the photographs of basketfuls of noses and ears as well as the number of cities in which there were major outbreaks of violence was given to me in personal conversation by Allen Whiting, deputy consulate general in Hong Kong from September 6, 1966, to September 5, 1968.

CHAPTER FIVE

p. 133 For reference to Yang Hansheng reading more than a hundred names of writers and artists who died during the Cultural Revolution, and for many of the speeches during the Fourth Congress of Writers and Artists, see Howard Goldblatt, ed., *Chinese Literature for the 1980s: The Fourth Congress of Writers and Artists* (Armonk, N. Y.: M. E. Sharpe, 1982).

p. 133 For figures on those the Gang of Four is alleged to have persecuted to death, see *A Great Trial in Chinese History: The Trial of the Lin Biao and Jiang Qing Counter-Revolutionary Cliques, Nov. 1980–Jan. 1981* (Peking: New World Press, 1981), pp. 20–21. The information on the bodies washing into Hong Kong is from a conversation with Allen Whiting, cited earlier.

pp. 133–4 The description of the death of Wu Han is by his son, Wu Zhang, in "Xing Cunzhe de Huiyi" ("Reminiscences of a Fortunate Survivor"), in *Wu Han he "Hai Rui Bagoan" (Wu Han and "Hai Rui Dismissed from Office")* (Peking: People's Publishing House, 1979), pp. 103–114.

p. 136 The stories of the atrocities in Tibet come again from John Avedon, *In Exile from the Land of Snow*.

p. 137 Lao She's novel was published in the United States as Lau Shaw, *Rickshaw Boy* (New York: Reynal & Hitchcock, 1945). For the "official" descriptions of Lao She's death, see Wu Boxiao, "Zuozhe, Jiaoshou, Shiyou" ("Writer, Teacher, Friend"), *Beijing Wenyi (Peking Literature and Arts)*, July 1978; and "Renmin Yishu Jia de Ai he Zeng" ("The Love and Hate of a People's Artist"), *Beijing Ribao (Peking Daily)*, August 24, 1978.

p. 138 For Tao Zhu's statement about suicide, see Tao Siliang, "Yifeng Zhongyu Fachu de Xin: Gei Wo de Baba Tao Zhu" ("A Letter Posted at Last: To My Father, Tao Zhu"), *Renmin Ribao (People's Daily)*, December 11, 1978. Until the Cultural Revolution, Gao Gang, leading official in China's northeast in the early years after Liberation, was the only high-ranking Communist Party official to commit suicide in political disgrace. The announcement of his death took his suicide as proof of his guilt and of his final betrayal of the revolution.

p. 140   Mao's 1965 statement on Jian Bocan and Wu Han can be found in Stuart Schram, ed., *Chairman Mao Talks to the People*, p. 254.

Fu Lei's letters to his pianist son, Fu Cong, while Fu Cong was studying in Eastern Europe and then living in England have been published posthumously. See *Fu Lei Jiashu (Fu Lei's Letters from Home)* (Peking: Sanlian Bookstore Publishers, 1981).

p. 142   Little has been written about the movement against the so-called May Sixteenth elements in the United States. For an analysis of the first movement in Peking, see Merle Goldman, *China's Intellectuals: Advise and Dissent* (Cambridge, Mass.: Harvard University Press, 1981), pp. 151–153.

p. 143   Yang Jiang describes the suicide of her son-in-law in *Ganxiao Liu Ji (Six Sketches from a Cadre School)*. For a translation, see Howard Goldblatt, trans., "Six Chapters from My Life 'Downunder.' "

p. 145   The suicide death of Wu Han's daughter is described in the previously cited piece by Liao Liao, "Xiangqi Wu Xiaoyan" ("Thinking About Wu Xiaoyan"). The description of the burning of the Guangdong hospital was reported to me in personal conversation by Allen Whiting, cited earlier.

p. 146   The description of the treatment of Liu Shaoqi by his doctors is from the previously cited article by his children.

The description of the death by medical neglect of Wu Han's wife is by their son, Wu Zhang, in the previously cited article in *Wu Han he "Hai Rui Bagoan" (Wu Han and "Hai Rui Dismissed from Office")*.

p. 147   The description of the death of Ba Jin's wife, Xiao Shan, is from the previously cited article by Ba Jin, "Huainian Xiao Shan" ("Reminiscences of Xiao Shan").

pp. 148–9   The death of Tao Zhu is described by his daughter, Tao Siliang, in the previously cited article "Yifeng Zhongyu Fachu de Xin" ("A Letter Posted at Last").

pp. 151–3   The death of Liu Shaoqi is described in the previously cited three-part article by three of his children.

CHAPTER SIX

p. 157   The filmscript of *Rashomon*, as well as the two stories from which the film derives, are published as *Rashomon* (New York: Grove, 1969). The quotation about everyone wanting to forget unpleasant things is on p. 103.

p. 180   For a discussion of the relationship between urban unemployment and the sending of youth to the countryside, see Thomas Bernstein's introduction to Peter Seybolt, ed., *The Rustification of Urban Youth in China* (White Plains, N.Y.: M. E. Sharpe, 1977).

p. 193   For the significance of the gift of mangoes, see Richard Baum, *Prelude to Revolution*, p. 152.

CHAPTER SEVEN

p. 210   The definition of a "disaster" is from Kai T. Erikson, *Everything in Its Path: Destruction of Community in the Buffalo Creek Flood* (New York: Simon & Schuster, 1976), p. 252.

p. 210   For the pioneering, seminal works on "extreme situations," see Bruno Bettelheim, "Individual and Mass Behavior in Extreme Situations," in *Surviving and Other Essays* (New York: Vintage, 1980), pp. 48–84; and Robert Jay Lifton, *Death in Life: Survivors of Hiroshima* (New York: Random House, 1967), p. 479.

p. 211   The statement by Ding Ling is quoted in Jonathan D. Spence, *The Gate of Heavenly Peace: The Chinese and Their Revolution, 1885–1980* (New York: Viking, 1981), p. 352.

For Lifton's discussion of "contagion anxiety," see Robert Jay Lifton, *Death in Life*, pp. 516–517.

p. 212   Many who have spent periods in solitary confinement have written about the constant "temptation" of suicide or insanity. For a sampling of these writings, see Jacobo Timerman, *Prisoner Without a Name, Cell Without a Number* (New York: Knopf, 1981); Eugene B. McDaniel with James L. Johnson, *Before Honor* (Philadelphia and New York: A. J. Holman, 1975); Arthur Koestler, *The Invisible Writing: The Second Volume of an Autobiography: 1932–1940* (London: Macmillan, 1969), and *Dialogue with Death* (New York: Macmillan, 1966); and Louis L. Snyder, *The Dreyfus Case: A Documentary History* (New Brunswick, N. J.: Rutgers University Press, 1973).

pp. 214–15 For the description of Tao Zhu's life in isolation, see the previously cited article by his daughter, Tao Siliang, "Yifeng Zhongyu Fachu de Xin" ("A Letter Posted at Last").

p. 218 For the argument that isolation is capable of producing madness, see Jules Henry, *Pathways to Madness* (New York: Vintage, 1965), pp. 447–449.

For an argument on the importance of social support in a stressful situation, see Glen R. Elliott and Carl Eisendorfer, eds., *Stress and Human Health: Analysis and Implications of Research* (New York: Springer, 1982), p. 67. For literature on the necessity of support in the concentration camps, see Terrence Des Pres, *The Survivor: An Anatomy of Life in the Death Camps* (New York: Oxford University Press, 1976), pp. 97–147, 181–209; and Patricia Benner, Ethel Roskies, and Richard S. Lazarus, "Stress and Coping Under Extreme Situations," and Elmer Luchterhand, "Social Behavior of Concentration Camp Prisoners: Continuities and Discontinuities with Pre- and Postcamp Life," in Joel E. Dimsdale, ed., *Survivors, Victims, and Perpetrators: Essays on the Nazi Holocaust* (Washington and New York: Hemisphere, 1980), pp. 240, 268.

p. 219 Many Chinese I interviewed describe friends who went insane during the Cultural Revolution, and they attribute the onset of that insanity to the pressures they suffered during that period. Moreover, many relate instances of insanity which began during the Cultural Revolution and persist today, as in the case described here by Bai Meihua. While psychiatrists recognize psychogenic psychosis as being, by definition, stress-induced, psychogenic psychosis is almost always acute and short-lived, leaving few long-term effects. Insanity has a technical psychiatric meaning of psychosis, which, according to many psychiatrists, has a strong biological basis and does not generally occur following acute stress. Thus, while the Chinese frequently use words like "insanity" and "madness" in describing reactions of relatives and friends, the more accurate description would simply be "mental illness" or "mental disorder." From the perspective of this research, attempting to understand the meaning the Chinese attribute to the Cultural Revolution, however, it is significant that the Chinese perceive a relationship between the traumas of the Cultural Revolution and insanity. I am grateful to Arthur Kleinman for pointing out the psychiatric view of the descriptions contained here.

p. 220 For the relationship between suicide and the onset of "adverse life events," see Glen R. Elliott and Carl Eisendorfer, eds., *Stress and Human Health: Analysis and Implications of Research*, p. 294. See also Jean Baechler, *Suicides* (New York: Basic Books, 1979), pp. 66–96.

p. 220 "Anecdote from the Western Front" has been cited previously.

p. 223 For the literary description of a suicide, see Zong Pu, "Wo Shi Shei?" ("Who Am I?"), in *Zong Pu Xiaoshuo Sanwen Xuan (Anthology of Zong Pu's Prose Fiction)* (Peking: Peking Publishing House, 1981), pp. 130–140.

p. 225 For the analysis of man finding meaning in suffering, see Viktor E. Frankl, *Man's Search for Meaning: An Introduction to Logotherapy* (New York: Simon & Schuster, 1962).

p. 234 The quotation about courage from Archbishop Bloom is in John Bowlby, *Separation: Anxiety and Anger* (New York: Basic Books, 1973), p. 322.

CHAPTER EIGHT

p. 243 For some of the best literature on the sequelae of extreme situations, see Kai T. Erikson, *Everything in Its Path: Destruction of Community in the Buffalo Creek Flood;* Leo Etinger, "The Concentration Camp Syndrome and Its Late Sequelae," in Joel E. Dimsdale, ed., *Survivors, Victims, and Perpetrators: Essays on the Nazi Holocaust*, pp. 127–163; Jim Goodwin, "The Etiology of Combat-Related Post-Traumatic Stress Disorders," in Tom Williams, ed., *Post-Traumatic Stress Disorders of the Vietnam Veteran: Observations and Recommendations for the Psychological Treatment of the Veteran and His Family* (Cincinnati: Disabled American Veterans, 1980), pp. 1–6, 10; and Ghislaine Boulanger, "Post Traumatic Stress Disorder: An Old Problem with a New Name," paper prepared for inclusion in Sonnenberg and Talbott, eds., *The Psychiatric Effects of War* (Washington, D.C.: American Psychiatric Association, 1983).

The symptoms of posttraumatic stress disorder can be found in *Diagnostic and Statistical Manual III* (Washington, D.C.: American Psychiatric Association, 1980), pp. 236–239.

p. 244 The figure of half a million Vietnam veterans suffering from posttraumatic stress disorder is from Jim Goodwin, "The Etiology of Combat-Related Post-Traumatic Stress Disorders," pp. 3–11.

p. 244 The argument that those responsible for the victims' suffering often face the world unencumbered by guilt is made by John P. Sabini and Maury Silver, "Destroying the Innocent with a Clear Conscience," in Joel E. Dimsdale, ed., *Survivors, Victims, and Perpetrators: Essays on the Nazi Holocaust*, pp. 329–357.

p. 245 For early discussions of survivor's guilt, see Bruno Bettelheim, "Trauma and Reintegration," in *Surviving and Other Essays*, pp. 29–35; and Robert Jay Lifton, *Death in Life: Survivors of Hiroshima*, pp. 489–500. For personal testimony to survivor's guilt, see Elie Wiesel, *Night* (New York: Bantam Books, 1960), pp. 86–87, 99–106. See also Kai T. Erikson, *Everything in Its Path*, especially pp. 156–173; and Jim Goodwin, "The Etiology of Combat-Related Post-Traumatic Stress Disorders," p. 15.

pp. 251–2 The story of Ba Jin's guilt over the death of his wife again is taken from the previously cited article, "Huainian Xiao Shan" ("Reminiscences of Xiao Shan").

p. 252 The scholar who has read Ba Jin's reminiscences of his wife as a contemporary equivalent of "J'accuse" is Leo Ou-fan Lee, in *Recent Chinese Literature: A Second Hundred Flowers* (Washington, D.C.: China Council of the Asia Society, July 1980). For background on the Dreyfus case, including the text of Zola's "J'accuse" and the quote from Clemenceau in the text, see Louis L. Snyder, *The Dreyfus Case: A Documentary History*.

p. 253 For examples of the fear of recurrence in other extreme situations, see Patricia Benner, Ethel Roskies, and Richard S. Lazarus, "Stress and Coping Under Extreme Situations," and Elmer Luchterhand, "Social Behavior of Concentration Camp Prisoners: Continuities and Discontinuities with Pre- and Postcamp Life," in Joel E. Dimsdale, ed., *Survivors, Victims, and Perpetrators: Essays on the Nazi Holocaust;* Kai T. Erikson, *Everything in Its Path;* and Jim Goodwin, "The Etiology of Combat-Related Post-Traumatic Stress Disorders."

p. 262 Liu Xinwu's "Awake, My Brother!" is translated in Lu Xinhua et al., *The Wounded*, pp. 179–205.

p. 263 The new symptoms of schizophrenic patients in China are discussed in Hsia Yu-fen and Tsai Neng, "Transcultural Investigation of Recent Symptomatology of Schizophrenia in China," *American Journal of Psychiatry*, vol. 138, no. 11 (November 1981), pp. 1484–1486.

p. 266 For Kleinman's study, and the quotation included here, see Arthur Kleinman, "Neurasthenia and Depression: A Study of Somatization and Culture in China," in *Culture, Medicine and Psychiatry* 6 (Boston: D. Reidel, 1982).

p. 268 That the stocktaking of old age is often accompanied by depression is argued in Patricia Benner, Ethel Roskies, and Richard S. Lazarus, "Stress and Coping Under Extreme Situations," pp. 246–247. See also Giuseppe di Lampedusa, *The Leopard* (New York: Pantheon, 1960), pp. 288, 290–291.

p. 270 See Glen R. Elliott and Carl Eisendorfer, eds., *Stress and Human Health: Analysis and Implications of Research*, pp. 55–69, 149–167 for models of response to stress. For literary treatments of individuals who have risen above their circumstances, see John Hersey, *Hiroshima* (New York: Bantam, 1959); and Arthur Miller, *The Crucible* (New York: Bantam, 1959). For the story of the dancer, see Terrence Des Pres, *The Survivor*, pp. 160–161; and Bruno Bettelheim, *The Informed Heart: Autonomy in a Mass Age* (New York: Avon, 1960), p. 258–259.

CHAPTER NINE

p. 276 See Aldous Huxley, *The Devils of Loudun* (New York: Harper & Row, 1952), p. 218.

The story of Song Binbin was widely disseminated at the time and was repeated by a number of people I interviewed. For a published account, see Stanley Karnow, *Mao and China*, p. 203. It is reported that Song Binbin is one of those Chinese currently studying in the United States.

p. 277 See Hannah Arendt, *Eichmann in Jerusalem: A Report on the Banality of Evil* (New York: Viking, 1964), pp. 294–295.

p. 279 The American who had occasion to teach her uncomprehending students the Ten Commandments was Norma Diamond of the University of Michigan. The Chinese university was Shandong University.

p. 281 For Fairbank's argument about the nondevelopment of capitalism, see John King Fairbank, *The United States and China* (Cambridge, Mass.: Harvard University Press, 1979), p. 47.

p. 289 For the experiments conducted by Stanley Milgram, see Stanley Milgram, *Obedience to Authority* (New York: Harper & Row, 1974).

p. 289 Albert Camus, *The Plague* (New York: Modern Library, 1948), p. 278.

EPILOGUE

p. 295 For the statement by Wang Bingzhang, see *News Roundup* (New York: Coordination Council for North American Affairs, 1982), no. 097.

p. 295 See Liang Heng and Judith Shapiro, *Son of the Revolution* (New York: Vintage, 1983), and *Intellectual Freedom in China After Mao, with a Focus on 1983* (New York: Fund for Free Expression Report, 1984).

p. 298 T. S. Eliot, "Journey of the Magi," in *The Waste Land and Other Poems* (New York: Harcourt, Brace & World, 1962), p. 70.

pp. 299–300 See Bai Hua, *Kulian (Unrequited Love)* (Taipei, Taiwan: Institute of Current China Studies, 1981), p. 102 (in Chinese), p. 83 (in English).

INDEX

A NOTE ON THE TYPE

---

on of
is face
ot based
period
nd thin
give a